D1530523

THE ARCHITECTURE AND ENGINEERING OF DIGITAL COMPUTER COMPLEXES

Volume 2

THE ARCHITECTURE AND ENGINEERING OF DIGITAL COMPUTER COMPLEXES

Volume 2

Boris Beizer
Director of Research and Development
Data Systems Analysts, Inc.
Pennsauken, New Jersey

ℚ PLENUM PRESS • NEW YORK–LONDON • 1971

First Printing — November 1971
Second Printing — March 1975

Library of Congress Catalog Card Number 71-141244

SBN 306-37152-9

© 1971 Plenum Press, New York
A Division of Plenum Publishing Corporation
227 West 17th Street, New York, N.Y. 10011

United Kingdom edition published by Plenum Press, London
A Division of Plenum Publishing Company, Ltd.
Davis House (4th Floor), 8 Scrubs Lane, Harlesden, NW10 6SE, London, England

Printed in the United States of America

CONTENTS OF VOLUME 2

Chapter 9
The Executive Processor

Chapter 10
The Nucleus

Chapter 11
Viability

Chapter 12
Viability Design

Chapter 13
System Analysis

Chapter 14
Implementation

CONTENTS OF VOLUME 1

Chapter 3
Hardware—The Central Processing Unit

Chapter 4
The Structural Elements of the Complex

Chapter 5
Programming Techniques

Chapter 6
Firmware

Chapter 7
Analysis

Chapter 8

COMPUTER COMPLEXES

> **Compromise,** *n*. Such an adjustment of conflicting interest as gives each adversary the satisfaction of thinking he has got what he ought not to have, and is deprived of nothing except what was justly his due.
>
> AMBROSE BIERCE
> *The Devil's Dictionary*

1. SYNOPSIS

The computer complex can be viewed from different aspects. Each aspect, when considered singly, may be given disproportionate weight. Hardware, software, function, and form must be blended and traded to achieve an optimum design. To each point of view there corresponds a distinct conceptual configuration. The several configurations of the complex must complement each other and be compatible.

Communications, be it of computers, programs, or persons, and the minimization thereof is a nexus of most complex designs that does not have its full impact until the complex is considered as a whole. The minimization of time or space or hardware costs as isolated elements of the complex is to be recognized for the subsidiary goal it is.

2. THE SEVERAL CONFIGURATIONS OF THE COMPUTER COMPLEX

The parable of the blind men and the elephant is pertinent to the design of computer complexes. One blind man, having considered only the elephant's ear, likened the elephant to a leaf; another, having examined only the tail, thought the elephant was rather like a rope; and so on. Similarly, one can see the computer complex as hardware or software, view it functionally or structurally, economically or operationally. A viable complex must be synthesis of these complementary views, lest it be lopsided and not meet its requirements.

The computer complex is elephantine, but unlike the blind men, having seen the component parts, we can effect their synthesis and achieve a perspective on the totality.

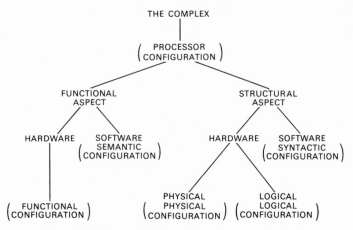

Figure 8.1. The several configurations of a computer complex.

A **configuration** is a graph that represents an aspect of interest of the computer complex. Its elements are processors, devices, or programs, connected by lines that denote communication paths, data paths, control paths, or physical wires, as appropriate to the aspect being considered. There are as many different configuration graphs of a computer complex as there are points of view and things of interest.

Figure 8.1 shows the relations that exist among the more important configurations of a computer complex. The first split in the graph could just as well have been between hardware and software, followed by the division between functional and structural aspects. Furthermore, the categories are not exclusive—between hardware and software we may have fuzzyware, while one man's function is another's structure.

2.1. Definitions

2.1.1. Processor Configuration

The **processor configuration** is a graphic representation of the complex's specification. Its elements are the identifiable processors of the complex—those required to do the job for which the complex is intended as well as those that are required for *any* viable complex independent of the particular application. The processors, it will be recalled, represent abstractions of both hardware and software, and are not differentiated as to implementation. The lines connecting the elements of the processor configuration are the various data or control paths. If only control paths are shown, the graph depicts a **processor control configuration**. If only data paths are shown, it is a

processor data configuration or, as it is more usually called, a **data flow diagram**.

2.1.2. Physical Configuration

The tangible complex consists of devices such as computers and memories. Every device is physically connected by wires to and through other devices in the complex. Each device and each cable can be considered to have an unchangeable number painted on it. These physical characteristics are what is depicted by the physical configuration diagram. The **physical configuration** is therefore equivalent to the wiring diagram used by the complex's installers.

2.1.3. Logical Configuration

At any one instant of time, a given physical tape station, say, may have a logical name which differs from the one painted on its cabinet. Typically, a tape transport will have a display which shows the momentary logical name assigned by the operating system. Not only may tape transports and disc drives have their logical names changed from moment to moment, but computers, memories, communication devices, printers, etc., may do so as well.

The various wires that connect the devices of the complex may be switched through a switching network, so that there may be many alternate paths that connect one device to another. The physical configuration shows the complete switching network, while the logical configuration shows the particular set of connections that happens to be implemented at the moment.

The **logical configuration**, then, is a description of the logical connections that exist among logical units. Every logical configuration is a subconfiguration of the physical configuration.[1] A given physical configuration may be used to establish many different logical configurations, and any one logical configuration can be implemented in many different ways. Figure 8.2 shows a physical configuration, two of its possible logical configurations, and two different ways in which one of the given logical configurations could be constructed. The two different ways of constructing a given logical configuration are examples of what we shall call **logical constructions**.

2.1.4. Functional Hardware Configurations

One computer in the complex may (momentarily) be assigned to a particular set of tasks. One might have an "input computer," an "executive computer," a "message computer," a "file search computer," etc., which is to say that the particular computer, say, the executive computer, is the one

[1] More formally, every logical configuration graph is a subgraph of the physical configuration graph.

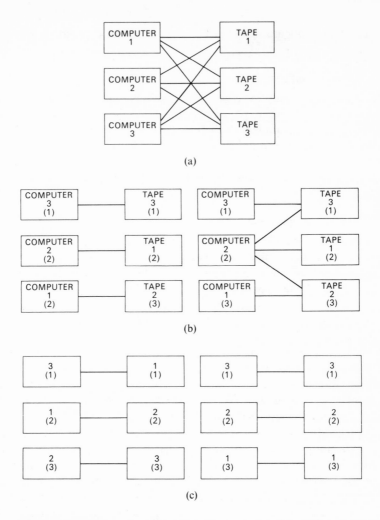

Figure 8.2. Physical and logical configurations. (a) A physical configuration; (b) two different logical configurations; (c) two different implementations (logical constructions) of a given logical configuration. The numbers without parentheses are the physical identifiers, the numbers in parentheses the logical identifiers.

in which most of the executive functions reside. The **functional hardware configuration** or, simply, the **functional configuration** shows the interconnection of logical devices as they are assigned to particular functional roles. The devices can be given functional names in addition to their logical and physical names.

Every functional configuration is also a subconfiguration of the physical configuration. Any functional configuration may have many different logical subconfigurations. Thus, the executive computer might at one moment be logical computer number 1 and at another moment logical computer number 2. It is not always possible to have a one-to-one correspondence between logical and functional names. A desirable characteristic of large computer complexes is the freedom to assign functional devices to logical devices, functional devices to physical devices, as well as logical devices to physical devices. Furthermore, a given computer complex, while having only one physical configuration, may have many different functional configurations, different logical configurations, and different constructions thereof.

2.1.5. Semantic Configuration

An aspect of a processor implemented as software which closely corresponds to a task for which the complex is designed (e.g., a file search routine, a payroll program, a data validation routine) is called a **semantic element**. The graph that shows the interrelation of semantic processors is called the **semantic configuration**. The semantic configuration is the software analog of the functional configuration.

2.1.6. Syntactic Configuration

An aspect of a processor implemented as software which is shared with other processors and is generally independent of the application (e.g., a storage allocation routine, a loader, a diagnostic program) is called a **syntactic element**. The graph that shows the interrelation of syntactic processors is called the **syntactic configuration**.

2.1.7. Review of Terms

These terms can be defined more formally as follows:

Physical Configuration: A representation of the interconnection of physical devices with physical names (painted on the cabinet).

Logical Configuration: A representation of the interconnection of logical devices with logical names (displayed on the device).

Functional Configuration: A representation of the interconnection of functional devices with functional names and functionally named connections.

Semantic Configuration: A representation of the interconnection of semantic program elements.

Syntactic Configuration: A representation of the interconnection of syntactic program elements.

Logical Construction: A particular mapping of logical names onto physical names.[2]

Physical Construction: A particular mapping of functional names onto physical names.

Functional Construction: A particular mapping of functional names onto logical names.

2.2. The Design Problem

The distinctions between the various configurations of the computer complex are not always apparent in a complex consisting of one computer. It is only when we consider the design of a complex of computers, in which functional and logical assignments can change from moment to moment, and in which there is a flexible relation between the various configurations that can be controlled by the complex itself, that these distinctions become important.

The specifications for processors must be transformed into subsidiary specifications for semantic and syntactic software. Similarly, functional and logical hardware configurations must be devised that are compatible with the requirements of the software. Finally, all of these must result in a physical configuration that can execute the software.

Trading can be done along any axis, the primary directions being that of hardware–software and function–structure. Ultimately, everything is physical (if we allow the pattern of magnetization in the memory). Abstract processors, or programs, cannot be executed save in the programmer's mind or in a physical hunk of hardware called a computer. Design is making the decisions as to the extent of hardware and software in the implementa-

---

[2] The following quotation from Lewis Carroll's *Through the Looking-Glass* is hoary in the annals of computer literature but most appropriate at this point:

"... The name of the song is called '*Haddocks' Eyes*.'"

"Oh, that's the name of the song, is it?" Alice said, trying to feel interested.

"No, you don't understand," the Knight said, looking a little vexed. "That's what the name is *called*. The name really is '*The Aged Aged Man*.'"

"Then I ought to have said, 'That's what the *song* is called'?" Alice corrected herself.

"No, you oughtn't: that's quite another thing! The *song* is called '*Ways and Means*': but that's only what it's *called*, you know!"

"Well, what *is* the song, then?" said Alice, who was by this time completely bewildered.

"I was coming to that," the Knight said. "The song really *is* '*A-sitting On A Gate*': and the tune's my own invention."

tion, the ways in which function will be sacrificed for structure and *vice versa*, and finally, how all of these factors will fit into a physical computer.

2.3. The Design Process

The design process is iterative, but proceeds in the general direction of processor to physical configuration. It begins with a specification, which is examined for redundancies and ambiguities, and is used to obtain a new, more formal specification, represented by the processor configuration. An examination of the processors in the processor configuration leads to a tentative assignment of functions to hardware and software. This may lead to a revision of the processor configuration. The tentative partition of the system into hardware and software elements leads, on the software side, to timing analyses and the development of an operating system (mostly syntactic). The semantic elements of the program, as well as those processors that lead to special-purpose hardware, dictate the functional configuration. The syntactic elements of the software leads to logical configurations. The functional and logical configurations must be reconciled. This may lead to further revisions of the functional–structural balance, and the hardware–software balance. A knowledge of the functional configuration(s) and the logical configuration(s) leads to a specification of the physical structure of the complex including its internal communications network. Cost considerations at this step may lead to revisions of the earlier steps. The procedure is repeated until the final configurations are settled.

3. TRANSLATION CRITERIA

Design, as we have seen, is a translation process—the translation of processors into hardware or software, the mechanization of a processor in terms of predominantly functionally oriented subprocessors, or as a sequence of calls and linkages of predominantly syntactically oriented processors. While there are no firm rules for what should be done when, there are predispositions toward certain kinds of implementations that hold in most cases. These indications and contraindications are discussed in the sequel.

3.1. Special-Purpose Hardware

A decision to implement a processor as hardware is typically equivalent to deciding to implement it as a special-purpose device. Similarly, a decision to implement a processor as software is equivalent to deciding to implement it within a general-purpose computer. While "general-purpose" is a technical term, connoting a particular computer structure, "special-purpose" denotes intention rather than construction. The use of general-purpose computers for implementing special-purpose functions has increased and will continue to do so. We should not be biased into thinking that a device, because its designers have decided to use a general-purpose computer, is operationally a general-purpose computer. If the device is marketed as a special-purpose device, it should usually be treated as such despite the details of its implementation. We shall use the term "hard-wired" to denote special-purpose devices not implemented as general-purpose computers.

A special-purpose device exists for a particular function. If the device is commercially available, tested, and accepted, it may be less expensive than an equivalent general-purpose mechanization of the same function. However, the existence of a commercially available special-purpose device is not the sole criterion used. The validity of an approach depends on the technological context of that approach. Very good special-purpose devices, while available, still can be obsolete. Alternatively, a special-purpose device might be introduced before it is economically viable.

An example is afforded by communication multiplexers. They were originally built as hard-wired devices. Each line had a character buffer that could detect and assemble a complete character. Characters thus collected were transmitted to the computer. This method was used because relatively few lines had to be serviced, and the cost of doing the job within the computer was excessive. Later, relative costs for hard-wired devices increased, cost performance of computers improved, and users required more lines. This led to the use of bit buffers, capable of assembling only one bit at a time. A computer was used to assemble these bits into characters. More recently, the trend has continued to the point where the computer handles everything, from sampling the bits to assembling and storing characters, under program control. In some cases, the communication multiplexing is done by a program within a computer of a complex. In other cases, it is done by a small computer, devoted solely to the multiplexing function.

Testing the validity of a special-purpose implementation should always be done by comparison with a similar implementation within a central computer of the complex. A timing analysis is done. The required memory is estimated. As a first approximation, the value of the special-purpose implementation can be estimated as the cost of replacing it by a program. Thus, if the processor requires 5% of the complex's time, and 2% of its memory, that proportion of the complex hardware cost is the value of the device. Similarly, the cost of developing the software is to be amortized over the number of such complexes. These costs establish a value for the processor. If the cost as software in the complex thus determined is $10,000, and the hardware implementation of the processor is available for $5000, special-purpose hardware is indicated.

One must be careful in such evaluations, because the $5000 could in reality be more expensive than the $10,000. Excess unusable capacity may exist in the complex. That is, the optimum computer for the application is larger than the required computer. It may have 30 to 40% excess capacity. In such cases, only the amortized software costs should be counted. The excess cycles and memory would be wasted if not used by the processor in question. On the other hand, if the computer is almost fully loaded, the small incremental memory and time required for this processor could well drive us into the next larger computer or memory or what not. The software implementation might then be far more expensive than the special-purpose implementation, even though it required a trivial amount of memory, time, and development.

Special-purpose devices tend to have a linear relation between cost and performance while general-purpose computers tend to follow a square law. Typically, the cost–performance characteristics of the special-purpose device is less advantageous than that of the general-purpose device. Servicing 1000 terminals through specialized communication devices might cost seven times as much as servicing 100 terminals. A computer used for the same purpose might only cost twice as much for 1000 lines as it did for 100 lines. The future needs of the complex must be considered in addition to the immediate needs. If the specialized device is, throughout the projected life of the complex, cheaper than a software implementation and such a device is available, it should be used.

A processor can always be implemented as a general-purpose computer program—it may be prohibitively expensive to do so but it is never impossible. In the same way that we investigate extreme solutions (e.g., maximum-space or minimum-time solutions of programs) we should examine the relative costs of a hardware design and a software design for each specified processor. The architect should know enough of *current* logic design practices and economics to make a reasonable estimate of a hardware implementation cost.

We must examine relative hardware and software costs, as long as technology continues to evolve as rapidly as it has. The architect should not be self-conscious about reversing his stand five times in as many years, first using hardware, then software, and then back to hardware, etc., for the same function, if indeed in each case the best predictions he could make about the technology led him to that conclusion. For this reason also, the history of the implementation of a particular function should be studied. The bad idea of a few years ago may merely have been premature, and the formerly good idea may become good anew.

Ultimately, the decision in favor of specialized or generalized hardware is based upon present and predicted comparative costs as determined over the projected lifetime of the complex.

3.2. Evolution of the Semantic Configuration

3.2.1. Specifications

The design of a computer complex begins with finding what it must do: that is, the specification. Ideally, a specification is consistent and (within theoretical limitations) complete. A specification should not presuppose its implementation. It should be worded in such a way that, were it possible, a hundred squirrels in a black box would be allowed to do the job. Thus, if it is a refinery control system that is wanted, the specification should include the number of lines, their characteristics, the kinds of differential equations that must be solved, the rate of solution, the accuracy and precision of the result, the reliability of the system, etc. If an analog computer can meet the requirements, it should be allowed. Each structural precondition in the specification reduces the implementer's freedom, and directly or indirectly results in an increased cost or reduced performance. The user might specify seemingly nonfunctional requirements such as: "it shall be a digital computer with 131K bytes of core memory," "constructed of integrated circuits," etc. In such cases, if the imposition of constraints is intentional (often it is not), the restrictions are to be taken as functional requirements.

It is in the best interest of the vendor and the buyer to determine the exact functional requirements, and to eliminate all nonintentional structural aspects of the specification. There is more than enough work in writing a good specification, so that there is little time for the buyer to be his own architect and engineer as well if it is not his intention to be so.

A specification should not be confused with the evaluation criteria used for a proposal. The former tells us what the job is to be; the latter are a method for estimating the credence of the vendor. Evaluation of proposals may require deep inquiries into the proposed structural configuration. The understanding and analysis of structures should not be confused with the generation thereof.

3.2.2. The Semantic Configuration

Functional elements must be isolated, grouped, and reorganized in a manner compatible with the needs of the system designer.

A typical example can be taken from a banking operation. The client specifies several functional processors: savings account, checking account, special checking account, mortgage, private loans, business loans, etc. All of these share a common compound interest calculation, bookkeeping procedures, etc.

The system designer must transform these into a set of functional components that are irredundant and complete. A possible transformation

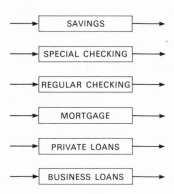

TRANSFORMED TO:

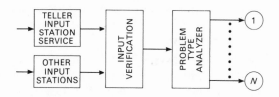

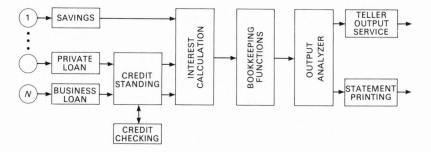

Figure 8.3. Transformation of functional specifications to semantic configuration.

is shown in Figure 8.3.[3] The particular sequence of processes specified may be procedural requirements or may result from the need to be compatible with existing systems and procedures. The transformation requires close coordination between the user and the vendor. Often, the transformation will require the user to examine his procedures and requirements to a greater depth than he has ever done before (sometimes with the embarrassing conclusion that a computer is not needed after all).

The conversion of the specification to a semantic configuration follows a sequence of well-defined steps.

  1. Functional Analysis: The several steps of functional analysis discussed in Section 4.1 of Chapter 5, that is, learning the language of the application (banking, biology, climatology, air-traffic control, communications, etc.), restating the specification, analyzing it logically for ambiguities and contradictions, and producing a functional data flow, are extended to the complex as a whole.

  2. Finding the Processors: The functional analysis will have resulted in the restatement of the specification to the finest possible functional level. Two things are sought: to eliminate redundant processors, and to identify independent processors and processor groups.

  3. Partitioning the Processors: The functional processors once found can be partitioned into independent or interdependent sets. These sets are what is required for the further steps in the design.

3.2.3. Elimination of Redundant Processors

One of the characteristics of bad systems, be they hardware or software, is the existence of accidental redundancies. Thus, the same or almost the same processor is found in several different places. Ultimately, the problem is one of managing the development effort. However, it is in the early stages of the system design, when the design team is small and manageable, that such unknown redundancies must be eliminated. If the team that does the initial functional analysis is small (no more than ten persons), such redundancies will show themselves and be apparent to all concerned.

More often than not, we are faced with almost redundant or rather almost identical processors and subprocessors. In such cases, data input or output formats may have to be changed (with the concurrence of the buyer). The things to look for in spotting potentially redundant processors are:

  1. Identical or nearly identical input data formats.
  2. Identical or nearly identical output data formats.

[3] The specification of a real banking system would never be so crude, nor would the resulting semantic configuration be so simple. Modern, large-scale bank data processing systems are among the most complex ever implemented.

3. Common files used.
4. Mathematically or logically identical functions.
5. Similar subprocessors used.
6. Similar data flow through subprocessors.
7. Common control functions.
8. Last, and usually least, similarity of intended application.

The last item is to emphasize the fact that the elegance of the design is rarely a result of spotting the obvious redundancies, but of spotting similarities among seemingly independent and different processors. In a somewhat deeper way, the following observations can be made or tested:

1. Input, output, and file information content.
2. Similarity of state diagram, sequential jump tables, mapping tables, or decision tables.

Eliminating redundant processors reduces the number of things to be considered and increases the designer's freedom. The fact that what were five processors in the original specification has become one processor with five entrances does not imply that only one copy of that processor will be used. It may well be in our interest to have five or ten copies in the final mechanization. But if this is so, let it be done by design and not by accident.

3.3. Semantic *vs.* Syntactic Configurations

The semantic configuration should parallel the functional specification. That is, there must be an element in the semantic configuration for each processor specified. That element may be a call to a subroutine, entries in a table, or a program.

The idea is to eliminate as much of the semantic programs as possible. The syntactic programs are more familiar to the programmer, and there is a greater possibility that they have been done before.

3.3.1. Tables

One of the first questions that should be asked in implementing a semantic processor as a piece of software is "Why not use a table?" The semantic configuration is the part of the complex most likely to change. There is not much chance that the methods used for storage allocation, buffering, I/O device control, etc., will be changed as a result of changes in functional requirements. However, the user's needs continually change, and the semantic configuration at the end of the complex's life may have little resemblance to what it was at the beginning.

Tables give us more freedom, increase the generality of the programs that are written (thereby decreasing programming costs), provide protection from obsolescence, increase flexibility, and are easier to maintain than coding. Furthermore, the table-driven program is more likely to have been written before.

3.3.2. Interpreters

One way of implementing a large hunk of semantics is to design a specialized language for it. Macro instructions and data elements particular to the application are defined. The semantic configuration then consists of a set of calls to these macros and subroutines.

The various processors are broken down into the most primitive sets of functional elements that can be defined. Each such element is given a name and a pseudoinstruction of the interpreter defined for it. The interpreter must have a simple parser to examine the commands and generate the call to the appropriate subroutine.

Taken to an extreme, this is an effective way of minimizing programming and testing costs at the expense of almost everything else (which may be appropriate in some cases). Everything that could be possibily defined as a subroutine is so defined. The subroutine calling tree becomes very large and deep. The excessive calls and depth take time as well as space, but the number of redundant processors is minimized.

3.3.3. Virtual Interpreters

One can start out by designing an interpretive system, with the intent of removing much of the interpretive stuff after testing is complete. The interpretation of the interpretive language command can be eliminated by eliminating the explicit appearance of that command in the final version of the program. The command is replaced directly with the proper calling sequence, eliminating a run-time process that was better done at design time. In this way, one might start with an interpretive system and end up with none but direct lines of code, table entries, etc. In doing this, we gain speed and reduce memory but lose flexibility.

One can, to advantage, go through all the steps of designing an interpretive system but not actually do so. That is, a set of commands is defined, with the understanding that the *programmers* are to perform the proper calls and linkages from the start without ever building the parser and such. Each programmer is his own interpreter. This approach requires careful controls, tight management over the programming effort, and standardization of labels and conventions.

4. PROCESSOR GRAPHS

Graphs are useful for depicting the relations that may exist between processors. Given a simple system with a few dozen significant processors, the relationship of these processors to each other can be readily seen with the aid of a diagram. In large-scale computer complexes, such as reservation systems, banking systems, or management information systems, where the number of significant processors is in the hundreds or thousands, such pictorial representations become unwieldy, and it is no longer possible to see what is going on. In such cases, elementary graph theory can be used to advantage.

The types of questions that might come up and for which graph theory is useful are:

1. What are the ultimate sources of inputs to this program?
2. Where do the outputs ultimately go?
3. Are these two processors independent?
4. Does it pay to have redundant copies of a given processor, and if yes, where and how many?
5. Should these processors coexist (i.e., be in the same memory)?

Graph theory will not give definitive answers to these questions, but will aid the programmer in discovering predilections for the proper solution.

4.1. Relations

A graph is a collection of nodes joined by directed line segments called links. The nodes represent items of interest, and a link indicates that a relation of interest occurs between two nodes. The links may or may not have weights, such as probabilities, or time, or space.

Of particular interest at this point are graphs in which the relations are **reflexive** and **transitive**. These laws are defined as follows:

Reflexive: For every node a of the graph, aRa. That is, every node is related to itself.

Transitive: If aRb and bRc, then aRc.

A relation such as "a is a descendant of b" is transitive but not reflexive (except for Mark Twain, who claimed to have been his own grandfather). A relation such as "a can be seen from b" is reflexive but not transitive on a spherical earth. The schoolboy's relation "Gozinta" is reflexive and transitive; for if "a Gozinta b" and "b Gozinta c," then "a Gozinta c."

The relation of interest in the analysis of processors is "b depends upon a," or, conversely and more conveniently, "a produces something that b needs." We can without loss of generality say that each processor produces something that it needs itself. The relation is obviously reflexive and transitive. We could for specific purposes narrow the relation, by considering such relations as

$$\text{``}b \text{ is controlled by } a\text{''} \qquad \text{or} \qquad \text{``}a \text{ controls } b\text{''}$$

or

"b obtains data from a"   or   "a's output is b's input"

or similar relations peculiar to the circumstances.

4.2. Matrix Representation of Graphs

Any directed graph with N nodes can be represented by a matrix A, called a **connection matrix** or **relation matrix**, whose entries are a_{ij} defined as follows:

$$a_{ij} = 1 \text{ if node } i \text{ has the required relation to node } j$$
$$= 0 \text{ otherwise.}$$

The following conventions are also useful:

I = the matrix whose diagonal entries are all 1,

U = the matrix of all 1s,

ϕ = the matrix of all 0s,

J = the matrix of all 1s except for the diagonal, whose entries are 0 (i.e., $J = \bar{I}$).

Furthermore, assume that the arithmetic operations performed on elements of these matrices are Boolean operations; that is

$$a + a = a, \qquad a \times a = a,$$
$$a + 1 = 1, \qquad a \times 1 = a,$$
$$a + 0 = a, \qquad a \times 0 = 0,$$
$$a + \bar{a} = 1, \qquad a \times \bar{a} = 0,$$

and that the commutative, associative, and bidistributive laws for Boolean algebras hold.

The sum of two matrices A and B is defined as

$$c_{ij} = a_{ij} + b_{ij}.$$

The product is defined as

$$c_{ik} = \sum_{j=1}^{N} a_{ij} b_{jk}$$

4.3. Idempotency Property

Connection matrices have the following interesting properties. If C is the connection matrix of a graph that denotes a transitive relation:

1. an entry c_{ij} of C denotes the nodes that are directly connected;
2. an entry of C^2 denotes the nodes that are connected by sequences of 2 links;
3. an entry of C^k denotes the nodes that are connected by sequences of k links.

Consider the matrix $\hat{C} = C + I$:

$$\hat{C}^2 = C \times C + C \times I + I \times C + I = C^2 + C + I.$$

Similarly,

$$\hat{C}^k = \sum_{j=0}^{k} C^j.$$

If the relation is reflexive as well as transitive,

$$\hat{C} = C + I = C \quad \text{since } C_{ii} = 1 \text{ for all nodes.}$$

We shall, unless otherwise stated, discuss only reflexive relations in the sequel.

The matrix C^k denotes (for reflexive relations) all nodes that can be connected by k *or less* links. It can be shown that if a graph has N nodes, and it is possible to go from node i to node j by some path, then the longest path between nodes i and j that crosses no node more than once has at most $N - 1$ links in it. It can further be shown that the following holds for any reflexive, transitive relation. There is an $n < N$ such that

$$C^{n+k} = C^n.$$

A matrix C, with this property is said to be an **idempotent generator**, because its nth power generates the matrix C^n, which is said to be **idempotent** (i.e., $C^{n+k} = C^n$). The idempotency of C^n is a useful property in calculating C^N. It can be done by successive squarings of C. If $N = 1996$, say, we calculate

$$C^2, C^4, C^8, C^{16}, C^{32}, C^{64}, C^{128}, C^{256}, C^{512}, C^{1024}, C^{2048}.$$

But since C^{1996} is idempotent, $C^{2048} = C^{1996}$. Consequently, the 1996th power of C can be calculated in 11 matrix multiplications rather than 1995.

4.4. Equivalence Relations

An abstract relation R is said to be an **equivalence relation** if the following is true:

(i) aRa —reflexive law,
(ii) aRb and bRc imply aRc —transitive law,
(iii) aRb implies bRa —symmetric law.

If R is an equivalence relation over the elements of a set (nodes of a graph), and subsets of the set of nodes are equivalent under R, the relation R is said to **partition** the set of nodes into mutually exclusive subsets. To illustrate, the relation "has the same birthday as" is clearly an equivalence relation. It partitions the human race into 366 mutually exclusive subsets.

4.5. Partial Ordering

An abstract relation R is said to be a **partial ordering relation** if it obeys the following laws:

(i) aRa —reflexive law,
(ii) aRb and bRc imply aRc —transitive law,
(iii) aRb and bRa imply $a = b$ —antisymmetric law.

The **antisymmetric** law states that if a has the relation R to b and *vice versa*, then a and b are the same elements. Partial ordering is as close to strict ordering as we are likely to get in a discussion of interesting graphs. Partial ordering relations have the following properties of interest:

1. The graph with arrows reversed is also partly ordered.
2. There are no loops.
3. There is at least one first and one last element.

4.6. Further Definitions

The **intersection** of two matrices A and B, denoted by $A \cap B$, is defined as the matrix C whose entries are

$$C_{ij} = a_{ij}b_{ij}.$$

The **transpose** of a matrix A, denoted by A^T, is the matrix with rows and columns interchanged. Its entries are

$$C = A^T$$

$$c_{ij} = a_{ji}.$$

4.7. Loop Connections and Equivalence

Let A be the connection matrix of a graph with a reflexive, transitive relation. Let $C = A^N$, where N is the number of nodes in A. The matrix

C is then the **chain connection matrix** of the graph whose connection matrix is A. Consider now the following matrix:

$$L = C \cap C^T = A^N \cap A^{NT}.$$

L is called the **loop connection matrix** of the graph. An entry of L is equal to 1 if and only if there is a path from node i to node j and back to node i again. Loop-connected subprocessors are interesting because they tend to be implemented in the same computer or assigned in such a way that their interaction will not be burdensome.

We have seen how a relation can be represented by a graph, and how a graph implies the existence of a relation that dictates where the links should be placed. Given a matrix, say L, there is a relation associated with it, say $\mathscr{L}$, that when applied to the graph would yield matrix L. The relation $\mathscr{L}$ associated with the matrix L defined above can be shown to have the following properties:

1. $\mathscr{L}$ is an equivalence relation.
2. It partitions the set of nodes into disjoint subsets, all of whose elements are equivalent under $\mathscr{L}$; such sets are said to be **equivalence classes**.
3. If the elements of an equivalence class thus defined are **associated**, that is, given a collective name, or called by the name of any one element in the class (alternatively, pick a **representative** of the set) the resulting reduced graph is partly ordered under the original relation C.

The properties of the matrices thus far discussed can be clarified by the following illustration:

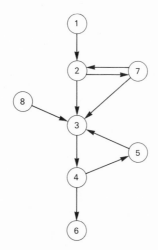

The connection matrix A of the above graph is

$$\begin{bmatrix}
1 & 1 &   &   &   &   &   \\
1 & 1 &   &   &   & 1 &   \\
  & 1 & 1 &   &   &   &   \\
  &   & 1 & 1 & 1 &   &   \\
  & 1 &   & 1 &   &   &   \\
  &   &   &   &   & 1 &   \\
1 & 1 &   &   &   & 1 &   \\
  & 1 &   &   &   &   & 1
\end{bmatrix}$$

Using the idempotency property, we obtain C, the chain connection matrix.

$$\begin{bmatrix}
1 & 1 & 1 & 1 & 1 & 1 & 1 &   \\
1 & 1 & 1 & 1 & 1 & 1 &   &   \\
  & 1 & 1 & 1 & 1 &   &   &   \\
  & 1 & 1 & 1 & 1 &   &   &   \\
  & 1 & 1 & 1 & 1 &   &   &   \\
  &   &   &   &   & 1 &   &   \\
1 & 1 & 1 & 1 & 1 & 1 &   &   \\
  & 1 & 1 & 1 & 1 &   & 1 &
\end{bmatrix}$$

L, the loop connection matrix, is

$$\begin{bmatrix}
1 &   &   &   &   &   &   \\
  & 1 &   &   &   & 1 &   \\
  &   & 1 & 1 & 1 &   &   \\
  &   & 1 & 1 & 1 &   &   \\
  &   & 1 & 1 & 1 &   &   \\
  &   &   &   &   & 1 &   \\
  & 1 &   &   &   & 1 &   \\
  &   &   &   &   &   & 1
\end{bmatrix}$$

This leads to the following node sets:

$$A = \{1\}$$
$$B = \{2, 7\}$$
$$C = \{3, 4, 5\}$$
$$D = \{6\}$$
$$E = \{8\}$$

Associating elements in the node sets, we obtain a new connection matrix, R, called the **reduced connection matrix**, with entries $[R_{st}]$:

$$
\begin{array}{c}
 \\
A \\
B \\
C \\
D \\
E
\end{array}
\begin{array}{c}
\begin{array}{ccccc} A & B & C & D & E \end{array} \\
\left[
\begin{array}{ccccc}
1 & 1 &   &   &   \\
  & 1 & 1 &   &   \\
  &   & 1 & 1 &   \\
  &   &   & 1 &   \\
  &   & 1 &   & 1
\end{array}
\right]
\end{array}
$$

whose graph is

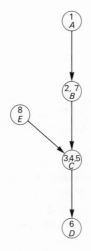

which is partly ordered, as promised.

4.8. Predecessors and Successors

The mth power of the reduced connection matrix, called the **loop set chain connection matrix** or **reduced chain matrix**, is also interesting. We

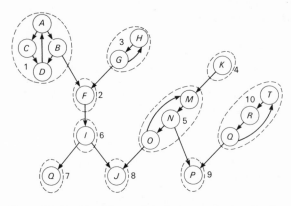

Figure 8.4. Partition of a graph by loop-connected node sets.

started with an $N \times N$ matrix, calculated its Nth power, evaluated the L matrix, and reduced it to obtain the R matrix, which shows the connection between loop-connected node sets. The R matrix is an $M \times M$ matrix. The matrix for R^M of the above example is

$$
\begin{array}{c@{\quad}ccccc}
 & A & B & C & D & E \\
A & \begin{bmatrix} 1 & 1 & 1 & 1 & \\ & 1 & 1 & 1 & \\ & & 1 & 1 & \\ & & & 1 & \\ & & 1 & 1 & 1 \end{bmatrix}
\end{array}
$$

The row corresponding to node i names the set of processors that depend on the outputs of node i. The column corresponding to node i shows the processors upon which it depends. The sets of processors that depend upon the set of processors denoted by node i (itself a set of processors) are called the **successor processor sets** of processor set i. Similarly, the sets of processors upon which the processors of node i depend are called the **predecessor processor sets** of the processor set i.

Given an arbitrary processor, and assuming that all other factors will not influence the design, there is a predilection toward having the successors and predecessors of processor set i colocated with those of i.

Consider the example of Figure 8.4. There are 18 defined processors, which can be partitioned into 10 sets of loop-connected processors as shown:

$$(1) = \{A, B, C, D\}$$
$$(2) = \{F\}$$

$$(3) = \{G, H\}$$
$$(4) = \{K\}$$
$$(5) = \{M, N, O\}$$
$$(6) = \{I\}$$
$$(7) = \{Q\}$$
$$(8) = \{J\}$$
$$(9) = \{P\}$$
$$(10) = \{Q, R, T\}$$

The tendency to keep the members of any one loop-connected processor set together is justified by the following observations:

1. If the component subprocessors of a set are all mechanized as hardware, the colocation will reduce the length and extent of communications and other interfaces. If the subprocessors are mechanized in a single piece of hardware, the interfaces are further minimized.
2. If the component subprocessors of a set are mechanized as software, then the particular software packages should be coresident. This will reduce buffer areas, communication areas, data transfer time, etc. If they are mechanized as a single program, the reduction in software interfaces is still greater.

The predecessors of processor set (6) are sets (1), (2), and (3). Its successors are (7) and (8).

The predecessors of (9) are (4), (5), and (10), while those of (7) are (6), (2), (3), and (1). It is clear from the diagram that (7) and (9), having no common predecessors, need never be colocated. That is, there is no inherent advantage in doing so. In a similar way, (10) has no common successors with (1), (2), (3), (6), (7), and (8), and consequently need never be colocated with them.

The preceding example is the kind of situation that would occur if every occurrence of a processor were shown separately. Assume that a particular processor occurred as a subprocessor in more than one processor. Implementing only one copy of that subprocessor would increase the number of cross-connections shown. The following arguments for the use of redundant copies of processors apply:

1. Redundant copies of a processor can be removed from within the same loop-connected set. To illustrate, if processors C and D of set (1) were redundant copies of the same processor, since there already

is a predilection toward implementing all of (1) as a unit, little will be lost, and perhaps something gained, by removing the redundant copy.

2. Redundant copies occurring in a direct path from some initial node to some terminal node are targets for removal. To illustrate, assume that B and I are two copies of the same processor. It is probably in our interest to remove one of these copies. Furthermore, the closer the copies are along the chain of loop-connected node sets that connect them, the greater the predilection toward merging them.

3. If the copies occur along disjoint chains, that is, two sequences of connected nodes such that no node in the first has either predecessors or successors in common with any node in the second, there is a strong predisposition toward using redundant copies. For example, the chains (1), (2), (6), (7) and (10), (9) are disjoint. Redundant copies of processors appearing in such chains are more likely to be justified than those appearing within a single chain.

4.9. Dependent and Independent Node Sets

The last remark in Section 4.8 leads us to define a new kind of relation between processors.

Predecessor-Independent Processors: Two processors are said to be **predecessor independent** if they do not have any common processor in their predecessor sets. That is, their inputs, traced back through the chain of processors that precede them, are derived from different inputs to the system. If two processors have at least one common predecessor, they are said to be **predecessor dependent**.

Successor-Independent Processors: Two processors are said to be **successor independent** if they have no common successor. If they have at least one common successor, they are said to be **successor dependent**.

Independent Processors: Two processors are **independent** if and only if they are both successor and predecessor independent. If they have at least one common successor or one common predecessor, they are said to be **dependent**.

Strongly Dependent Processors: Two processors are **strongly dependent** if they have both a common predecessor and a common successor.

Independence of processors implies a tendency toward redundant implementation. Successor dependence implies irredundant implementation, additional use of storage, or other forms of internal communications. That is, the outputs of the given processor will ultimately be used more than once and consequently the output space used by the processor cannot be immediately released. Predecessor dependence implies that the inputs to the processor may ultimately be derived from a source that will have to be used by some other processor. Consequently care should be taken in destroying those inputs. Strongly dependent processors imply that caution will have to be used in modifying both inputs and outputs.

Matrix methods can be used to identify the various forms of dependence and independence. It is convenient to deal with the reduced loop connection matrix of the original node set.

Reviewing the steps thus far, we have

A = connection matrix of the processor configuration,

$C = A^N$ chain connection matrix,

$L = C \cap C^T = A^N \cap A^{NT} =$ loop connection matrix,

R = reduced connection matrix,

$S = R^M$ = reduced chain connection matrix.

The R matrix of the graph of Figure 8.4 is

	1	2	3	4	5	6	7	8	9	10
1	1	1								
2		1				1				
3		1	1							
4				1	1					
5						1		1	1	
6						1	1	1		
7							1			
8								1		
9									1	
10									1	1

The reduced chain matrix $(R^M = S)$ is

	1	2	3	4	5	6	7	8	9	10
1	1	1				1	1	1		
2		1				1	1	1		
3		1	1			1	1	1		
4				1	1			1	1	
5					1			1	1	
6						1	1	1		
7							1			
8								1		
9									1	
10									1	1

The entries in a row of S denote the successors of the node corresponding to that row. For example, the successors of (3) are (2), (6), (7), and (8), as can be verified from the graph. An outway is clearly a node that has no successor except itself. Algebraically, the outways are defined as follows. Let

$$V = S \cap J. \tag{1}$$

A node i is an outway if

$$\sum_{j=1}^{m} v_{ij} = 0. \tag{2}$$

Similarly, the entries in the column denote the predecessors of a node, and an inway is a node for which

$$\sum_{i=1}^{n} v_{ij} = 0. \tag{3}$$

Two nodes i and j are predecessor dependent if and only if they have at least one common predecessor. This is clearly obtainable as the intersection of their corresponding columns. Define the matrix P with entries p_{ij}:

$$p_{ij} = \sum_{k=1}^{m} s_{ki}s_{kj} \tag{4}$$

The P matrix of predecessor dependencies is

	1	2	3	4	5	6	7	8	9	10
1	1	1				1	1	1		
2	1	1	1			1	1	1		
3		1	1			1	1	1		
4				1	1			1	1	
5				1	1			1	1	
6	1	1	1			1	1	1		
7	1	1	1			1	1	1		
8	1	1	1	1	1	1	1	1		
9				1	1			1	1	1
10									1	1

The matrix is symmetrical, as would be expected. The relation depicted by the P matrix is reflexive and symmetric, but not transitive. An interesting property of this matrix is that it can be partitioned into subsets that have only the same predecessors. This is done by grouping according to those elements whose rows (or columns, since the matrix is symmetric) are identical. Such a grouping yields

$$\{1\}, \{3\}, \{2, 6, 7\}, \{4, 5\}, \{8\}, \{9\}, \{10\}$$

Note that the predecessors of $(2), (6),$ or (7) are (1) and (3), in addition to elements of the same set.

In a similar way we can define the successor matrix Q by

$$q_{ij} = \sum_{k=1}^{m} s_{ik}s_{jk} \tag{5}$$

This yields Q as

	1	2	3	4	5	6	7	8	9	10
1	1	1	1	1	1	1	1	1		
2	1	1	1	1	1	1	1	1		
3	1	1	1	1	1	1	1	1		
4	1	1	1	1	1	1		1	1	1
5	1	1	1	1	1	1		1	1	1
6	1	1	1	1	1	1	1	1		
7	1	1	1			1	1			
8	1	1	1	1	1	1		1		
9				1	1				1	1
10				1	1				1	1

Chapter 8

Partitioning as before, we obtain

$$\{1, 2, 3, 6\}, \{4, 5\}, \{7\}, \{8\}, \{9, 10\}$$

as those sets that have common successors.

The independent processors are given by

$$\overline{P \cup Q} \qquad \text{or} \qquad \overline{P} \cap \overline{Q}. \tag{6}$$

The strongly dependent processors are given by

$$P \cap Q. \tag{7}$$

Applying this to the present example, we obtain

	1	2	3	4	5	6	7	8	9	10
1	1	1				1	1	1		
2	1	1	1			1	1	1		
3		1	1			1	1	1		
4				1	1			1	1	
5				1	1			1	1	
6	1	1	1			1	1	1		
7	1	1	1			1	1	1		
8	1	1	1	1	1	1	1	1		
9				1	1				1	1
10									1	1

Partitioning, we obtain $\{1\}, \{2, 6, 7\}, \{3\}, \{4, 5\}, \{8\}, \{9\}, \{10\}$ as the strongly dependent modules. Combining these results, we see good reasons for implementing $\{2, 6\}$ and $\{4, 5\}$ within their own modules.

The matrix of independent processors $(\overline{P \cup Q})$ must be interpreted carefully. In the above example it is

	1	2	3	4	5	6	7	8	9	10
1									1	1
2									1	1
3									1	1
4						1				
5						1				
6									1	1
7				1	1				1	1
8									1	
9	1	1	1			1	1			
10	1	1	1			1	1	1		

This matrix yields the following noncontradictory observation:

$$\{1, 2, 3, 6\} \neq \{9, 10\},$$
$$\{4, 5\} \neq \{7\},$$
$$\{7\} \neq \{4, 5, 9, 10\},$$
$$\{8\} \neq \{10\},$$
$$\{9\} \neq \{1, 2, 3, 6, 7\},$$
$$\{10\} \neq \{1, 2, 3, 6, 7, 8\},$$

where $\neq$ symbolizes lack of dependence. These observations, obtained directly by an examination of $P \cup Q$, specify the various ways in which the sets of processors can be partitioned with impunity.

4.10. Applications

Independent processors form natural subdivisions of the design task. We have seen how to take the processor configuration and extract from it those sets of processors that are independent of each other. The analysis can be done in two different ways. In the first case, no redundant copies of processors are included in the processor configuration. This tends to maximize the dependencies and increase the size of the loop-connected processor sets. The second analysis is one in which redundant copies of processors are placed in as many places as makes sense—the copies being labeled as, say, A.01, A.02, . . . , A.98. This tends to increase independence, maximize redundancies, and decrease the size of loop-connected sets. The final solution will generally lie between these two extremes.

It is easier and more revealing to start with the second analysis (redundant copies shown explicitly) than with the first (no redundancies), because it is easier to contract the matrix to reduce the redundancy than to expand the matrix to introduce the redundancy. Assume that a matrix has entries for two redundant copies of a processor, say A.05 and A.06. We wish to combine these to obtain a new matrix, with only one copy of the processor, called, say, A.00. The new matrix will have one less node, and hence will be of a lower order. The row corresponding to A.00 in the new matrix is found as the sum of the rows of A.05 and A.06 in the old one. Similarly, the column for A.00 is found as the sum of the columns of A.05 and A.06 in the old matrix. It can readily be seen that expansion is not unique, and does not necessarily lead to the same graph. That is, if a graph is reduced by removing a redundancy and then expanded again, the resulting graph does not necessarily equal the original graph.

If two node sets are independent in the irredundant graph, we have almost complete freedom as to their implementation. One can be done in hardware and the other in software. Similarly, if both are software elements, there is freedom as to which computer they should be in, since there will be no communications between them. The independence of node sets gives us insight as to the ways in which we should partition the design tasks. It is clearly safer to give two independent sets of processors to two different groups or individuals than it would be to split up a strongly dependent set of nodes. Independence gives us an insight into whether the processor should be built or bought. It is safer to buy a processor that is independent of most of the rest of the configuration than one that is strongly dependent on the rest of the processor configuration.

The number of other processors that a given processor is dependent upon is an indication of the importance or the degree of dependence and therefore a measure of how safe the partitioning can be. This leads to another design time *vs.* run time decision. If we wish to minimize design time, it is the number of connections and not the mass of data that will be communicated that concerns us. The measure of dependence is therefore weighed by the number of links. If run time and space concern us, then the mere existence of a logical connection is not as important as the mass of data that will be communicated, or the amount of memory that must be used for data transfer because of that connection.

One should be wary of seemingly independent processors, especially those that show up on the irredundant processor configuration. It is expedient to check that independence with the buyer. About half the time, such independences are indicative of an ambiguity or ellipsis in the specification and not of true independence. After all, one is more prone to forget to mention a relation than to mention a nonrelation.

The strongly dependent nodes have generally converse properties to the independent nodes. That is, they should be kept together, implemented in the same manner, by the same persons, and purchased the same way.

Not only should we be aware of loop sets and dependent and independent processors, but of what particular links in the graph make the nodes loop connected, or dependent. We may have a perfectly lovely graph, in which there is only one link that makes the whole graph into a single loop-connected node set. By breaking that link we may considerably reduce the size of loop sets and the number of dependent nodes. In reality, the link, if it is essential, cannot be broken without changing the specification. By mentally breaking that link, or making a **cut**, we commit ourselves to an explicit interface between two or more processors. Such cuts can be made at links in which the amount of communications is known to be small, slow, simple, or unimportant. Such cuts may also be made where we know that, for practical reasons, the cut must be made, e.g., when one processor (node) *must* be hardware and the other *must* be software. On the other hand, if we have such information in advance, it is probably best to start the original analysis with the cut already in place, and not obscure the issue by having a link that we know we will remove.

The star-mesh transformation discussed in Section 6 of Chapter 7 is helpful in identifying such cuts, as well as other dependency relations among pairs of nodes. The statistical equations are replaced with simple Boolean equations (i.e., $1 + 1 = 1$, etc.). Diagonal entries are all zero and are removed whenever they occur. Otherwise, the incident, excident, and total star-mesh transformations remain the same. They again tell us what is connected to what. The transformations are not to be considered as substitutes for the full matrix operations, but rather as shortcuts for giving us a relation between two given nodes, or finding the successors or predecessors of a particular node. If a diagonal entry occurs, it merely means that that node is included within some loop-connected node set.

Much of what we have described analytically the seasoned architect does by intuition tempered with experience. Lacking that intuition, we can still proceed one step beyond where everything seems to depend on everything else, and begin to see where the tangle can be unraveled.

4.11. Extensions and Generalizations

The methods described in the above sections can be extended or generalized in several directions. Each such extension further reduces the problem of deciding what goes with what and when (that is, gives us sharper slices of the problem), but at an increased analytical cost.

4.11.1. Functional Connections

The existence of a link between two processors may depend upon an input or some other external factor. In general, we can say that a link entry, rather than being a simple 0 or 1, is a Boolean function. Each entry of the matrix then specifies the conditions under which the nodes will be connected. A typical example might be nodes representing application programs that are called as a result of a decision table. The decision table processor, for such an analysis, may be considered to be outside the configuration. Each valuation of the variables in the decision table establishes a different connection matrix for the processors. If there are N such input or decision table variables, the matrix (with Boolean functional entries) represents 2^N graphs simultaneously.

Procedures for finding loop sets, predecessors, successors, etc., can be defined but are beyond the scope of this book. They are closely related to those described here. The use of such more generalized procedures allows us to weigh dependence, independence, etc., by significant logical conditions.

This sharpens the notion of dependence even more, and allows a yet more rational decision to be made about implementation, cuts, and partitions.

4.11.2. Probabilistic Weighted Boolean Functions

Given a graph in which the connections of the nodes are Boolean functions of N variables, we can establish the dependencies of its nodes. Furthermore, it is often possible to associate a probability with the occurrence of each combination of those variables, if not as N independent probabilities, then certainly as 2^N probabilities. The sum of the product of the probabilities and the 2^N dependency matrices gives us a probability weighting of the dependency. This kind of weight will tell us what will be important at run time, but not at design time, since the probabilities given are usually related to run time parameters. At design time, all existing links are equiprobable, since they must all be implemented somehow.

4.11.3. Numerical Weights

Analogous methods can be used in which we keep track of the number of links or the number of paths that make two particular nodes dependent upon each other. This kind of analysis is biased toward design time problems.

4.11.4. Other Weights

The links can be weighted by the amount of communications that will occur between the two processors, and the probability that the transfer will occur, in a manner analogous to that which was used for performing timing analyses. However, the star-mesh transformation equations as described in Section 6 of Chapter 7 do not apply. The primary reason is that a branch (that is, simultaneous excident links from a node) does not necessarily depict the occurrence of mutually exclusive events. In general, such branches depict *simultaneous* events. The analysis, while possible, is considerably more complicated and beyond the scope of this book.

It is possible to extend the methodology presented here further and further to the point where very elegant functions or algorithms are used to depict dependencies among processors. Each such extension reduces the power of the mathematics that can be brought to bear, while increasing the validity of the model. One can foresee (with horror) a benighted analyst producing a "connection matrix" of processors, each of whose entries is an n-dimensional array having n different series, parallel, and loop connection algorithms, with $n(n - 1)/2$ different distributive laws, and so forth. Even if such a mathematical grotesquery were not to collapse under its own weight(s), it would still be useless. Recall that all of the above analysis can and is often done well by intuition. If the model does not aid that intuition, or if it is more difficult to achieve a valid answer using the model, the intuitionists among us will reject the model as a mere curiosity. The overeager analyst has made a major blunder—he has refused to take slices— and (if the kindly editor will accept another unforgivable mixed metaphor) has attempted to swallow the elephant whole.

5. PARTITIONS

The allocation of processors to computers or special-purpose hardware is a partition of the processor configuration. That is, it has been decided, for each processor in the configuration, how (in general terms) it will be implemented. If a decision has been made to implement, say, processors A, B, and C as hardware, it must further be decided whether there should be N devices, each of which does a little of A, B and C, or three devices, one doing A, another B, and the last C. Analogous decisions must be made for the allocation of processors to computers when they are implemented as software.

If the amount of special-purpose hardware is small, there will not be a significant partition problem. Similarly, if the complete software configuration can be executed by a single computer, partition is simple. It is only when the complex consists of more than one computer that partitioning becomes a significant design problem.

5.1. Extensive and Functional Partitions

Consider a set of processors that are to be implemented in the same way, i.e., either as hardware or as software. The very fact that these processors are recognized as distinct processors means that there is something about their functions that we wish to distinguish.

The performance of each processor of the set can be measured in a sensible manner: for example, a message processor implemented in a FAFNIR-880 can handle 30 transactions per second, etc. Typically, the statistically specified processing load of the complex will imply a required performance value for each processor in it. Generally, a processor may have more than one performance parameter specified. Given a statistical specification of incident load for a given processor, whether its performance is characterized as a single number or a set of parameter values, we can arbitrarily say that this complex load represents "one unit of load."

The load presented to the set of processors can be distributed in one of two ways: functionally or extensively. A **functional partition** is one in which different functions are allocated to different devices. An **extensive partition** is one in which the load of a processor is distributed among several devices. The extent of a processor's implementation is the percentage of the

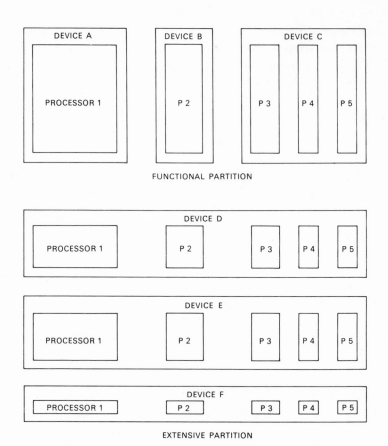

Figure 8.5. Functional *vs.* extensive partitions.

total load for that processor handled by the implementation. Thus, if 500 lines are to be terminated, and five devices are used, each one has an extent of 20%. Similarly, if a task is to be distributed equally among N computers, each computer has an extent of $100/N\%$ for that processor. The difference between extensive and functional partitions is shown in Figure 8.5. Note that processors need not be allocated to devices on a one-for-one basis, and that an extensive partition need not be uniform, i.e., require equal allocation of a task to several devices. Furthermore, a purely functional or a purely extensive partition will rarely occur. For example, in addition to the extents of processors 1, 2, 3, 4, and 5 that they already implement, device D in Figure 8.5 might be used to implement a processor 7, while device E might also implement processors 8 and 9.

5.2. General Advantages and Disadvantages

Several general observations can be made about the relative merits of functional and extensive partitions. One cannot say that functional (extensive) partitions are better than extensive (functional) partitions. We can, however, review the factors that one would have to consider to come to a decision in a specific instance.

5.2.1. Customer Acceptance—Marketability

Functional partitions are more meaningful to the nontechnical buyer. A functional partition allows the user to point to a device and say that it and it alone is performing a particular task. Each device can be given a name which truthfully reflects the tasks that the device is performing. No such assignment can be made for predominantly extensive partitions.[4]

Fortunately, as users become more knowledgeable, the marketability of functional partitions becomes less important. What we are saying is that there are many good reasons for having some processor sets functionally partitioned, but that intellectual palatability to the user, at the expense of his pocketbook, should not be one of them. To ignore this fact leads to a sycophantic subordination of the customer's needs to his (sometimes naive) desires.

5.2.2. Design Simplicity

The functional partition has more explicit interfaces than does the extensive partition. Because of this, it is easier to design. Furthermore, it is more likely that the implementation of the processor is already available (i.e., as a device or as a program). Design costs are lower, implementation time is reduced, design administration is simpler, progress can be more readily judged, and testing is easier than in an extensive partition. Crash programs tend to favor the use of functional partitions, as do relatively small jobs.

5.2.3. Functional Growth

Functional growth is relatively easier to accomplish in a functional partition than in an extensive one. One adds functions by adding devices or program modules. Functional partitions are generally more flexible than extensive ones. If the tasks to be performed cannot be well specified, a more functional orientation is indicated.

[4] We recall an instance of a computer complex in which the partitions were functional and extensive across several computers. Furthermore, the design was such that the physical, logical, and functional constructions could change from moment to moment as a result of computer failures and repairs. Yet, each computer had a little card (for the benefit of visiting firemen) proclaiming it to be the function A computer, the function B computer, etc.

The addition of new functional processors to an extensive partition requires modification of several copies of the device or, more commonly, the addition of a new, functionally oriented, element.

5.2.4. Efficiency

Extensive partitions tend to be more implicit because there are fewer explicit interfaces. In this respect, they are more efficient than functional partitions because the designer has more freedom to exploit syntactic elements of the problem and implicit mechanizations. On the other hand, extensive partitions are more redundant than functional partitions. Clearly, if the extent of a partition were made microscopically small (e.g., one complete independent devices for each line, one copy of a program library for each user), overhead and unnecessary redundancy could drive the efficiency down to the point of absurdity. Balancing this is the fact that the explicit interfaces of a functional partition increase the amount of explicit communications and therefore reduce efficiency by increasing internal communications.

5.2.5. Crosstell

The indications and contraindications of either type of partition can be explained in terms of **crosstell**. Crosstell is a measure of the dependence that may occur among the units of processing that make up the extent of a function. It is a generalized concept that can best be described by example. Consider a complex that must service a number of lines or terminals. Such a complex might be doing numerical machine tool control, factory control, message switching, passenger check-in, reservations, on-line banking, etc. Each input will be processed and generate outputs (typically) for the same line (or for the return line of a pair of duplex lines). If the output of line A is relatively independent of that of line B, the system has little crosstell. If what comes in at A can significantly affect what goes out at B, then the crosstell is high. One can measure crosstell statistically by finding the extent to which the outputs of lines are correlated to the inputs on other lines. A chemical–petrochemical process control system has relatively little crosstell, a reservation system or banking system has intermediate crosstell, while a message switching system has high crosstell. Crosstell as a concept can be also applied to nonphysical processing units. Consider a banking program, say, used to calculate the accounts of the various depositors. There is relatively little crosstell among the depositors, as transfers of money from one to the other are relatively rare. Thus, one could implement the letters A to H in one computer, the letters I to P in another, and Q to Z in a third. The relatively low crosstell implies that there will be little communication across the extensive partitions.

To reiterate, the extent of a function is measured in terms of functional units peculiar to that function (messages, records, transactions, lines, etc.). If the crosstell among these units is high, a functional partition is indicated. Low crosstell militates for an extensive partition.

5.2.6. Extensive Growth

An extensive partition is more capable of orderly extensive growth than is a functional partition. One can add extensive elements in smaller increments than are possible in adding a device that will perform several functions. Typically functions do not grow at the same rate. For example, processors A, B, and C are implemented in one device. An increase in load for A might lead to unwanted redundancy because B and C were increased unnecessarily. If the growth in extent is relatively uniform among the processors implemented in the same device, extensive partition will not be deleterious. If, however, the functions do not grow proportionally, functional partitions might be preferred.

5.2.7. Viability

A system with extensive partitions is less prone to total failure than one with functional partitions. If the partition is predominantly functional, the loss of one device can mean the loss of the complete complex. If the partition is predominantly extensive, the loss of one device means the loss of only that extent of the several functions.

5.2.8. Maintainability

Functionally partitioned elements are simpler to maintain in some respects than extensively partitioned ones. To the extent that the functionally oriented element is intellectually simpler than its extensively oriented counterpart, it is easier to maintain. However, since there must be more of these elements, the complex as a whole tends to have many different kinds of elements, to the point where it is difficult to become expert in all of them. The extensively partitioned system tends to have fewer but larger elements, that are more intellectually complex and individually more difficult to maintain than functional elements. But since there are fewer of these elements, the complex as a whole may be easier to maintain. Since the extensively partitioned system is less vulnerable to failures than the functionally partitioned one, it is more likely that in case of a failure there will be elements available that can aid in diagnosis and repair.

5.2.9. Operational Simplicity

Training and staffing of operators can be more readily done with functionally partitioned systems. The relative intellectual simplicity and the explicit correspondence between elements and functions requires less training for operators. Given a poorly designed functionally partitioned system and a poorly designed extensively partitioned system, the functional system will be easier to operate. Given well designed systems, the differences are likely to be insignificant.

It is generally desirable to recruit operators of a complex from among those who are familiar with its applications rather than from among programmers and system designers. Thus, factory control personnel are trained in the operations of a factory control system and communications personnel in a communications system. The reason is that these individuals are more capable (in an emergency) of making those decisions for which the complex was not programmed, or to recover from unexpected situations, than are computer professionals. Yet the operators must learn much about the system. It is not a question of the relative intelligence of designers and operators, rather it is a question of asking people to learn another discipline in addition to their own. The extensively partitioned system demands more of its operators in terms of learning the computer complex in a professional way. The functionally oriented system is easier to learn.

Systems designed for relatively short life spans and limited productions tend to be more functionally oriented than those designed for multiple production or long lifetimes.

5.3. Partitions in Hardware

The question of functional *vs.* extensive partitions of hardware occurs in two contexts: the design or use of special-purpose hardware, and the selection of computers out of which to construct the complex. We shall see that it is not expedient to use a different computer type for each functional task, even if this means losing efficiency in each execution of every function. Furthermore, the selection of the computer depends critically on the software partition and on viability considerations discussed in Chapters 11 and 12. The specification, selection, or design of special-purpose hardware components, however, does depend upon the kinds of partitions—functional or extensive—that are used.

5.3.1. Customer Acceptance

Customer acceptance plays a bigger role in promoting favoritism toward functional partitions in hardware than it does in software. Often the customer cannot point to any hardware element of the complex, other than those that are functionally oriented, and say that this device does a specific task. Programs, being seemingly insubstantial whether functionally or extensively oriented, are equally (un)acceptable in either form. The increasing trend toward submerging a general-purpose computer within a special-purpose system and marketing that system as a device, despite the fact that it could be programmed to perform many other functions, bears witness to these attitudes. On the other hand, extensively partitioned hardware, if multifunctional, is complex. For this reason, special-purpose hardware is partitioned both functionally and extensively. The extent of the device is set at an optimum economic point, and the device is constrained to perform only one or two simple functions.

5.3.2. Design Simplicity

Both types of partitions are used in a successful special-purpose hardware device. Typically, the offer is not of a single device, but of a product line of modular devices that are compatible, contain interchangeable components, have similar operating principles, and perform relatively narrow functional assignments.

Multifunctional hardware devices are more difficult to design properly than the single-function devices—witness the difference between designing a computer and, say, designing a communications multiplexer.

5.3.3. Functional Growth

Special-purpose hardware devices tend to have little or no functional growth abilities. The discreet designer will include "open doors" much in the same way that the knowledgeable software designer will. That is, if possible, not every state of a control counter will be utilized, and decoding networks will not be completely assigned. He will tend to design the device to allow functional growth, but will rarely stray far from the intended application. Thus, a multiplexer may be given the inherent ability to handle different codes, speeds, and formats; a terminal device will allow different signaling procedures; a motor control will not be restricted to one kind of motor; but it is not likely that the communications multiplexer would have the ability to control motors, or that the motor control could be functionally expanded to perform data logging. Functional growth is then very narrow. If functional growth must be achieved among the special-purpose hardware elements of the system, it will invariably be done by the addition of new devices rather than by the modification of old ones.

5.3.4. Efficiency

We have said that extensive partitions are generally more efficient than functional ones. This may be true in general, but is only partially true for hardware. A multifunctional device would be more efficient than its extensively oriented counterpart of a set of single-function devices. The multifunctional extensive device would benefit from common power supplies, cabinets, reduced wiring, reduced line drivers and receivers, fewer cables and connectors, and so forth. However, the more multifunctional the special-purpose device is made, the more desirable a computer appears, or alternatively, the less marketable that device is. Consequently, the multifunctional orientation leads to smaller production, concomitant higher costs, and, therefore, less performance at a given price than the higher-production, single-function, extensively oriented device. Every special-purpose device contains compromises between theoretical efficiency and the realities of compatibility with the rest of the world.

5.3.5. Crosstell

The crosstell problem of special-purpose devices is generally solved by pushing the problem back to the computer which controls it. This is why such devices are peripheral devices. They funnel data to the computer and distribute the computer's outputs. Typically, crosstell problems that are not solved by the computer are solved by using an interposed device controller for this purpose. A disc file controller may (but usually does not) contain a buffer memory to allow disc-to-disc transfers without going through the central computers of the complex. A digital communication line controller may have interposed a circuit switching system to allow subscribers to converse with each other directly if this is possible and required. These instances, however, are rare in a computer complex. One of the reasons for using a complex, with its centralized memory and other similar facilities, is the existence of inherently high crosstell. If every terminal of a banking system could work out of its own little account, with no need to go through a centralized file, the complex would probably not be needed—the whole job could be done by a bunch of elaborate piggy banks.

Crosstell, then, is not usually solved at the special-purpose hardware level.

5.3.6. Extensive Growth

Extensive growth is the natural domain of special-purpose hardware. It should, however, be recognized that such growth comes in discrete lumps, dictated by the manufacturer of that hardware for good reasons. One can rarely obtain exactly the number of anything that one wants. Servicing 17 lines may cost 1.75 times as much as servicing 16 lines, while servicing 32 lines may cost only 1.95 times as much. The evaluation of a special-purpose device within a computer complex can start with the assumption of continuous growth ability but should go through the following successive phases:

1. Use average values for the cost as a function of capacity, such averages being determined in the neighborhood of the present and projected requirements.

2. Use a continuous but proper approximating formula for cost as a function of capacity. Typically, such formulas will follow a cost *versus* capacity law of the form

$$\text{Cost} = K_1 + K_2 N + K_3 N \log_2 (N + K_4),$$

where N is a measure of capacity. The appropriate law is derived from the manufacturer's price list and many conversations with his customer engineer. Use such laws as first approximation to trades and the evaluation of alternative schemes and suppliers.

3. Use the actual, nonlinear, cost *versus* capacity relation in the neighborhood of the optimum derived in step 2, recognizing that it is not desirable to have present or projected capacity bound near the extensive limits of the device.

Extensive growth of special-purpose hardware is summed up in one word, "modularity." Few hardware manufacturers are simple enough to devise nonmodular hardware. The modular element may consist of a single unit; that is modularity in the highest (but not necessarily most economical) sense.

Typically, the device will accommodate a number of units and be capable of **physical** and **logical growth** up to that maximum number. The distinction between physical and logical growth is important. The fallacious assumption that these are the same can result in a rude shock at some later data. **Logical growth** is the ability to accommodate the maximum logical number of subunits. That is, there is room in the address structure of the device for 2^N units because an N-bit address register and associated decoding logic are included. If the device does not have logical growth up to the maximum required number, it is not usually possible to make the modifications that would be required to provide this growth.

Physical growth is the ability to physically accommodate the required maximum number of units. That is, there is enough room in the cabinet, the output drivers can handle that number of lines, there is sufficient room to mount the connectors and run the cables, etc. Physical growth ability is generally designed into the device from the beginning. Thus, a special-purpose device may be designed to terminate up to 256 lines. The 256-line device is what is first designed. This assures that there will be enough physical, electrical, and logical capacity to accommodate the 256 lines. It may, however, be marketed in modules of 16 lines. The additional physical growth may require additional cabinets, power supplies, cables, etc. If this is included in the original design, and if that design also has the logical growth ability, then the device will be capable of extensive growth. Logical growth ability is typically less expensive than physical growth ability. For this reason, the logical extent of the device typically exceeds its physical extent. The rude awakening of the buyer occurs because he has been led to believe that logical and physical limits were identical. Having bought the advertised logical growth, he is surprised to find that the physical ability does not exist. Such discrepancies between logical and physical extent are typical in computers and associated devices—computers that can "address 20,000,000 bytes directly," terminate 2^{32} peripheral devices, 256 tape transports, 512 disc drives, drums with 16,384 heads, etc. It is essential, when considering the applicability of a special-purpose device, computer, or peripheral device, to inquire into and insist upon obtaining a clear description of the differences between the logical and physical extensive limits of that device. One should always count on the lesser of the two limits as being the correct limit of the device's extensive ability.

5.3.7. Viability

The factors contributing to viability will be discussed in detail in Chapters 11 and 12. Extensive partitions are less vulnerable to failure and result in a more viable system than do functional partitions.

5.3.8. Maintainability

Again, extensiveness contributes toward improved maintainability. This is true for hardware, because multifunctional devices that are not computers are not generally built in quantity by the manufacturers of special-purpose devices.

5.3.9. Operational Simplicity

To the extent that modularity of special-purpose hardware contributes to reduced maintenance, it also contributes to operational simplicity. Special-purpose hardware generally is not an important operational element. The controls of computer complexes are generally effected via software elements, and the special-purpose devices are not important unless they fail. Operational simplicity of special-purpose devices is measured primarily in terms of the device's viability characteristics and not by its internal complexity or modularity.

5.4. Partitions in Software

A comparison of extensive and functional partitions is not particularly germane to computer complexes having only one CPU. Software can be partitioned primarily in terms of time, space, and channel utilization. An extensive partition of software in time cannot be done in the single computer, because the computer can only execute one instruction at a time. If processing N items requires kN milliseconds, it will require at least that, no matter how that kN milliseconds is divided. While there may be some question about how to break up a lengthy function into several smaller intervals, this is not properly an extensive partition. The one computer is still doing the whole job. There is no purpose in having redundant copies of a program or tables within one memory of a computer. Consequently, extensive partitions of program space within a given memory are pointless. It may be sensible to partition tables across several memories to improve memory bandwidth matching, but the programs will not be so affected. The main purpose of redundant copies of a program in a single computer is to improve viability, and not to improve the efficiency of the program. Extensive partitioning of channels is done to improve bandwidth or to reduce memory access delays. Again, it is not a question of how the processors are partitioned, but how the implemented processors are used and use the facilities they require.

The question of extensive $vs.$ functional partitions of software is then primarily one of deciding how the several processors that are to be implemented as software are to be allocated to the several computers of the complex. The job is made more difficult by the fact that the computer has generally not yet been selected when software partition questions first come up.

The partition of the software processors is used to specify the computers, which in turn may change the partition.

5.4.1. Customer Acceptance and Marketability

As in hardware, the customer would emotionally prefer to have each computer of the complex perform uniquely assigned tasks. He wants a clear functional configuration. But this is not likely to occur, and the proper configuration is generally a result more of extensive partitions than of functional partitions. Since the software is not well understood, and often distrusted, the adroitness of an extensive partition or for that matter a functional partition of software is likely to be lost on the user anyhow, and generally will not figure much in the acceptance of the design.

5.4.2. Design Simplicity

Every computer that must execute the functional mix represented by the extensive partition must have all the software required for that set of tasks. If in addition to this there is a substantial amount of crosstell between the extensive elements, additional design burdens will be imposed because there will be need for additional communications, buffer areas, constants, tables, etc. It is more likely that a functionally oriented partition can be obtained as a proprietary program or as firmware. Design costs and time are generally higher for an extensive partition than for a functional partition of the software.

5.4.3. Functional Growth

The use of extensive partitions implies that each computer is loaded nearly to the maximum point in performing the functional mix of the extensive partition. If loading were not high (at least 50 to 60%, and generally 75 to 80% per computer), we should inquire as to why the extensive partition was used at all.

The extensive partition is used when it is clear that one computer cannot handle the complete job. The processing load could have been partitioned functionally or extensively. If it was partitioned extensively, the complex will typically employ the fewest computers that can handle the total job. Consequently, they are as near to being fully loaded as can be. The extensive partition of functions presupposes that the major growth will be extensive rather than functional. If functional growth is required in a processor set that has been partitioned extensively, the extensive partition must be further increased, to make room for the new functions. Thus, if four computers were used for the original functions, five may be required to handle the load with the added function. That function must be incorporated in each computer of the extent.

Functional additions to a set of software-implemented processors requires us to attenuate the load by extending the partition and then to add the function in each computer of the extensive partition. This is somewhat more difficult than adding a function to a set of computers that have their software functionally partitioned because the interfaces tend to be more explicit, already exist, and are consequently easier to change.

5.4.4. Efficiency

Extensive partitions of software are generally less efficient than functional partitions. First of all, there is a redundancy of programs, constants, tables, work areas, etc. Memory is therefore increased. Secondly, each computer must execute the same overhead functions and consequently have the same overhead programs. This tends to increase both time and space usage. If there is a substantial amount of crosstell, there will be more explicit communications among the several computers than if the interfaces were functional. On the other hand, the communication among the several processors that make up the functional mix of the extensive partition is more implicit than it would be in a functional partition. This tends to reduce interprocessor communications.

No reasonably designed complex is either wholly functional or wholly extensive with regard to the partition of its processor configuration. Generally, a two-stage system is constructed, where one stage is functionally partitioned and the other is extensively partitioned. Furthermore, there is a clearcut functional separation between the two stages. Thus, if a system must do a lot of communication with remote terminals and not much internal processing, the first stage will be extensively partitioned and comprise those functions for which crosstell is not severe, while the second stage will be functionally partitioned and take care of crosstell-related functions, total system control, etc. If, on the other hand, the system is processing dominated, the modest communication load may be the functional center of the system, with an extensive partition of processing among several large number crunchers in the back. The idea is to keep interprocessor dependencies and crosstell away from the intercomputer interfaces.

5.4.5. Extensive Growth

Extensive growth for extensive partitions is natural and simple if the ability has been designed into the system from the start. Extensive growth for functional partitions is messy at best. If the extent of the processing load accommodated by a set of processors has grown beyond the ability of the computer that is used to implement them, some of the functions in that set will have to be relegated to other computers to make room for the additional load. If neither the computer nor the memory is overloaded by the addition, the question is not worth dwelling upon. It is generally possible to increase space, and generally very difficult to increase processing speed. Moving processors around to make room for others is difficult. The programs of the computer from which the processor is to be excised must be purged of all traces of that processor. This can be as difficult as patching in a new processor. Internal interfaces such as calling sequences must be converted to external interfaces such as data transfers or control messages. The computer which receives the function that has been transferred must be similarly transformed.

5.5. Mixed Partitions

The general case can be seen from the above discussion to be the use of mixed partitions. Those processors that have little direct crosstell and/or for which it is expected that there will be more extensive growth than functional growth are partitioned extensively. Those processor sets for which crosstell is high, that are highly dependent upon other processors, that have a lot of overhead, and for which functional growth is expected are partitioned functionally. The result is a multistage configuration with recognizable functional separation between stages.

5.6. Crossed Partitions

A **crossed partition** is one in which a processor is implemented in two different ways, in order to meet load requirements. For example, part of one function is implemented as software, and extended into hardware, e.g., a line scanning function is done by a hardware multiplexer for 15 lines, and directly by the computer for 5 additional and almost identical lines.

In general, crossed partitions imply a lot of redundancy. There must be overwhelming reasons to justify the duplication of design effort, testing, integration, training, maintenance, interface, etc., that such dualistic mechanizations imply. One more often ends up with the worst of the two worlds rather than with the best of the two. Attempts at this have typically been in the interest of increasing viability. Where this is appropriate, the primary way of accomplishing the task may be through hardware. The backup for the hardware may be an equivalent processor implemented as software. The system is either in a state in which it is using the hardware version or in a state where the software version is in use. This could be a proper form of crossed partitions, but as usually implemented it is not.

The cases in which, for reasons other than viability, hardware and software implementations of a processor are simultaneously used to accept a greater processing load are few. Most often they have come about as a result of extensive growth requirements that could not be otherwise met, and which for financial reasons it was not possible to upgrade completely to one or the other implementation. It may occur as an interim situation in transition between two forms of implementation. It is rarely designed beforehand, rarely desirable, and not often successful. It is a patch; and patches tend to come loose.

6. THE INTERNAL COMMUNICATION STRUCTURE OF MULTI-COMPUTER COMPLEXES

The internal communication structure of a computer complex consists of those wires, gates, registers, busses, etc., whose primary function is to transfer data from one unit of the complex to another. The units of a complex are to be understood as individual CPUs, memories, etc. The internal communication facility is to be distinguished from the external facility, which is charged with communication of data to and from the world external to the complex.

The physical communication network consists of the actual wire paths which exist between the various units of the complex. The logical communication networks are those wires which are called upon in the program. While the physical configuration is constant during the operation of the complex, changed only by the addition of other CPUs, memories, or equipments, the logical configuration may be variable, depending upon the health of the various units, the program load, etc. We will exclude for now those configuration changes brought about in the interest of viability. We can distinguish between systems in which the logical facility is changeable under program control and those in which the logical communication facility is static. A parallel processing system in which several CPUs have their own memories and operate independently on several programs is an example of a static communication facility. A system with shared memory in which data transfers can occur among CPUs and memories is generally considered to have a dynamic communication facility. It is clear that the physical communication network must allow the implementation of all possible logical (and functional) configurations; i.e., one cannot call for the use of a communication link which does not physically exist.

The internal physical communication structure of the complex is determined by the logical communication facility and the degree of unit interchangeability required by considerations of viability. If no interchangeability is required, then the logical and physical communication facilities can be identical. If total interchangeability is required, the physical communication facility must allow the logical communication for any construction of the units.

6.1. Generic Internal Communication Topologies

Six basic internal communication topologies can be recognized. They are the radial system, the tree system, the bus system, the matrix system, the iterative system, and the symmetric system, illustrated in Figure 8.6. Each type will be considered in turn and the factors which lead to its adoption and/or rejection will be discussed.

6.1.1. Radial and Tree Systems

The predominant structured complex type found today is the radial system. The radial system is a direct evolutionary product of the mainstream of commercial computer design. Earlier systems consisted of a single CPU coupled to a variety of specialized I/O controllers. The I/O controller varied in complexity from a simple interlock between the I/O device and the central computer to a sophisticated computer in its own right. Examples are tape multiplexers, corner turning buffers for punched card equipment, file search systems, etc.

As the number and complexity of I/O devices grew, it became apparent that there were several processes common to almost all I/O controllers, viz., buffering, data format and code conversion, automatic address assignment for writing, block transfers of data, data searching, multiplexing and demultiplexing, etc. While a generalized I/O controller was not justifiable for any one of these functions or for any one I/O device, in aggregate, the hardware that the individual I/O controllers represented amounted to

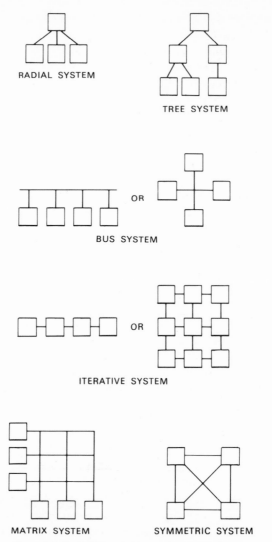

Figure 8.6. Basic internal communication topologies.

more than the main frame of the computer itself. Therefore, there evolved a sequence of more and more generalized I/O controllers, culminating in the use of stored-program digital computers for this task as well.

The majority of large-scale data processing systems are of this sort. The units in this case are computers as such. As usually programmed, the peripheral or I/O control computer is assigned all routine I/O control jobs. General instructions are given to the peripheral control computer(s), which are then interpreted and converted into the detail instructions of the I/O routine. For example, the I/O controller may be given an instruction to read the twenty-seventh through thirty-third blocks of tape on tape transport 17. The I/O control computer interprets the instruction, examines availability of the transport, takes care of the fact that logical tape 17 is located on physical tape transport number 12, formats the data, and perhaps does some simple searches, sorts, or other preprocessing.

Among the various individual computers and computing systems using a radial structure are BIZMAC, IBM 7090/1401, CDC 7600, and SAGE.[5]

The tree structure is a natural extension of the radial structure, and many large systems use it. The SAGE system is a tree with respect to the AN FSQ-8/AN FSQ-7/radar computer hierarchy.

It should be noted that no computer complex is a pure example of any of the structures described. Thus, it will be convenient to call a given complex a tree structure (SAGE), radially structured (SAGE), or iteratively structured (SAGE again), depending upon what is to be explicated.

Many factors enter into the effectuality of a radial or tree physical structure. It is to be recognized that the root of the tree (the center of the radial structure, or that device which has no other device at a level parallel to it) is the natural place at which to implement the central control or executive functions. This structure is effective if the tasks performed by the various devices are fairly well distinguishable, either by function or by extent.

The following is a list of factors that militate for and against the use of a radial structure. The factors discussed below are valid for all radial structures, not just those in which the units are full computers.

Factors which favor tree or radial structures:

1. The system can be cleanly partitioned either in extent or by function, and there still remains a substantial amount of coordination required for the individual units, but not much communication among them.
2. Individually complex tasks that must be performed by individual subsidiary CPUs, with infrequent intercomputer communication as far as bandwidth is concerned, but sufficient coordination required to justify a central communication control.
3. Basic data coming in from the outside which for the sake of efficiency and security must be preprocessed simultaneously with distribution to central processing thereafter. This is generally a partition

---

[5] With respect to the relation between the AN FSQ-7 and the radar data processors, and the AN FSQ-8 and the AN FSQ-7s.

by extent at the lower levels of the tree with a partition by function among the levels of the tree.

4. A semantic configuration in which the cost of internal communication is extremely high and must be minimized through the use of a large central processor.

Contraindication for tree or radial structure:

1. The problem is not easily partitioned in function or extent.
2. Very heavy (high bandwidth) internal communication requirement.
3. Viability a major factor.
4. Extensive partition is possible, but communication is geographically constrained, i.e., each unit need communicate only with its neighbor.

6.1.2. Bus Systems

A bus-structure system is one in which all communicants share a common communication facility. That is, there is a party line. Only one element of the system can transmit a message to the bus; however, all addressed parties can receive. Bus systems are a common internal structure of many computers, particularly the earlier machines. Bus structures, by their very nature, require a bus controller or coordination routines. If communication can be batched and service is infrequent, this type of structure can be effective. Partition of tasks by function or by extent is far more flexible than in the tree structure. Queuing problems are more critical, however.

Factors that favor a bus structure:

1. Modest internal communications required.
2. Primarily batched communications.
3. Distribution-type communications—each source goes to several destinations, each destination receives from at most one source at a time.
4. Central control of bus either by hardware or software is justified.
5. Great flexibility in the way of functional and/or extensive growth within the limits of communication capacity of the bus, without modification of the elements already on the bus.

Contraindications for a bus-structured system:

1. Heavy and/or randomly distributed communications required.
2. Station-to-station rather than dispersive communications.
3. Growth pattern well understood, flexibility not required.
4. Central control used for nothing except bus control but remains major item in the system.

5. Communication between elements is over long lines, and bus structure cannot be electrically implemented at the required speeds.

6.1.3. Matrix Systems

The matrix-oriented system is an extension of the bus-structured system. It consists of several busses that can be shared by many elements of the system. Communication is, therefore, more flexible, and the system can handle much higher bandwidths. Examples of matrix-structured systems are the RW 400 and B 8500. The factors which favor the use of a matrix system are the same as those that favor a bus system, with the exception of the requirement for modest internal communication. The contraindications are also the same, with the exception of 2, which is not an important factor. The matrix system is to be looked upon as something between a bus-structured and a symmetrically structured system. It lends itself well to the use of modular units. Full communication flexibility is not provided, but the problems and constraints are such that the limited communication facility is acceptable.

6.1.4. Iterative Systems

In iterative systems, the internal communication is highly constrained, so that each unit can only talk to its neighbors (in one or more topological dimensions). Such structures have limited applications. The major indication for them is that there is a similarity or analog of the problem and the internal structure of the complex. Thus, a two-dimensional iterative structure is applicable to the solution of partial differential equations by the relaxation method (ILLIAC IV). An air defense system can coordinate the various area controls along a defense perimeter via an iterative structure since, in general, a complex need only communicate with its immediate neighbors. If there is no strong geometrical-communcation analog, the iterative structure tends to get glutted in its own communication, and intermediate units waste time relaying messages. Iterative structures are best applied in extensively partitioned systems with low crosstell that can be constructed of modular subunits.

6.1.5. Symmetric Systems

The symmetric system, in which everything can communicate with everything, is by far the most sophisticated, flexible, effective, and expensive form of internal communication structure that can be built. The primary purpose for using it is to achieve total interchangeability of components from the points of view of viability. As the system gets large, internal communication becomes a major part of the system's cost.

6.2. Channel Structures

Communication between the hardware elements of the complex is accomplished via channels. Manufacturers can and do offer channels of various types with a broad range of capabilities and bandwidth. Our interest at this point is not in the specific control functions that may be performed by the channel and its associated controller, or in the code, format, and speed conversions that may be performed. Our emphasis will be on the bandwidth of the channel, its hardware cost, and the cost (in memory cycles executed) of character transfers from unit to unit. We can assume that we will not inadvertently force the use of incompatible channels, controllers, and devices, or overload the physical or logical limits of a hardware unit with respect to the number of channels of various types that it can handle. These assumptions tend to reduce the problem of channel assignments to the point where it is tractable even if still difficult.

We have seen that the way in which processors are assigned to hardware or software implementations and the way these in turn are implemented as functional or extensive partitions are to a large extent directed toward the reduction of internal communications. But in the discussion on partitions, we were not too specific about what precisely it was that was to be reduced—was it the memory space, memory cycles, instructions, channel bandwidth, or what? It is all of these, as usual, as a compromise, and at the expense of each other.

6.2.1. Generic Channels

The simplest type of channel is a **direct channel**. A direct channel is one that is used or activated directly by the action of the control of the central processing unit. The memory switch and all its associated gear is a direct channel. The various interrupt lines of the complex are also direct channels. In each case, the communication of data along the channel is ancilliary to the execution of an instruction. While there may be explicit instructions for such communications (e.g., STØRE, FETCH), the actions of a direct channel may be initiated as a result of any and all instructions.

The bandwidth of a direct channel is at least as high as that of the computer(s) it services. The direct channels of a computer may be activated simultaneously with other channels—in fact, they usually are. Thus, a bulk-to-main-memory transfer requires the use of the channels used to control both the disc and the memory switch. In the discussion of the memory switch in Chapter 4, it might have been inferred that the memory switch was used only between the computer and the main memory. This is not always the case. In some computers it is possible to tie a device that is neither a computer nor a memory directly to the memory switch. In fact, in early computers this was the predominant way in which communications were carried out. The memory switch, internal register transfers, channels, etc., were nothing more than different ports to a central memory bus. Everything coming in, going out, or moving around within the computer did so over the central memory bus. For some contemporary systems, the high-speed transfer channel and the memory bus are one. In such cases, the distinction between channel types is one of intent and usage rather than one of structure.

Contentious transfer channels or **autonomous transfer channels** are those channels for which a contentious transfer between devices and the main memory can be established. They are characterized by high transfer rates (broad band) and block transfers. Their bandwidth is limited to that of the memory switch ports that they use. Contentious transfer channels, while typically broad-band, can come in a variety of sizes and shapes. Typical are multiple words in parallel; word parallel, character serial; or serial by bit. The transfer per memory cycle could range from one bit to several words. Speed is also available in a wide range, from full main memory speed to a few tens of bits per second. The important characteristic for us is the ability to establish contentious transfers.

Explicit channels are those for which an explicit instruction must be issued for each unit of data transfer, and for which the instruction execution is not complete until the transfer has been completed. That is, the transfer is not autonomous, and the next instruction in sequence is delayed until the completion of the transfer. Explicit channels are typically the least expensive as far as hardware costs are concerned, and the most expensive in terms of the number of memory cycles required to transfer a given number of words.

A comparison of the three channel types is instructive. Let us say that the unit of data transfer in all three cases is a word, and that a block of words is to be transferred. A transfer of N words would take the following number of cycles:

Direct channel:	1 instruction (FETCH AND STØRE N WORDS) . . .	2 cycles
	1 cycle per word	N cycles
		$N + 2$ cycles
Contentious channel:	1 instruction (TRANSFER N WØRDS)	2 cycles
	2 cycles per word	$2N$ cycles
	15 cycles for the termination interrupt service . .	15 cycles
		$2N + 17$ cycles
Explicit channel:	1 instruction per word to fetch	$2N$ cycles
	1 instruction per word to store	$2N$ cycles
	2 instructions per word for index testing (one of them a jump).	$3N$ cycles
		$7N$ cycles

The particular values required for the three different channels will differ from computer to computer.

It is clear that for a given machine there are values of N for which one of the three channels is less costly than the other two. Suppose that in the above example the minimum amount of data that the FETCH AND STØRE instruction could transfer is a complete block of 64 words, while the other channels were not so restricted. From 0 to 3 words, the explicit channel would be preferred: and for more than 24 words, the direct channel would be the most efficient.

Other types of channel may exist that fall between those discussed above or that have characteristics that overlap more than one of the above categories. The important principle to be learned is that the cost per bit of data transfer, as measured in cycles per bit transferred from the source to the ultimate destination, can vary with the number of bits being transferred. This cost, however, is readily determined. Such a determination results in a comparison similar to the one above. From this comparison, one can obtain the range over which a particular channel is most effective. If the distribution of lengths of the data packages to be transferred is known, the channel to be used can be chosen to minimize the total processing load presented by the data transfers. Remember, however, that in addition to the three generic types there are variations as to the number of bits simultaneously transferred (bit, character, or word interface), the number of data units that can be transferred using a single instruction, the delay in the transfer, and the priority of the transfer. It could be that a particular manufacturer will give a choice of twenty or more channel types to use for transfer of data among the hardware units of the complex.

Relatively few manufacturers will allow any kind of device on any kind of channel. For example, it may be that two computers can only communicate over a special contentious, computer-to-computer channel, or that a card reader can only be connected by an explicit channel with a character interface, or, most often, that there is no choice in the channel structure for a computer-to-main-memory connection, e.g., it must be via a direct channel. These restrictions will tend to narrow the choice somewhat. Such narrowing asides, there is usually more than one way to communicate between two units available in standard hardware. If specialized interface hardware can be constructed, the choice of channel types is significantly extended.

6.2.2. Bandwidth Matching

The choice of channel is not always made in the direction of minimizing transfer costs as measured in cycles required per bit transferred. The most economical channel available can be too fast. As an example, consider a computer capable of executing 1,000,000 cycles per second which is to be connected to a core with an inherent transfer rate of 250,000 words per second. If 2 cycles are required per word, for a contentious channel transfer the maximum load that the mass memory presents would be 500,000 cycles per second. This is probably enough to allow other functions to go on as well. Suppose, however, that there are four such memories to be serviced. The aggregate load would be 2,000,000 cycles per second, substantially more than the computer is capable of executing. If now the data transfer were required very infrequently, say, only 1000 words per second from each mass memory, it might well pay us to use the costlier explicit channel. The aggregate load for the explicit channel might be 28,000 cycles (using our previous model), compared to 8000 cycles for the contentious channel. While the 8000 cycles could not be executed, the 28,000 cycles could, since it is possible to schedule them over the second. Even if only 500 words had to be transferred and the computer could execute the 4000 cycles in the available 4000 microseconds, there would be an intolerable period of 4000 microseconds during which interrupts could not be serviced and during which other critical functions would have to be deferred. The choice of channel structure can therefore be a choice of *increasing* the total number of cycles used for a transfer in order not to momentarily overload the capabilities of the machine. The statistical load (including a judicious number of σs) presented to the computer by the channels should be less than the total number of cycles that the computer is capable of executing. It is not unreasonable to limit the momentary transfer rate of the aggregated channels to less than 50% of the capacity of the memory.

The choice of channel can be made to obtain a proper bandwidth match between the computer and devices, and devices and other devices. In addition to this, overlap and interlace can be used to further improve the bandwidth match by effectively increasing or decreasing the apparent transfer rates of the communicants.

6.2.3. Communication Costs

We have seen two of the cost items that enter into evaluating the cost of internal communications; cycles per bit transferred, and peak bandwidth requirements. In addition, the program and data space required by the channel must be considered. Program space is minimized for direct channels. Contentious channels require instructions for setting up the transfer and for servicing the termination interrupt. Explicit channels need instructions for fetching, storing, and for incrementing and checking block counts. The use of re-entrant coding, the existence of good loop control instructions, EXECUTE instructions, and elegant interrupt hardware can make the program space required vary widely, to the point where it is not possible to make generalized statements. Storage space depends mostly on the statistics of the data being transferred and the frequency with which the transfer takes place. It does not differ much among the three channel types.

The major cost item to be considered is the cost of the channels themselves. Broad-band channels, using single-word or multiword parallel transfers, are usually more expensive than single-bit channels. This is true for all three generic types. For a given **data unit width** (number of bits transferred in parallel), the direct channel is typically more expensive than the contentious channel, which in turn is more expensive than the explicit channel. The ratio in hardware costs could be 20 or 30 to 1.

Software design costs are usually highest for contentious channels and lowest for direct channels. The contentious channels programming cost is higher than that for explicit channels because the contentious channel usually has an interrupt that must be serviced, which the explicit channel usually does not have.

Reliability is another item worth considering. If a direct channel fails, it is likely that the computer has failed, as well as all other channels. Many computers are constructed in such a way that one contentious channel could fail without harming the others. That is, various contentious channels serving the same computer are relatively independent. Explicit channels usually contain the least amount of hardware per channel. The direct channel and the explicit channel are more likely to fail as groups, but having little hardware devoted to a particular channel, assuming that the computer itself has not failed, are less likely to fail than the contentious channel. The contentious channel, while less reliable than either the direct or the explicit channel, tends to fail independent of other channels, allowing some processing to continue despite the failure. Here again, we have the typical kind of choice that continually plagues the architect.

The optimum choice is only to a first degree of approximation that which minimizes the cost of communications. The cost of communications is a weighted sum of the various items such as cycles, memory, reliability, bandwidth, etc., that affect the cost. The optimum from the point of minimizing internal communications is not necessarily the optimum from the point of view of optimizing the complex. For example, a potential for extensive growth of a particular processor may force the use of a particular channel because the other channel types have a logical or physical limit that is inadequate. A particular channel mix that minimizes processing load may increase delay to the point where it is intolerable. Maintainability may be improved by using a single channel type throughout the complex, to such an extent that the reduced maintenance costs and increased system viability may more than compensate for the reduced efficiency of any one channel. The selection of a channel type to meet the communications requirements of two devices is a decision for which it should not be assumed that the local optimum is the global optimum.

6.3. Communication Analysis

6.3.1. Communication Models

Given a tentative allocation of processors to computers, the partitions thus created induce communication requirements. An analysis of the flow charts of the various processors, in which links are weighted by the amounts of data that are to be transmitted from the given processors to other processors, allows one to form a communication model for the complex as a whole. From that model, channel bandwidth requirements can be established. Next in the design process, channels can be allocated as to number and type, and the additional processing burden established by the service of these channels evaluated. The result can then be used for a further iteration in which revised processing loads are used to revise the partition of the processors. If all goes well, this process converges to an optimum allocation of resources.

The model starts with the design flow charts. Each processor in each tentative partition must be reanalyzed (by the methods of Chapter 7), using a model in which the link weights are the numbers of bits whose transfer is initiated upon achieving that link. A separate analysis is required for each destination outside of the set of processors tentatively in that partition. However, this is not as tedious as it appears because relatively few links will initiate communication to more than one destination. The same trick that was used to simplify memory evaluation can be used here. The flow chart is simplified until only those links that initiate the transfer of data (and the nodes they span) remain. All weights not belonging to the particular destination being considered are then removed, leaving only those destined to the place of present concern. The flow chart is then analyzed, giving us the probability that a transfer will occur, the mean value in bits for that transfer, and the standard deviation or higher moments as required. If, on the basis of external data or other timing analyses, we can determine the probability that the particular processor will be executed, we have a model of the communication situation.

Figure 8.7 shows the situation as it might occur within a given computer and its associated processor set. For simplicity's sake we have left out the communications among the processors within the set. Processor 2 generates "messages" of given statistical characteristics destined for destination 3. We have shown two such sets for reasons that will be apparent shortly. Processor 5 generates messages for destinations 3 and 2. The case of processor 2 is important. It may be in our best interest to segregate the kinds of

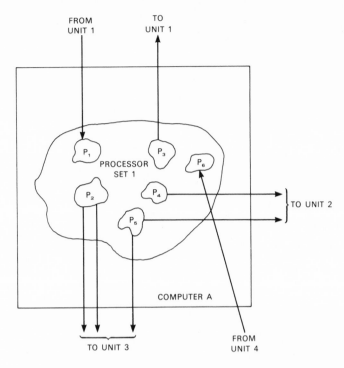

Figure 8.7. Processor set communication and computer-to-subsystem communication.

messages being transmitted, e.g., data, control, verification signals, etc. If we do not segregate in this way, the mean value of the transfer of data from processor 2 to destination 3 will still be correct, but the peculiarities of the distribution will be obscured. We generally have a pretty good idea of what kind of channel we shall use anyhow. The segregation could be functional or according to tentative channel assignments. By summing the distributions obtained for each processor in the set for the same destination, we obtain the distribution of messages for that destination as initiated by that computer. Separate analysis can be performed to obtain bits per second, characters per second, messages per second, transmission blocks per second, etc., as required.

Bits per second are worthy of special attention if different code lengths are used for different channels or if there is a choice as to the degree of parallelism available for data transfers. Characters per second are needed for a similar reason, and words per second—if appropriate to the possible channels—are needed to properly evaluate the number of contentious transfer cycles that will be used. Messages or functionally complete data transfer units may initiate interrupts in the receiving destination, which in turn may elicit further interrupts or acknowledge signals in the originating processor sets. Messages may be broken up into transmission line blocks or message blocks, each one of which can initiate termination interrupts or other actions. Fortunately the analysis of the individual processors is simple and relatively few categories are required. The collection of this information results in a diagram somewhat like that of Figure 8.8.

We have depicted the complete collection of statistical data regarding the transfers symbolically by μ and σ, recognizing that several distributions may in fact be required. We must select an allocation of channels for each link in the graph of Figure 8.8. The obvious place to start is with the channels that we are committed to; e.g., "an explicit channel pair must exist between each pair of computers." We shall see later, in the chapters on viability, that we are committed to far more than might be supposed at first glance. If the precommitted channels are sufficient, we have a tentative channel assignment. If not, we attempt to find a minimum cost allocation of channel types and number to each link in such a manner that all communication requirements can be accommodated at a reasonable cost, within the physical and logical limits of the complex, with the assurance of satisfying the requirements with a sufficiently high probability.

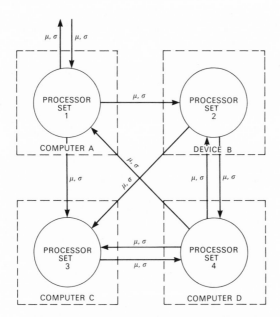

Figure 8.8. Interprocessor set and intercomputer communications.

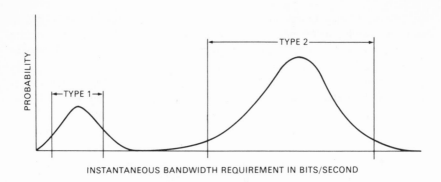

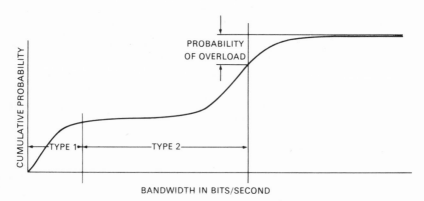

Figure 8.9. Allocations of channels to match bandwidth distributions.

The probability distribution and its integral, the cumulative distribution, are useful guides in selecting the channel mix. Figure 8.9 shows a typical bandwidth distribution and its associated cumulative distribution. We note that there are two populations of data transfers, perhaps corresponding to short and long messages, character or word interface, or high and low frequency of transmission initiation. We might have, for the sake of simplicity, a choice of two different channel types—say, type 1 and type 2—each with its characteristic bandwidth. In this example, most of the distribution can be covered by two channels, one of each type. These could be superposed on the bandwidth distribution as shown. The cumulative distribution is used to determine the probability of a channel overload. This is simply done by marking off a distance equal to the bandwidth of each of the channels used. The point at which the furthest channel crosses the cumulative distribution tells us the probability that the bandwidth requirement will be met, or, equivalently, the probability that there will be an overload. If the overload probability is not sufficiently low, because of unwieldy queue buildup in the various processors, we might add a third channel, say, of type 1, to obtain the results shown in Figure 8.10. The addition of a channel significantly reduces the overload probability. Proceeding in this way, we can obtain an assignment that satisfies the requirements to within any desired probability.

Associated with each channel type there is a cost. Each channel has a discrete, known bandwidth. Furthermore, the load distribution can be found or approximated. There is therefore a clear assignment problem here: find a minimum cost mix of channels that satisfies the probability requirements. If this were all there was to the problem, life would not be too difficult. However, several additional facts come into play which tend to reduce the selection of channels to a predominantly cut-and-try procedure rather than a formal algorithm.

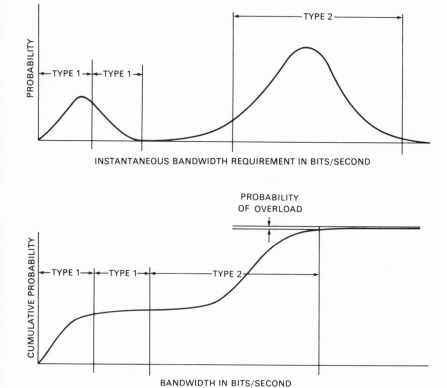

Figure 8.10. Channel allocation for reduced overload probability.

Channels usually come in a package. There will be a channel with several ports, going to all destinations. Thus, the sum of the distributions of the excident links may have to be used. Some channels may have single ports and can be independent. The assignment of one kind of channel may require the sum of the excident distributions, while that of another kind of channel may require only the incident or excident distribution for that destination. Bandwidth is not the only factor to consider—the number of cycles stolen per bit transferred, the nature and the complexity of servicing acknowledgment interrupts, the logical and physical limits of the channel, and viability requirements can drastically change the picture. When all is said and done, we end up with a cut-and-try procedure. The use of the distribution, however, is important, even for cutting and trying. In many cases, particularly with the bimodal and trimodal distributions that occur in things like bandwidth requirements or message lengths, the use of simple averages rather than the distribution can result in a 20% to 30% underestimation of the requirement.

Given a tentative channel assignment, we must determine the amount of additional communication generated as a result of that assignment. This means the processing of interrupts, the stolen cycles, and other processing such as buffer assignment and manipulation that may be required for the acknowledgment processing. This adds to the processing burden of each computer in the complex, in some cases to the point where one or more computers are overloaded or uncomfortably near the upper loading bound that we have established to allow for future growth or peak requirements. This in turn may result in a new channel selection. Fortunately, there is usually not too much choice. We can arrive at a tentative channel assignment and generally make only slight modifications in the processor partition and in the channel assignment. The value of the analysis is to assure us that we have not blundered. With so many other things to think about, we should welcome every tool that helps us avoid errors. Many badly designed complexes are bad because of inadequate intercomputer channels. Colloquially, such a system is said to be "strangled" or "choked." Big CPUs must be connected by comparably big pipes, lest they grind to a halt. Unfortunately, we still suffer from undue emphasis on the CPU. One of the characteristics of a multicomputer complex is that there are relatively more channels per CPU than there would be in a single-computer system using the same hardware. Consequently, the channel costs tend to reduce the share of the cost allotted to the CPU, with the result that while in the single-computer system the channel costs may be minor, in the complex they tend to be as important as that of the CPU itself. The selection of a CPU for application to a complex is therefore influenced as much by channel structure as it is by CPU design, repertoire, speed, etc.

6.3.2. Block Factor Evaluation

One characteristic of most channels is their ability to transmit blocks of data rather than single characters or words. It is usually possible to transmit only as many characters as are actually contained in the message. However, data are usually organized in memory as blocks of fixed length. These blocks may be strung together by various means to allow longer messages to be accommodated. The specific mechanisms by which this is done is discussed in Chapter 10.

For the moment, it suffices to say that each segment of data is divided into blocks. The first block of a string of such blocks may contain administrative data relating to the chain of blocks, while each subsequent block contains a lesser administrative area. Whether or not the administrative area is actually part of the block (it usually is not) is not important for now. If the block is very small, the administrative area will dominate, and space will be wasted as well as processing time. If, on the other hand, the blocks are very long, space again will be wasted, but processing overhead will be reduced. This leads to a channel–time–space trade which is worth evaluating.

Two approaches may be taken toward the use of chained blocks and their transmission. We could transmit the complete block, whether it contained useful data beyond a certain point or not. This would result in wasted transmission cycles, which must be compared to the cost of building a special I/O instruction for each transmission such that only exactly the right number of characters would be transmitted. It is usually less costly to use a uniform transmission length. If a variable-length transmission is used, then the memory block that receives the data will also have invalid characters in it. If, say, the block length is 64 characters, and only the first 48 locations are in use for a particular block, an I/O transmission instruction containing the number 48 would have to be constructed. The number of memory cycles required to construct that instruction must be compared to the number of memory cycles wasted in transmitting garbage. In many cases, once a block has been selected, the complete block must be transmitted. Thus, the length of the block not only affects the allocation of memory, but the communications requirements as well. Further, we should not forget that each block termination will also generate an interrupt, whose processing must also be accounted for.

Some comments are in order here. The analysis does not depend on whether or not the administrative areas are contiguous to, or part of, the block. It does not matter whether the first, or last, or both of these distinguished blocks have specialized extra administrative areas. If the last block requires administrative areas over and above those required by a middle block, those extra areas can be added to the extra administrative areas of the first block. Similarly, if the administrative areas of middle blocks,

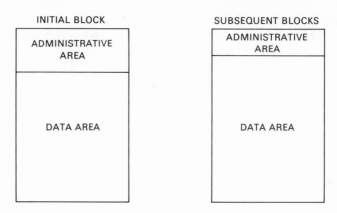

Figure 8.11. Block model for dynamic storage allocation block size
determination.

such as links (forward or backward links to other blocks, links to drum blocks, etc.), are not stored on the blocks themselves, they must be stored elsewhere and accounted for in the evaluation of the total storage requirement for a record. The block model is shown in Figure 8.11.

It is assumed that the length of the records to be stored can be described by a probability distribution which states the probability associated with any record length. The block length is chosen to fit the distribution. We do this by partitioning the distribution in segments of net block length and reducing the actual length by the number of characters used for administrative purposes. Table 8.1 shows this for a block length of 256 characters in which the first block requires 32 administrative characters, and in which subsequent blocks require 16 administrative characters each.

Table 8.1. Block Length Selection Example

A	B	C
Message length	Number of blocks used	Message probability
0–224	1	$P(L = \ \ 0–224)$
225–464	2	$P(L = 225–464)$
465–704	3	$P(L = 465–704)$
705–944	4	$P(L = 705–944)$
945–1184	5	$P(L = 945–1184)$

We must also evaluate the probability that there will be messages of such lengths. This is more easily done on the cumulative distribution.

The average number of blocks used per message is the product of the probability of having messages of length lying between the figures in column A and the number of blocks shown in column B, summed over all numbers of blocks. For example, if the probabilities involved were uniformly 0.2 for all five record length ranges, the average number of blocks used would be

$$0.2 \times 1 + 0.2 \times 2 + 0.2 \times 3 + 0.2 \times 4 + 0.2 \times 5 = 3.0.$$

If, on the other hand, the distribution were sharply peaked, resulting in probabilities of 0.1, 0.6, 0.2, 0.1, 0.0, we would have

$$0.1 \times 1 + 0.6 \times 2 + 0.2 \times 3 + 0.1 \times 4 + 0.0 \times 5 = 2.3.$$

If the record length distribution were bimodal, with probabilities 0.0, 0.5, 0.0, 0.0, 0.5, we would have

$$0.5 \times 2 + 0.5 \times 5 = 3.5.$$

To evaluate the optimum block structure, we write down columns A and B and evaluate the associated probabilities from the cumulative distribution of the record length. Repeating this for each block length, we can see that at some point the optimum size will be found. The average number of blocks is then multiplied by the block length (gross, not net) to determine the number of characters used per record. If we wish to deal with two possible block lengths, the problem is further complicated in that we must try the various combinations of the two lengths. The whole business can be considerably simplified by programming the procedure and entering the distribution and block structure as parameters. Figure 8.12 shows the results of such an analysis for record lengths typified by an exponential distribution.

Having chosen a block that minimizes the total memory requirement, we will have obtained a block structure that can be used to evaluate the effect on channel transfers. The original distribution is now used to obtain a block distribution. That distribution is that which is given as columns B and C of Table 8.1. Given the block length distribution, the two policies (fixed-length transmission $vs.$ variable-length transmission) can be compared. The primary difference between the two is the cycles wasted (in the fixed-length transmission case) to transmit the unused space in the last block of the chain. If we have optimized the space, we shall also have optimized the transmission, since (typically) both the data and the associated administrative data (or equivalent) must be transmitted. We can, from the original transmission length distribution and the block length distribution chosen, obtain a wasted transmission distribution. The number of cycles for the wasted transmissions is compared to the excess of the number of cycles required to build, transmit, and receive a variable-block-length message over the number required to transmit and receive a fixed-block-length message.

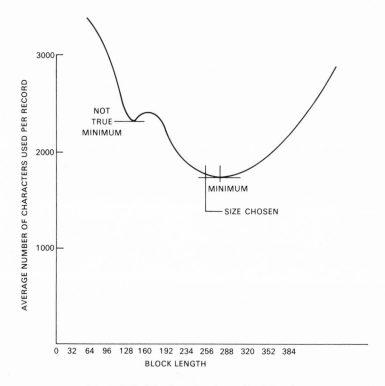

Figure 8.12. Selection of optimum block length.

The interrupt processing can be obtained from the block distribution, i.e., there is a certain probability that there will be 1, 2, 3, 4, 5, . . . , N interrupts per message. Assuming that the interrupt processing time is known, the expected processing time (per second, say) for interrupts can also be evaluated.

It will often be the case that the processing for a beginning block, an end block, and a middle block is not the same. A given block could be a beginning block, a middle block, an end block, or for that matter a beginning *and* an end block. The probabilities associated with each kind of block are therefore interesting.

Let P_i be the probability that a message will require i blocks. Then

$$P_{\text{beginning}} = P_{\text{end}} = \sum_{i=1}^{N} \frac{P_i}{i}$$

$$P_{\text{middle}} = P_1 + \sum_{i=1}^{N} \frac{(i-2)P_i}{i}$$

The total number of cycles used to transmit the data is therefore the number of cycles used to set up the transmission, to process the termination interrupts, and to perform what special processing is required for beginning, middle, and end blocks of a string of blocks. We must also evaluate the total number of cycles required to receive the data at their destination if that destination is a memory. The cost of the channel and transmission mode used is the sum of the cycles used on *both* sides of the transmission. To this must be added any coordinating chitchat which may be required to set up the transmission or acknowledge its receipt.

If the effectiveness of one channel type over another is analyzed without consideration of blocking factors, the result could be incorrect. One may have to develop each tentative choice of channels to the point where the true cost of transmission, reception, interrupt, and setup cycles as well as space has been properly determined.

6.4. Memory Placement and Communications

Transfers of data to and from the complex (that is, inputs and outputs) are usually to or from a main memory. The statistically significant "intercomputer" transfers are typically from the main memory associated with one computer to that of the receiving computer. Most other statistically significant intracomplex messages are from a main memory to a bulk memory, from bulk memories to other bulk memories, and from bulk memories to main memories. For a processor which is mechanized as a program to manipulate data, those data will have to be transferred from perhaps a bulk memory to a main memory, to a scratchpad memory, and finally into

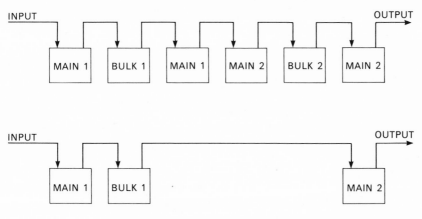

Figure 8.13. Bulk storage as a data transfer medium.

the registers of the computer, and back out again by a similar path. If any one of these memories is accessible to another computer of the complex, that memory can be used as communication channel between them. Memories used in this way offer a significant reduction in cycles required to transfer the data. Figure 8.13 shows a typical comparison. By sharing the bulk memory, the number of cycles required to get data from the input to the output could be cut in half. If there is no bulk memory required, and only main memory is used, the data transfer cost can be cut in half yet again. While the use of memories as an implicit communication facility can reduce processing cycles, there may be administrative problems that can erode the advantage thus gained.

6.4.1. Various Types of Memory Transfer Schemes

One of the simplest and most elegant ways of getting data from one computer into another is placing them on magnetic tape or removable disc, and mounting the tape or disc on the receiving computer's drive. If, once the writing computer has finished, it has no need to re-examine what it has written, this method is valid. A slightly more elegant variation on this theme occurs in those systems in which it is possible to assign devices such as tapes or discs to more than one computer. At any time, a given physical tape or disc drive is electrically connected to a specific computer. That connection is made by a circuit switching device such as a crossbar switch. The switch is controlled by the operating system programs, or manually by the operator. An automatic or semiautomatic switching facility that can accomplish a memory transfer in one second has a large bandwidth. For example, a reel of magnetic tape might contain 92 million bits and could therefore be transferred at an equivalent rate of 92 megabits/second. A disc drive transferred in this way will have a comparable equivalent bandwidth. The larger the capacity of the memory being transferred, and the faster the transfer is accomplished, the higher the effective bandwidth. However, this type of scheme is predicated on the fact that once the writing computer has finished writing, it need not read the data again. This scheme is therefore promising for predominantly one-way communications, in which the switching delay can be tolerated. It is used for transferring historical files to another computer of the complex, for transferring statistical data, accounting data, stale recovery data, or other information that will have a low probability of being re-entered into the main stream of the processing.

If two-way communication is needed, a special controller can be used, with two control ports (i.e., having its own memory switch) allowing several computers to have access to it. The first computer can write the data, and then the other computers that have access to the device can read the data, or modify them, as appropriate. The effective bandwidth is much higher, because the "transfer time" is the time required for the one computer to relinquish control, and for the other computer to obtain control. The transfer of control is done in milliseconds or microseconds. Cost, however, can be high, because control hardware must be duplicated, and much of the unduplicated hardware must be considerably complicated if conflicts between the computers are to be avoided. The software is also more complicated because there are now two computers that can modify the data, two computers that can fail, and two computers that might have to administer the memory. For this reason, a direct connection of a memory to more than one computer is often limited to "you read, I write," or "I write, and either one of us can read." Variations on this theme in which certain areas are written only by the one computer, while other areas are written by another, with all areas read by both, etc., are possible. There is a qualitative distinction between systems in which the computers cannot write in each other's areas and those in which the computers can.

If the hardware works, reading will not harm the data. It is primarily writing by more than one computer that must be administered. As more and more freedom is given to the several computers having access to the same memory, the administration increases in complexity, to the point where it can be more expensive than had a memory-to-memory transfer via a channel been used. One must be assured then that there are no conflicts or, if conflicts are possible, that the resolution of such conflicts is still less costly than using memory-to-memory transfers.

We have seen an intermittent transfer method, using memories as an intermediary and an alternating transfer method. A quasi-simultaneous transfer method can also be used. Computers can communicate with other computers by simply having them share the same main memory. If all main memories are accessible to all computers of the complex as in the B-8500), there need be no explicit computer-to-computer data transfers. Any location in memory is accessible as soon as the computer is given access by the memory switch. The complex is inverted; that is, the memory is the center and the various computers are merely devices that service the main memory. Since any computer is as good as any other (assuming that they are all the same), the relation between physical names and logical names, or functional names, can change from instruction to instruction. In fact, this is done in the B-8500. The executive computer is that computer which happens to be performing the executive program at that moment. In fact, at any instant in time, upon the termination of a task by a computer, it will in turn become the executive computer. There could be several executive computers in operation at once, or for that matter, any functional computer could have multiple simultaneous existence. This approach reduces most of internal communications to trivia, at the expense of greatly complicated software design. Priority structures are more complicated, administration must be made more explicit, re-entrant coding is required throughout, interrupt control hardware is greatly complicated, etc. The software of such systems is typically much more explicit than it would be were the main memories distinct. The explicitness of the software, tables, and data tends to reduce the communication advantage of the method.

6.4.2. Where to Place Intermediary Memories

The destination graph must be re-examined to determine where the intermediary memories (if any) should be placed. To do this, one must be more specific about the data transfer. It is not adequate to say that we want to transfer data from computer A to device B. One must also know what the device will do with them in turn. We must go back to the data flow diagram and determine the genesis and subsequent disposition of each item of data that must go into and out of the tentative intermediary memory. That unfortunately is a matter of semantics. One has to understand the processes that are taking place and why they are taking place. Presumably any time data go from one computer to another via bulk memory, that bulk memory is a candidate for a role as a shared intermediary memory. If it is possible to maintain simple administration by prohibiting two or more computers from writing in the same place, if administrative traffic generated by the shared use of memory (e.g., to tell the other computer that the data are stale) is small compared to the number of cycles saved by the use of a common memory, if the flow of data is generally unidirectional, and if the data that satisfy these criteria are a significant portion of the data transfer into and out of the memory, then it may pay to interpose that memory between two or more computers. The administrative problems, however, tend to grow as the square of the number of computers having access to the same memory. Programming costs, testing costs, and documentation costs are also significantly increased. These costs are defrayed by the reduced number of channels, reduced processing time for transfers, reduced delays, and reduced redundant storage.

7. SUMMARY

Each aspect of the computer complex leads to a different configuration. The primary configurations of the complex are: the processor configuration, which is a formalization of the system specification; the physical configuration, which is the way the physical units of the complex are connected; the logical configuration, a subconfiguration of the physical configuration, which describes the interconnection of logical units; the functional configuration, which is an assignment of functions to physical devices; the semantic configuration, which is the software analog of the functional configuration; and the syntactic configuration, which represents the inter-connection of syntactic program elements. The implementation of a processor is reflected in each of these configurations. For each processor there are proclivities that will dictate the use of predominantly functional vs. structural or semantic vs. syntactic implementations.

The processor configuration can be examined using elementary graph theory. In particular, graph theory can be used to find "natural" groupings of processors, to evaluate the use of redundant processors, to find dependencies of processors, and in general to begin to form tentative configurations as a part of the design process.

A given set of processors can be partitioned functionally or extensively. Indications and contra-indications for extensive or functional partitions of general processors, hardware implementations of processors, and software implementation of processors have to be considered.

The internal communication structure of the complex is a characterizing nexus of the complex. Radial, tree, bus, matrix, iterative, and symmetric structures each present particular advantages and disadvantages. Three types of generic channels for internal communications were introduced: the direct, contentious, and explicit channels. A combination of graph theory, the timing analysis techniques of Chapter 7, and elementary probability can be used to obtain reasonable assignments of channel types to the internal communication network of the complex. Methods of obtaining optimal data transfer blocks were also discussed. Memories are then seen to be yet a fourth form of communication channel, whose proper use can do much toward optimizing the complex.

8. PROBLEMS

1. Establish cost–performance relations for disc memories, drums, main memories, channels, communication buffer units, multiplexers, etc. Do so on the basis of theoretical logic design considerations and compare the results with advertised catalog prices. Understand and explain the differences.

2. For any one such device, project expected technological changes over the next ten years and obtain a predicted relation between cost and performance as it may be over the next ten years. Use a Delphic technique.

3. Compare cost–performance of a processor that can be competitively implemented as hardware or as software from the point of view of extensive growth as in Problems 1 and 2 above.

4. Compare cost–performance of a processor used in Problem 3 from the point of view of functional growth as in Problems 1 and 2 above.

5. Perform a partition and generation of various configurations and internal communications (in miniature) for any of the following systems: on-line banking, air-traffice control, automatic power plant control, automobile assembly plant control, automated supermarket, automated warehouse, municipal traffic light control, remote-access time-sharing system, electric power distribution, telephone central office, reservation system, real-time student class roster and registration system, stock-market system, check clearing system, on-line system for voting booths in the national elections, automated parking lot, irrigation and flood control computer complex, central hotel computer, central hospital computer, central home computer, central nervous system. In all cases, assume that the available CPUs are too small to handle the job individually. The job should be large enough that at least three computers of the type selected will be needed.

6. For those functions that are to be implemented as software in the example of Problem 5, compare and contrast the resulting configurations obtained by maximizing the degree of semantic processors *vs.* maximizing syntactic processors.

7. For the Boolean operations defined on page 410, prove that the commutative, associative, and bidistributive laws hold for matrices if they hold for individual elements of the matrices.

8. Prove that connection matrices as defined have the idempotency generation property.

9. Prove contentions 1, 2, and 3 of Section 4.5 (page 412).

10. Prove assertions 1, 2, and 3 of Section 4.7 (page 413).

11. Refer to Section 4.9. Prove that expression (2) (page 420) is a proper criterion for outways. Similarly, prove that expression (3) does describe inways. Prove that the matrix defined in equation (4) does satisfy the definition of predecessor dependency and that the matrix defined in equation (5) (page 421) similarly satisfies the definition of successor dependency. Similarly, validate the expressions for independent processors (6) and strongly dependent processors (7).

12. Develop the extension discussed in Sections 4.11.1 and 4.11.2. [*Difficult.*]

13. Extend the star-mesh transformations to allow nonexclusive-or probability connections. [*Open problem.*]

14. Prove the formulas on page 460.

9. REFERENCES

1. Benes, Vaclav E., *Mathematical Theory of Connecting Networks and Telephone Traffic*, Academic Press, New York, 1965.

   This is a compact and thorough book dealing with the design of circuit switching networks. The internal communications of the complex are indeed a circuit switching network. Cost–performance relations, blocking probabilities, and multistage network designs are covered in this book. In general, the internal communications network of the complex is a trivial example of the kinds of networks discussed by Benes.

2. Chestnut, Harold, *Systems Engineering Methods*, John Wiley, New York, 1967.

   This book, while oriented to the design of simpler, primarily analog systems, is a cogent presentation of the steps involved in getting a system design done. It is good correlative reading to this chapter.

3. Hall, Arthur D., *A Methodology for Systems Engineering*, Van Nostrand, Princeton, N.J., 1962.

   As with most books on systems design, there is an analog system flavor. Nevertheless, the philosophy is appropriate and well presented. The application of theory of games to decision making in system design is worth reading. Good parallel reading for this chapter.

4. Hare, Van Court, Jr., *Systems Analysis: A Diagnostic Approach*, Harcourt, Brace & World, New York, 1967.

   This book, like many others on systems analysis, tends to have an analog system flavor.

However, the discussion of graph-theoretic concepts, statistical concepts, games theory, and mathematical programming is readable and easy to apply. The problem section is particularly well developed and could be used for supplementary problems.

Chapter 9

THE EXECUTIVE PROCESSOR

1. SYNOPSIS

The executive processor is the central control of the complex. It directs the facilities of the complex toward the execution of its appointed tasks in concert with the desired goals. The executive is not necessarily itself complicated, but the subprocessors that it directs can be. They include job control, scheduling, file control, maintenance, viability, priority, security, accounting, and statistics. The executive programs can range from simple sequential jump tables to complex scheduling algorithms that continually perform optimization analyses intended to maximize the utilization of the complex's resources. The complexity of the executive and its associated subprocessors is directly related to the diversity of tasks that the system will execute, and the uncertainty in the characteristics of those tasks. The more diverse the application and the more uncertain the knowledge of the characterizing distributions, the more complex the resulting executive program will be.

2. SYSTEM FUNCTIONS

If we were to list the different syntactic processors of various systems, we would find that most of them are present in one form or another in every system, although some may be vestigial in some complexes or may be the semantic processors of others. System design (other than the design of the semantic processors) is the design of the syntactic processors and their interrelation. An operating system is the aggregation of these processors.

2.1. The Executive

The executive processor is the central control of the complex. It is, on a grander scale, to the complex what the control is to the individual computers

469

within it. The executive processor and most of its subprocessors are almost always implemented as software, but need not be. The job of the executive processor is to schedule and coordinate subprocessors in a manner compatible to the goals set for the complex.

2.2. Job Control—Accountability

Each **job** (i.e., discrete set of tasks to be performed) will draw on the facilities of the complex. The **job control** function will assure that the various processors that must be activated to perform the job are activated in the proper sequence. Job control is a logical function, i.e., a specification of a sequence; it is not to be confused with scheduling, discussed below. **Accountability** refers to the fact that the system must keep track of the job and know its status at all times: While the system might be allowed to lose the job or fail to do it, it must not lose the fact that the job was lost.

2.3. Scheduling and Optimization

The scheduling function is based on the set of sequences of demands made on the facilities of the complex by the various jobs within it. The object of scheduling is to attempt to utilize these facilities at the optimum efficiency. If the system is to run only one job at a time, there is no significant difference between job control and scheduling. When the system does several jobs concurrently, interlaces processing and I/O operations, and maintains the integrity of interwoven jobs, scheduling becomes a significant processor in its own right.

Some form of optimization (i.e., a directive to maximize an objective function) is implicit in the design of every complex. While optimization is usually diffused throughout the complex, it may be an explicit processor. It most often appears as an explicit processor in the scheduler.

2.4. Priority, Authority, Security, and Privacy

Since the complex has limited facilities, there will be, especially in times of peak loading, priorities imposed or implied by the complex's user. Not every job has the same urgency. More urgent jobs will generally be performed first. However, one should not assume that the priority of a job remains fixed. It may vary from moment to moment. Juggling urgency, timeliness, conflicting priorities, and shifting priorities is the job of the priority control processor.

Priority control also exists within the complex, especially for interrupt processing. A given job, therefore, may have several different priorities, depending upon what is being done at the moment. Even if there are no externally imposed priorities, the complex needs an internal priority control processor for interrupts.

Authority and priority should not be confused. High authority does not necessarily mean high priority. Authority is a question of what element is in control, priority relates to the sequence in which things will be done. Authority is primarily a question of establishing which processors can be allowed to modify what files or other processors. Authority can be autocratic, democratic, stratified, unstratified, fixed, or variable; it can be delegated, abrogated, or circumvented. It means the same within the complex of machines as it does within human complexes.

Security is a reflection of authority. Those aspects of the complex relating to security exist to maintain the authority structure, so that it cannot be destroyed unwittingly or by design. Security may be externally imposed, as in the protection of files from unwarranted examination (privacy), or may be internal, e.g., protection against a program bug.

2.5. Operations Monitoring, Statistics, and Accounting

The operations monitor is an interpretive processor (some kind of partial trace) that gathers the sequence of times at which predefined events occur. This may be done by hardware or software, or as a combination of both. The output of the operations monitor can be used as a log of the system's activities for statistical purposes, for accounting purposes, or as a legal record of transactions.

One nice thing about computer complexes is that it is relatively easy to obtain design statistics that would have been useful before the complex was built. Operational statistics are gathered to predict required modifications in the system or to prepare a specification for the system's replacement. The gathered statistics are boiled down by the statistics processor. The functions of the operations monitor and the statistics processor may overlap.

The complex is expensive. Jobs are run concurrently, each one making various unpredictable demands on the complex's facilities. Many systems, particularly those serving a heterogeneous user population, require accounting procedure so that the cost of the complex may be properly allocated according to use. Accounting and billing may be based on information gathered by the operations monitor, or may be statistical. The accounting functions therefore can overlap with the monitoring and statistical functions.

2.6. Operations

The complex will interface with its human operators. Despite the slowness of the operator relative to the computer, the inevitable errors made by the operators, and the occasionally malicious treatment attempted by human users of the complex, the complex must survive and continue to communicate in a sensible manner. The operations functions are the means by which this communication is established and maintained.

2.7. Maintenance

Despite our best intentions, it is not likely that the programs of a computer complex will remain unchanged throughout its lifetime. There will be bugs to correct, new functions to add, desirable enhancements, etc. It is rarely possible to take the system completely out of service while such changes are made. Furthermore, it is not realistic to reassemble or recompile the complete software for every change. The maintenance processors allow us to make changes under the above conditions.

2.8. Memory Management

There are two aspects of memory management: dynamic allocation of memory to processors or jobs, and optimum scheduling of memory transaction requests. The latter is particularly important for drums, discs, and tapes, or other nonrandom-access memories. Memory management will be discussed in Chapter 10.

2.9. Queue Control

A common feature of a system used for concurrent job processing is the maintenance of job queues. A job queue is a list of job or data identifiers presented to the various processors of the complex.

The output of the scheduler is the placement of a job identifier (or sometimes the job data themselves) on queues of the processors that are to work on that job. The queues are a means (not the only one) by which a job is transferred from processor to subsequent processor. Queues, however, must also be controlled, maintained, require space, etc., leading to a queue management task. Queue control will be discussed in Chapter 10.

2.10. I/O Control and Buffering

A necessary feature of an operating system is common control over I/O operations. The collection of I/O driver routines, together with their error recovery routines, interactions, etc., is sufficiently well developed in the operating system of a modern complex to warrant calling it a processor. This function also will be discussed in Chapter 10.

The fact that devices do not operate at the same speed as other devices or that files and records may have variable or undeterminable lengths leads to the establishment of communication areas in memory called **buffers**. Since memory is usually at a premium, buffer areas cannot be dedicated to each job or each interface. Buffering can be centrally administered as part of I/O control or as part of memory management.

2.11. File Management

A file is an organization of data which is to be distinguished from memory. A file is to memory what a processor is to a computer. Files are created, destroyed, moved, converted, or otherwise manipulated in the course of executing a job. Since equipment may fail, files may be modified, and files may be shared by more than one job or processor, a file management subprocessor is a feature of many computer complexes. File management will be discussed in Chapter 10.

2.12. Communication

Communication is a specialized form of I/O control. Communication is now so ubiquitous that some sort of communication processor is a feature of most computer complexes. While there is a continuum of communication problems stretching from internal I/O to external telegraphic communications, we shall restrict our discussion of communication to that which is done over telegraph or telephone lines. Communications will be discussed in Chapter 10.

2.13. Viability

Every complex can and will fail. The role of the viability processor is to maintain maximum performance despite such failures. Viability will be discussed in detail in Chapters 11 and 12.

2.14. The Firmware Library

The complete library of firmware—the loader, assembler, translators, test and diagnostic programs, etc.—is properly considered part of the system functions.

3. THE EXECUTIVE PROCESSOR

The executive directs the action of a number of subprocessors which do the actual work. These subprocessors may call each other or may, via a sequence of calls, call themselves recursively. Most of these subprocessors are more complicated than the executive, and may have higher priorities. Many of these subprocessors would be significantly simpler or nonexistent except that the facilities that the executive manages are spartan for the tasks at hand. Management in the absence of constraints and with unlimited facilities is trivial. The fact that the complex has neither unlimited time or space is what makes most of the executive necessary. The executive, then, is the processor that decides the what, with which, and to whom of the sub-processors (hardware and software) of the complex.

While the executive is the coordinating nexus of the complex, it is not necessarily the most important, most critical, or most difficult processor to design. The mere fact that it has the highest authority does not mean that it should be programmed by the *programmer* with the highest authority. One should not confuse the authority of a program or its position on a calling tree with the amount of experience required to code it, or with the position of the programmer in the programming organization. The most difficult thing about the design of the executive processor is deciding what it is supposed to do.

3.1. Executive Parameters

There are no design parameters exclusive to the executive. It can be implicit or explicit, table-driven, straight-line-coded, etc. The same design trades apply to it as apply to other programs. In this sense, there is nothing esoteric about it. Its design, however, is sensitive to the statistics that characterize the tasks to be performed by the complex—not more so than with other programs, but more noticeably. The processing load that the complex will contend with can be represented statistically by an appropriate set of distributions. These distributions may be correlated, and may be narrow or broad. We could, under appropriate assumptions, at least hypothetically, reduce the complete characterization of a processing load to a number of distributions. The broader the characterizing distributions, the more random the job to be performed, and hence the less *a priori* information we have on which to base an optimum design. This will necessarily lead to a more complex executive. The simplest executive results when the job is precisely known beforehand. In such cases, the executive can be completely implicit, being nothing more than the succession of instructions or calls in the program.

As the characterizing distribution gets broader, the design of the executive, if it is to optimize under these haphazard conditions, becomes more elaborate. As it becomes more elaborate, less time and space are available for honest work. Clearly, the law of diminishing returns is operative here. The (ridiculous) extreme would be an experimenting executive, which tried to sequence jobs in every possible way (based on a random search, say), executed the jobs, and monitored the results. Picking from these the experimentally derived optimum sequence of operations, it would then proceed (needlessly) to do the jobs. If it were our intention to obtain perfect optimization, the executive would never get done—which is to say that there would be no time left for processing. The cost of the executive, as measured in time, space, channel utilization, delay, or other parameters of interest, is to be subtracted from the savings of these facilities obtained through the use of the executive.[1] It is that sum that we wish to maximize. The elegant executive is one that is optimum in this sense.

3.2. The Isochronous Executive

Assume that the complex is to perform a completely repetitive set of tasks in which there is little variability of input or output. A data logging system is an example. Input are sampled at predetermined instants, a predefined calculation is done for each input or set of inputs, and predefined outputs are recorded. While the numerical values of the inputs and outputs change, the processing does not. One can predict what processor will be active at what time. The sequence of operations is repetitive and could conceivably (but not practically) be driven by an externally derived, constant-interval clock. Each processor is allotted a number of clock intervals. At the conclusion of each clock interval the processor is either allowed to continue or, if its preordained time is up, the next processor in line is activated.

If the mechanization is to be explicit, it is readily done as a table-driven processor. The executive consists of little else but a clock interrupt service routine, a counter for the interrupts, and a table that specifies how many clock periods the present processor should be allowed and which processor is to be activated next.

A tendency toward this type of executive structure is indicated for narrowly distributed jobs. It is used in logging systems, for polling communication lines, factory control, or process control. A truly isochronous executive however, cannot really be used. It is not practical to synchronize I/O devices, data will be in error, operator interventions occur unpredictably, equipment will fail, timings will be varied, the speed of the computer varies,

---

[1] The cost of finding the optimum is a complicating factor that tends to minimize the effectiveness of mathematical programming (e.g., linear or dynamic programming) in the design of scheduling or executive algorithms. Mathematical programming is used to find the optimum blend of peanuts or fuels, to schedule trucks and locate warehouses, to find an optimum pipeline network, or to find an optimum schedule for a set of jobs to be performed on several machines. In classical mathematical programming problems, be they linear or nonlinear, the cost of finding a solution is assumed to be negligible.

as does the clock interval—in short, everything conspires to make the ideal goal of true predictability untenable. Yet, the executive *is* trivial, being mostly a set of design-time decisions rather than run-time decisions. It is highly optimizing; one can optimize the schedule of events to achieve the maximum concurrency of operation.

The isochronous executive (or rather the extent to which the executive is made isochronous) is vulnerable to changes in processor execution times. Data-dependent processing time for any processor will cause either wasted time if the processor finishes early, or improper processing if the processor finishes late.

3.3. The Asynchronous Executive

Consider a single computer consisting of a CPU, memory, various peripheral devices, and externally derived input lines on which inputs occur according to some distribution. For the sake of simplicity, assume that there are three priority levels in operation. The highest level is used to service the interrupts, all of which have the same priority. The next lower level is used for the executive, and the lowest level is used for the semantic processors. Assume that the computer is operating at the lowest level. An input occurs, causing an interrupt and the resulting entrance of the interrupt service routine. The interrupt service routine performs what is required and transfers control to the executive routine. The executive routine may decide that the interrupted process is to be resumed, or that a new process is to be activated. If the old process is to be resumed, the executive restores the computer to the conditions that prevailed prior to the interrupt and executes a jump to the proper place in the interrupted routine. Suppose, however, that on the basis of examining the interrupt it is decided that the old routine is to be temporarily suspended and that a new routine is to be entered. The executive then establishes the conditions that should prevail for the new routine and causes it to be entered. Note that the "new" routine could be one that had previously been interrupted and is now resumed. Every interrupt can cause a similar action to occur. At any moment, the computer is in the middle of many different routines. If a routine should finish its work, it terminates by calling the executive, perhaps through an internally generated interrupt. The executive then treats this as just another interrupt and again performs the actions required to execute or initiate the process that should be next executed. The details of how this is done need not concern us for the moment. Let us say (for the moment) that the executive contains, either as tables or as sequential lines of code, the logical structure required to properly sequence the processors it controls. Suppose that a particular program was originally designed or expected to take N milliseconds of running time, but that it turns out to take $2N$ or $N/2$ milliseconds instead. While this would destroy the synchronous executive, it does not materially affect the asynchronous executive. The relation or sequencing of processors in the asynchronous executive is sequential, and not temporal as in the synchronous executive. Consequently, variation in processing time of individual subprocessors does not affect the logic of the executive. It is, as is the asynchronous computer, speed independent and totally impervious to timing dispersion. We gain great freedom from data dependencies by this structure. Given unpredictable data dependencies (characterized by a large σ), an asynchronous executive has an advantage over the synchronous executive. However, it is not obtained without cost.

First of all, every processor termination will cause the equivalent of an interrupt and will require executive action. Taken to an extreme, every subroutine termination will require examination by the executive. Furthermore, every subroutine termination will require us to store the full complement of registers, memory locations, etc., required to restore the computer to the conditions that prevailed before the given subroutine was interrupted. Since there is no way to predict how many times a given subroutine might be interrupted, or how many interrupted subroutines may exist at any one time, some sort of interrupt stack must be maintained. Typically, the interrupt stack will be maintained in dynamically allocated space, and there is also an additional processing attendant to fetching and modifying data so stored. If taken to a further extreme, each subroutine or program terminates whenever it has completed one pass through the routine. That is, the routine does not have a loop in it that allows the multiple processing of data units. Each unit (say John Doe's paycheck) will create an internal interrupt or an equivalent form of call to the executive. Taken to this extreme, we will pay for the initialization calculations each time the routine is used. In other words, we forego the advantages obtainable by batch processing of similar items, gaining in exchange the freedom from temporal dependencies. The smaller the processing unit that is allowed to create a call to the executive (be it smaller in time or space), the more internally generated calls to the executive there will be, and the closer will the running time required by the executive to process that call approach (or exceed) the running time of the process. Similarly, the space required to store the interrupt or to otherwise administer the routine will also increase and may approach or exceed the space of the routine or the data, or both. Therefore, the efficiency decreases as the partition is made finer.

There are some other disadvantages to this kind of executive structure. The average delay for processing a job increases. There is also an increase in the uncertainty of the time at which the process will be complete.[2]

---

[2] This should not be confused with the delay, as they are different concepts. For example, the delay of the isochronous executive might be 150 milliseconds, but the sigma of that delay is of the order of microseconds. The delay of the asynchronous executive could be shorter, say, 50 milliseconds, but the sigma is large—of the order of milliseconds.

3.4. The Anisochronous Executive

We can take a point of view midway between the two above executive structures and not generate any internal interrupts, but also not run the executive from an external clock. Instead, we shall allow the time between events to vary, but maintain a strict sequence of operations as we had in the hypothetical isochronous executive. We now have some tolerance to variations in processing time. If there are no externally generated interrupts, or if those that do occur can all be predicted (as in an I/O operation), the strict sequence of operations, with the attendant efficiency inherent in batch processing, can be maintained by the simple expediency of going into a loop while waiting for the anticipated interrupt. Thus, we execute a disc seek, and go into a wait loop until the interrupt occurs. The executive is not bothered, but the scheme does not allow something else to take place while waiting. The executive is simple (in fact it may be nonexistent or vestigial) and incurs very low overhead, but much time and space is wasted. We are back to the situation we had prior to having an operating system.

The executive structure here maintains a sequence of operations rather than a slavishly followed schedule. The sequence will be repeated in a regular fashion, and the executive, like the isochronous executive, will have a flow chart that is generally a loop.

3.5. The Real Executive

The isochronous executive was impossible to implement because it presumed total temporal control over the occurrence of external interrupts and totally predictable processing times. These objections were overcome by using the anisochronous executive, in which the temporal variations were compensated for by wasting time. The same objections were overcome in the asynchronous executive by imposing a complex structure to keep track of things (stack, interrupts, etc.). The asynchronous executive becomes top-heavy if the subdivision of processing units and data units is made too small. It also suffers from not having a time sense. That is, it does not allow for the possibility that the system may have to perform certain functions according to a fixed, preordained schedule.

We see from the above discussion that the proclivity toward either an isochronous executive, on the one hand, or an asynchronous executive, on the other, is determined by the expected variability of the tasks that the system is to perform. The broader the characterizing distributions, the stronger the tendency toward an asynchronous executive.

The real executive is a combination of all three ideas. It will have certain functions that will be performed according to a strict schedule, others that will follow a generally asynchronous scheme, and, as we shall see, despite the wasted time and the possibility of performing useful work, occasionally the executive will execute a diddle loop while waiting for certain actions to take place (see Chapter 12—*Ledgering*).

3.5.1. Dedicated *vs.* Generalized Systems

One can distinguish between two kinds of computer complex applications: those in which all programs are fixed (over a period of days or months, say), called **dedicated systems,** and those in which the programs to be executed are not predictable and can vary from moment to moment (**generalized systems**). The former are exemplified by systems used for communications, air-traffic control, reservations, order entry, process control, factory control, data logging, or simulation. The latter are exemplified by commercial and scientific data processing systems, or time-sharing systems. The characterization, however, is not necessarily fixed and may vary in the course of a system's life.

Consider for example a large-scale airline reservation system. It is subjected to peak loads during daylight hours, especially during the tourist season, that far exceed the load at night or off-season. Furthermore, the system must operate twenty-four hours a day, seven days a week. This means that the system will have much time and space available during off hours. During peak hours, there is a proclivity toward the dedicated system with its narrow data distributions and almost no execution of new programs. During the off hours, it is used for program development and perhaps a totally different set of data processing jobs. Furthermore, the complex may not be implemented all at once, but may be established in stages. During the early phases it is used for program development, while later new program development falls off to a trickle.

A commercial time-sharing system may be used almost exclusively to develop new programs. Many of these programs are run only once or twice. More time is spent in program development and testing than in executing production runs. Not only are the processing time and space requirements broadly distributed, but the processing time for any one job is not predictable either.[3] The distinction between systems that run programs and systems that manipulate programs then lies not in the fact that programs are manipulated, but in the fact that the distribution of running time and space is broad.

We may occasionally observe dedicated systems that appear to have broad time or space load distributions. However, closer inspection will reveal that the distribution is composed of a small number of distributions,

---

[3] It would not be reasonable to perform a timing analysis for each user program.

which are individually narrow. For example, a communications system may contend with two populations of messages—short ones and long ones. These are two distributions which combined have a large σ, but when examined in detail are in fact narrow distributions.

3 5.2. Executive Design Pitfalls

What then is the right structure for an executive? The only reasonable answer one can give is: "It depends." Several common errors are made in the design of executive systems, particularly for dedicated systems.

1. Confusing the executive structure that is optimum during the development phase of the complex with the optimum executive over the operation life of the complex.
2. Confusing efficiency during peak loadings with efficiency in handling subsidiary tasks, or improperly trading one for the other.
3. Confusing generality with efficiency, or simplicity with efficiency.

An executive structure appropriate to a time-sharing system is poor for message switching or process control. Similarly, the executive structure of a complex used for information storage and retrieval is poor at servicing the requirements of a research and development laboratory. The highly efficient reservation system executive is grossly inefficient in doing payrolls and management reports, and the darling of the programming staff that designed the complex for a dedicated system is operationally inadequate. Similarly, the development staff may have to struggle with the inefficiencies of the ultimate executive used in the dedicated system when it is used for program development. The resolution of these differences can be that a different executive is used for development than for running, or that a different executive is used during off hours than during peak hours.

3.5.3. Executive Design and Weights

The design of the real executive then must be based on a proper weighting of the uses to which the system will be put. One has to decide what the complex is being built for, and the relative importance of each function. One can take the characterizing distributions and weight them with the importance of the associated functions measured on a scale from 0 to 1 (i.e., the "probability" of that function).

To illustrate, consider a process control system that will be installed at 20 different locations. The development machine, test machine, and target machine are of the same kind. The development effort will last two years, and the systems are to be amortized over a ten-year period. We have therefore 200 years of system operation compared to 2 years of development. The weight given to the operational characterizing distributions is therefore

0.99, while that given to the development distributions is 0.01. Suppose, however, that the system is to be amortized over only five years and that there will be only one system produced. The relative weights are now 0.715 and 0.285, respectively—the efficiency of the system during development is relatively more important.

It also makes a difference who pays for the machine time and when. The buyer might assign a weight of 0.0 to the efficiency of the system during development, while the builder assigns a weight of 1 to that phase of the development effort.

There are relatively few "bad" executive systems. There are, however, many that are inappropriate to the tasks at hand and are therefore operationally bad. One of the reasons that many dedicated systems use unique executive structures is that the one supplied by the manufacturer is designed to handle the totality of applications for which the complex is marketed. The manufacturer has a dilemma in the design of the operating system comparable to that which he faces in designing the computer. He cannot practically examine each individual sale and provide that complex with an optimum executive lest he have N different executives to design and maintain. Even if the largest computer manufacturer were willing to do this, he could not obtain enough programmers to implement such a plan, and very few users (other than those who buy a dedicated system) would be willing to pay the price of an operating system that is optimum for them. The manufacturer, then, designs an executive structure that is optimum for the characterizing distributions of his intended market, knowing full well that any specific application will not fit that distribution. It is therefore always possible to "improve" the standard operating system—that is, improve in the light of the specific requirements, but at the cost of degrading its efficiency with respect to the average requirements. It is not fair then to label a standard operating system as bad or inefficient. Given a rational consideration of the constraints facing the manufacturer, most competent designers would come up with something that was not much more efficient.

Many new executive systems touted as radically more efficient than last year's model, or characterized in the literature as "breakthroughs," are often nothing more than a recognition of the fact that the assumed statistics are not what they were thought to be. After all, the designer of the operating system or executive of a commercial computer no more performs a thorough statistical analysis of user requirements and habits for the executive system than he does for laying out the computer's instruction repertoire. Intuition is the byword here. In some cases, where the manufacturer has improperly assessed the market requirements, he comes out with an elegant operating system that satisfies no known need, resulting in a predictable commercial disaster.

3.6. The Cyclically Structured Executive

3.6.1. The Cyclic Structure

Most systems perform their functions according to a generally aniso-chronous, repetitive cycle. The system performs **transactions**, that is, a sequence of operations consisting of input, processing, and output. Each transaction can be traced through the system by using the data flow diagrams: The structure of the cycle is not totally inherent in the **transaction flow**; its design is an important aspect of the system design.

A cyclic structure appropriate to the transaction flow shown in Figure 9.1 is depicted in Figure 9.2. Note that the sequence in which the functions appear in the basic cycle does not necessarily correspond to the sequence indicated in the transaction flow diagram. The sequence of operations carried out for each transaction individually will, of course, be as indicated in the transaction flow diagram.

The duration of the cycle is not fixed. Any one of these functions could take more or less time. If input is heavy, the input phase, and probably all subsequent phases, will be stretched out. Similarly, the variability in access time for the disc reads and writes will affect the duration of these phases during any particular cycle. The occurrence of invalid data formats or other input errors will also affect the cycle length.

3.6.2. Technical Basis for the Cyclic Structure

The basic cycle, or **system cycle**, design is based on the expected duration of each process to be performed and the characteristics of the data or

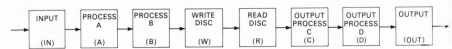

Figure 9.1. Illustrative transaction.

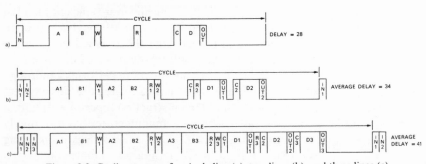

Figure 9.2. Cyclic structure for single line (a), two lines (b), and three lines (c).

programs on which those processes operate. Knowledge of the system load statistics and a timing analysis performed for each processor allow us to obtain an expected or average transaction flow. That is, we take a sufficient number of paths through the system flow diagram to account for 95 or 99% of all processing. From this, we can structure a hypothetical (perhaps functionally meaningless) **average transaction flow**. The input statistics tell us how many such average transactions will occur per unit of time. The number of such average transactions can be based on the average transaction rate or, more commonly, reflect a peak transaction rate for which the system is being implemented (e.g., $\mu + 4\sigma$).

The basic cycle is designed as if the executives *were* isochronous and as if the average values *were* absolute. It is later refined to correct this perhaps fallacious assumption.

The design load of the system is critical. There is no *a priori* reason to believe that the cycle structure that is optimum for low load conditions is also optimum for high load conditions and *vice versa*. In fact, this is rarely the case. The system designed for high efficiency under peak conditions is generally wasteful when the load is low. Similarly, high efficiency under low load conditions leads to a nonlinear degradation of capabilities under high load.

The efficiency of the system under low load conditions is meaningless if the load model is complete. That is, if we properly account for *all* functions that the system must perform (so-called subsidiary and opportunity functions as well) and give the appropriate weight to all such functions, the system will either be fully loaded or not. *In either case the system will always execute instructions at a maximum rate.*

As an example, consider a reservation system whose primary function is to process the reservation agent's transactions. Under low load conditions the system is used for lower-priority functions such as compiling program changes or processing operational statistics. Peak conditions occur for three to four hours at midday, and the primary functions at midnight are 1% of the load during the peak hours. The choice of computers will be dictated by the needs of the peak hours and not the efficiency during the off hours. Program changes are infrequent and statistics processed one day are as good as those processed another. Consequently, it matters little how efficient the system is for these functions.

Higher efficiency for the low-priority functions, if bought at the expense of degrading the performance for high-priority functions, will increase the system's required capacity but not necessarily the system's throughput for critical functions. Clearly then, the idea of weighting all functions by their importance is crucial—only then can one obtain a proper perspective for cycle design. That perspective is gained by defining the average transaction, which is where the cycle design is started and where the efficiency at various tasks is built in. The *load*, then, to which we refer is the total, statistical load, including all auxiliary functions, given their proper weight. In this light, it is worth exploring what it is the system does when it is not "fully loaded."

Computers are not normally turned off. If the computer is capable of executing N instructions per second, it will execute that many instructions even if it has nothing to do. The instructions will be expended in test programs, exercisers, diagnostics, initializing the system cycle, diddle loops, or a combination of these things. In any case, the wasted cycles during no-load periods are indeed wasted—and nobody should really care.

An analogy is offered by a suspension bridge. It is built to take the stress imposed by wind and a few thousand automobiles. This represents an enormous reserve of tensile strength. We do not take the bridge down when there is no traffic, nor do we bewail the loss of all that "holding power" (substitute "computing power") when there is no traffic to handle. The bridge has zero "efficiency" under zero load—it is totally wasted. What we really care about is what will happen when there are several thousand cars stuck on the bridge during a hurricane.

Another source of failure in a large-scale computer complex design is the unrealistic attempt to harness the unused capacity of a dedicated system. The generalized system is designed as a compromise and is perforce less efficient than the dedicated system designed explicitly for a specific task. Similarly, the dedicated system is grossly inefficient as a generalized system, even though it has the apparatus required to perform the generalized system functions. What may happen though is that the designer loses sight of the proper weights or attempts to justify a large system by holding out the chimerical promise of being able to handle N subsidiary functions during off hours. The result is merely a chimera. Still, all that unused computer capacity is seductive—a siren that ever lures the unwary architect to grief. The system must be designed to match its characterizing load distribution, be it broad or narrow. It cannot practically be designed to be both simultaneously. If the auxiliary functions are not included in the load model, with their appropriate weights, from the very start, their subsequent addition must be understood to be conditional upon the acceptance of either poor efficiency in the performance of the subsidiary tasks or a degradation of the system in the performance of the primal tasks. The proper load model and weights *will* lead to the commercial operating system if that is the load, or to the highly specialized executive of the dedicated system if that is appropriate.

3.6.3. Cycle Design—An Example

We shall develop an example of a basic cycle design for a system performing the rudimentary functions shown in Figure 9.1. The evolution of the cycle is shown in Figure 9.3. We shall in this example assume that all functions can be accommodated in a single computer and ignore the effects of priority levels, malfunctions, interrupts, and other complicating factors. We shall assume the following characteristics.

1. Input can be initiated in 1 unit of time but will take 5 units to accomplish. Each input line requires its own initiation, but inputs can be overlapped.
2. Output can be initiated in 1 unit of time but will take 10 units to accomplish. Outputs can also be overlapped. Line utilization should be maximized. Input and output on the same line cannot be overlapped.
3. Process A takes 3 units of time.
4. Process B takes 4 units of time.
5. Process C takes 1 unit of time.
6. Process D takes 3 units of time.
7. Processes cannot be split up.
8. Disc reads or writes can be initiated in 1 unit of time but will take 6 units of time to be accomplished.
9. A given record cannot be read until it has been written.
10. Multiple reads and writes can be overlapped.
11. Cycle overhead can be ignored.
12. There are 10 lines to be serviced.

We could start the cycle design by incorporating these rules into the processing for a single line. The result is shown in Figure 9.2a. The cycle has a duration of 38 units of time of which only 15 are actually used; 23 units are wasted. Furthermore, we are far from our goal of maximizing the utilization of the lines. To rectify this, we can do two lines at a time, to yield the cycle shown in Figure 9.2b. The cycle is increased to 46 units and the wasted time is 16 units. The cycle length can be increased further by processing 5 lines at a time, to yield a cycle 84 units long, with only 9 wasted time units. The average delay, however, has increased to 56 units of time.

This approach leaves much to be desired. We are not achieving the required line utilization. There is still dead time left over at the end of each cycle. We are not taking possible advantage of batching that could occur if the several instances of each use of a processor were contiguous. Another problem with such "piecing in" is that the cycle becomes overly complex, nonrepetitive, and difficult to change.

We have seen that as we increased the efficiency, the delay increased. If we are allowed a large delay, we can substantially increase the processing efficiency and almost totally eliminate wasted cycles, while keeping the

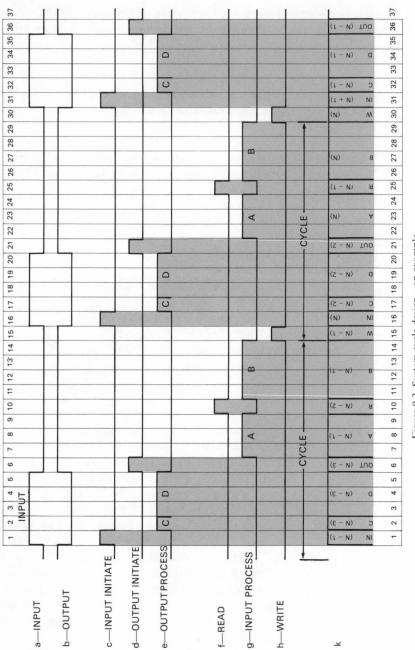

Figure 9.3. System cycle design—an example.

inputs and outputs busy. It is not necessary to do the output of the data gathered in one cycle during that cycle. We can perform output functions on the data gathered in previous cycles.

The cycle design is started by specifying the most critical commodity first—in this case, the necessity to keep inputs and outputs busy. Since the elapsed time for input and output averages 15 units of time per line, and since the average processing per line takes 15 units, we should be able to achieve complete line utilization as well as no CPU wastage.

We shall again arrange a schedule with only one line for the moment (see Figure 9.3). We have shown input starting at $T = 1$, 16, and 31, and output starting at $T = 6, 21$, and 36. Therefore, input and output must have been initiated at these times, as shown in lines c and d. The total output processing takes 4 units of time and can therefore precede the output initiate as shown in line e. A read must precede the output processes and be initiated early enough to allow for the 6 unit time delay. This would place reads at $T = 11$ and 26. This however will not leave 4 contiguous units for B. Consequently, we place the reads as shown in line f at $T = 10$ and 25. Note that we have made a time and delay trade with space. Had we placed the read at $T = 11$ and $T = 26$, we would either have wasted time or, more likely, have delayed the output by yet another cycle. To avoid this, we have the data area for the output present one unit of time before it is actually used, therefore increasing the expected memory utilization. We can then place the input processes as in line g and the write as shown in line h. We have thereby achieved a cycle in which all time is profitably spent, and the inputs and outputs are kept going at the maximum rate.

The cycle can be made to start at any starting point of a process. However, the cycle design is not complete until we specify to which cycle the various reads and writes belong. This is shown in line k of Figure 9.3. In working this out, we find that during the input cycle N we are outputting the data gathered during cycle $N - 2$ and doing the reads for the data gathered in cycle $N - 1$. We have achieved our requirements at a cost of an average delay of 35 units. Our less efficient pieced-together cycle had an average delay of 28 units. We see that the "sacrifice" of delaying the output for two whole cycles was not too large. The cycle is regular and the delay is load independent.

We have shown the cycle for a single line. There are several ways in which we could expand this cycle for N lines. It is clear, however, that under the present assumptions it is impossible to keep all lines busy simultaneously. The reason is that each line has an elapsed time of 15 units and requires 15 units of processing. If, however, we made the transmission and reception time for each line equal to 50 and 100 units, respectively (by changing the problem), we would have enough processing time to keep all lines busy all

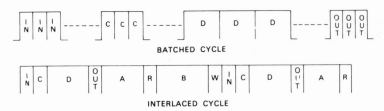

Figure 9.4. System cycle designs—examples of batched and interlaced cycles.

the time. The two main ways in which we can expand the cycle is (1) to have individual serial cycles for each line operating quasi-concurrently and (2) to batch the processes for the several lines. The two basic schemes are shown in Figure 9.4.

The batched cycle is more efficient because it allows us to take increased advantage of possible initialization and common overhead. It will typically require less program space but more data storage. The delay for the batched cycle is also longer than that for the interlaced cycle. The interlaced cycle is typically faster, has higher overhead, more program space, and less data space, and has a more complicated executive program.

The time–space–delay trade is basic in the design of the system cycle. Consider a read operation. The earlier the read operation is initiated, the less the delay will be and the less likely that time will be wasted while waiting for the data to be ready. On the other hand, the earlier the read operation is initiated, the longer will the data be resident in the main memory, and thus, the more memory is required.

3.6.4. Base-Sequence Program Design Considerations

The real executive system is driven by a base-sequence program or schedule. That program may be large and explicit or minor and vestigial. Typically, it contains many subcycles and decisions at which parts of the cycle may be by-passed. A typical structure is shown in Figure 9.5. While there is a basic cycle structure, at every point possible, and where it is relatively easy to test, an opportunity to by-pass the next part of the cycle is presented. Should there be nothing for the system to do, it will spend most of its time in cycle overhead functions. Each process within the cycle may itself be cyclically structured. Furthermore, a given process may appear in several places in the cycle. Thus, in a system required to serve high- and low-speed lines, the low-speed line service routines might be engaged only once during the cycle, while the high-speed line routines might be engaged four times.

Shortcuts in the main cycle are taken where possible. The time saved by these shortcuts must be weighed against the time spent to see if the shortcut can be taken. A subprocessor, say, that performs function A may contain

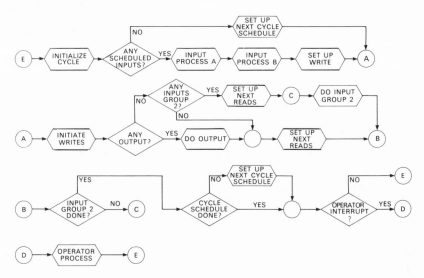

Figure 9.5. Typical base-sequence program flow chart.

its own test to determine if there is anything (more) to do. In this case, the test performed for that function is redundant when there is something to do. In other words, it takes extra time when the system is loaded and saves time when the system is not. For this reason, it may pay to assume that there is something to do, go through the calling sequence, and let the subprocessor exit with nothing done. This results in a simpler cycle structure (e.g., a straight line). The choice is determined by the relative probabilities of having something to do and the relative costs of going through an unnecessary calling sequence as compared to testing a switch (and setting or resetting that switch). The trade is a familiar one and can be evaluated by the methods discussed in Chapter 7.

3.7. The Multilevel Executive

We have been discussing the executive as if it consisted of only one program operating at a single priority level. In reality this is not the case. The executive functions can be distributed among several different levels. Furthermore, there can be more than one base-sequence programs.

3.7.1. Urgency, Authority, and Priority

Interrupts are created by malfunction detection hardware, alarms, normal termination of I/O operations, requests for additional memory, and special conditions of I/O devices peculiar to the device. An interrupt is an expression of relative urgency. That is, the program being executed is interrupted because it is not possible or practical to wait until the program is complete prior to returning control to the executive. Urgency is measured by the time allowed for the interrupt response and the cost of failing to respond to the interrupt in a timely manner. The cost is high if the interrupt is caused by an I/O device requesting memory for an irreproducible input. The cost is low if the interrupt is caused by a low-speed output device (say, a typewriter) signaling that it is ready for the next output.

Urgency only partly depends on the device. It also depends on the application. For example, failing to respond to a radar track signal in an air traffic control system or failing to respond to a pulse in a process control system is not serious. The air traffic control system has been integrating the track and can afford to miss a pulse every few hundred milliseconds. Similarly, the input of the process control system is incremental, the system has feedback, and will compensate for missed pulses. A missed interrupt in a communication system, however, may mean the loss of a message, which, if it comes from an unattended station, may not be reproducible. The value of the message, and hence the urgency of the interrupt, is clearly related to the nature of the message.

A missed device termination signal will only result in a momentary loss of efficiency, assuming there is a method by which the status of the device can be determined. Failure to respond to an error condition interrupt could result in the loss of the whole system. Urgency, then, is partly measured by the importance associated with the interrupt as measured by the cost of missing it, or alternatively by the cost of correcting the situation if the interrupt is lost.

Urgency is also measured by the probable time between interrupts for the same line. A controlled termination signal for output devices cannot recur until another output command has been given. That command will not be given if the termination interrupt for the previous command has not been serviced. Consequently, for some devices, a second interrupt will not normally occur unless the previous one has been serviced. Input devices, however, may cause any number of interrupts in a row, that cannot be readily controlled. Thus, a process control system may create a stream of interrupts spaced a few milliseconds apart, as could a high-speed communication line. A carriage return character may trigger an interrupt in a time-sharing system that could recur every 20 milliseconds. The higher the urgency of the signal the higher the priority level that will be assigned to that interrupt. The urgency, however, is measured by a combination of factors and not just the speed with which the response must occur.

Priority and urgency should not be confused. Priority is assigned to an interrupt or process in response to urgency; i.e., priority is the cure for urgency.

Priority and authority should not be confused either. While it is generally true that higher priorities are associated with higher authority, this is not immutable. How often do we hear of a peculiar circumstance in which the lowest member of a hierarchy is given top priority, or in which the highest authority is justifiably made to wait while an underling performs a critical task. It is with our machines as it is with organizations. Authority in a computer complex is measured by the ability to write or modify the contents of memory. That program which can modify any memory location has the highest authority. We can produce a memory modification graph, showing which processors can modify which. Authority relations are typically reflexive, antisymmetric, and transitive—which is to say they form a partly ordered graph.[4] Consequently the analysis of authority relations can be performed by using the methods and techniques of graph theory appropriate to partial ordering relations.

There is a paradox, however, with relation to the exercise of authority. The computer can execute only one instruction at a time. Assume that the executive (which has supreme authority) is placed at a low priority level. If the computer should happen to be executing the executive program, then the executive program, through the use of privileged instructions and having unrestricted access to memory, could set switches, mask registers, and perform other acts to disable (temporarily) all processors at higher priority levels, and thereby exercise its authority. However, if the executive program is *not* being executed by the computer, and if it is at a lower priority level than some other program, there is no way for it to exercise its authority (e.g., to modify the contents of memory locations pertaining to the higher priority levels). An answer (albeit a poor one) to this dilemma is to place the executive at the highest priority level. This can be wasteful, reduce the amount of implicit programming possible, and increase the delay for urgent functions. Another way is to have the executive entered periodically in response to certain higher-level interrupts, such as a clock interrupt or watchdog alarm, in addition to the more usual interrupts that would require its attention. This implies that part of the executive exists at more than one level. The higher-priority-level portions of the executive contend with those situations that require executive action because of urgency or impending catastrophe, while the lower levels are devoted to the processing associated with the base sequencer. The high-priority-level portions can be used to block interrupts of

---

[4] Typically, since most systems will have one supreme authority that has precedence over all others, the authority graph will have a maximum element and consequently have an upper lattice property. Since it is not necessarily true that there is a processor of lower authority than any two other processors, the graph does not necessarily exhibit a lower lattice property and is therefore not necessarily a lattice.

those levels that are higher than the executive, allowing the low-level portion of the executive to exercise its authority.

3.7.2. Interrupt Levels and Program Levels

The priority level of an interrupt is normally determined by hardware. The occurrence of the interrupt stops activities at a lower level and initiates a program (perhaps vestigial, consisting of only a jump instruction) whose function it is to service the interrupt. In a simple system, the level of the program is determined by the levels of interrupts that can or cannot interrupt the program. The interrupt level currently in force in the computer is specified by the contents of the interrupt register. The occurrence of a higher-level interrupt will cause an automatic change of the interrupt state. The SELECT NEXT PRIØRITY instruction, or its equivalent (such as resetting the mask registers and attendant cleanup work, in the less extensive mechanizations), is used to make a downward change of the interrupt state of the machine.

Consider now a computer in which there are no external interrupts. The machine, however, is assumed to have the ability to generate internal interrupts. That is, a working program can generate an "interrupt" to call the attention of a higher-level program. A low-level program, upon executing an instruction that requires it to wait, issues an internal interrupt instruction to the higher-level program. The usual interrupt cycle is followed. The higher-level program performs what it must and then executes a NEXT PRIØRITY instruction to revert back to the lower level. We could then construct a complete internal interrupt structure, level indicator register, mask registers, etc. A race resolution network and priority selection network are not needed because only one program can be running at a time. We have then two distinct concepts, that of an (external) **interrupt state**, which refers to the levels of external interrupts that will be accepted, and that of **program state**, which refers to the levels of programs that can be activated. "Priority level" is a generic term covering interrupt level and program level. "State" and "level" will be used interchangeably in this context (e.g., "internal interrupt level"). The two structures could be independent but usually are not. One scheme used is to have the instructions that cause changes in the internal state (program state) automatically set up the mask register for the external interrupt state. There is no inherent reason why these two different states need be coordinated or why they should not be distinguished. Thus, external interrupts at levels 1, 2, 3, and 4, could be serviced by programs at program states 4, 3, 2, and 1. While such extreme differences would tend to erode the usefulness of the interrupt mechanism, they are not impossible.

It is occasionally desirable to distinguish between instructions that change the interrupt state and those that change the program state. Conceivably, a machine could have a complete set of equivalent instructions for both.

In a computer complex consisting of only one computer the program state can only be changed by the program that is currently being executed (assuming still that there are no external interrupts). Associated with each state must be a flip-flop (the analog of the interrupt flip-flop) that specifies whether there is any activity to be performed in that state.[5] To leave a state, the program executes a kind of WAIT instruction, which is then followed by a program state change instruction. The execution of a WAIT instruction will cause the activation of the highest active program state. The WAIT instruction is not interruptible.

Should a program operating at a particular level wish to suspend processing at that level because there is nothing to do, it would execute a QUIT instruction, which would have the effect of resetting that program state's activity flip-flop, followed by a shift to the highest active state. Alternatively, the execution of a state selection instruction will cause the entrance of the named state.

The entrance of a new program state can be done in two different ways. On the one hand, the state can be entered to the conditions that prevailed before it was interrupted or executed a WAIT instruction. On the other hand, the entrance can be to a specific, fixed point of the program of that state. In external interrupt processing, the former is usually implied. Both methods can be used for program state changes, for distinctly different reasons. A transition to a fixed point of the program (usually the beginning) allows that program to be entered many times in a particular state without having run to completion. For example, a program at level 2 executes a WAIT instruction. The prevailing register conditions are stored and control turned over to level 1. Level 1 performs some operations and decides that that which level 2 was waiting for is not yet ready. However, it reinitiates the level 2 program (with new data), which again proceeds to (perhaps) the same WAIT instruction. This could continue until there were several entries on the stack at level 2. At some point, the level 1 program might decide that one of the entries in the level 2 stack (not necessarily the oldest) can now continue. This time, the level 1 program makes the transition to level 2 by restoring the conditions that prevailed when that instance of the execution of the level 2 program issued the WAIT instruction. If the transition had been from level 2 to a lower level, say 3, the return from level 3 (by the issuance of a WAIT or QUIT instruction) would require knowledge of how that return should be accomplished—that is, either to a fixed point or to one of several conditions stored in the

<hr>

[5] Since in many systems there is no distinction between program state and interrupt state, and program states are equivalent to interrupt states, an interrupt is equivalent to having that particular program state activated.

stack of the level 2 program corresponding to the level 2 and 3 interface. Clearly this can readily get out of hand, requiring stacks for every possible combination of program state and transition direction. For this reason, upward transitions are usually to a fixed point while downward transitions are usually to a restored point.

In single computers or in multicomputer complexes that do not share the main memory, internally generated interrupts (i.e., changes of program state) are primarily administrative conveniences that use much of the same hardware that would be required for managing the external interrupts anyhow. In shared-memory computer complexes, such as the B-8500, these capabilities approach necessities. CPUs are allocated to program states as needed. There can be several CPUs simultaneously executing the same program at a given level on different data. A CPU executes a level change by issuing a WAIT or QUIT instruction (as appropriate), causing a shift to the highest active level. If that level is currently being serviced by a CPU the entrance may merely be added to the stack. On the other hand, one, two, or more CPUs might be assigned by the hardware to the new level, allowing parallel processing of independent stacked entries. While in a single computer a state can only be left voluntarily (after all, there is only one program active at a time) by issuing a WAIT or QUIT instruction, this is not the case in a shared-memory complex. A voluntary QUIT or WAIT on the part of CPU A could cause the interruption of the program being executed by CPU B. In this case, the return must be to a restored point rather than a fixed point.

One should not confuse the program level with location of the program. A common subroutine used by several different levels could, if re-entrant coding is used, appear only once in the memory. While each level that had occasion to call the subroutine would need a work area and parameter transfer area unique to that subroutine at that level (indeed to that particular call), the subroutine body could exist any place in memory. The program state is determined solely by the instructions that were executed to change the state and not by the program which is currently being run. While the concept of tying an area of memory to a particular state is not essential, it is often done. Normally, associated with each program state there will be memory allocated for the unique use of that state. The occurrence of a program state change will cause the fetching of register data from a predetermined subarea of the memory associated with that state. If this approach is taken to an extreme, a program can only be executed at a given level if it resides in the area associated with that level. Some computers, unfortunately, have been constructed with these restrictions. More usually, only the areas required to properly administer the state are associated uniquely with that state. All other areas of memory are in a shared pool. Interrupt and program state and authority are not based on the memory location now being executed, but are rather stored explicitly in registers for that purpose. Thus, a given subroutine may be in a common area and be executed at any of several different program levels or authority levels. This allows a potentially harmful subroutine shared by all users to be used by a program at a low authority level, without causing damage.

3.7.3. Level Assignments

Levels are assigned to interrupts on the basis of urgency and the facilities that the computer has for servicing the interrupt. The response to an interrupt action can consist of several different steps.

1. **Interrupt acknowledge**—The action required to turn off the interrupt and allow another interrupt to occur on the same line. This includes the processing required to store the registers and conditions of the interrupted program.

2. **Interrupt stacking**—The processing required to record (implicitly or explicitly) the source and/or store the sequence number of the interrupt.

3. **Interrupt service**—The processing required to allow the interrupt stack entry (if any) to be discarded.

4. **Interrupt process**—The completion of the processing associated with the interrupt.

As an illustration, consider the interrupt caused by a disc read indicating that the buffer area in which the data are being placed is about to be filled up. The response to that interrupt will be complete when a new memory area is allocated to the disc, or when the old area is allowed to be overwritten (e.g., when the data have been moved).

The interrupt acknowledge and interrupt stacking could be performed by hardware. However, in a small computer, all registers will have to be stored and the identification of the particular interrupt placed in a common work area for all interrupts. The next step might be to place a sequence number and an interrupt identifier in a processing stack for that kind of interrupt (e.g., "the seventh memory request interrupt for drum 4"). The interrupt service might be a transfer of the appropriate command to the memory allocation processor, the interrupt process itself being performed by the memory allocation processor successfully assigning more memory to the disc input buffer area.

Each of these actions could be done by processors operating at different program states. Furthermore, the sequence in which the operations occur is not necessarily as shown. For example, it is not likely that the stack entry would be cleared until the memory allocation has been completed. The interrupt stacking program WAITS by calling the interrupt service program,

Table 9.1. Interrupt Level, Program Level, and Authority

Interrupt level	Program level	Authority level	Function
1	1	8	Malfunction indicators—acknowledge, stack, service
	2	1	Viability executive
2	3	8	Irreplaceable interrupt acknowledge, stack, service
	4	6	Interrupt executive
3	5	8	High-urgency interrupt ACK and STACK
4	5	5	Abnormal I/O termination interrupt ACK and STACK
	6	4	I/O executive
5	7	8	Medial-urgency interrupt ACK and STACK
	8	9	High-urgency interrupt service
	9	9	Medial-interrupt service
	10	3	Memory management
6	11	8	Low-urgency interrupt ACK and STACK
	12	7	High-urgency executive
	13	5	High-urgency processing
	14	7	Medial-urgency executive
	15	10	Medial-urgency processing
	16	9	Low-urgency interrupt service and processing
	17	2	Main executive
	18	10	Main program
	19	9	Background executive
	20	10	Background programs
	21	2	Exerciser and test routines

which in turn calls the memory allocation program. The completion of the memory allocation causes a re-entrance of the interrupt service, which in turn clears the stack entry. The completion of the stack clearing might be the first point at which the interrupt is acknowledged.

A representative level assignment is shown in Table 9.1. It should not be taken as an ideal assignment. Furthermore, one should not assume that all levels shown are mechanized as hardware.[6] Violations of authority will typically produce a program level change to the malfunction indication level shown in Table 9.1, and the correspondingly high authority and program level. The highest interrupt level and program level is used for functions related to malfunction and error conditions. The authority level for the malfunction indication interrupts is kept relatively low because there is no reason to have such interrupts cause modifications of all other programs.[7]

[6] In small systems, where most of the mechanization is done as software, the interrupt executive also controls authority and program levels and is therefore at the highest level.

[7] By placing authority violation alarms at a low authority level, should the malfunction interrupt routines (e.g., authority violation interrupt) also fail, the system will probably go into a loop. This is desirable as it gives a positive indication of an unrecoverable condition.

The next program level, however, is used for the viability executive functions, which in order to either recover from errors or to effect an orderly termination of ongoing operations must have the ability to modify or read all conditions in the system. The highest authority clearly belongs here, as does the highest priority and program. The reason that the interrupt ACK, STACK, and SERVICE occur at higher levels is that there is nothing much for the viability executive to do until these interrupts are ready for processing. Furthermore, under conditions of failure we may want to interrupt an ongoing viability-related program because of yet another failure, one that could negate the viability efforts underway. The viability executive, having the highest authority, can readily inhibit those interrupts that it does not wish to examine. The high priority position of the viability executive is required—there is certainly not much point in continuing any other processing until the malfunctions have been examined and corrected. For example: a memory parity error makes all other programs suspect. Note that the viability executive may call exercisers and test routines if needed. These must have the authority to examine all of memory (save those areas used by the viability executive itself).

Program levels and interrupt levels generally keep pace but need not. The typical program levels shown for interrupt acknowledge, stacking, servicing, and processing will be respectively lower, as shown. There does not appear to be valid reason for having interrupt stacking operating at a higher program level than interrupt acknowledgment. High-urgency interrupts will occur at higher interrupt and program levels than low-urgency functions, in a manner generally related to relative urgency. However, we have pointed out that urgency can vary dynamically, so that while the level of an interrupt line will remain fixed by wiring for most computers, the program level, when implemented as software, may be allowed to vary dynamically.

The next program level may be devoted to programs used to acknowledge irreplaceable interrupts. These are short-term interrupts (typically pulses rather than levels) which if not acknowledged in sufficient time will disappear or are in danger of being masked by another interrupt on the same line within a short time. The acknowledge and stack programs perform only the work required to acknowledge and stack the interrupt and to transfer control to the next program. The centralized interrupt executive program, if there is one, may also appear at this level. The irreplaceable interrupts are followed by high-urgency interrupts such as requests for additional memory by an I/O device, a drum or disc termination, requests for another block of data, etc. High-urgency interrupts may be ignored at the expense of having to redo part of the processing.

High-urgency interrupts may be followed by lower-urgency abnormal terminations (e.g., tape breakage, stuck paper tape, out-of-paper attention) that will typically continue until acknowledged. The responsive processing can be delayed. The corresponding program level may also be the level at which the centralized I/O executive (if there is one) resides.

The system may possess several executive programs and associated base-sequence programs. We have, for illustrative purposes, shown a system with six such executive base-sequence programs: interrupt, I/O, high-urgency, medial-urgency, normal, and the background executive. Conceivably, there could be an executive program and base sequencer at every program level. Typically, we have shown the executive programs at the same priority level and at the next higher program level as the bulk of the programs they direct. They could occur either at a higher level or at a lower level. If the program functions are relatively fixed (reflecting the narrow distribution of a dedicated system), having the main programs and the base sequencer at the same program level allows a more implicit structure to be designed and reduces the amount of processing required for internally generated interrupts. If the executive is at a higher level, control is simplified but additional processing time is required to make the level shifts. If the executive is at a lower level it will not be able to interrupt the ongoing program unless there has been an external interrupt or a termination of the now completed program, or through the agency of a **wake-up interrupt**. A **wake-up interrupt** is a delayed internal interrupt triggered by the executive or other programs with sufficient authority. The executives may command that it be interrupted after N memory accesses have been executed. If the executive is at a higher level than the operating program, the transfer is direct. If the executive is at a lower level than the operating program, the reassumption of executive program execution must be made indirectly through some higher-level program that momentarily blocks all other interrupts. If, for example, the occurrence of a wake-up prevents the interruption of the next several instructions, and the executive is the only program that has the authority to block all interrupts, then it can still exercise priority even if it is at the lowest level.

The lowest levels may be devoted to low-priority programs, background functions, etc. Typically, the lowest level is that which the computer executes if there is nothing else to do. If there is truly nothing else to do, the system should be set to performing exercising and test routines. It is not generally desirable to put the computer into a tight loop or into a halt state for any prolonged period. Either situation can cause repeated biasing of the same components in the same way. This can induce hot spots, and can cause impurity migrations within the transistors that lead to their premature failure. It is generally best to keep the machine busy executing a randomizing sequence of instructions. A test routine is a good choice.

3.8. Determination of Level

3.8.1. Authority Level Assignments

Authority levels form a partly ordered system. Consequently, we can use graph theory to obtain the relative authority levels for the various processors in the system. Authority levels should be determined on the basis of whether or not it would be harmful to have a given program modify another program. Thus, if program A could damage program B due to a bug in A, they should not have authority over each other. The second point in determining the authority level is deciding whether or not A *must* have the ability to modify B, despite the possibility of malfunctions. Clearly, the executive must have the ability to operate in user areas.

The relative authority of all pairs of processors in the system should be determined and used to form an authority matrix. That is, $a_{ij} = 1$ if program i must have the ability to operate in j's area. Clearly, $a_{ii} = 1$. We can then take the Nth power of this matrix, discover authority loops, resolve them, and thereby obtain a partly ordered authority graph. This graph must then be mapped onto the hardware facilities that the system provides for authority control. The hardware authority facilities must be expanded through software to the point where the proper authority graph is mechanized, or to the point where it is felt that a reasonable compromise with the ideal graph has been achieved.

3.8.2. Interrupt Level Assignment

Interrupt levels are assigned on the basis of a relation of the form "A is more urgent than B." This relation is clearly transitive, but not necessarily reflexive or antisymmetric. It can be shown that the chain extension of an arbitrary transitive relation (i.e., $A + A^2 + A^3 + \cdots + A^N$) can be used to generate a partly ordered set as shown in Chapter 8. We can obtain groupings for interrupt levels under the urgency relation in much the same way we obtained groupings for processors based on the dependency graph. This will result in a partly ordered interrupt level assignment, which must be mapped onto the (usually) strictly ordered hardware interrupt structure. If the strict ordering of the hardware interrupt structure is not adequate, then it must be extended by software to achieve the desired partial ordering.

It is not always possible to say that a given interrupt is indeed more urgent than another. We might have a situation in which interrupt A is more urgent than B and another condition during which the urgencies are reversed. If interrupt levels can be dynamically assigned, such problems can be resolved, albeit with difficulty. In the more usual case, however, interrupt levels have fixed assignments and cannot be modified on line. In such cases, we must resort to subsidiary criteria to decide which interrupt should be placed at which level.

○ *Frequency*

Given two interrupts, with everything else equal, the higher-frequency interrupt should be placed at the higher interrupt level. This, no matter how small the effect might be, decreases the amount of time spent processing interrupts. Typically, an interrupt processing program will examine interrupts existing at the same interrupt level prior to returning control to a lower priority level. This means that all interrupts current at that level will be processed without taking the time to stuff registers, etc. Furthermore, the restoration of the level that was interrupted is now amortized over the several interrupts that were current during that level. By placing the higher-frequency interrupt at the higher level, we increase the probability that the system will be at the corresponding program level when the interrupt occurs.

○ *Processing Times*

Given two incomparable interrupts, with all other aspects the same, placing the interrupt having the longer processing time at the higher level will reduce the delay for the processes related to that interrupt. This, however, is done at the expense of increasing the time and delay for the lower-level processes. Placing the short-processing-time interrupts at higher levels increases the probability that the processing routine will complete its operation without being interrupted. This saves space, and may save time since there is generally less processing required for a normal termination of a routine than for an interrupt.

○ *Space and Residence*

If both service programs are not normally resident, in a space-bound situation the short program is given the higher level while in a time-bound situation the larger program is given the higher level.

○ *Authority*

The service program having the higher authority should have its interrupt placed at the higher level. This allows the higher-authority program to exercise direct control over the lower-authority program and reduces the number of wake-up interrupts.

3.8.3. Program Level Assignments

Program level assignments will generally have the same relation as the corresponding interrupt levels. It is not likely that one can justify having the interrupt levels for devices A and B at levels 3 and 4 respectively, with the corresponding service programs at levels 4 and 3 respectively. Program level assignments can be determined by graph theory in much the same way as interrupt level assignments. Similarly, the criteria for resolving the relative level of two otherwise incomparable programs are analogous to those given for interrupt levels. The graph-theoretic relation used is of the form "program A should be completed before program B."

The program levels and the interrupt level assignments must be reconciled. Certain common points are obvious. It is clear that the interrupt acknowledge programs should be at the same relative program levels as their corresponding interrupts. As a result of such mandatory correspondences, the two schemes will be brought into almost complete conjunction. The little freedom remaining must be determined on the basis of the peculiarities of the situation.

3.8.4. How Many Levels?

The number of levels may be optional. Typically, the more hardware levels, the higher the price of the system. The more levels are implemented, the more memory will be used for dedicated areas. We know that neither interrupt levels nor program levels are necessary. Let us for the moment ignore the difference between program levels and interrupt levels and assume that they are the same. We shall make the following common assumptions: (1) An interrupt at a given level will not interrupt the processes underway at that or higher levels and (2) the interrupt service processors at each level will process all other interrupts at that level which were activated prior to the completion of the given interrupt. Under these assumptions, and provided we know the incident interrupt rates for each level, the processing time for each interrupt, and the noninterrupt processing that must go on at that level, we can compare the effects of various numbers of interrupt levels.

Each program level can be considered as if it were a distinct state. By representing program levels (states) as nodes, and the transitions caused by interrupts as links, we can represent a system as a state graph, in the manner shown in Figure 9.6. At any given instant of time, the system is in exactly one state. It remains in that state (the self-transition) until one of two things happen: there is nothing more to do in that state, in which case it executes a transition to a lower state, or an interrupt for a higher level occurs, in which case it executes a transition to a higher state. Associated with each upward transition (transition from a lower state to a higher state) is a transition cost equal to the cost of terminating the operation in the lower state and starting the operation in the higher state. Associated with each downward transition is the equivalent cost for the opposite direction.

If we assume that there are a sufficient number of levels to service all interrupts and to maintain maximum utilization of the system's resources, is there any advantage in increasing the number of interrupt or program levels? Each level added to the system will perforce increase the number of

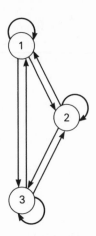

Figure 9.6. Interrupt
state graph.

transitions that will occur, reduce batch processing in each level, and increase program space. It does, however, reduce the delay for high-priority functions at the expense of low-priority functions. High-priority functions will be resident for shorter periods, while low-priority functions will reside for longer periods; therefore, the space may increase or decrease. The effect of fractionating levels is to increase almost everything except the delay of higher-priority functions.[8]

If a level must be fractionated into two levels, there still remains a choice as to whether hardware or software should be used for the purpose. If the fractionation is done by hardware, the cost is readily determined from the manufacturer's catalog. If it is done by software, we must include the transition cost excess over the cost of hardware-controlled transitions and compare this with the fraction of the system facilities used for these additional transitions.

Generally, trading among the number of levels is difficult to do analytically. Often we can readily justify employing the maximum number of levels available but cannot justify the specialized engineering required for still more levels.

3.8.5. Deferred Processing

Increasing the number of levels, whether interrupt levels or program levels, increases the processing and the delay for all functions except those occurring at the higher levels. Paradoxical though this may sound, *it can*

---

[8] The detailed analysis requires a knowledge of Markov process theory, which is beyond the scope of this book.

lead to a net reduction in processing load. Let us assume that a given system structured with N levels requires 300,000 memory cycles per second for interrupt handling during a high-intensity burst. Furthermore, let us assume that normal processing will require 900,000 cycles per second. The net requirement then is 1,200,000 cycles per second. Let us now introduce an additional level that allows us to defer part of the 300,000 cycles over the next several seconds. Say that only 100,000 cycles must be expended immediately and 200,000 can be deferred to a later time. In so doing, we may increase the original 300,000 to 350,000 cycles. This would seem to increase the net load to 1,250,000 cycles. However, if the burst is not likely to last more than one second, and if in the nonburst condition the total processing load is only 600,000 cycles per second, by deferring the processing we obtain an average of 850,000 cycles per second, and a burst requirement of 1,000,000 cycles, a net reduction of 200,000 cycles in the burst. By deferring peak processing for a few seconds we can reduce the required machine capacity.

The longer the bursts the less the payoff for deferred processing. In the above example, placing external interrupt acknowledge, stacking, service, and processing at four different levels was an example of deferred processing. The delay was increased, the processing for any given function was increased, and the amount of memory required was increased, but the average required processing capacity was decreased.

It is not unusual for a busy-hour load to be ten times the off-hour load, and to have 50% of the processing done in a 4-hour period. If we could average the load over a 24-hour period (which would be intolerable for most systems), the required capacity would be only $\frac{1}{5}$ of the peak-hour requirements, while the 24-hour average might be only $\frac{1}{10}$ or $\frac{1}{20}$ of the peak-second requirements.

We should not make the mistake of assuming that requirements of 100 cycles per millisecond, 100,000 cycles per second, and 3.6×10^8 cycles per hour are the same requirements. Typically, 3.6×10^8 cycles per hour is ten times more stringent than 100,000 cycles per second, which in turn is ten times more stringent a requirement than 100 cycles per millisecond. A detailed knowledge of burst distributions and expected burst histories allows us to trade deferred processing against delay, increased processing, and increased memory, to achieve a net reduction in the required hardware capacity. By knowing the characteristics of the bursts, we can do some timely procrastination.

The use of additional levels in order to defer processing is a convenience rather than a necessity. It has the advantage of simplifying the overhead processing required to defer high-priority processing. The use of multiple levels makes this automatic and implicit.

3.9. Multicomputer Executive Structures

Computer complexes can be divided (roughly) into two classes, those in which the CPUs share the main memory on a memory-cycle-to-cycle basis, and those in which the main memories are momentarily devoted to the sole use of a single CPU. A given complex may have both types.

In the latter case, computers can only execute instructions out of their own memories. The processors have been partitioned and assigned to each computer according to some rational scheme, which among other things is intended to minimize the explicit communications required between the several computers of the complex. One of the computers in the complex is designated as the executive. It performs a base-sequence program to which all other computers are tied, albeit loosely. The other computers in the complex also run under their own (typically simpler) base-sequence programs, which are optimized for the performance of their functions. There are then several executive programs in operation, and the interrelations between the various executives and their structure depend upon the logical topology of the system.

3.9.1. Logically Radially or Tree-Structured Systems

Whatever the physical structure of the complex, we are presently concerned with its logical structure. It is clear that tree, radial, bus, matrix, or symmetric physical structures can all be used to implement a logical tree structure. The discussion of Chapter 8, Section 6, applies to logical topologies as well as to physical topologies. The various proclivities, indications, and contraindications for the structures described there apply also to logical structures, no matter what physical structures are used to implement them.

In logically radial or tree systems the central executive is typically placed at the central node of the tree. This is the common point of the system and the point at which communication and mass memory can most readily be centralized. Three generic situations are shown in Figure 9.7.

In Figure 9.7a the executive is shown in a centralized position communicating with several front-end computers. A **front-end** computer is one which is devoted primarily to, or accomplishes the majority of, externally applied urgent tasks such as communications with the outside world.[9]

---

[9] Which is another and perhaps long-winded way of saying that these computers perform the "real-time" functions of the system. The reader will note a studied avoidance of this term. First of all, all time is "real." Secondly, there is so much ambiguity as to what "real time" is, and the concept as used in the literature is so context-dependent, that it is unlikely that agreement as to what this term means will be achieved in the next decade. We prefer to say that the front end is concerned with processing the majority of uncontrolled, externally applied, or urgent functions.

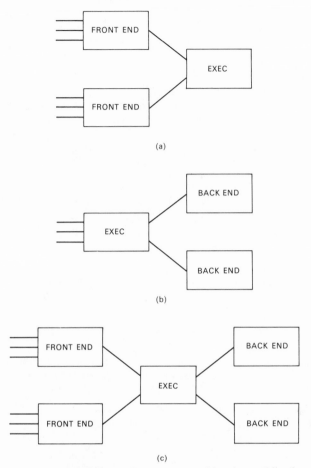

Figure 9.7. Possible executive computer positions in a multilevel system: (a) rear-end executive; (b) front-end executive; (c) middle executive.

In this arrangement, deferred processing is not only done by using additional levels, but by deferring the processing to another computer. The executive computer, by virtue of the burst-ameliorating activities of the front-end computers, will have a steadier load and therefore a more efficient executive. Each computer in the scheme of Figure 9.7a will have a base-sequence program that runs quasi-independently of those of the other computers. Communications between the front end and the executive is done by blocks of data that are transferred to and from the executive. At appropriate points in the base-sequence programs of the front-end computers, their executives will request additional data for output processing, or will request that the central computer take data that are ready for central processing. While the executive cannot directly effect control over the inputs to the front-end computers, it can control the processing load in those computers. It can do this by the simple expedient of denying the front end additional output. By deliberately delaying output data it frees the front end to spend more time on input. This also has the effect of transferring memory to input processes that would otherwise be used for output. If input is solicited by the front end (i.e., polled), the executive can control the input rate indirectly if *it* is the computer that establishes the polling schedule. By refusing to give the front-end computer a polling schedule, more time is allotted to input processing. There are many other implicit methods to control what the front end is working on, without having to direct its activities in detail. It is of course possible and necessary to allow the executive computer to exercise direct, imperative control over the front end. This is normally done by relatively high-priority interrupts to the front-end computers. The executive can measure the length of the front-end cycle and thereby determine the processing load of each computer. This is done by having the front end report to the executive (by an interrupt) at a predetermined point in the front-end cycle.

The system shown in Figure 9.7b is one which is typically dominated by processing tasks and has comparatively low communication tasks. The role played by the executive and the method by which it communicates with and controls the activities of the outlying computers is similar to that used for the system of Figure 9.7a. This position for the executive will, however, result in lowered efficiency. The executive base-sequence cycle is typically more complex than that of the nonexecutive computer. The executive, being concerned with a multitude of functions contends with a broadly distributed load. By adding to this the vagaries of uncontrolled inputs and external communication tasks, the distribution is broadened still further. It is therefore desirable to allow the back-end computers to perform as much of the executive functions as they are capable of doing for themselves, restricting the central executive functions to those that perforce must be placed there, i.e., those concerned with or affecting the interaction of the two back-end computers.

The scheme shown in Figure 9.7c is a hybrid of the other schemes. This structure will occur when both front-end and back-end functions must be extensively partitioned. In this case, the executive computer is likely to perform only executive functions, that is, the coordination of intracomplex communications. Indirect control over the activities of the outlying computers can be achieved by denying them necessary data, trusting to the executive of each outlying computer to assure that it will be gainfully employed.

3.9.2. Executive Philosophy

We see that the primary mode of control exercised over the activities of outlying computers is indirect. The executive and the outlying computers operate each under its own executive program, with direct control reduced to a minimum. This is analogous to the light touch on the reins required to control a team of horses—it would be ludicrous to direct their every step. Therefore, in addition to the direct commands ("do this or that"), there is indirect, implicit control that can be exercised by delaying or denying data or information. Concomitantly, by increasing the rate at which information is supplied to high-level programs within an outlying computer, the executive can reduce the work being done on lower-priority programs in that computer.

This relationship can be formalized by considering the set of programs complementary to a given program. The **complement** of a program or processor is the set of all other programs or processors. By denying data to a program we increase the proportion of time spent on its complement. By overloading a program we decrease the proportion of time spent on its complement. Explicit and direct control over the activities of an outlying computer can be achieved by addressing ourselves to a program—implicit and indirect control can be achieved by addressing ourselves to the complements of a program. Since implicit control usually entails less processing, space, and data transfer, it is more efficient. Implicit control, by manipulating the complement of a program, however, requires greater design time efforts and a better understanding of the interrelations and the dynamics of the system. It is the design cost *vs.* efficiency trade.

3.9.3. System Executive *vs.* Computer Executive

The executive of the system and the executive program of the computer which embodies the system executive are not necessarily one and the same. This would be akin to saying that the admiral of the fleet is the captain of the flagship. There can be two base-sequence programs within the computer that houses the executive—one for that computer and one for the system as a whole. In most cases, the two different functions will be merged into a single base-sequence program. However, one should start the design by explicitly separating the two functions. The computer running the executive functions will also be doing nonexecutive tasks. In Figure 9.7a it is performing data processing, while in Figure 9.7b it is performing communication functions. If the two executive programs are at different program levels, it is easy to see this distinction.

The executive design criteria that apply for the central computer do not necessarily apply for the system as a whole. The system executive program is concerned with maximizing the effectiveness of the system—it allocates the resources of the system. The executive computer executive program is concerned with maximizing the executive computer's facilities, which are typically less than those of the system. The initial design should be done under the tentative (and soon to be discarded) assumption that the two functions will be done in two separate computers, and only later should it be decided how these functions may be merged within a single computer or even within a single executive program. Getting back to our analogy, the functions of the captain and the admiral are distinctly different. Those functions should be clearly defined and only then should we worry about what happens on the flagship. Remember also that the flagship of a fleet is whatever ship the admiral happens to be on.

3.9.4. Shared Memory Systems

Some or all of the main memories of a multicomputer complex could be shared by more than one CPU. The principal advantage of this scheme is the reduction of explicit intercomputer crosstell and the ability to handle burst conditions. There are, however, significant disadvantages with respect to viability.

The shared-memory system is similar to the single computer except that there can be more than one computer performing any particular task. Not only must the priority control processor determine what level a particular computer should be operating at, but also how many computers should be operating at that level. This system (which physically is perforce a bus, radial, or symmetric system) can be adapted to any of the various logical topologies. Computers participating in a shared-memory system are symmetrically structured and physically undifferentiated. The processor being executed by a computer is determined solely by the area of memory it is working out of. The control over what the various computers are doing, and how much resource is allocated to what function at any one time, is done by the priority assignment hardware and software. The indirect control methods (denying outputs) used for the independent computers can also be used here. Data must be marked as ready for processing to achieve indirect control. This increases space and time because the receiving processor must examine the tag. Another way of doing this is to delay placing the data descriptor on the processing queue for the function that we wish to delay. A more direct form of control over the processing activities of all computers is afforded through blocking the priority levels, or restricting the number of computers that can operate at them. The priority control program can designate the number of computers that should be allowed to work at a particular level. Thus, if there are N computers, a number from 0 to N can be designated. At any one time there could be several computers working at the same level, in fact, using the same programs. For this reason, re-entrant code must be used throughout.

Administration is more complex and must be explicit to prevent simultaneous, redundant processing on a given task. The increase in administrative costs is (hopefully) paid for by the reduction in explicit data transfers.

4. JOB CONTROL

4.1. Jobs and Tasks

The system exists to perform processing on externally supplied data. Data can be partitioned into sets which are (relatively) independent of each other. The processing that is to be done on that data set is called a **job**. A job might be processing one airline ticket, interpreting one line of JOSS, compiling a FORTRAN program, running a particular program, performing one iteration of a control loop, etc. That which constitutes a job can only be defined in the context of the application of the complex. We can say the following: the job starts at the first command or upon the receipt of the first item of data for that job and terminates when the final output has been produced. Each job makes demands upon the complex—demands for memory, for I/O, for computers, for mass memory, etc. Rarely does a job go from beginning to end without interruption. Aside from cycle stealing, the job will be interrupted by jobs of higher priority. The job will pause while waiting for slow operations to complete. Jobs are not necessarily processed in the order in which they arrive.

The later job may finish first, the shorter before the longer, or *vice versa*. The system is attempting to maximize the utilization of its resources. It does this by chopping jobs and intermixing them in a way to achieve that optimum. The resulting mess is the responsibility of the **job control processor**. Job control consists of **job assessment, error control and recovery**, and **interjob control**. Since files will be created, accessed, and destroyed as a result of a job, it is expected that the job control processor will interact with the file management processor. The main mechanisms used for job control are **job queues** and **task queues**, as well as a number of tables and directories. A given job may be broken down into one or more parts. While a job could be defined and described as a tree or a more general graph, the typical system allows jobs to be defined only as strictly linear sequences of tasks.

4.2. Job Assessment

While the unit of work presented to the system as a semantic element is the job, the system consists of predominantly syntactic processors. The job could be: "Do my eigenvalue program on this file." This job specification must be converted to requests for loading certain programs, data files, allocations of memory, requests for bulk storage, performance of I/O operations, etc. Each of these internal work units is called a **task**. Job assessment is analogous to interpretation of instructions and the subsequent definition of the sequence of microinstructions that will be executed to accomplish the instructions.

Job assessment may be implicit or explicit. The more dedicated the system, the more likely that most of the jobs will be defined implicitly. Thus, in an air-traffic control system, it is known *a priori* that inputs coming in on line 17 are from the radar and should be treated accordingly. Similarly, inputs on a certain line of a communication system may not only specify implicitly what is to be done to the message, but may specify the destination, code, and format of the resulting output message as well. On the other hand, the input to a time-sharing system could represent anything from a request to talk to the operator to a request to clear 500 files.

Job assessment begins with the interpretation of commands (if explicitly given) and ends with requests for facilities. In a general system, a job may contain within its definition a request for a certain amount of memory, for tapes, mass memory, printouts, etc. A compiler or assembler will extract such information from the source program and make it an explicit part of the job definition, even though not supplied by the job requester. Job assessment is not necessarily done in one place or at one time. In many cases, the requirements for facilities cannot be established *in toto* until the job is running. Facility requirements may also be data-dependent.

In commercial operating systems, part of job assessment is the establishment of a list of the separately compiled subroutines that are needed for each job. Job assessment also determines which tasks must be performed or, if this is not possible, which is the first task to be performed. For example, a request to run a program which is about to be entered can only be partially analyzed. Job assessment will establish a need for buffer areas, the use of the communication processor, mass memory, file processor, etc. Upon having accepted the program it will go through another phase of job assessment, viz., use of the compiler. This in turn will result in further task definitions, e.g., a call to the loader. If the job assessment processor fails to determine the tasks, or at least the initial tasks of the job, it must abort the job with appropriate notification to its originator.

The job progresses as a sequence of generally sequential tasks. In a multicomputer complex, it is possible to establish a nonsequential (i.e., partially parallel) sequence of tasks, to allow maximal utilization of parallel computing capabilities. At present, the algorithms for deciding (without running the job, or the equivalent) how the job may be done in parallel are too cumbersome to warrant their on-line utilization.

4.3. Error Control

Any task might be completed improperly. The possible errors are legion: overflow, attempt to execute privileged instructions, attempted violation of authority, nonexisting routines, missing data, data in the wrong format, invalid instructions, etc.

The abortion of any task must be signaled back to the job control processor so that it can alert the job specifier of what went wrong where. The failure to complete a task does not necessarily result in scrapping the job. Part of the job definition may include instructions as to what to do under certain error conditions. Other forms of recovery action may be implicit in the job definition. The task failure could be due to a transient malfunction or a catastrophic failure in the task processor. The very failure of the task might be the point of the task. As an example, the task could be part of a diagnostic program testing authority. The program would deliberately attempt to execute a boundary violation in order to test the boundary controls. The "failure" of that task would be welcome. If the task were successfully accomplished, it would result in a notification of a hardware malfunction and probably call in another test routine as the next task.

4.4. Interjob Control

Jobs are presumably independent. In actuality they may not be. As an example, consider a time-sharing system which provides an elegant accounting system for each user company. At the end of the month, the accountant closes the files and generates the invoices for that month. The invoice contains, among other things, the computer usage up to the time of closing. The individual users have their machine utilization automatically dumped into one of the files that the accountant is using. Since the world is not nice, the accountant may have good reason to call in the master file more than once during a session. That file could have been modified by one of his company's employees as the invoices were being calculated. Either a positive indication of such events or a method for preventing such race conditions must be provided. As long as more than two jobs can call on the same files, it is possible for the jobs to interact. Therefore, some sort of interjob control must be provided.

As another example, we can take a communication system which operationally appears to be several independent communication systems, each with its own doctrines, procedures, and formats. While at first the various users will not require interconnection, it is likely that at some time they will see the possibility and desire it. As a final example, consider again a time-sharing system. Two different users log into the system. The system provides facilities whereby they can communicate with each other.[10] This also creates the possibility of job interaction.

Every system which allows a breakdown of jobs into subjobs effectively has an interjob control problem at the lower level of the job hierarchy.

Interjob control requires that each file and each task of each job be tagged with one of several states. The following states are representative:

○ **Loaded and running:** It cannot be interfered with.

○ **Loaded and ready to run:** It can be interfered with if this is allowable under the doctrines of the system. Notification of interference is required.

○ **Loaded and blocked:** The task is waiting for some other operation to be completed. Since the completion signal will probably be at a higher priority level and cannot be controlled, the task cannot be interfered with.

○ **Not loaded and ready to run:** This will require an executive action to load. Interference is possible if allowable under the system doctrines.

○ **Not loaded and blocked:** Since executive action will be required to load the task, interference could be allowed.

○ **Loaded and complete:** Interference is possible if allowable.

○ **Unloaded and complete:** The job is no longer in active storage, is no longer being processed, but is still within the system, if only as an item to be administered.

○ **Not resident but not yet completed or accounted:** The job is not yet closed.

○ **Closed**

This last state does not really exist because the closure of a task is tantamount to its disappearance as an explicit data element.

The primary danger with allowing interjob communication is the possibility of **job lock-up**. One can readily imagine a situation in which two jobs call each other recursively and somehow both are waiting for each other before the next step can be taken. Both jobs are active, both jobs are blocked. One way to prevent this is to allow job interaction to take place only via files, where such lock-ups are more readily resolved. Another way is to provide reasonableness checks or limits on the duration of the job residency and to turn over to error control all jobs that have exceeded the allowable

---

[10] Time-sharing systems typically provide operator controls via just another user terminal (albeit a privileged one). These systems also provide the ability of an external user to talk to the operator. This is sufficient to allow all users to "talk" to each other.

residency. If some sort of control for preventing or detecting lock-ups is not provided, the system will eventually (in a matter of days) become glutted with blocked jobs.

4.5. File Management Interface

File management is performed by a processor to be described in Chapter 10. At this point we are concerned with the interface between the job control processor and the file management processor. The job control processor communicates to the file management processor requests for existing files by name, commands to create files, to delete files, or to modify files. The file management processor in turn obtains the files, or notifies the job processor if the files do not exist, creates and deletes the files, or modifies them if that is required. Attempts to create a file with an already existing name are also brought to the attention of the job control processor.

4.6. Job Status

The **job status** is a dynamic description of the job in terms of the tasks that have been or are scheduled to be performed. The job status data and the files associated with the job at any instant of time should be sufficient to re-establish the job at exactly that point. That is, should the system fail, the job status table and the contents of the various files are sufficient to restart the job, except for those tasks that were in progress at the time of the failure. The job status data *are not* a history of the job. They do not tell us how that particular status was achieved, the time at which the tasks were performed, or in general, even the sequence in which they were performed. One error made in the design of job status tables is to provide a detailed history of the progress of the job. There may be systems in which this kind of microscopic trace is required, but these are relatively rare and typically restricted to military or financial applications. The following information can be included in the job status table:

1. The status of all tasks that have been identified but not yet closed.
2. The status of all files that have been identified but not yet closed.
3. The units (physical) that have been assigned or scheduled for the performance of those tasks.
4. The physical and logical identification(s) of the memories in which unclosed files may reside. Note that any given file could have several simultaneous existences (e.g., in core, on drum, disc, and tapes, as well as redundant copies in the interest of reliability).

Much of this information is not kept in explicit job status tables. For example, the status of a task may be implicitly specified by the fact that it appears on the queue of the processor that will process that task.

4.7. Accountability

Every system can and will fail. Consequently, we can expect that at times transactions, messages, data, and jobs or parts thereof will be lost. In many systems, if data are lost, they can be recovered, providing it is known that the loss has occurred. To run the job we must have it. To be accountable for a job, we need only have the job status. The job itself can be lost without losing our accountability for it. Job accountability is lost when the job status can no longer be trusted. If the system maintains proper job accountability, it can, upon discovering the loss, request a retransmission of the pertinent data, or take other appropriate corrective action. However, if accountability is lost, not only does the user not know what has happened to the job, but the system itself does not know. This will cause problems when the job is rerun, may permanently leave unusable space in memory, or otherwise tie up facilities for a long time.

In communication systems, there are message retrieval activities that allow a message to be traced and recovered from the source if accountability is maintained. In reservation systems it is generally considered more important to maintain accountability than to honor all transactions. If accountability is lost, a seat may be reserved but not sold. If a transaction is lost, but not its accountability, the worst that will happen is that the same seat will be sold twice. It is considered more desirable to have a full aircraft, taking the risk that very rarely a passenger will be inconvenienced. In a time-sharing system, loss of accountability may lead to a bad run, while the loss of an input without loss of accountability may result only in a request for a reproduced input.

The simplest way to achieve accountability is to defer the closure or acknowledgment of a task until redundant copies of the job status table changes have been made. A discrepancy in the several copies of the job status table is used to determine that there has been a malfunction or an error. The last thing done in a task, prior to returning control to the executive, is to change the job status table. The first thing done by the executive upon resuming that job (after a malfunction) is to examine the validity of the job status table entries for that job.

5. SCHEDULING AND OPTIMIZATION

At any instant there are a number of tasks ready for processing, but only a few devices that can be used to process them. Scheduling is the matching of facilities to tasks. The job control processors make requests for devices, but it is the scheduler that allocates those devices. While most scheduling processors are designed to optimize the utilization of the facilities, there is much for the scheduler to do even if optimization were not attempted.

5.1. Objectives

The primary objective of the scheduler is to fill the requests for devices made by the job control processor in the proper sequence, despite the fact that the duration for which any particular device will be busy is not known. Scheduling trains is relatively simple, since the deviation in run time is supposed to be very small. Consider the difference in performance of a railroad or an airline under normal conditions as compared to what happens in a snowstorm or similar disruption. Scheduling in the computer complex is scheduling under uncertainty. The following functions are performed by the scheduler:

○ *Device Allocation*

Allocation of the proper device to the jobs as requested and when needed to perform the tasks. In this larger context, devices are to be taken to include mass memory, main memory segments, channels, tape units, computers, printers, terminals, communication lines, etc.

○ *Concurrent Job Device Allocation*

Allocation of devices to jobs for concurrently operating jobs, in which it cannot be told which of two competing jobs will need the facility first, nor how long that facility will be used.

○ *Dynamic Priorities*

Maintaining control and allocating devices according to predefined, possibly dynamically changing job priorities. The job priorities are not to be confused with the interrupt priorities or program levels described above. In a commercial time-sharing system, all user jobs may operate at the same program level. However, the time-sharing company might offer three different rates corresponding to three different job priorities such as "interactive immediate," "remote batch immediate," and "deferred." A complete job priority system might be imbedded within the executive program, typically as part of the scheduler.

○ *Optimization*

Performance of the above functions with the intention of meeting a set of desired optimization criteria. These could include the following possibly contradictory requirements: maximization of the utilization of the facilities, minimization of delay, maximization of income, equalization of the performance as seen by the user.

○ *Subsidiary Functions*

Subsidiary functions that can be included under the scheduler are: initialization of units (including memory) such as cleanup, returning a tape to the load point, etc.; initialization of programs or subroutines.

5.2. System Status Tables

The scheduler must at all times either maintain or have access to the status of the system. This means that it must know the state of each job, and each task within that job, the status and location of each active file, and the physical condition of each device. The latter means knowing whether a device is working or not, whether it is on-line or off-line, busy, not busy, etc.

The status tables for devices must specify if the allocation of a device to a job or task is to last for the duration of the task or job, or if it can be reassigned prior to the completion of the task. For some units this is inherent, while for others it may depend on the job assessment. For example, if a task requires a printer, it is not likely that that printer can be assigned to any other job, lest the outputs of several jobs be interlaced, resulting in garbage. If, however, the printer is used solely to alert the operator as to what to do in case a task is aborted, and if there are several jobs using it in this manner, the allocation can be temporary. In the first case, the allocation is fixed for the duration of the job; in the second case, the allocation is limited only to printing one page or just one line.

The system status tables will normally also contain the amount of elapsed time since the unit was allocated to the task or job and/or the amount of time that the task or job has been waiting for a free unit. The time that the device (say, a computer) has been in use may be used to prevent hogging of facilities by a job. The elapsed time while waiting for a free unit may be used to prevent excessive delays by changing job or task priorities.

As each change occurs, typically because of an interrupt or because a task has become blocked, the scheduler must examine its available facilities to determine the next incremental step in the schedule. Let us assume that an I/O processor has signaled that a particular operation has been completed. The I/O processor has been given a task of the form "TRANSFER BLØCK 85 FRØM DRUM TØ MAIN MEMØRY." The successful completion of that task frees a channel and the drum, and probably unblocks the task that was waiting for these data. The I/O handler does not know to which task or job that block belongs. Given this information, the scheduler will perform the following steps:

1. Find the job and task for which the transfer was done.
2. Examine the job to see what should be done next, if anything—perhaps there are several blocks to be transferred before the task can be unblocked.
3. Change the task status (e.g., from unloaded and blocked to unloaded and ready to run).
4. Schedule the reloading of the task according to the present priority of the task. This may require a run through the job priority sub-processor, which too might have to be scheduled.
5. Examine the device status in the light of the job status to see if the device can be released, and, if it can be released, change its status.
6. Change the status of the channel to reflect the fact that it is free.

If the termination was an abnormal one, a similar set of steps will occur, allowing (if possible) the recovery of the task, or its abortion if that is the only thing that can be done.

The complete set of system status tables is not necessarily directly under the aegis of the scheduler. More often, these tables do not exist as centralized tables, but rather as tables distributed throughout the system and managed by individual processors. Thus, the drum and disc management processors may maintain their own tables and in fact may perform the details of the scheduling for those devices. Similarly, the file management processor maintains files, correlates their identity on various devices, and may schedule their movement in the system.

The scheduler of a dedicated system and the base-sequence program of a dedicated system tend to be one and the same. As the characterizing distributions get broader, the base sequence program is transformed toward the scheduler described above. They can be looked upon as opposite extremes.

5.3. Optimization Methods and Goals

The primary mechanism used by an optimizing scheduler is the attempt to maximize the utilization of the units of the complex. Ideally, no memory cycles would be wasted, all channels would be continually busy, in short, all devices would be running at full tilt. If the expected durations of tasks are known, and tasks are known in advance, there are a number of analytical methods that can be used to obtain an optimum schedule. The classical form of this problem is called the "allocation problem." In its classical form, the problem deals with the allocation of tasks to machines in a job-lot production shop, e.g., a small machine shop. It is assumed that the sequence of operations (machines or units) required for each job is known in advance, as well as the durations of the tasks for each job, the cost of doing the jth job on the ith machine, the number of machines of each type, their capacity, etc. Under these assumptions, the optimum schedule can be obtained by using linear programming. Given a computer, with twenty or so units to be allocated, and a similar number of jobs, the cost of solving the linear programming problem would constitute a noticeable perturbation on the operation. However, since none of these factors is known in advance, and they all are at best known statistically, change from moment to moment, and are subject to changing priorities during the course of execution, analytical methods are not very useful for basing the design of a scheduler. At present, the problem of finding a scheduling algorithm for the realistic situation encountered in a computer complex is unsolved. If we further complicate the issue by including the cost of obtaining the optimum schedule, and the uncertainties associated with the tasks and jobs to be scheduled, we are still further from a solution.

Optimization is therefore applied locally. That is, we attempt to optimize various subprocessors of the system and trust that if we schedule a task for a device as soon as possible, so that each device will be kept busy, the system as a whole will be reasonably efficient.

The problem then of minimizing wasted facilities is not yet solved. However, this is only the simplest optimization goal. We must, in reality, optimize with respect to a goal that consists of many factors. We could optimize individual jobs, minimize job delays, average delays, etc. In reality, then, we deal with a more complex goal than that of maximizing unit utilization.

5.4. Spooling

One form of local optimization that can be used is called **spooling**. The philosophy behind spooling is to attempt to batch things so that the batch can be optimized. As an example, consider a multicomputer complex that has only two high-speed printers. Let us assume that the printer can printed 10 lines per second. A program that uses the printer might only provide an output every 200 milliseconds. If a printer is assigned to that program for the duration of the job, its effective speed will only be 5 lines per second. Another program might slow the printer down to a few lines per minute, while yet another program might be constantly blocked while waiting for the printer. A similar situation occurs with card readers, card punches, terminals, and tape units. The slower peripheral devices, then, can markedly increase the processing delays and increase the number of tasks on queues. Conversely, the fast devices may not be utilized to their full capacity.

In spooling systems, tasks are not given real peripherals to work with. Instead, all ouptuts to and inputs from the slower peripherals are to or from the mass memory at the maximum possible rate. The program "prints" a line in a file stored in the mass memory. Similarly, it "reads a card" from a file where that card has been previously stored. In this way the action of the slower peripheral is not bound by the processing and can occur at the maximum rate. When the job is done, all of its print file is printed. As soon as the present job has been printed, the next job in the printer queue is printed. This way, the peripheral device is bound by the speed at which the file can be fetched. The number of lines to be printed, or cards to be punched, is known prior to printing the first one, and the schedule can be somewhat better.

The result of spooling is an increase in the capacity of the system, at the cost of increasing the delay for any one job, and the total main and mass memory in use. The additional costs are increased processing to store the outputs and fetch them back again for the true output. Since these are usually contentious transfers, the costs are more than compensated by the increased efficiency.

6. PRIORITY, AUTHORITY, SECURITY, AND PRIVACY

These functions are not so much accomplished by explicit processors as they are a reflection of a design philosophy that must pervade the system. The advent of large-scale centralized systems that contain vital data on most persons in the United States, central credit clearing houses, systems that handle large representative cash transfers, and the coming check-less society make these formerly minor aspects of system design increasingly important. In this context, we are not concerned with priority, authority, security, and privacy from the point of view of internal system requirements, but rather from that of the user.

6.1. Priority

6.1.1. Internal vs. External Priority

The internal priority given to a task is only roughly a reflection of the external priority assigned to it. A priority structure can be established for jobs that is as rich as the priority structures established for internal processors. Strict ordering, partial ordering, etc., are all possible. It is important, however, to note that the external priorities typically are distributed at several different internal levels. Thus, external job priorities may be assigned as 1, 2, and 3. At internal level 5, these jobs may be assigned priorities in relative order 3, 1, 2, while at yet another internal level, the ordering of priorities may be 1, 3, 2. Typically, the external priority ordering of jobs and the internal priority ordering of jobs will coincide only at the base program level. The reason for such seemingly haphazard differences between internal and external priority ordering is that each job makes different demands on the system resources. Job 1, while having the highest external priority, may never need the drum. Job 3, on the other hand, uses the drum. The drum will probably be given a higher priority than the disc, resulting in the kind of priority permutations shown above.

6.1.2. Dynamic Priorities

Priorities are not necessarily constant throughout the history of a job. We have seen that the priority of a task may differ from the base priority of a program in the interest of maximizing the utilization of the facilities that the complex represents. In many systems, priority levels (which effectively reflect a reaction to a specification of maximum allowable transaction delays) are established fairly grossly. Thus, external priority levels 1, 2, 3 might be specifications for delays of three seconds, three minutues, three hours respectively. A characteristic of most users is a highly nonlinear annoyance function. While not a peep is to be heard from the user who expects a delay of two hours when the actual delay is one hour, 59 minutes, and 58 seconds, his annoyance with an additional delay of four seconds is usually dispro-portionate to the amount of time he has been waiting. Studies made of tele-phone user habits, for example, show that the point of explosion is reached 15 seconds after failing to hear a dial tone.

Within the complex, jobs, and even tasks, are implicitly or explicitly assumed to work against a deadline established by how close to the maximum expectabie delay for that priority the job is. Thus, as a job approaches the deadline, its priority may be increased. This implies that the length the job or task has been in the system must be maintained as part of the job status. The system may also, separately, maintain the length of time the job or task has been on the processing queue. The sum of the lengths of time on the queues is usually less than the time in the system. As the job gets staler, its internal job priority is shifted upward, to the point where it may usurp jobs or tasks of higher external priorities. This kind of shifting priorities repre-sents a qualitative change in the scheduling processors. What it means is that the job of scheduling must be interrelated with job control processors. Not only is there scheduling, but there is rescheduling as well. The scheduler is committed to examining all queues and all entries on all queues to determine if positions should be changed. This means that all the difficulties associated with moving queue entries or relinking queues exist.

This is an area where associative memories can be effective. The position on the "queue" is determined by the particular priority queue the task is on and by the age indicator for the task or job. One can establish a function of the external priority and the staleness that redefines the internal priority of the task. By searching for the "hottest" such item, shifting priorities are readily implemented.

6.1.3. Priorities and Facilities

Priority assignments as discussed thus far reflected the user's point of view. However, the facility may cause changes in the priority to suit its own requirements. As an example, consider the main memory of a computer. It has, by whatever priority/scheduling algorithm in force, loaded memory with certain tasks. Typically, there will be areas of memory left over that cannot be filled except by small tasks. In order to maximize the utilization of the memory, the scheduler may temporarily increase the internal priority of small jobs, using them to fill in the chinks. In a similar way, small, low-priority jobs, may advance ahead of larger, higher-priority jobs in the use of mass memories, channels, and CPUs. The idea is that if something can be fitted into the schedule, it will be, despite the fact that priorities in the fine may be upset. The point of view should be that if nothing else of high priority can be accommodated, the leftovers should be allocated to lower-priority tasks, with the intent of keeping the complex as busy as possible. If the scheduler always maintained strict priority and service in the order of arrival—a so-called "fair" system—it would not achieve the optimum utilization of the complex's resources.

6.1.4. Probabilistic Priorities

We see by the above that externally imposed priorities are at best probabilistic. That is, in the interest of providing a good system, external priorities may occasionally be compromised. The priority should be specified by a probability distribution that states the expected probability that the particular job will be accomplished sooner than a job of a lower priority of comparable size that is entered at the same time. Conversely, there are applications in which the job order must be strictly maintained, lest meaningless results occur. Thus, a reservation should precede the reservation's cancellation, an update should follow an input, and no one should receive credit prior to payment or be billed prior to incurring an expense.

6.2. Authority and Security

We have defined authority as a specification of what areas in which medium a program is allowed to modify or read or both. As with priorities, there are both internal and external specifications. Again, the internal and external structures do not necessarily coincide.

6.2.1. Security and Authority Hierarchies

Who has access to what can be described by a graph. However, the specification is not simply one of stating that a particular subprocessor has the ability to modify or examine a subsidiary processor. To each link of the graph must be appended a logical expression (hopefully combinational) that specifies the conditions under which that link exists. Thus, we may say that processor A has the ability to modify B if a key has been set, or if it has been verified by the proper party. The possible structures of such graphs, the conditions under which they change, and the logical expressions that are used to open the locks are as complex as human imagination. Each additional element of security imposed on the system means an additional term in a Boolean function that is to be evaluated, either by hardware or software or both. Each such addition increases costs and decreases the efficiency and flexibility of the system. Security can vary by user request or by operator intervention. But even the ultrasecure file to which the key is lost must be recovered somehow.

6.2.2. Locks, Keys, and Passwords

The implementation of security is a matter of building locks and keys. Such locks can be implemented in the hardware or software or as a combination of both. A simple scheme is based on the use of passwords. The user must specify the appropriate password prior to gaining entrance to a file. An attempted access without the proper password is cause for the temporary termination of the job. Files can be fitted with time locks that prevent their being accessed except at certain predefined times. Hardware keys can be implemented in terminal devices such that the program requests the originating hardware to identify itself prior to executing the task. Sequential locks can be employed. That is, successive activation of the processor will require different keys or passwords, the keys being generated by an algorithm known only to the accredited users of the processor. The algorithm might be calculating a term of the Fibonacci series based on the residues of a specified random number. In short, the kinds of locks used can be as simple as an 18th century skeleton key lock, as sophisticated as a modern bank vault, or as complex as the procedures used to initiate a nuclear attack. Again, the more complex the scheme the more cumbersome it becomes and the larger a penalty it extracts from the efficiency of the system.

Security measures should not be imposed beyond the value of the security. Thus, security in a commercial installation which can only be accessed by bonded employees can be less than the security of a public time-sharing system. In each case, one must establish a price (or get an insurance company to do so) for each kind of security violation. One must determine whether it is protection from malfunction, illicit modification, or illicit reading that is desired. In short, the complexity of the measures imposed should be proportional to the severity of the consequences of not taking such measures.

6.2.3. Breaking and Entering

The only system with perfect security is the one that does no useful work, just like the safest aircraft is made of poured concrete—it cannot fly. Given a determined "thief," every lock can be picked, every safe blown, and every security measure compromised. The idea is to make it more expensive to break in than the expected value of doing so. We know that it is not possible, and certainly not practical, to design a system that is free of bugs. There will always be an input sequence that will cause the system to crash, that is, an input sequence which causes the undetected, illicit modification of at least one memory location. Furthermore, it is likely that there are an infinite number of such sequences. The software might be perfect, but the particular sequence of instructions executed causes the crosstalk to disable the memory protection devices, or some such thing. If there is a sequence that causes the system to crash, there is a closely related sequence of inputs that modifies the system without causing it to crash. By extension, there is a sequence of inputs that allows the illicit modification of the executive processors, in particular, the security-related processors—which is to say that security can be broken.

One would not consider trying to crack a safe by trying all possible combinations, because the time required to do so would be too great. However, this method, while not practical for safe cracking, is practical for "system cracking," because the system itself can be used to generate the appropriate illicit sequences. Therefore, it is not valid to say that a particular security measure is good because the thief would have to try five million times before succeeding. With a computer, this might be done in a matter of minutes. The countermeasure for this kind of attempted entry is to alert the operator whenever such attempts occur. That is, not only put locks in, but create an alarm system as well.

A common security hole exists in many systems because of improper cleanup of memory. With main memory, mass memory, tapes, discs, etc., being allocated to various tasks from moment to moment, the probability that a particular block of memory will have been previously used to contain passwords, keys, combinations, or valuable data is high. If each memory area is not scrubbed clean prior to being turned over to a new user, a potential security violation exists. The user has only to read the "garbage" that he finds in that file with the appropriate format. If he tries enough formats on enough garbage files, he will eventually hit paydirt. If this kind of illicit entry is to be prevented, every user whose security must be protected must pay for the cleanup of his scratch files or temporary residences in memory. Furthermore, since control over the executive is tantamount to control over every user, the areas used by executive functions must also be scrubbed.

Other methods, such as encryption and decryption, self-destruct files, ingenious and ingenuous combinations of hardware and software, can be implemented at great cost. Security like everything else is only probabilistic and we must pay dearly for every additional σ.

7. STATISTICS, OPERATIONS MONITORING, AND ACCOUNTING

The complex is expensive and is designed on a base of imperfect data. The parameters on which the system is based are projections which are typically two to three years old by the time the system is in operation. Operating statistics may be used to "tune" the system to provide better performance. Operating statistics gathered over a period of time can be invaluable for establishing the parameters of the system's replacement.

The system and its operators are also imperfect. There will be procedural errors and malfunctions which combine to spoil runs. Sometimes, the only way to reconstruct vital data is to trace exactly what went wrong and when. A log of the system's activity can be helpful for this purpose.

The complex, be it commercial, private, or military, is often shared by several users. The cost of the complex is allocated to each user on a rational basis that properly reflects the value of the facilities he uses. Whether the cost is actually charged, or whether the user is merely told how much usage he has had free of charge, there is usually some sort of "accounting" function to properly determine how much of the complex was used by whom and when.

The data used in all three cases are much the same and are gathered and manipulated in much the same manner. The distinction is typically one of the intent, that is, the use to which the data are put rather than something inherent in the way the data are gathered.

7.1. Logging

7.1.1. Transaction Logs

The simplest form of operational data gathering is to produce a running log of all transactions. This log may be produced for viability purposes, for legal purposes, or for accounting purposes, or may be a by-product of the normal operation of the complex. The data are typically stored on magnetic tape. A transaction entry will contain the point of entry of each transaction, the complete sequence of chit-chat that occurred between the external operator and the system, and descriptors of the internal operations that may have occurred as a result of the transaction. While the operational data thus gathered may be adequate to the needs of the user, for whatever financial, legal, or other reason, they may not contain the critical data required by the designer. For example, such logs will not usually contain the error rate information, mistakes, garbled messages, garbled commands, etc. If the time and place of the transaction is not required, the log will not contain this information. Such things as operator delays, key-in rates, etc., will also not be gathered. If a rich log is to be kept, it may pay to increase it somewhat to provide design data that may be needed in the future.

7.1.2. Operations Logs

The logging can be done from the point of view of the user, tasks, and jobs. Associated with each user, job, or task can be the complete history of that user, job, or task. This could include references to all files created, their names, their size, the time of creation, the time of destruction, the media on which they were stored, etc. Similarly, the devices used by the job can also be logged, as can the standard programs used by the job. A ludicrous extreme of a log would be an interpretive trace of the whole system.

7.1.3. Facilities Logs

Logging can be done from the point of view of the facilities of the complex. Typical in such logs would be: a record of all failures and the time at which the unit was again available; the amount of memory used in each system cycle; the duration of the cycle; the amount of mass memory in use; the channel utilization; the number of calls to each processor; the number of transactions occurring in a unit of time; the number of simultaneous external operators; the length of all internal queues; etc. Such data (intended primarily for design purposes) should be gathered in such a way as to minimize the perturbations to the system. Internal logs of this sort can be supplied as commercially available hardware or software monitoring systems.

7.1.4. How Much?

One of the difficulties with total logging is that there may be a lot of it. It is not unusual for a complex to generate four to ten reels of tape per day. At $25.00 per reel, the cost might be $35,000 per year for tapes alone. Adding to this the cost of storage and handling, the total cost of a year of data logging could be $100,000. For this reason, detailed logs must be destroyed at some point and replaced with summary logs containing less information. Logs that are maintained for the user's or accounting purposes can be reduced by an appropriate program which reflects predefined operating procedures. The rate at which stale data are discarded will depend upon the data's value and legal requirements of the complex. A complex used for income tax return analysis will probably keep detailed logs for many years. Banks and reservation systems will keep logs for lesser periods, while a commercial data processing installation or a message switching system might be required to keep such logs for only 30 days.

7.2. Statistics

7.2.1. How Much?

The logs kept for statistical data gathering are the easiest to take care of. We must only be assured of having a statistically valid sample. The simplest scheme is to retain a small sample of the log reels at random. The discarding should be done by the system and not by the operator. If a person is allowed to choose which tapes will be kept and which will be discarded the data may be biased. The operator might choose "hairy" situations that would lead to an overestimate or overdesign of future systems. Another operator might be biased toward tapes that showed a quiet period. In general, a small sample of 0.1% should be adequate. The sample should be chosen to properly reflect the full spectrum of activities, including daily, hourly, and seasonal variations. It should also be taken continually throughout the system's life so that long-range trends can be established.

7.2.2. When?

Statistical data gathered in the first few months of operation should be mistrusted. It takes anywhere from 3 to 6 months for a system to settle down. That is, the external operators and users are no longer trying to make the system fail; the internal operators have learned sundry bitter lessons; bugs have been removed; people are no longer fascinated by the various tricks the system can do. In short, the system ceases to be a toy and becomes the tool it was designed to be. Until the break-in phase is over, the system statistics are dubious at best.

The early statistics can be a guide to the validity of the statistics. If there are major qualitative and quantitative differences between the nature of the transactions experienced and the predicted transactions for the same period, it may indicate that the break-in period is not over. It is not unusual for a system to go live with a 100% or higher load than anticipated, settling down after a few months to a more reasonable 25 to 50% overload.

The trend in the transactions for the first few months should be watched. If the trend is qualitatively and quantitatively toward the predicted statistical load, all is well and good and tuning of parameters can begin. If the trends diverge from the anticipated statistics, special care must be taken. Each act of tuning (i.e., choosing new buffer sizes, reallocating memory areas, changing internal priorities, modifying the base sequence, adding or deleting queues, etc.) will be reflected in a performance change, which will in turn affect user habits and therefore the traffic load. If too many changes are made at once, an unstable situation may occur in which the system appears never to be right.

7.2.3. Category Logs and Counters

A simpler form of logging is to provide counters for critical parameters. Thus, if we wish to gather statistics on transaction lengths, we could log all transactions. On the other hand, we could set aside a number of memory locations that can be incremented every time a particular value of transaction length is observed. In this way, the system builds the characterizing distributions directly. These distributions are then logged, rather than the actual transactions. Thus, we might have twenty counters for transaction lengths, ten for transaction types, thirty or so for failure types, and a similar number for failure durations. In all, the system might contain several hundred such counters. This kind of scheme can be further extended to the point where a complete data reduction system is employed. This can include various correlations, distributions, adaptive sampling schemes, and other calculations limited only by the ingenuity of the statistician. Elaborate data gathering and reduction, when done on-line, perturbs the statistics gathered by the additional load required to gather them. Unfortunately, since the peak load statistics are the most important, it is under those conditions that the perturbation will be the greatest. An overly elaborate data gathering system may perturb the data so much that they become useless.

7.2.4. Mode Switches

It is often desirable to have controls or commands that allow parts of the statistics gathering to be turned on or off. The capability for gathering elaborate statistics is incorporated but the operator is allowed to determine what shall be gathered when. In this way, as critical situations come up, which demand detailed examination, the pertinent statistics gathering can be activated. If mode switches are implemented, it may prove costly to test these each time for every processor providing such statistics. The mode switches implemented in this way are also a perturbation.

7.2.5. Implementation

It is more desirable to gather the statistics from tables required by other processors than to create special statistics tables. The statistical processor then gathers from these tables what it needs without perturbing the other processors. This approach requires additional standardization of formats, which may indirectly reduce efficiency. The statistics processor should be invoked by the executive and the various interrupt executives. The executive can direct the gathering of statistics prior to turning control over to the next routine. In this way, perturbation can be reduced if not eliminated completely when there are no statistics to be gathered. As the system becomes older, the incremental value of additional statistics becomes minuscule, things tend to settle down, and only very light or occasional sampling is required to establish long-range trends. For this reason, it should be possible to eliminate statistics gathering and analysis later in the life of the system. In one system consisting of five computers, one computer was devoted to statistical processing. The application is justified to allow an optimization of the network of lines through which the system communicated since that network cost substantially more than the whole complex. After sufficient statistics have been gathered, the computer will be used to enlarge the system to meet increased loads.

The format of the final output is important. It is not unlikely that the final data reduction of the statistics will be done by a computer not in the complex. The standard formats of a generalized system will probably be compatible with most commercial computer installations. However, the formats provided in a dedicated or miliary system may differ substantially. It is generally much easier to write data in oddball formats than it is to read them. The typical errors made in such logs are: using codes that will not be accepted on a commercial computer, or that have specialized control meanings; writing "infinite"-length blocks, e.g., 5 million characters; too many blocks between file marks; not checking after writing for drop-outs; using different formats within a block, such as binary intermixed with hexadecimal and alphanumeric; using different codes, such as ASCII, EBCDIC, and Baudot, on the same type of record without indicating that fact; requiring different parts of the log to be interpreted in different ways without designating what that interpretation is to be (e.g., letting one record be an actual transaction and another record be the contents of various counters, with no way to differentiate the two; making program changes that inadvertently change the statistics formats. The writer of the statistics generation subprocessor should proceed as if he were the one who had to write the statistics data reduction program. Putting it another way, "Have a heart, fellows!"

7.3. Accounting

Accounting is ideally done by evaluating an arithmetic expression or function of the data associated with the user and the facility logs. The cost of each unit used by the job is determined, the amount of time it was in use is determined, the overhead cost of the complex is known, and consequently an equitable charge can be established. If it were so simple, no lengthy discussion would be required. In practice the creation and administration of accounting schemes are as elaborate as those of the priority and authority schemes employed by the complex.

7.3.1. Accounting Objectives

The basic objectives of accounting is to charge fairly for facilities as used. If the system is not a commercial one, accounting may be a matter of properly allocating costs to various departments. It may be a means of allocating a scarce facility to its users in an equitable manner even though there is no "charge." The commercial time-sharing system contains accounting aspects common to almost every system in which some form of accounting is employed. Consequently, we shall use it as a model for accounting practices and methods.

7.3.2. Accounting Factors

The most obvious aspects of accounting is the cost of the facilities employed by a user or a job. We start with the unit costs and, applying some amortization policy, obtain the cost per unit time for each unit. To this must be added the cost of maintaining and supporting the entire complex. Units with high failure rates will have higher maintenance costs and should be billed at higher rates. Expensive units such as memories and computers will have higher charges than terminals, say. The complex is run by people who have salaries, overhead, take up floor space, get sick, etc. Furthermore, there may be advertising, publicity, development, and other costs associated with the complex. Needless to say, the accounting department can obtain a cost rate for each unit of the complex, considered as a hunk of hardware sitting on the floor. Similarly, we can trust the accounting department to come up with a comparable development cost for each program in the complex. The more primitive accounting schemes are based on an equitable apportionment of costs based on normal accounting practices.

It is clear that higher-priority programs and tasks should be charged at a higher rate than lower-priority programs or deferred tasks. Similarly, files that are stored readily accessible (say, on the disc) should be charged at a higher rate than inaccessible files stored on off-line tape. Large users that present or are committed to highly repetitive and predictable loads present an opportunity for closer tuning (because they narrow the sigma of the load distribution). Therefore, such users can expect and demand a lower price. Users requiring extensive security measures, privacy, reliability, redundant storage, or special features and facilities can expect to pay a higher price for these features. Users at the low end of the distribution and users at the high end (i.e., users at $\pm 3\sigma$) can expect to pay a premium price for not being within the majority of the predefined user categories. That is, we can expect prices to increase as the job deviates from the mean for which the complex was designed.

7.3.3. Dos and Don'ts

A job run twice under identical conditions should be charged at the same rate, even if the peculiarities of the operating system have led to different numbers of swaps, interrupts, etc. The price should be predictable by a simple routine. One user should not be penalized for the vagaries of another user. If the price is established as a function of the time of day, a user should not be penalized or charged extra during high-load intervals, unless he can predict the relation between cost and load and is made aware of the load in advance.

7.3.4. Equitable Accounting and Implementation

By considering all the factors that are required in an equitable accounting scheme, as well as the mutually contradictory dos and don'ts, we obtain an impossible accounting situation. The algorithm for accounting becomes as complex as the scheduler itself. The simplest and most usual approach is to make some sort of simple allocation, recognizing that it is not equitable for all parties.

A fixed rate is charged per unit transaction, or per line of print, or per memory used, or for CPU usage, etc., or a combination of these. Only operations directly ordained by the user are charged for, with overhead and system operations allocated according to CPU, memory, and elapsed time usage. Another approach is to provide flat-rate services based on statistical evaluation of user habits. Thus, a function of the major parameters may be employed and the user categorized by this function. He is then charged a fixed rate for all facilities based on what his usage function has been over a previous period. Other schemes abound.

No matter what scheme is used, there will always be a way to beat it. That is, if the scheme is established to be statistically equitable, there is always a user who will find out about it and will choose the inconvenience of operating at a 3σ point to "beat" the system. This is not unusual and is a factor in almost every utility system from electric power to telephones. If the way to beat the system is obvious and harmful, the accounting scheme will be modified to correct it. As the users become more skilled, they will find subtler ways to beat the system. The answer is not to engage in an increasingly expensive and marginal countermeasures game, but to define flat rates sufficiently high that a fair return can be obtained even if *every* user is beating the system.

7.3.5. Private Accounting and Statistics

It is often the case that an external user may wish to impose his own accounting scheme or statistics gathering scheme. Three basic approaches can be taken here.

1. Give the user access to his log.
2. Do it for him.
3. Give him standard options.

The first is the simplest and the least restrictive. By allowing the user to create programs that enable him to read (but not modify) his own logs, he can obtain sufficient data to run the most elegant accounting or statistics scheme he desires. This method is the cleanest because the program that is used for the private accounting is just another user program and is charged accordingly.

The second method is most prone to abuse. There is always a hassle about the cost of the accounting features, the efficiency of the data gathering methods, and what not. The third method, while superficially more attractive than the second, has an unfortunate tendency to degenerate under user pressure to as many standard options as there are users.

7.3.6. Hereditary Billing and Royalty Schemes

The increased usage of proprietary programs may require that the system (be it commercial or not) provide accounting for such programs. If the programs are leased or sold at a fixed rate, there is no more difficulty than there is for hardware cost allocations. If, however, the program is charged on a usage basis, substantial complications will ensue. For example, how does one properly allocate costs for a re-entrant routine that can be used by many different programs? How does one determine and allocate costs for recursive routines? Each such routine becomes part of the "equipment" roster and must be accounted for accordingly.

A further complication ensues if a routine calls yet another routine and both require billing. Thus, Program A calls proprietary subroutine B, which in turn calls proprietary subroutine C. A must pay royalties to B, who in turn pays royalties to C. Again, the additional complications of recursive calls, multiple calls, calls at different levels in the calling tree, etc., can make this kind of billing messy.

7.3.7. Collection Cost

The guiding principle to all accounting schemes should be a proper estimation of the collection costs, that is, the cost of properly accounting for each dollar of revenue. The more precise the scheme, the more expensive the next increment of revenue. If the cost of collection approaches $\frac{1}{2}\%$ of the revenue, it is no longer worthwhile to increase the precision of the billing scheme.

8. OPERATION

The system, whatever its job, should be under the ultimate control of human operators. There will be one or more interfaces by which the complex can inform the operator what is going on and by which the operator can direct the operation of the complex. The particular form of interface device used is not important—it can be a CRT with a light pen and full keyboard, a typewriter, or a sophisticated gadget not yet invented. For the sake of discussion we can assume that the interface is a typewriter. Whatever the nature of the system, the following subprocessors will exist: communications, interpretation, and execution. In addition to this, there may be a specialized subprocessor for training operators.

8.1. Communications

The specifics of the mechanical processors used to communicate with an operator are not different from those of processors used to communicate with a terminal. What concerns us here is not how a character gets printed or read, but rather *what* characters get printed or read.

The operator is human and should not be forced to converse with the complex in an inhuman tongue. The crudest form of communication is by means of numbers and meaningless mnemonics. While the programmer may perfectly well know that "XJIB707" means that a certain program step has been reached which signifies the completion of a prescribed action, the operator, who is not necessarily a programmer, may not remember. The complex should communicate with the operator in a human language, with reasonable grammar and spelling.

The number of different messages that the complex may be able to print may be excessive. Two approaches may be taken to reducing the storage: off-line storage and data pools.

8.1.1. Off-Line Storage

Each action in the complex requiring the operator's attention can be predetermined and an appropriate line of print established for it. That line may contain blank areas for inserting numbers or qualifying parameters. For example, a message might be formed as:

PHYSICAL TAPE NUMBER _____ ASSIGNED TØ JØB ___ .

The totality of such messages might exceed the main memory capacity, or otherwise be overly large. In general, the frequency with which messages are printed is low compared to the speed of the complex. There is usually sufficient time to obtain a copy of the proper message from a disc or drum or other bulk memory and bring it into main memory as required. Only critical messages related to equipment malfunctions need be stored in the main memory. The message is activated by transferring its identifier to the operator communication subprocessor. It in turn requests the message from the file management subprocessor, inserts the proper values in the blanks, and turns the result over to the I/O subprocessor that prints the message.

8.1.2. Pools and Vocabularies

It may be that the total number of possible messages, not counting the expansion due to different parameter values, may exceed the capacity of the bulk memory as well. It may be that the message possibilities are reasonable, but for other reasons the messages cannot be stored in the bulk memory. In such cases, a **pool** or **vocabulary** can be used. A vocabulary is a table of words. Basic English consists of only 1500 words. It is possible to communicate with other humans with this limited vocabulary. In the case of a computer complex, a total of 300 words or less will suffice. A message then consists of a call to these words in the appropriate sequence. This sentence has five words. The command to the file processor might be "BRING 73, 88, 54, 12, 90." The proper words are fetched and placed in an area where the operator communication subprocessor builds the messages. The vocabulary scheme has several advantages besides saving space. It is flexible and allows an unlimited number of messages; it allows centralization of all operator communications, including internal diagnostics of the various processors; and it is readily modified, increased, or reduced.

8.1.3. Communication Style

There is a trade between explicit messages and abbreviations or mnemonics. As the operator becomes more skilled, he finds messages such as "XJIB707" less annoying than the long time that it may take for the clearer messages to be printed. For this reason, shortened versions, less explicit messages, may be used for high-frequency situations, while as the probability of the message becomes low, it is made more explicit. Thus, a routine acknowledgment of a command by an operator might be

"YØUR CØMMAND IS ACKNØWLEDGED—THANK YØU"

or

"ACK"

or simply

"*"

Similarly, a response to a meaningless command might elicit

>"I DØ NØT UNDERSTAND, PLEASE REPEAT THE CØMMAND"

or

>"NACK"

or simply

>"?"

The first example in each case is too verbose, while the last is open to misinterpretation and subject to misunderstanding if there has been a malfunction. It is generally preferable to use a terse response consisting of a single word, such as "RØGER," where the probability of having all characters garbled is small.

Several things can be done to make the job of communicating with the operator easier:

1. Leave a blank space either before or after every word in the vocabulary so that the insertion of blanks between words is automatic.
2. Use indentations to inform the operator of the level of the respondent. For example, use no indentation for the executive, 5 spaces for the application program, and 15 spaces for subprograms of the application program. There are after all many processors trying to talk to us, and we need a method for recognizing their "voices."
3. Use a bell or other positive indication for errors or alarms. Most teleprinters have bells that can be so used.
4. Place headings and page numbers on each page of the communication. Do not print on the fold of the paper.
5. Provide a control so that the operator can abort the message in progress (i.e., turn off a long printout).
6. Provide controls that allow the operator to rescind commands not already acted upon.
7. Allow operator functions to be performed at any reasonable terminal. That is, the operator should be able to go to any terminal and designate it the master control.
8. Avoid cute phrases, ambiguities, slang, double entendres, misspellings, poor grammar, and inadvertent four-letter words or their homonyms. When all hell has broken loose and the operators are trying to get things working again, such little jokes may not be appreciated.

8.2. Interpretation

Commands must be given to the complex by the operators. Where those commands are provided by means of predefined pushbuttons, there is relatively little interpretive processing. The identification of the push button can be used as an index to the appropriate routine. Typewritten commands, however, will require interpretation. Here, as in output, it is desirable to have sensible commands rather than obtuse codes that can be readily forgotten. Again, an overly lengthy command will be annoying after a while. The possibility for both long and curtailed commands should exist.

8.2.1. Forgiving Formats

One way of doing this is to have commands given as English words. Typically, a four- or five-letter code will suffice to allow unambiguous commands in English. Thus, the command to execute a function might be given as "EXECUTE," and the command to stop might be given as "TERMIN-ATE." The advantage of using longer words is that it is less likely that two commands will begin with the same letter sequence. This allows the possibility of accepting curtailed commands. The following commands could be interpreted as equivalent:

EXE, EXEC, EXECU, EXECUT, EXECUTE, EXECUTEWXZ

or

TER, TERM, TERMI, TERMIN, TERMINATE, TERMINATINELELTIZC.

In the above example, we have used only the first three characters of the word as significant. A good choice is the number of characters that can be stored in a single word. The choice of commands should be made on the basis of words that can be readily curtailed without causing ambiguity. It is also reasonable to provide synonymous commands. Thus, a command or phrase referring to a teleprinter could be accepted as one of the following forms:

TTY, TELetype, TYPewriter.

By allowing synonymous commands, we may take a few more words of memory, which are more than repaid by increased operator efficiency and ease. Single-character commands have the advantage that a search need not be used to interpret them. They can be directly used as the index of a jump table. Searching, however, can be reduced with word commands by performing an appropriate mapping of the command onto the index of a table. One can use the numerical values of the four characters as coefficients in a polynomial generated by a number of shifts and adds to obtain a residue, that is, one can use a hash code. This will leave undefined places in the table which can lead to error routines if activated. The cost of such a polynomial evaluation should be compared with the mean value of the cost of the table search.

8.2.2. Sentential Schemes

A useful scheme for operator commands ensues if we examine the grammar of commands. The typical form is:

$$\text{(ADVERB)}^n \text{ VERB THE (ADJECTIVE)}^m \text{ NOUN.}$$

Other forms of commands might be used in which one or more of the adjectives or adverbs do not appear. The intention here is to make use of a limited vocabulary to simplify the interpretive task, while allowing reasonable communication with the system. There is again a trade to be made between clarity of operation and operator patience.

8.2.3. Human Foibles

The most explicit command scheme is one in which the system signifies by positive action that which is required next. Thus, a sequence to rename a file might be as follows:

> *Ready*: RENAME
> *Specify file name*: ALMA
> *Specify new file name*: JANE
> *Is old file to be saved?*: YES
> *Roger*:
> *Ready*:

A less explicit command sequence more prone to error is

RENAME ALMA TØ JANE AND SAVE ALMA.

Still less explicit is

R$ALMA$JANES.

The novice operator will prefer the first of these schemes, but upon gaining experience he will lose patience with it and tend to favor the third scheme. The interpretation of the first and third schemes is simpler than that of the second because they both have explicit delimiters. The second scheme will require some additional processing to extract the commands and parts thereof because the blanks are used as delimiters. The more general and forgiving the command structure, the more internal processing there will be. The trade here is not with time or space, but between programming cost and operator convenience. Statistically, operator commands occur so rarely that they do not contribute significantly to the processing load. Similarly, the programs required to interpret the operator commands are small compared to the programs required to perform the indicated processes.

8.2.4. Dos and Don'ts

In addition to the things mentioned in the preceding section, we can add the following:

1. The format and vocabularies of the commands should be the same as those used by the system to communicate to the operator. The fewer the formats the better.
2. There should be an explicit indication to distinguish a command from a response: use two different-colored ribbons, special delimiters, upper and lower case, etc.
3. Each command should be terminated with an explicit delimiter such as ".", "$", ":", or carriage return. If possible, two delimiters should be used, such as a period followed by a carriage return. If any other delimiter or end character sequence is used, that is, if the characters preceding the carriage return are not a period, say, followed by N blanks, the command should be ignored and the sequence repeated. In any event, there should be an easy way to rescind the command.
4. If full duplex lines are available it is best to have the computer rather than the operator type the character. The operator presses the key, the character is accepted, and the received character is typed by the computer. This form of echo transmission reduces errors due to line noises. Alternatively, the system should repeat the command for verification.
5. Critical commands should have explicit multistep procedures intended to require several conscious steps prior to execution. Thus, a command to erase all memory should involve three or more complicated steps even if it could be done in one command. By the time the operator is ready to respond to a system emergency that requires drastic action, it is all over, and what the computer wants is directions on how to pick up the pieces. In such cases, the extra few seconds are well spent to avoid inadvertent action.
6. Panic buttons should not be placed on the console used for normal commands. Such buttons should be guarded by a shield and should be prominently labeled. Low-pressure switches should not be used.
7. The command vocabulary should be table-driven and be readily changeable. It is likely that the initial command format will not be acceptable after operational trials and will be changed several times before it is settled. It should not be cast in concrete.
8. Caution should be used in establishing command structures and computer response sentences for a system intended for installation in a foreign country, even if the commands and responses are in

English or if the country in question is an English-speaking country. It is best that the language be cleared by a bilingual national of the country lest innocent phrases be introduced that have earthy connotations.[11]

8.3. Training Modes

Most large computer complexes will have a number of operators. In a reservation system or a banking system there may be several thousand operators (three shifts, seven days a week means 4.2 operators per terminal).

These operators must be trained. There may be external operators (those at a terminal) and internal operators of the complex itself. All of them require training. While the command structure should be designed to be error tolerant and not to allow malicious attempts at wrecking it (e.g., "let's push all the buttons simultaneously and see what happens"), if operators in training are allowed access to the actual system, they may inadvertently destroy part of the data base. The system operators might temporarily decommission the system. For this reason, one or more training modes should be provided. The training mode for the external operators is essentially the same as the normal programs, but the files to which the operator has access are restricted to training files. A command should be incorporated that will change the interpretation of the commands from a designated terminal from live commands to training mode commands. Once the training mode has been established for that terminal, all commands should be interpreted in the training mode. This means that dummy files will be substituted for real files and that dummy processors will be substituted for some real processors. Strict segregation of files must be maintained to prevent data generated during training sessions from becoming part of the real data base. It should not be possible for the trainee to initiate the nontraining modes. This should be done only by special commands and passwords.

The training mode could be anything from a simple segregation of files and deactivation of critical processors to the incorporation of a complete teaching program for the purpose. In a widespread system with many external operators, such as a banking system, a reservation system, or credit clearing system, the use of a training program can be justified. The trainee is paced through the various functions of the system, alerted to each error, and the step repeated. He is given specific tasks to accomplish such as posting a check, entering and checking an income tax return, or booking a passenger on a flight after checking reservations. A teaching program represents a

---

[11] We recall a British associate who was working a time-sharing system with what appeared to be an inordinate amount of trouble. What the system had been printing was "INVALID CARRIAGE RETURN." Our associate was interpreting this as a meaningless request to return the "*in*valid carriage," or wheelchair.

complete processor in its own right, which is generally much more complicated than the basic command interpretation processor. For still more elaborate systems, where operator performance is important (such as in air-traffic control systems), it may be necessary to keep grades, mark progress, and test the trainee. The system should be designed so that the experienced operator can obtain information on how to perform a little-used function. Thus, if a clerk does not know, or has forgotten, the procedure for a foreign bank draft, he should be able to query the system and obtain a synopsis of the procedure.

Training the system's operators is far more difficult. Much of that training has to do with handling emergency procedures, special cases, etc., that will rarely come up. The system operator, being allowed to exercise high-level authority, is not readily accommodated. A training mode or program for him will only teach him a small part of what he should know. Furthermore, as in the case of on-line program testing in a live system, it may not be feasible to provide dummy processors and simulated exercises lest the training software exceed the operational software. This kind of training program is akin to a simulator of the system.

9. MAINTENANCE

One must accept the fact that the system, no matter how narrow its characterizing distributions, if it is not trivial will continually be changed. There will always be new bugs found, new conditions to contend with, and new capabilities and functions to be added. Hardware will be changed, increased, or modified, necessitating concomitant changes in the software. Wherever possible and reasonable, such changes are anticipated so that it is parameters that are changed rather than programs. However, going overboard on parameters will leave us with a flexible system that is not capable of doing much processing.

Life tends to be somewhat harsher in the environment of the installed system than under the conditions that prevailed during its development. The system is doing a job, and it is not possible to take it out of action to make corrections. Maintenance must be done with the system in operation. The program changes will of course contain their share of bugs. Maintenance, then, is to be done on a running system in such a way that even if there are bugs in the new programs, the system itself will not be jeopardized.

As each new program is introduced into the operating complex, it must be tested, without the possibility of destroying the system. As a first step, it is given a low level of authority. Most bugs will result in an attempt to read or write a location that is not allowed for that program. Unit testing can be accomplished in this manner, allowing the complete program to be tested without interfering with the complex. A second step of protection is required when we attempt to integrate the program. This can be done by having the scheduler provide the proper inputs to the program and by spooling all outputs from the program. The old program and the program that is to replace it both run in the system; however, only the old program is allowed to produce usable outputs. The outputs of the new program are diverted to storage for checking. If the system in question has no redundancy, the next step—that of actually replacing the program and trying it live—will be risky. However, many (in fact, most) large complexes have redundant computers, memories, and peripheral units. Final testing is accomplished by running the new program in the standby system. If it performs properly there, the operator will simulate a failure of the running system and turn control over to the standby which contains the new program. All of these abilities, however, imply that there are facilities in the executive that allow it to distinguish between a program that is undergoing test and a program that is actually running. This necessitates a test mode in the executive. The test mode or test processor may simulate the entire system, replacing actual devices with logical equivalents, actual program with dummy programs, etc.

It is not feasible to make program modifications that will require a reassembly or recompilation of the entire system. The ability to incorporate separately assembled subroutines or programs is essential in any rationally designed computer complex. Therefore, the complete mechanism for sub-routine linkage and relocation, with the attendant hierarchy problems of local and global labels, is required if there is to be reasonable maintenance, even if this is not required to simplify the programming.

10. SUMMARY

The control of the computer complex resides in a specialized set of processors called collectively "the executive processor." It is seen in reality to consist of possibly many different executives. In any one computer of the complex there may be several executives operating at different priority levels, serving different functions. Furthermore, there may be a system executive and a viability executive that do not necessarily correspond to the executive program of the central computer of the complex.

Executive structures are seen to extend over a spectrum from the simple base-sequence control program to the more complex queue-driven asynchronous executive structure with a centralized scheduler. Dedicated systems, or systems having narrow load-characterizing distributions, have executives that tend to take on the characteristics of the base sequencer. Generalized systems or those in which the load distributions are broad are seen to tend toward the more complex asynchronous executive structures.

Interrupt priority levels, program priority levels, and job priority levels are seen to be distinct and relatively independent concepts. Furthermore, the independence of authority and priority levels has been established. The assignments of functions to high-priority levels has the effect of decreasing the processing delay for those functions. The value of deferred processing as a means of timely procrastination is a central concept. By trading deferred processing in a burst against raising overall processing, the average processing time of all functions is increased but the peak processing load is decreased. Guides to the assignment of functions to levels and methods for establishing the base sequence are also presented.

Job control, scheduling, and optimization are three primary functions of the executive. External priority control, authority control, statistics, operations monitoring, accounting, operator communications, and program maintenance are ancillary functions of the executive processor(s).

11. PROBLEMS

1. Establish the executive functions required for any of the following systems: on-line banking, air-traffic control, atomic power plant control, automobile assembly plant control, automated supermarket, automated warehouse, municipal traffic light control, remote-access time-sharing system, electric power distribution, telephone central office, reservation system, stock-market system, check clearing system, automated parking lot, central hotel computer, centralized hospital computer for physiological monitoring of patients in operating rooms and intensive care units, petrochemical process control, central passenger automobile control and diagnosis. In each case assume that the available CPU is small, so that at least three computers will be used.

2. Group the systems of Problem 1 according to the characterizing load distributions for each and design a base sequence or queue-driven centralized scheduler, as appropriate.

3. Examine the applicability of a commercially available operating system (say, IBEX for the Belchfire-500) in each of the above applications. State the sacrifices, advantages, and disadvantages of using a commercial operating system in each application. Estimate the performance increase that might be obtained were a specialized operating system or executive to be used.

4. Examine, and prove in general the relation between the σ of the characterizing load distributions and the efficiency of the executive system. Consider using information theory. [*Open problem.*]

5. Apply the theory of asynchronous switching networks to the design of asynchronous queue-driven executive systems. [*Open problem.*]

6. Establish an optimum base sequence for the example of Section 3.6.3 under the following alternative set of assumptions:

    1. Inputs and outputs require 100 units of time to be accomplished and there are 8 lines. All other assumptions remain the same.

    2. Same as 1, but disc reads and writes cannot be overlapped.

    3. Same as 1, and reads or writes, but not both, can be batched and overlapped.

    4. Same as 1, reads and writes can be intermixed and overlapped, and the output order need not correspond to the input order: i.e., line 7 can be outputted prior to line 3 even though the input occurred in the reverse order.

Maximize the throughput.

7. Do Problem 6 under the additional assumption that each cycle has an overhead of 35 units; 100 units; 400 units.

8. Calculate average delays and delay distributions for the various solutions in Problems 6 and 7. Examine the relation between cycle length and delay quantitatively.

9. Under the assumption that everything is fixed, devise a generalized (nonheuristic) algorithm for base sequence layout that minimizes wasted processing time.

10. Establish the interrupt priority levels, the program priority levels, and the authority levels for the various executive subprocessors of Problem 1.

11. Why is the sum of the lengths of time spent on the several processing queues not equal to the delay of the transaction?

12. Design an equitable billing scheme for a commercial time-sharing system; a reservation system shared by several hotel chains; a communication system.

13. What authority should be given to a common subroutine used for several different authority levels, highest or lowest? If the wrong one is given, how far could the process go before an authority violation occurred?

12. REFERENCES

1. Beizer, Boris, "In Each of Us a Monster Dwells," *Datamation*, Volume 14, Number 6, F. D. Thompson Publications, Inc., Greenwich, Conn., June 1968, pp. 48–52.

   A not so funny story about the uses and abuses of computers and associated security problems.

2. Hoffman, Lance J., "Computers and Privacy: A Survey," *Computing Surveys*, Association for Computing Machinery, Inc., Baltimore, Maryland, June 1969, Volume 1, Number 2, pp. 85–103.

   A review of security and privacy problems and solutions. The table of countermeasures is worth thinking about. Good bibliography.

3. *IBM Systems Journal.*

   Despite the fact that this journal is a house organ with the inevitable biases toward IBM equipment, technologies, and philosophy, almost every issue has something worthwhile for the reader. In particular, Volume 5, Number 1, 1966, describes the structure of ØS-360.

4. Martin, James Thomas, *Design of Real-Time Computer Systems,* Prentice Hall, Englewood Cliffs, N.J., 1967.

   Many detailed descriptions of operational procedures with various real-time systems. Section III has a description of many different applications of computer complexes. The section on queuing theory is good.

Chapter 10

THE NUCLEUS

He immediately ordered his engineers to make a machine to hoist these two extraordinary men out of his kingdom. Three thousand learned scientists worked at it; it was ready in a fortnight and only cost about twenty million pounds sterling in the money of that country.

FRANCOIS-MARIE AROUET DE VOLTAIRE
Candide

1. SYNOPSIS

Concurrently running jobs require a variable amount of memory. Dynamic storage allocation is provided, allowing the peaks of one job to be compensated by the lulls of the other. Several methods are presented for the allocation and management of storage. The system must also have the ability to provide an effectively infinite memory. The efficiency of a rotary memory depends on the way transactions are scheduled for it. Various memory scheduling techniques are discussed in this chapter.

Buffering is an integral part of most I/O operations, and the primary buffering methods are presented. The logical structure of jobs is maintained through processing queues. Where these queues should be placed and how they should be managed and stored is discussed here. The maintenance and search of files are two interrelated problems also discussed in this chapter. Finally, since communication is part of most computer complexes, a generalized communication system is discussed. This last discussion also shows the ways in which the various processors of the system are interrelated.

2. MEMORY MANAGEMENT

2.1. Why Memory Management?

The cost of the memories in a complex can exceed the cost of the CPUs by an order of magnitude. Infinite memory is no more practical than infinite speed. Since memory will be shared, there must be processors that will disburse memory as it is needed. Other processors are required to collect used memory and make it available for redistribution. There are two main methods used for allocating memory, **dynamic storage allocation** and **paging**.

The way in which read and write transactions are scheduled for drums or discs can materially affect the processing capabilities of the complex. A poorly designed system may be **transaction bound**, that is, unable to keep up with the required number of reads and writes. Part of memory management is the optimum scheduling of memory transactions to avoid transaction binding.

2.2. Dynamic Storage Allocation

The memory is divided into several areas:

1. Dedicated space required by the hardware for registers, interrupts, etc.
2. Space for permanently resident programs.
3. Data areas for permanent tables, constants, and communication between processors.
4. Variable program space that can be used by more than one program.
5. Variable data space that can be allocated as needed to tables, data, queues, etc.

Each processor requiring memory requests it from the memory allocation processor. The memory allocation processor examines the available memory and assigns part of it to the requesting processor. At some time, the processor returns the space (or rather requests its return or destruction by the memory allocation processor). It is then available for subsequent use by some other processor.

2.2.1. Direct Allocation

Let us conceptually subdivide a portion of the memory (called the **dynamic memory pool**) into convenient segments. The segments need not be uniform in length. If a processor requests 187 characters of memory, the memory allocation processor (MAP) determines which part of the pool is available and gives the requesting processor the start and end addresses of a contiguous block of 187 characters. The MAP then marks that area as being in use. This conceptually simple approach is an administrative nightmare. Each request may be for a different amount of memory, in no way related to the previous request or to the requests made by other processors. As things progress, it becomes increasingly difficult to find contiguous areas of memory of the proper size. Memory becomes increasingly fragmented. Small pockets of one or two locations build up which cannot be used by any processor. Eventually, the memory consists of nothing but such pockets and the areas of memory required to keep track of how the memory has been subdivided. Thus, in an attempt to optimize the usage of memory by giving each requester only what is needed, we ultimately waste memory by arriving at a finely divided partition useful to no one.

This could be corrected by periodic reassignment of memory to requesting processors by repacking the data. But the cost of repacking is spurious data moves and the need of informing each active processor of how the memory it uses has changed. If the repacking is done with every request, time is wasted. If it is done periodically, space is wasted.

2.2.2. Linked Lists

Figure 10.1 shows the *conceptual* structure of a **linked list**. Each block contains its length and the address of the first location in the next block (the **link address**). The blocks themselves may be scattered throughout the memory and need not be contiguous. Each block contains its own administrative data. A separate request for dynamic storage is not needed for such administrative data.

If the using processor must fetch or place data in successive locations, it must be aware of where the administrative areas are. Thus, every access of dynamic storage (by this scheme) requires an examination of the address and a calculation to see to it that data are not inadvertently placed in or retrieved from an administrative area. A correction is required to skip over such areas and reset the base address for the block when going to the next block.

We can remove most of the objections to variable-length blocks by fixing the block length. The optimum block length is chosen in much the same way as the optimum block length for data transmission is chosen, that is, it is that fixed block length which minimizes the expected space wastage. While the using processor must still test for the end of the block, the test is made against a predefined constant rather than against a variable length. An arbitrary but fixed block length does not have a simple relation between the identifier of the block (i.e., its name) and its starting location. The optimum block length might turn out to be 187 characters. Thus, blocks 1, 2, 3, and 4 could start at locations 0, 187, 374, and 561 respectively. While there is an algorithm for deriving the initial address of the block from its identifier (i.e., multiplication), it is needlessly time consuming. We can minimize this calculation by making the block length equal to a zero residue modulo the weights of the number representation system of the computer. Thus, in a binary machine we select block lengths from among 1, 2, 4, 8, 16, etc., while in a decimal machine we select the optimum block lengths closest to a power of 10. The initial address of the block is obtained from the block identifier by shifting and then adding the first address at which dynamic storage starts.

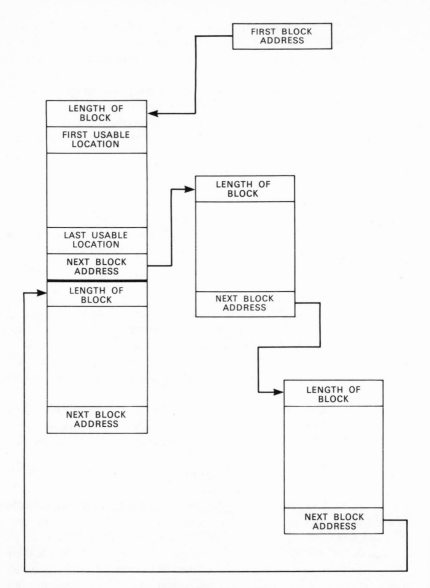

Figure 10.1. Linked list.

To further simplify matters we place the first word of each block at a location whose address is 0 modulo the block length. This has the added advantage of finding the actual address of a location in dynamic storage by ØRing the initial address of the block with the relative position of that location. That is, the 27th location in each block is always in some memory location whose address ends in 27.

Administrative data are required in addition to the link. Since the blocks are of fixed lengths, the data contained in the last block of a chain may not be valid. The user processor must also be aware that the block in question is the last block of the chain. The link area can be used for these purposes. Since the link ends in zero (modulo the block length), a nonzero entry in those address bits can designate that this is the last block. In particular, that entry can be the relative address of the last valid character or word in the block. Alternatively, a special administrative area may be used.

2.2.3. Link Positions and Link Tables

We have conceptually placed the link in the last location of the block. It could just as well be placed in the middle, at the beginning, or not in the block at all. Placing it in the middle offers no obvious advantage and is a nuisance. Placing the link as the first item in the block has a distinct advantage over placing it at the end. It allows the address of the link, the name of the block, and the location of the link to be the same. In particular, the address of the next block's link can be obtained by an indirect fetch using the present block's link.

The situation is depicted in Figure 10.2. It can be seen that the address of the next block can be obtained indirectly from the address of the present block. The particulars will depend on the address structure of the computer and the number of addresses contained in a word. It may be possible to place the administrative data in the bit positions used by the op code (if the computer will still perform indirect operations properly when this is done). An ANALYZE instruction extends the ease with which linked lists can be examined if the link is placed in the first word of the block.

It is not possible to get away with a simple link and a few bits of administrative information in most systems. The next block in the chain might not be in the same memory (e.g., it may be on disc). The block may require status data or extensions to more than one other device. It may also be necessary to have equal ease in moving backward along a chain of blocks as in moving forward—that is, a back-pointer to the previous block in the chain of blocks may be required. As each additional bit of administrative data is placed in the block proper, the area which must be skipped over (and the processing associated with determining such boundaries) is increased.

There is no inherent reason why the administrative data should be placed *in* the block itself. There are many reasons why they should not. This can be done by creating a table which contains an entry for each block in the memory. To simplify the processing, we make the administrative area analogous to the blocks by choosing an administrative block length equal

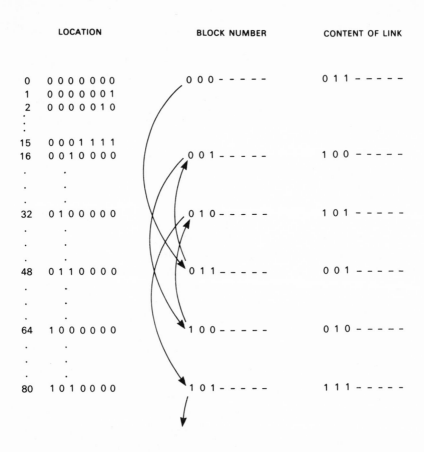

Figure 10.2. Relation between block name, pointer location, and pointer content (block length = 16).

to zero modulo the number representation system weight. Again we place the first administrative block in a "zero" location. This is depicted in Figure 10.3. In this example the data block length is made a binary multiple of the administrative block length. The advantages of indirect addressing to obtain subsequent block addresses are retained. The cost may be additional wasted space required for nice administrative block lengths.

Another advantage obtained by separately storing the administrative information and the data block is that it is possible to transfer the complete linking pattern in the memory by a simple contentious transfer of the administrative table.

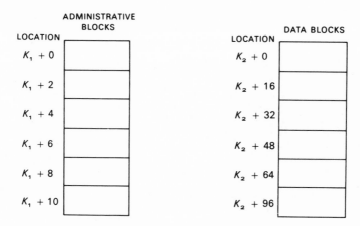

Figure 10.3. Separate data and administrative blocks.

While the previous discussion has been slanted toward the allocation of main memory, the same principles apply to the allocation of space in bulk memories. Separation of the two functions allows the storage of administrative data in a different memory. The drum administrative data can be kept in core and the administrative data of the disc can be kept on the drum. If the administrative data are kept in the same medium, every request for additional space requires reading the last block on the chain and modifying its administrative area to include the new link. The number of disc or drum transactions can readily be doubled by using the conceptually simpler approach of keeping the administrative data in the block that they administer.

Unless the system possesses elegant hardware facilities that get around the various problems discussed above, or unless there are unique extenuating circumstances that dictate the contrary, the following principles apply to the layout of dynamic space:

1. Separation of administrative and data areas.
2. Binary (or decimal) lengths for both with a fixed power of 2 (10) ratio.
3. Initial location chosen as zero modulo the length of the data block.

2.2.4. The List of Available Space

The memory management processor must know what blocks of memory are available at all times. The conceptually simple way to do this is to set a bit in the administrative area of the block. When a block of memory is requested, the memory allocation processor searches the administrative areas until an unoccupied block is found. Similarly, the occupancy flag is reset when a block is returned.

This approach is operationally poor. The larger the memory the longer will such scanning take. If the administrative areas are part of the blocks for a drum or disc, each memory allocation could require several thousand read operations. Separating the administrative area alleviates but does not eliminate the problem. Since there are additional delays while searching for free blocks, the memory in use increases with increased load. Therefore, memory allocation will take longer under high-load conditions than under low-load conditions.

One way of overcoming these disadvantages is to link all unused blocks in a master **list of available space** (LAS). When a block is returned, it is linked to the last block in the LAS. When a block is needed, it is the first block in the LAS that is taken and linked to the requesting processor's chain. Systems having both backward and forward pointers can do requesting and returning from either the top or the bottom of the LAS. The time required to obtain a block of space is independent of the amount of space in use.

The LAS is suited to main memory allocation but is not as convenient for the allocation of blocks in bulk stores such as drums or discs. If the bulk memory is small, or if it is subdivided into relatively large blocks, it may be feasible to maintain the administrative data (or at least a copy thereof) in the main memory. If, however, the bulk storage is large or is subdivided into small blocks, there may not be enough room in the main memory to store the complete administrative data. One could compromise and store only the links of the LAS. However, since each entry in the LAS must contain at least one drum or disc block address, the LAS could still be too large.

One approach is to keep the LAS on the drum or disc, and to keep only one block of links for the beginning and one for the end of the LAS in main memory. As each block of the disc is removed from the LAS and assigned to the requesting processor, a counter which specifies the topmost valid location of the LAS is incremented. As blocks are returned to the LAS another counter which marks the bottommost entry of the LAS is incremented. When the top block of the list is exhausted, the next block of the LAS pointers is fetched from the disc and the counter returned to the top of the new block. Similarly, when the bottommost block is filled, the block is written to the disc and the appropriate links made.

2.2.5. Garbage Collector

Another approach can be used which is a combination of the LAS and the conceptually simpler tagging of unused blocks. Blocks are tagged as free by the processor that returns them. The fact that the block has been returned is ignored at the time. The storage allocation processor has a list of available space and distributes the blocks that are in that list. Should the list become exhausted, a memory collection routine called the **garbage collector** is activated. The garbage collector goes through the administrative areas and finds all unused blocks, which it then links to the LAS. Garbage collection is certainly activated whenever there is no more room. It can also be activated periodically during a time interval in which there is available processing time that would otherwise be unused (see Chapter 12, Section 4, *The Ledger*). The advantage of garbage collection is that the return of a block does not require a call to the memory allocation processor. Time is saved. Furthermore, the garbage collector can be made more efficient than can an individual return of a block. Garbage collection is a form of deferred processing.

The disadvantages of garbage collection are several. More space may be required. This can be avoided by activating the garbage collector before the LAS is exhausted. When a block is needed and the LAS is exhausted, the ensuing delay of the garbage collector may be intolerable.

2.2.6. Memory Maps

Another approach to the administration of the available storage is to maintain a bit table. This is often called a **memory occupancy map** or **memory map**. A unique bit in the memory is reserved for each block. If the bit is set to 1, the block is available, if it is set to 0, the block is in use. The linking and administrative data are kept elsewhere, perhaps in the block itself or in an analogous table. The bit table is also analogous to the memory which it serves. In machines having explicit bit addressing, the bit address concatenated with the lower-order bits of the word address when shifted is the address of the block. This allows a simple conversion from the memory map to the block address. Blocks can be examined for availability as fast as words can be tested for zero. If there is one free block indicated in a word of the bit table, the value of that word will not equal zero. It is then a simple matter to scan that word for the first nonzero bit. If the word length of the machine is 32 bits, the table can be examined 32 blocks at a time. If the computer has repeat modalities or table searching instructions, scanning the bit table is faster yet.

A disadvantage is still that it will take longer to find an available block when the memory is crowded than when it is unoccupied. This disadvantage can be alleviated by keeping track of the last word at which a free block was found. The scan for available blocks is cyclic. The allocator does not at first examine words which on the previous scan were found not to contain free blocks.

Another disadvantage is that there may be three sets of analogous areas: the bit table, the administrative data area, and the blocks themselves. Each such analogous structure restricts the possible places at which other programs or data may be placed. One can only find so many contiguous areas of memory starting with addresses whose lower-order bits are zero. Furthermore, there are many functions other than memory management for which this is desirable. In fact, almost all tables which are used to administer things that can be given sequential names (1, 2, 3, etc.) such as lines, devices, interrupts, and registers, etc., can benefit from such placement.

The memory map is usually laid out in a manner which allows the simplest conversion from the bit location to the block address. However, it may be in our interest to do otherwise. Consider a drum that has 32 tracks and 32 sectors. Let us make each block 1 sector long. The memory map will consist of thirty-two 32-bit words. The successive bits in a word could be analogous to tracks, in which case the words would represent sectors. Alternatively, the bits could represent sectors while the words represent tracks. If the bits represent sectors there will be a proclivity toward assigning successive blocks to the same track. This can improve the operation of the system by increasing the probability that two or more blocks can be fetched in the same revolution. If, on the other hand, the bits represent tracks, the tendency is to assign successive blocks to the same sector on different tracks. This increases the probability of waiting a revolution between blocks of a chain. These proclivities are not usually significant in generalized systems. In dedicated systems, however, where the pattern of storage allocation may be predicted (small σ), there may be a noticeable advantage in sacrificing the ease of conversion from the bit address to the block address in order to minimize the delay in fetching successive blocks.

2.2.7. Mixed Pools and Shared Pools

It may be that the length distributions are bimodal or multimodal. The use of a single block length can therefore be wasteful. An optimum fit might be obtained with two different block lengths. It is not unusual to have four different block lengths: a basic block length for internal allocation of 256 characters, a buffer block length of 4096 characters which is analogous to blocks on disc, administrative blocks of 16 characters, and communication blocks of 128 characters. Maintaining several different pools, each having its own block length, is not a problem. The difficulties occur when it is desired to share these pools.

Subdivision of blocks leads to memory wastage by excessive fragmentation because a larger block cannot be reconstituted until all of its components have been returned. The finer the allowed subdivision the greater the fragmentation waste. If, for example, we allow a 256-word block to be subdivided 256 ways, we are back to variable-length storage allocation with all of the attendant pitfalls plus the additional administrative burden of keeping track of subdivided blocks.

One method of getting around the problems of shared pools is called the **buddy system**. The buddy system restricts the subdivision of higher-level blocks into two half-sized blocks at the next lower level. Thus, blocks of length $2^k, 2^{k-1}, \ldots$ are allowed. A separate LAS is kept for each level. Block allocation for a 2^k-sized block is made by examining the 2^k LAS. If no block is found, the next-larger-sized block's list (2^{k+1}) is examined. The block found on that list is split into two "buddies" of length 2^k; the one is given to the requester and the other is placed on the 2^k LAS. If no block is found at the 2^{k+1} level, the procedure is continued upward until a block is found. Return of the blocks is done in the reverse manner, attempting to merge a block with its buddy (if the buddy is free) until the highest-level block possible has been reassembled. The surprising thing about this algorithm is its efficiency. Simulation studies have shown that the wastage due to fractionating is small.

2.2.8. Overflow

There is always the possibility that the momentary memory requirements will exceed the available capacity. The memory is then said to be in **overflow**. Every system using dynamic storage allocation should have a potentially infinite memory. Thus, as core is exhausted, the drum is used; as the drum gets filled, the disc is used; and the disc itself is extended onto tape or removable disc packs. We can always get another reel of tape or another disc pack, providing us with the desired potentially infinite memory.

Overflow protection is the ability to continue processing even though there is a shortage of memory blocks. Several reactions to impending or actual overflow can be programmed.

1. Detect impending overflow and curtail the processing that causes it.
2. Direct the scheduler to give high priority to those processors that release memory in use.
3. Direct the scheduler to give high priority to delay-producing processors that indirectly keep the memory in use.
4. Extend the memory to some other medium.
5. Overwrite active blocks.

The last of these measures, while the simplest, is rarely acceptable. It may be feasible for applications in which one second's worth of data is as good as another or in which stale data are of little value. To illustrate, consider a data acquisition system performing a noncrucial function. The data might be updating information. Only the latest information is valuable. There might be no objection to having stale data overwritten by more recent data. If the information is related to the track of aircraft in an air traffic control system, there is more interest in where each aircraft is now than where it was a few seconds ago. The new data are given a higher priority than the old and the old are discarded, alleviating the memory shortage.

A combination of the first four schemes is used in most systems to contend with overflow. Overflow control consists of four phases: detection, alleviation, overflow operation, and recovery. The detection phase is continuous. Its purpose is to warn the executive or the operator that an overflow condition may occur. Alleviation measures are taken prior to actual overflow in order to prevent its occurrence. Should it not prove possible to prevent the overflow, the system must go into an overflow mode of operation. Once the overflow has disappeared, the system must resume normal operation in an orderly manner.

○ *Overflow Detection*

It is possible to know at all times how much memory is in use. Each time a block of memory is assigned, a memory occupancy counter is decremented. Each time a block is returned, the counter is incremented. The same principle can be used for main memory, drums, or discs.[1] The contents of this counter can be used to trigger an impending overflow alarm. In communication systems, drum overflow can lead to a serious degradation of the system's processing ability. It usually occurs because messages have been queued for a line which is out of order. An impending overflow alarm is used to alert the operator, who can then "drain" the messages for that line onto magnetic tape. Comparable overflow controls can be built into any system.

The overflow alarms should be adjustable. Furthermore, they should be changeable from the control console and not require reloading or reprogramming. The initial settings of the overflow alarms are almost never right. Prudence dictates that they be conservative. The operator, having gained some experience and intuitive knowledge of the statistics of the bursts that cause the overflow, may set the alarms closer to the overflow limit. He may in fact disable some of the overflow alleviation procedures *in toto* by setting the alarm that triggers those procedures to a point beyond overflow. Setting the overflow alarm limits is one way in which the system can be "tuned" to better match the actual situation.

○ *Alleviation Techniques*

The intention of alleviation is to prevent overflow. Overflow almost always occurs during periods of high processing load such as momentary

---

[1] Overflow is the usual state of things for tapes. There is typically a tape reel sensor that warns us that the tape has only a few hundred feet of space left. The normal tape closing procedure is used. The operator is warned to mount a new tape, etc. The term "overflow" does not normally apply to tapes. The operator can be signaled to prepare a new disc pack much in the same way that tapes are handled. We shall confine ourselves to a discussion of the more difficult problems associated with the overflow of memories that cannot be so simply extended.

bursts. As processing delay is increased, the elapsed time between the assignment and the release of a memory block is also increased. This in turn means that more memory will be in use. Therefore, high processing demands from the point of view of time imply increased memory utilization. The point in question is not obvious. It is true that if the system has to handle more transactions in a period of heavy loading, extra memory will be needed for the additional transaction. However, each individual transaction requires more memory under heavy load than it requires under light load. As an illustration consider a system in which several different kinds of transactions must be processed. One of these transactions takes T memory cycles to process. The elapsed time for the process is K seconds. Each transaction requires M units of memory. The transactions arrive at a rate of N per minute. The average memory required is NKM units for this function. If the elapsed processing time (delay) per transaction is increased to, say, $K + k$, the memory will be increased by NkM units.

To decrease the memory in use, then, we can prevent inputs (make N smaller), raise the priority of the function that is causing the overflow (make K smaller), or defer the complementary functions by reducing their priorities. Preventing inputs can be done in several ways. Input can be prevented in a polling system by not polling. In systems in which each input requires acknowledgment before the next input can be sent, we delay the acknowledgment. In some systems it may be necessary to alert the sources of input (be they humans or machines) that they should wait before sending new inputs. Techniques used for discouraging or preventing inputs are known collectively as **input choking** techniques; the inputs are said to be "choked." Occasionally the term "throttling" is used instead of "choking." Choking can be made implicit by placing input-initiating functions (such as polling) or input-acknowledging functions at a lower priority level than output functions. Thus, while the input functions themselves may be at a higher priority level than the output functions, the input-acknowledging or initiating functions may be placed at lower priority level than the output.

Auxiliary functions such as statistics gathering or accounting, which are normally at a lower priority level than outputs, are automatically suppressed.

If a function that requires the assignment of memory blocks (a memory creator) has been initiated, its suppression will increase the elapsed time and therefore increase the amount of memory in use. This is exactly the opposite of what we want to do. It is therefore desirable to split the process so that the parts that create memory are separated from those that destroy it. This allows us to suppress the initiation of the function without suppressing its completion.

The penalty paid for such alleviation techniques is increased processing time, increased programming time, increased number of program interfaces,

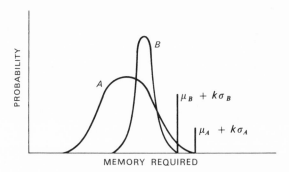

Figure 10.4. $\mu + k\sigma$ trade for memory.

and more queues, all of which tend to increase the amount of memory in use. In exactly the same way that we traded time now for increased time later, we can trade less memory in use now for more memory in use later. This is a typical $\mu + k\sigma$ trade. The situation is depicted in Figure 10.4. Distribution A shows the case in which we have minimized μ, while distribution B shows a $\mu + k\sigma$ minimization. The overflow condition should (by design) be an extreme, low-probability condition, that is, what we expect at $k\sigma$. Distribution A has a lower mean and higher standard deviation than distribution B. However, the sum of the mean and the standard deviation for the same number of sigmas is lower for distribution B. The processor characterized by distribution B will use less memory than the processor characterized by distribution A. Alternatively, if both processors are assigned the same amount of memory, B will have a lower overflow probability than A.

Overflow for critical processes can be alleviated by extending the less critical processes onto another medium. There is no need to wait until an actual overflow does occur. Thus, when a certain alarm condition is reached, low-priority functions are no longer given memory in the primary medium, but are given it from the back-up medium to which the primary will overflow.

If the executive contains a centralized queue control or if scheduling is done by the centralized control over the transfer of tasks from queue to queue, alleviation can be implemented by delaying the linking of data from the output queue of one processor to that of the next. Thus, if we know that a processor which can tolerate the delay has a high probability of requesting the assignment of memory blocks, we will deny it input by allowing its input queue to dry up.

To summarize: impending overflow can be alleviated implicitly by the priority levels assigned to interrupts and the program levels assigned to processors; explicitly by operator intervention, dynamic priority assignment, scheduling, or queue control; directly by attacking the memory problem; or indirectly by reducing the time during which the memory blocks are in use.

○ *Memory Extension*

A control character or bit in the administrative area of the last (which is perhaps also the first) block of a chain is used to indicate that the next block is to be found on some other medium. A pool of memory is established in the extension memory, each of whose blocks is homomorphic to those in the memory which is to be extended. Each processor using dynamic space checks the extension bit prior to fetching the next block in the chain. If the extension bit indicates that the particular block is not in the main memory, it must request that the block be fetched from whichever extension memory the block is in. The fetching is done by the processor that manages the extension memory. The processor is blocked while waiting for the fetch to be completed. This gives the executive an opportunity to delay that process in order to save time or to suppress the further creation of space. Similarly, a processor requesting additional memory can be suppressed or delayed by blocking while waiting for memory. While it is possible to explicitly inform a processor that it is no longer working in the main memory but in the extension, it is more effective to do this indirectly by marking the administrative area of the block. The memory allocation processor is simpler, as is recovery from overflow. From the point of view of processing time these are much the same. In the first case the processor will have to test a mode switch to see if it is extended, while in the latter it must test the link to see if it is extended.

○ *Operation during Overflow and Recovery from Overflow*

The difficulty with overflow is not only with the increased time, space, or programs required for testing for overflow mode, or with the mechanics of extension, but also with the maintenance of processing sequence when the system is in overflow and recovering from overflow. Most processes operating on a string of data start at the beginning of that string and go to the end of it. The first block to be returned to the memory pool is the first block of the chain. This is the opposite of what we want during overflow. As the process proceeds down the chain, it returns memory blocks, thereby alleviating the overflow condition. By the time the process reaches the last block in the chain, there is plenty of memory available and the overflow condition has long been corrected. However, that last block is still on the extension memory. Unless something is done, the processor will be blocked while waiting for the fetch to be accomplished. The processing delay will be increased, and therefore the space in use will be increased. The net result will be that recovery from overflow will be slower than might otherwise be possible. If the block length has been properly chosen, the single-block chain is the rule and the multiblock chain is the exception. Therefore, most data will be wholly in the main memory or wholly in the extension. This fact tends to reduce the number of fetches required in recovery from overflow.

It may be that the delay associated with the extension of the block cannot be tolerated. In some systems it is possible to break the sequence of the chain and process the data in a different order. As an example, in a communication system messages are normally processed in FIFO order. However, the user may allow the FIFO order to be broken after an overflow has occurred. New messages are linked to the primal chain, the end of which is linked to the extension. Those messages that were unlucky enough to have gone out to overflow may wait several hours until the chain reaches the extension. At that point, a message may be cleared. By then, the chain may have grown again. Thus, for every five or ten messages in the primal memory, only one or two in the extension may be transmitted.

We can begin the recovery from overflow when enough memory has been replaced to make the effort worthwhile. Some processors are operating in the overflow mode (that is, they are assigned memory locations in the extension memory). As memory is recovered, first the more urgent functions are given space in main memory, then the less urgent functions, and so on. As the available pool builds up further, and as the time is available, we can begin to bring blocks back from the extension. A type of garbage collector can be used. The garbage collector goes through the administrative area looking for blocks that are extended. As it finds such a block, it fetches the extension block and writes it in a block of dynamic space. It then links the new copy of the block to the the block that had been extended, destroys the copy of the block on the extension memory, and resets the extension bit. By keeping count of the number of blocks that had been extended, the garbage collector knows when to stop.

Since there is no point in hurrying to recover an extended block which is not being used, recovery can also be done on an *ad hoc* basis. Fetching the extension of a block accomplishes most of the recovery since that block must be written in dynamic space. The fetching processor could also continue fetching blocks in the extended chain until the whole chain had been fetched from the extension memory.

2.2.9. Indexing and Moving in Dynamic Space

Indexing through sequences of words or characters in dynamically allocated space is more complicated than doing the same thing in fixed data areas. The difficulties arise from the fact that the blocks are linked. This means that tests for the end of the block must be made for each increment. When the end of the block is reached, the next block in the sequence must be accessed. The base address of the new block must replace the address of the old block. In addition, since the end block may not be filled with valid data, a test for the logical end of the block must be performed. The general problem to consider is moving a string of characters or words from one area in dynamic memory to another.

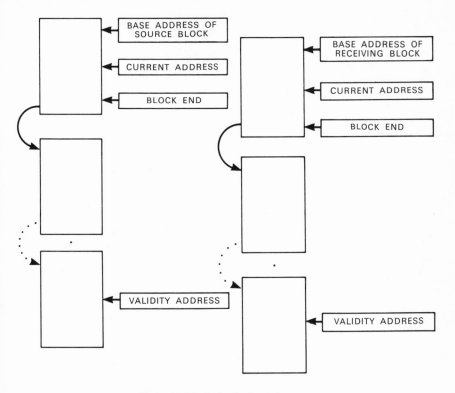

Figure 10.5. Indexing in dynamic space.

The indexing problem is shown in Figure 10.5. Eight addresses are used. The base address of the block is the address of the first word in the block and is used as a relative address for all operations in that block. The base address of the receiving block is different and is similarly used. Unless there are hardware facilities for the purpose, the block end of the source and the destination blocks must be tested. Since the transfer is not necessarily to and from locations whose addresses are equal relative to the beginning of the block, two separate block end tests must be made. A current position pointer must be maintained for each block. Finally, we can expect that the last block of the chain (or, for that matter, any block in the chain) is not filled. Consequently, there is a validity delimiter which must also be tested to tell us when the transfer is complete.

A double indexing modality is particularly useful here. The base address of the block can be kept in one index register, the current address in another, and their sum used to find the address of the character or word. Since it generally takes less time to test a register for zero than to compare its content with a stored constant, we could perform the operation using the following registers:

1. Current address on the source block, incremented for each move.
2. Source block end counter, decremented for each move.
3. Source block valid area delimiter, decremented for each move.
4. Destination block current address, incremented for each move.
5. Destination block end, decremented for each move.
6. Destination block valid area delimiter, decremented for each move.

This means six index incrementation operations and four tests for each move. We have reduced the processing by counting down the block ends and the validity counters—the move is still done in the forward direction.

The move can be further simplified by observing that the validity pointer must always precede the block end. Therefore, it can be used to substitute for the block end test. If the logical end of the block is reached by testing the validity pointer, it can then be compared with the source and destination address respectively to see if this was an internal delimiter or if the end of the block had been reached. Doing this removes two incrementation operations and two tests, but increases the amount of preliminary and subsequent processing. This is a typical inside-the-loop *vs.* outside-the-loop trade.

If either double indexing or address modification is possible, we can further reduce the number of incrementations and tests by combining the current address and the block end indexing. The idea is to do the move backwards. The index register (for the source or destination block) is used for both block end testing and for determining the address. Since we are doing the move in reverse, only the one source and destination register must be decremented. Thus, we have reduced the number of register operations to two as well as the tests. However, additional setup is required to test the validity counts before the move is started.

Table 10.1

FETCH (0)
STORE (0)
FETCH (1)
STORE (1)
FETCH (2)
STORE (2)
.
.
.
FETCH (N)
STORE (N)
JUMP

A final approach, which requires no incrementation or testing, can also be used. A sequence of fetch instructions and move instructions is used, with one entry per position in the block. The scheme is shown in Table 10.1. Here the source and destination relative addresses are assumed to be the same. The base addresses of the blocks are placed in index registers which are used to modify the sequence of instructions. A different register is used for the source and destination blocks. The scheme can start at any point in the block, which can be established either on the basis of a validity pointer or in order to test for the end of block. The test is accomplished by virtue of having reached the terminating jump instruction.

Table 10.2

	Location	Instruction	Location	Instruction
EXECUTE (0 + (L))	0 + (L)	FETCH (0 + (M))	0 + (K)	STORE (0 + (P))
EXECUTE (0 + (K))	1 + (L)	FETCH (1 + (M))	0 + (K)	STORE (1 + (P))
EXECUTE (1 + (L))	2 + (L)	FETCH (2 + (M))	2 + (K)	STORE (2 + (P))
EXECUTE (1 + (K))	3 + (L)	FETCH (3 + (M))	3 + (K)	STORE (3 + (P))
EXECUTE (2 + (L))				
EXECUTE (2 + (K))				
.				
.	N + (L)	FETCH (N + (M))	N + (K)	STORE (N + (P))
JUMP		JUMP		JUMP

In Table 10.2 a more generalized approach is used which allows relative displacement of the contents of the two blocks. Again, the base addresses can be used to establish the source and destination blocks. Execute instructions allow us to perform a further index modification which can account for the relative displacement of the two sets of data. A comparable scheme can be implemented in machines having multiple indirect and indexing modalities.

2.3. Segmentation and Paging

2.3.1. General

Some systems, such as time-sharing systems or commercial data processing systems, are designed to be constantly in overflow. The memory is partitioned into predefined, equal segments. The partition may be established either by convention or by hardware. A segment of memory is said to be **overlayed** when the loader moves a new program or file into the segment. If prior to the move of the new data, the content of the segment is written on some other medium such as the drum or the disc, the segment is said to have been **swapped**. Swapping is used when the data must be saved for a subsequent reswap. Overlays are used when the data can be discarded. Overlays are normally used for system and library programs or fixed tables that are stored elsewhere. Swapping takes at least twice as much work as overlaying.

2.3.2. Dedicated Systems

Swapping and overlays present no particular problems in systems with narrow load distributions. Overlays are used for seldomly used programs or permanent data, based on logical conditions which are part of the program, or according to a fixed schedule incorporated into the base sequence program. Special hardware or administrative routines are not needed. While the system itself may not be dedicated, certain aspects of the system may be characterized by narrow distributions and predictability that allow the use of simple overlays and swapping.

Consider a set of files that contain information for establishing air travel fares between the various cities in the world. Of the thirty-thousand-odd pairs of cities, perhaps only 500 different trips account for 90 % of the fare requests. Fare tables can be permanently established in main memory for these trips. Another area may be shared by the less frequent trips. When a fare is requested between a pair of cities, the city names are used to generate a table index. That table entry specifies either the location of the information in the main memory or the block address of the information on the drum or disc. If the file is not resident, it will be fetched from the appropriate medium and will overlay the file now in the shared area.

A similar scheme can be used for programs. A jump to a nonresident program is not done directly. Rather, the jump is made to a routine which will fetch the required program, store the return address of the calling program, and cause the required program to be loaded and initiated.

In both cases there is a trade between the cost of residency and the cost of overlays. The resident program, when not being executed, consumes only memory. Its cost is readily established as the fraction of the cost of the memory that it uses. Thus, if we amortize the cost of the memory over a ten-year period, taking into account the fair share of maintenance costs, etc., we might obtain a residency cost of 1/1500 cent per second for a 1000-word segment. If the segment is to be overlaid, there will be a residency cost on another medium, which might be 1/10,000 cent per second. There will also be the cost of overlaying, which will include the channel use cost, the CPU cost for setting up and performing the overlay, as well as the amortized programming cost required for the increased complexity of the overlay.

2.3.3. Displacement and Migration

It may happen that it is not possible to perform the trade analysis for all files, since the required file usage statistics are not known at the time of design. The system can be used to tune itself, to obtain an optimum location of the files based on actual usage. The intention is to have the most used files in the main memory and the less used files in more inaccessible memories. As each file is accessed, a counter is incremented for that file. The loader overwrites the file with the smallest count. The counts can be periodically modified so that they contain a running average of their utilization. The scheme can be extended to questions of storage between drum and disc as well as between main memory and drum.

In this way the high-usage files will eventually migrate toward the main memory, while the low-usage files will migrate toward the bulk memory. The end result is an optimum placement of the files. At that point, it may pay to fix the permanent locations of the files and discontinue the automatic migration. The files must of course still be fetched to the main memory if they are to be used.

2.3.4. Virtual Memory

When it is not possible to predict what files a particular program will need or, in fact, which programs will be running, a more complicated form of segmentation is used. This typically occurs in generalized systems in which there are user programs whose characteristics are not known in advance. The user is given a subjective memory which may or may not coincide with the physical memory of the system. The apparent or **virtual** memory that the user may have access to might be 38K words in a computer that has a main memory of either 16K words or 256K words. The user does not know how much physical space he may have at any one time. The complete swapping or overlay mechanism is transparent. That is, the user is not aware of its existence and can program as if the complete virtual memory were directly available to him. At any instant of time he might actually have only a fraction of the virtual memory resident in the main memory.

2.3.5. Virtual Memory Mechanization

The part of the main memory that will be used for the virtual memory is divided into equal-sized segments (called **pages**). Each page can be considered as a block of dynamic memory. Associated with each program that uses the virtual memory is a table. The most significant bits of every main memory address in the program are used as an index to the table. The table contains the base address of the memory block currently used for that segment, control information, and the address of the block on an extension memory if it is not resident. The base address of the block in current use may be kept in a base address register to avoid an additional memory reference for every normal memory reference. A separate base address register may be used for operand addresses and instruction addresses. The base address(es) modify every memory reference.

Every reference to the virtual memory is compared (after suitable transformation) to the base address of the current segment(s). If the reference is within the current segment, the instruction is executed in the normal manner. If the reference is not in the current segment, the table for that program is examined. If the access is to a segment which is resident, the base address register is loaded with the address of the segment found in the table and then the instruction proceeds in the normal manner. If the required segment is not resident, the operating system will be alerted, the instruction aborted, and the program blocked until the missing segment has been fetched. The operating system must then place the proper entries in the segmentation table for the program. When all of this has been accomplished, the program can be reinitiated at the instruction that was interrupted.

The extension address need not be an actual address, but can be the name of the segment. The segment itself might be obtained by first searching a directory of segments to see what the extension address is. The table itself can be stored in dynamic space, in which case it may have extensions onto other media.

None of the above hardware is absolutely essential. We could execute all programs interpretatively and test the boundaries of the pages as part of the interpretative routine. This would, of course, be extremely wasteful. If the virtual memory scheme is to be reasonable, the computer must at the very least create a boundary violation interrupt. That is, there is hardware to test every address prior to its transmission to the memory address register.

Automatic segmentation is an alternative to dynamic storage allocation. However, because a table must be kept for each active program, it is suited only to gross partitions of the memory.

2.4. Memory Scheduling

2.4.1. Transaction-Bound Systems

Systems that use serially accessed memories such as delay lines, drums, discs, and tapes can be bound by the rate at which these memories can be accessed. There is a delay associated with the fetching or writing of data to a drum or disc; typically the delay is one-half of a rotation. We shall for the remainder of this section discuss **memory transactions** rather than read or write actions. If the system must perform N transactions per second (i.e., reads or writes) but can only perform less than N transactions, it is said to be **memory transaction bound.**[2] There may be adequate space, time, and channel available, but the computer spends most of its time waiting for needed

[2] We shall often, in context, where there is no possibility of confusion with semantic transactions, drop the word "memory" and use "transaction" alone.

transactions. If all transactions must be performed strictly in the sequence in which they are generated, and they are stored randomly, there is very little that can be done about transaction binding. If, however, the transactions are not all dependent, and ordering among the independent sets is not critical, then it is possible to schedule the transactions in such a way as to almost completely eliminate transaction binding. Such optimum scheduling can be done in the overwhelming majority of systems. Every dedicated system has sufficient independence among the memory transactions to make an optimum schedule possible. In those systems in which strict order must be maintained, transaction binding is avoided by allocating the memory in such a way as to minimize the latency, much in the same way as programs were designed to minimize latency in the earlier drum machines (see Chapter 3, page 63).

2.4.2. Basic Principles

The basic principle used is that of ordering the transactions in a manner analogous to the movement of the device. Consider a drum which consists of N tracks and K sectors. Assume for the moment that it takes no time to switch between tracks and that there is no apparent interlace (that is, if there is interlace, it is mechanized in hardware).

If we knew which sector of the drum was about to become accessible, we could examine all pending transactions and initiate the one that could be performed at that time. The average latency would be reduced to the time it takes to traverse one sector. As we shall see, it is neither necessary to know the current position of the drum nor to examine the waiting transaction queue.

By ordering the transactions in a manner analogous to the movement of the device, the number of transactions that can be executed for each rotation approaches the number of sectors on the device. The average latency for each transaction is approximately one-half a revolution, but the system is no longer transaction bound.

2.4.3. Drum Scheduling

Transaction requests are presented to the drum control processor on its input queue. The order of requests on that queue is not optimum. The drum control processor could scan the queue and pick out transactions in the proper order (i.e., in rotational address sequence), and place these in a new queue which is used to request the transactions. As the drum processor is executing the instruction that starts the transaction, several more transaction requests can come in that could be executed during the ongoing rotation. For example, transactions are scheduled for all sectors except 13, 17, and 45, and a request for a sector 45 transaction comes in. If the drum has not yet gotten to sector 45, we can still schedule it and decrease its waiting time. To take advantage of this, we can insert the new transaction into the transaction queue. Thus, every transaction request that comes in requires the examination of the transaction queue to see if the new transaction should be fitted into the queue. If it is to be fitted in, the preceding and succeeding queue entries must be relinked. Alternatively, we can batch the transaction requests and sort them in sector order.

While either of these methods will work, they both can be cumbersome. A simpler approach is to use a **transaction table** or "spin table."[3] A table is established with as many entries as there are sectors. The address of the drum block (all drum blocks are assumed to be the same or multiples of a fixed length) can be considered as consisting of two parts, a track address and a sector address. The sector address portion of the drum block address is used as an index for the scheduling table. The track address of the drum block, the command (read or write), and the appropriate core memory locations are placed in the location corresponding to the sector address generated index. The general scheme is shown in Figure 10.6. By permanently assigning space to this table, it is not necessary to link and unlink queue entries, or to sort the queue in the optimum order.

As each transaction is examined by the drum scheduling processor, the sector address is extracted to obtain the index on the schedule table. A control field on the schedule table is examined to see if there has already been a transaction scheduled for that sector during the coming revolution. If there is a transaction scheduled, the new transaction will be delayed until the following revolution. The drum transaction processor executes the transaction instructions in sequence as fast as it can, typically one at a time, followed by a transaction completion interrupt.

As usually implemented, there are at least two such tables, which are used alternately. If this were not the case, it might not be possible to build the new table in the elapsed time between the termination of the transaction for the last sector and the initiation of the transaction for the first sector. Therefore, if the scheduler finds the transaction on the present table occupied, it attempts to place the transaction on the next table. If this is not possible, the transaction remains on the queue. Because it is the topmost location requesting that sector, it will be serviced on the next rotation after that corresponding to the second table.

Scheduling tables take space. If the drum has been divided into many sectors, or if the transaction rate is relatively low, a linking and unlinking

---

[3] It is interesting to note that the spin table technique was used as early as 1960 at RCA in the design of COMLOGNET. (It may have been used earlier still, but that has not been verified.) The first formal description of the scheduling doctrine did not appear until 1966 (see References 2 and 8). By that time, some 30 systems using this scheduling method were in operation.

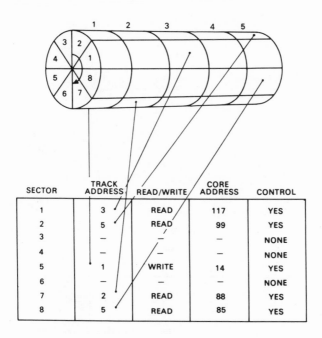

SECTOR	TRACK ADDRESS	READ/WRITE	CORE ADDRESS	CONTROL
1	3	READ	117	YES
2	5	READ	99	YES
3	–	–	–	NONE
4	–	–	–	NONE
5	1	WRITE	14	YES
6	–	–	–	NONE
7	2	READ	88	YES
8	5	READ	85	YES

Figure 10.6. Drum transaction schedule table.

scheme may be more effective than a table. The scheduling processor must scan the table, and if the table has few entries, the scanning time may be larger than the linking time. The linking scheme and the table scheme can be combined to yield some additional advantages which are applicable to disc scheduling as well as to drum scheduling. A two-way linking scheme is shown in Figure 10.7. A single table is constructed which contains only a link address and control information that specifies whether or not there is a transaction for that sector. The sector number is again used as an index to the entry in the sector control table. The scheduling processor then scans down the small linked list or queue for that sector (possibly by multiple indirect addressing) and places the transaction on the queue for that sector. Little space is wasted. The advantage of this approach is that since the queues are in dynamic space, there is no limit to the effective number of spin tables. In the example shown, it would take nine tables to accomplish the same thing.

The work required to issue the commands, however, is somewhat greater than with the simpler tabular approach. The processor that issues the transaction commands scans the sector control table. As it finds an entry

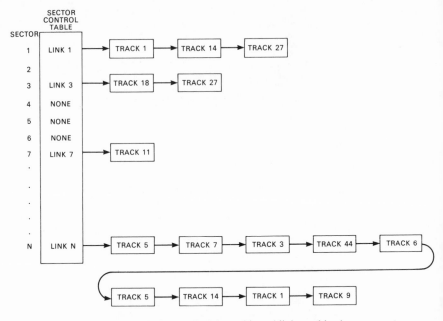

Figure 10.7. Drum schedule—table and link combined.

(i.e., a link to an entry for a transaction) it issues the transaction and relinks the head of the queue to the sector control table.

If the number of entries for each sector is likely to become large, the repeated scanning through each queue to place a new transaction can be eliminated by storing the address of the last entry on the queue in the sector control table.

A read transaction may not be allowed to follow a write transaction directly, or *vice versa*. A gap of at least one sector may be required by the hardware. This problem can be solved by establishing two sets of tables or queue sets, one for odd-numbered sectors and one for even-numbered sectors. This approach, while simple, halves the number of transactions that can be executed in one revolution. Another approach to read–write conflicts is to establish separate read and write tables or queues and perform the reads and writes on alternate revolutions. A similar restriction on transactions is that it may not be possible to switch tracks between transactions. Thus, two adjacent sectors cannot be scheduled unless they are for the same track. Again, an odd–even scheme can be used, with the same penalty.

A somewhat more elegant approach to the read–write conflict problem is to allow the following entries in the table rather than the simple "scheduled or not scheduled" approach:

AVAILABLE FØR READ,
AVAILABLE FØR WRITE,
SCHEDULED FØR READ,
SCHEDULED FØR WRITE,
AVAILABLE FØR READ ØR WRITE.

If we place a read transaction in a sector, the entry for the next sector is marked as "available for read," and the present sector is marked "scheduled for read." Write transactions are handled similarly. The normal state of the entry is "available for read or write." The read–write conflicts are eliminated without sacrificing the number of transactions that can be performed in a single revolution. The reason there is no significant sacrifice is that the number of transactions required per revolution is rarely comparable to the number of sectors on the drum. As the transaction density is increased (i.e., begins to approach the number of sectors on the track), the scheme begins to approach the odd–even method. The effect, however, will be that alternate revolutions will contain mostly read transactions and will be followed by revolutions dominated by write transactions. The delay will tend to be double what it would have been with pure read or pure write transactions, as in the case of odd–even segregation, but the number of transactions per revolution is the same as in the pure read or pure write case.

The track conflict problem can be solved in a similar way. If multiple spin tables are used, the entry following can be marked as

AVAILABLE FØR TRACK 7.

Since many systems have both of these restrictions, the status of the sector can be

AVAILABLE FØR READ ØN TRACK X,
AVAILABLE FØR WRITE ØN TRACK Y,
SCHEDULED FØR READ ØN TRACK X,
SCHEDULED FØR WRITE ØN TRACK Z,
AVAILABLE FØR READ ØR WRITE ØN TRACK W,
AVAILABLE FØR READ ØR WRITE ØN ANY TRACK.

While we have described the resolutions of the conflict problem in terms of schedule tables, the same concept can be applied to a mixed table–queue scheme such as was shown in Figure 10.7. A simple way to avoid control problems is to use dummy queue entries wherever there are restrictions. The specific nature of the restriction is entered in the dummy transaction. A scan of the queue for that sector will allow us to place the transaction in the first dummy queue entry for which the restrictions do not affect the particular transaction. If there are no dummy entries, the transaction is placed at the end of the queue. However, since placing a new entry on the queue establishes restrictions on the previous and next sectors for the same revolution, it is necessary to scan along the previous and next sectors' queues to place the restrictions. Dummy entries for these queues containing the restrictions must be placed as far out on them as the new entry.

Since each entry establishes both previous sector and next sector restrictions, each entry requires that three entries be made.

Another form of restriction can occur in which we may wish to limit the number of revolutions that will be devoted to this particular set of transactions, i.e., we may wish to limit the system to five revolutions per system cycle. This may come about because the drum is being independently read or written by some other computer or because an area of the drum is to be manipulated which has a different layout. The explicit table approach does this implicitly. With the table–queue combination, we must explicitly keep track of the number of entries on each sector queue.

It may also be necessary to allow high-priority transactions to usurp lower-priority transactions. If there are no restrictions, the problem is readily solved by pushing down all transactions for that sector. If, however, there are read/write or track switching restrictions, the usurpation of entries in a schedule by higher-priority transactions will require a complete re-examination of that schedule. Each change will propagate to the previous and succeeding sectors, to the point where the complete schedule is upset. Furthermore, it is possible to establish unresolvable conflicts or lockouts by pushing the schedule about. It may be simpler to redo the whole schedule.

2.4.4. Effectiveness

The advantage gained by this kind of scheduling is dramatic. The following results are taken from Denning (Reference 2).

Let N be the number of sectors on the drum, t the rotation time for the drum, and n the number of transactions waiting on the queue. If the locations of transactions are randomly distributed on the drum and there is no delay required to initiate reads or writes (i.e., no restrictions), then the expected delay per transaction is

$$T = \frac{t}{n+1}\left[1 - \frac{1}{2N}\right]^{n+1}$$

The number of requests serviced per unit time is

$$Q = \left[T + \frac{t}{N}\right]^{-1}$$

A comparison of the optimum schedule to the FIFO schedule shows a dramatic improvement. The optimized schedule is typically an order of magnitude better. Furthermore, the efficiency of the scheme improves with increasing transaction load. The system is only transaction bound when the number of transactions per rotation approaches the number of sectors on the drum.

2.4.5. Disc Scheduling

Individual cylinders of a disc can be treated as drums and therefore require no further explication. Fixed-head discs are logically identical to drums and are scheduled the same way. Movable-head discs, however, are different. The limiting factor to disc scheduling is the head motion. Head motion is analogous to track switching. If the track switching time of a drum is very large, or if the head motion time for a disc is small, the two devices behave similarly. Usually the head motion time is sufficiently large to warrant optimization.

One method is to seek the cylinder that can be most quickly reached from the present position and schedule all transactions for that cylinder as with a drum. If two or more cylinders are equidistant from the present cylinder, the one with the greater number of transactions is scheduled first.

The difficulty with this kind of scheduling is that if there are many transactions requested on a group of adjacent tracks, the system will tend to remain in that area, ignoring the transactions that are further away. There is bias against tracks at the edges. The policy can be improved by weighting the ties by the number of transactions waiting in a given direction. Thus, the "nearest track next" policy is modified to a policy of "the nearest track in the direction that has the greatest number of transactions." This policy can be further improved by weighting transactions by the number of revolutions that they have waited. Thus, we might give one revolution a weight of 1, two revolutions a weight of 2, three revolutions a weight of 4, etc. The direction in which the next track will be chosen is based on the sum of the weights in that direction. The particular succession of weights will affect the rates at which the edges will be serviced. The weighting scheme must be based on transaction statistics. The net effect of this policy is that the arm will tend to drift back and forth uniformly across the disc. The cost of calculating the weights prior to each track motion must be balanced against the time wasted by not having the transaction performed at the maximum average rate.

The scheduling problem is more complex for systems that use a single channel to service multiple discs with independent seek mechanisms. Transactions are made at a rate compatible with the available channel capacity. The intention is no longer merely to maximize the number of transactions per unit time from the point of view of having the heads properly located, but to assure that the channel will be used to capacity as well. The time required to perform optimum scheduling calculations in such cases becomes sufficiently large to warrant a special-purpose computer devoted to this task. Several manufacturers offer hardware schedulers for this purpose.

2.4.6. Tape Scheduling

Consider a single tape reel containing a number of blocks of approximately equal size, some of which are to be read. If we must read every block on the tape in order to identify it, the processing time would dominate the problem, and optimized scheduling would be a comparatively minor issue. Special administrative blocks on the tape may be used in conjunction with skip commands to reduce the number of blocks to be read. A skip-block command will not actually read the block but will create an interrupt after the block has been traversed. Most tape transports having a skip-block command allow the blocks to be skipped in the reverse direction as well as in the forward direction.

At any moment, by keeping track of what we have done, we know which block we are at. It is further possible to determine the distance to any block. The tape can be considered as if it were a band that can be traversed in either direction. The same kind of scheduling techniques that are used for disc track optimization can be used here. That is, we move in the direction for which the accumulated weight is maximized.

Another policy is to treat the tape as if it were a single-track drum. The tape in effect "rotates," or rather scans back and forth (see Figure 10.8). Transactions occurring in "front" of the present tape head position are scheduled for the forward pass, while those in "back" are scheduled for the reverse pass. If the tape is outbound (skipping forward), transactions are ordered such that the most recently written blocks are first. When the tape beginning is reached, the ordering of the transactions is reversed. Since multiple skips over blocks can be almost as fast as the continuous reading speed, the tape can be traversed at almost the reading speed. In many transports, the reading speed is as much as half of the rewind speed.

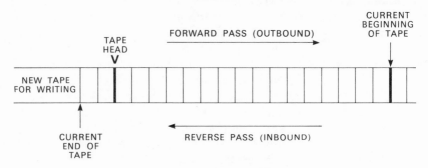

Figure 10.8. Tape scheduling scheme.

If writing must be done, it will occur only at the home position of the tape (i.e., the current end of tape) since it is not possible to overwrite individual blocks in the middle of other blocks on most tape transports. The new blocks are incorporated in the next scan. Similarly, we can ignore blocks beyond a given point. The controls are established to ignore those blocks and to begin the return trip as soon as the last valid block has been reached.

There is a disadvantage to this scheme. It is wear and tear on the tape transport and the tape. Each time a block is traversed, the pinch rollers will be activated. This stresses the tape and can cause premature wear. The tape transport itself sounds like a child running a stick along a picket fence. If the transport is not built for this kind of service it will require excessive maintenance. A disc should be used if many such transactions are expected.

3. BUFFER METHODS

3.1. What and Why

A **buffer** is an area of memory used to allow devices of disparate speeds to communicate with one another. Buffering is used to reconcile the high speed of the central computer to slower speeds of its peripheral devices. Communication between devices is almost always accomplished by an intermediate sojourn in memory. The primary buffering problems are those concerned with moving data between peripheral devices and the main memory.

The intention of a good buffer design is to obtain timely service of the device without using too much memory. A secondary goal of buffer design is the avoidance of unnecessary internal moves.

3.2. Fixed Overwriting Buffers

The simplest approach to buffering is to establish a dedicated area of memory for the purpose. Typically, that area will depend upon the format of the data being moved and the device to which the data are going or from which they are coming. Thus, a buffer for a card reader or punch is 80 characters long, a buffer for a printer has 135 characters, while a buffer for a teleprinter might have 85 characters. The buffer size is chosen according to the expected length of the records being transferred. If that length is fixed and known in advance, the following simple scheme will work. The issuance of the next command to the device must be forestalled until the content of the buffer has been moved to a work area and the buffer is again cleared. This has two disadvantages: an internal data move is required, and it may not be possible to keep the device operating at maximum speed. Its primary advantage is simplicity.

If the block is long or if the block length is distributed, the fixed-buffer scheme is seriously deficient. It requires high-priority processing as soon as the buffer is filled. During the interval between the "buffer filled" (or "empty") signal and the next character, the system must transfer the data to another area lest the new data destroy the old, or lest the device miss characters which were to be transmitted to it.

The inadequacies of fixed buffers with respect to handling long, unpredictable blocks of data can be partially alleviated because programs can be executed while the buffer is being filled. To take advantage of this possibility, a warning is needed to alert the computer that the buffer is about to be filled. This can be done by hardware. An interrupt is mechanized which occurs when the buffer address counter (which controls the contentious transfer) is a fixed number of characters from the end. If the warning is given sufficiently in advance, the buffer service program can begin to move the data out of the buffer into a work area or into the buffer from a work area, as appropriate to an input or output transfer, respectively. In most cases, the buffer filling speed will be less than the speed at which the internal moves can take place. The internal move can keep ahead of the contentious transfer. The primary difficulty with this approach is that of keeping them synchronized so that neither overruns the other. One way of doing this is to allow the internal data move program access to the buffer address counter. By testing it prior to each data move, the internal move program can be assured of never overrunning the buffer. This means that the internal program will probably waste cycles in diddle loops while waiting for the contentious transfer to get sufficiently far ahead of it to transfer more characters into or out of the buffer. Should other interrupts occur, the contentious transfer may completely fill the buffer (or empty it) before the internal program has had a chance to service the buffer. Therefore, single buffer overwriting schemes are typically restricted to slow devices such as teleprinters, card readers, card punches, and high-speed printers in which it is possible to keep up despite the occurrence of higher-level interrupts or higher-priority programs.

3.3. Alternating Buffers

Alternating buffers are also known as **toggle buffers** and **ping-pong buffers**. Two or more buffers are assigned to the task. While the one buffer is being used for the transfer, the other buffer is being serviced. When the buffer-filled interrupt occurs, the interrupt service program has only to modify the main memory address being used for the transfer and reset the control counters. Control is shifted to the alternate buffer, which is then used for the transfer. In the meantime, the other buffer is serviced. The primary advantage of this scheme is that it is not necessary to synchronize the internal data move with the contentious transfer except when the buffer is actually expended. This eliminates the comparison of the buffer position with the internal program's index for that buffer. It is no longer possible to overwrite the buffer. Alternating buffers can be used with higher-speed devices such as tapes, drums, and discs. It is again possible to use an alerting interrupt to warn the system that the buffer is about to be expended and thereby activate the service of the alternate buffer. The buffer-filled (empty) interrupt is essential since control should not be shifted to the alternate buffer until after the active buffer has reached the end. Alternating buffers need not be restricted to an alternation between two buffers. Three or more buffers can be used. The fixed, overwriting buffer is a special case in which only one "alternating" buffer is used.

3.4. Dynamic Buffers

The logical extension of alternating buffers is the use of dynamic storage. This effectively allows indefinite-sized data transfers. Furthermore, if the programs that are to use or produce the data that are contained in the buffer are designed to work with dynamically allocated space, internal data moves can be eliminated. The price paid for the increased efficiency is the necessity of linking a new block to the buffer function in addition to transferring control to the new buffer block. As each buffer is filled, a new block must be assigned to the buffer chain. This means that the vacancy chain or other form of occupancy record must be examined, and a vacant block found and linked to the active block, prior to its being filled. In some machines, this processing can be as great as the internal moves required for alternating buffers.

3.5. Mixed Schemes

It is sometimes convenient to use a combination of several schemes. For example, fixed buffers can be used in conjunction with dynamic buffering, or in conjunction with alternating buffers. The fixed-plus-dynamic scheme is the most prevalent. A typical application occurs in communication systems. There are, for the sake of this discussion, two types of messages: small fixed-length control messages and textual messages of several hundred characters. Furthermore, the preambles of the textual messages have the same form as the control messages. A fixed buffer whose size is equal to the length of the control messages and textual message preamble is assigned to each line. An interrupt signals the filling of the fixed buffer. The interrupt service program can then examine the content of that buffer and determine if a control message has been received or if the preamble of a textual message has been received. If it is a textual message, the fixed buffer is linked to a buffer block in dynamic space and the transfer control is set up for the newly linked block.

On output, the procedure is somewhat simpler. If the message in question is a control message, it is created directly in, or moved to, the fixed buffer. If a textual message is to be transmitted, output can proceed directly from the block in which the preamble starts.

3.6. How Much? How Big?

A first approximation of the amount of dynamic space devoted to buffering functions is obtained from an analysis of the creation and destruction of space. No special distinction need be made between blocks used for buffering and blocks used for processing. A number of blocks sufficient to satisfy the required number of standard deviations for memory is used. The size of the block is determined by the block sizing procedure described in Chapter 8 (pages 457–460). The combination of fixed-plus-dynamic buffering introduces a new wrinkle into size selection but not a major complication. The use of fixed buffers implies that their space will be forever allocated to the buffering function. The total space should be small by virtue of a small fixed buffer size. The size should be based on the length distribution. A distribution which has a fixed lower bound (e.g., all messages exceed 23 characters) is a good candidate for fixed-plus-dynamic buffering.

Fixed-plus-dynamic buffering is not without its headaches. In the communication system example discussed above, we took advantage of the equal length of the control message and the preamble of textual messages. It was further implied that it would not be necessary to move the preamble into dynamic space. If the data in the fixed buffer must also be moved to dynamic space for processing, several complications will occur. The data that were in the fixed portion of the buffer are moved to dynamic space. If the fixed buffer is not the same size as the blocks in dynamic space, there will be at least one block which is not filled somewhere in the middle of the chain. If the fixed buffer is smaller than the dynamic blocks it will be the first block of the chain. If the fixed buffer is larger than the dynamic block, it will be a block somewhere in the middle of the chain. The result will be that every block will have to contain a valid data delimiter. This will complicate subsequent indexing and all other serial operations on those data. The partially filled block represents a waste of space. Since the fixed block will be typically smaller than the dynamic block, we can always expect to waste the difference in their length.

3.7. Alert and Control

There are two distinct points of concern in the control of a buffer: the point at which we are alerted that the buffer is about to be filled (exhausted), and the point at which the filling (emptying) has actually occurred. Interrupts are used for these purposes in most systems. It is usually possible, either under program control or by wiring modifications, to select the point at which the alert will occur. The earlier the alert occurs, the more time there is to react. The selection of the alert point is another parameter in the buffer scheme design. Alerting presents slightly different problems for input and output.

3.7.1. Input

The very least that can be done when the block-filled interrupt occurs is to modify the channel control words to the parameters of the new block on the chain. In some systems, two areas are provided for this purpose, and the channel control words are themselves alternated. In such systems it is only necessary to set a switch (i.e., complement a bit) to indicate that the alternate channel control data are to be used. All other functions associated with setting up the new block can be done at the time of alert. The following functions are required:

1. Find a vacant block.
2. Link that block to the input chain.
3. Set up the new transfer control data.
4. Move them to the alternate transfer control words.

There is not much point in examining a vacancy if the new block is not going to be assigned when found. The earlier the new block is linked, the more memory will be wasted. The use of an alert signal is similar in concept to deferred processing—it is a form of **anticipatory processing**. Deferred processing is a trade of memory cycles under duress for more memory cycles at leisure. A secondary cost is additional delay and therefore additional space. Anticipatory processing is a trade of space before it is needed for memory cycles under duress. It is also a time trade—time in anticipation of duress for the possibility that the space will not be needed after all. If the new block is assigned, say, ten characters from the end of the old block, not only will the block assignment time have been wasted, but so will the time required to return the block to the vacancy chain. In addition, for the duration that the unneeded block was reserved, the additional space will have been wasted. Given the probability distribution that represents the input transmission lengths, and the dynamic block size, it is relatively easy to determine the cumulative probability that a block will be wasted for any position of the alert signal. If we know the rate at which the block is being filled, it is possible to determine the expected space wastage.

The proper selection of the alert interrupt position depends upon the rate at which the block is being filled and the expected delay between the occurrence of the interrupt and the time at which the setup of the new block will have been completed. The faster the block is filled, the earlier the alert interrupt must be placed. For slow devices such as teleprinters an alert interrupt may not be required at all. There may be enough time to service the block-filled interrupt and get a new block linked before the next character comes in. High-speed devices may require considerable advance notice (in terms of characters remaining to be filled rather than in terms of time). Faster lines require more memory than slower lines even if the transmission length distributions are identical. It would be reasonable to expect that if we were to double the speed of all devices inputting to the computer, the memory required for their buffering would only double. We see, however, that the memory increase is somewhat greater than double since the alert interrupt must be moved up a few characters.

As the speed of transmission is increased, the alert interrupt position approaches the beginning of the block. At that point it can be eliminated

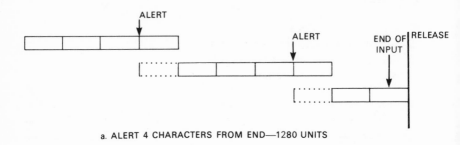

a. ALERT 4 CHARACTERS FROM END—1280 UNITS

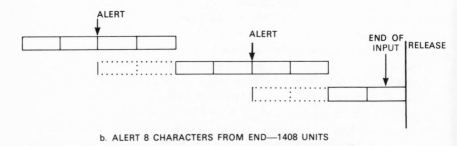

b. ALERT 8 CHARACTERS FROM END—1408 UNITS

Figure 10.9. Effect of alert location on memory use.

altogether because the linking of the next block can be done when a block termination interrupt occurs. The program first transfers transmission control to the new block and immediately goes about obtaining another block. If the alert is even earlier, three or four blocks can be tied up.

The sensitivity of alert interrupt location can be gauged from the example shown in Figure 10.9. Sixteen character blocks are used in both cases. We shall assume that the blocks are destroyed or are transferred to some noninput function two character times after the last character has come in. The first case (Figure 10.9a) shows the alert occurring four characters from the end of the block. If the character rate is one character per second, the total space-time used is 1280 character-seconds. In Figure 10.9b, the alert occurs eight characters from the end. The total space-time used is 1408 character-seconds.

3.7.2. Output

The alert pointer position is not nearly so critical on output. It should be placed far enough in advance of the end of the block to assure that the new block will be set up in sufficient time. There is no block assignment to perform, and the return of buffer blocks to the pool can take place at relative leisure compared to the time available for assigning blocks. In many systems the alert position for both input and output is wired into the hardware and is the same for both. Consequently, there may be no choice once the input alert position has been decided.

4. QUEUES

4.1. Why Queues?

The most common way of organizing data transfers from task to task is to place the data on queues. Whether it is the actual data or an identifier of the data which is placed on the queue need not concern us for the moment; it is convenient to discuss queues as if the actual data were on the queue.

We can generalize the concept of queues by defining a **queue** to be an ordered list of data or data descriptors. The overwhelming majority of processors in a system examine queue entries in order and perform the appropriate operations on all entries of the queue until there are no more entries left. Under the more general definition of queues given above, a fixed table or list, such as a polling sequence for terminals, can be considered as if it were a queue.

Scheduling, in the last analysis, is the placement of data descriptors or data on appropriate queues in a fashion that optimizes the resources of the system. A predefined table is a fixed schedule or, alternatively, a fixed queue. The prevalence of queues as a processing organization technique is due to their simplicity and implicity. Queues could be replaced by connection matrices or other representations that could accomplish the same things. However, such matrices would be sparse, and sparse matrices can be more conveniently implemented as linked lists of connections—which is to say, as queues.

Another advantage of queues is that it is not necessary to know precisely how many items of a given type are going to be processed by a processor in any one system cycle. Queues, which are most naturally stored in dynamic space, can have variable length. As one processor, either because of the large number of entries on its input queue or because of data that take a long time to process, slows the system down, queue entries of other processors increase. Similarly, a fast processor or a fast run for a processor will cause its input queue to be quickly exhausted, while the number of entries on its output queue will increase. Queues can be looked upon as speed matching devices between processors having disparate processing speeds—which is to say that they perform an internal buffering function while maintaining the logical structure of the jobs and the sequence of tasks that data are to go through.

4.2. Where and What

Associated with each physical device, there is at least one processor (perhaps a trivial one consisting of only one instruction) that manages or otherwise uses that device. We can therefore consider processors only and not be concerned with the specific device. One could have a different queue for every identifiable processor of the system.[4] This approach is extreme and has several attractive features and serious deficiencies. It is flexible because processors can be changed or added without affecting the logical structure of the system. Its primary disadvantage is that every termination of a processor will cause a return to the scheduler. The overhead is correspondingly high. Generally, the various processors have been partitioned and grouped, thereby defining new, compound processors. It is *these* that require the individual queues.

If a task is to be scheduled for a processor, it is placed at the end of the input queue for that processor, with the appropriate status changes. Neither the task, nor its data, or even its entries in the status table need be placed on the queue. Typically, the queue contains an identifier and perhaps an instruction. The instruction is not necessarily a machine instruction, but is

---

[4] In a commercial installation, or in a time-sharing system, user programs are not considered processors of the system.

rather a specialized grouping of data (within a few words) that will be interpreted by the processor for that queue. That processor will in turn use the identifier to obtain the details of the task. The identifier may in turn point to a master job queue, which in turn points to the several tables that the processor will have to use. Continuing in this indirect manner, the processor will obtain the relevant addresses and perform the required task.

This degree of indirection is required for several reasons. The relevant data may not be in the main memory and will have to be obtained by the file management processor. The master job queue itself may not be in the main memory. For that matter, the processor's own queue may not be in the main memory. The location of the data, the descriptors of the data, the queues, the queue entries, and the processor may be continually, dynamically re-allocated and reloaded. Logically contiguous memory areas (from the point of view of the processor) may not be physically contiguous. Relocation may not necessarily be performed through the use of a relocation register. The programs may be re-entrant, necessitating indirect operations. They may be used at more than one program or priority level, or by more than one computer simultaneously.

4.3. Dedicated Systems and Generalized Systems Queues

The more queues there are and the more explicit and specific the function associated with each queue, the simpler it is to manage them, but the longer it takes. Dedicated systems are characterized by few queues of short, relatively predictable, length. Fixed schedule tables are used in the extreme case. Generalized systems tend to have many queues.

4.3.1. Dedicated Systems

In a dedicated system, in which the processor sequence is known at design time, the individual processor maintains the queue entries. Each processor can be looked upon as having three types of queues: the input queue, the output queue, and the error queue. Task descriptors are placed on the input queue. The process is performed and, if successfully terminated, the new task descriptor is placed on the appropriate output queue. If the process is unsuccessfully terminated, the task descriptor (again modified) is placed on the error queue. In the dedicated system, the output queue of one processor is usually the input queue of the next processor in the sequence. The scheduling is thus implicit. Each processor is responsible for the transfer of the task descriptors to the next processor in the line. It is relatively more difficult to change the sequence operations or to add new functions in the dedicated system. Such changes may require the construction of new queues and the modification of many subprocessors.

4.3.2. Generalized Systems

As the system becomes more generalized, the number of input queues and output queues tends to increase as the second power of the number of processors, that is, in the extreme case, everything could go to everything else, resulting in N^2 queues. Furthermore, if each processor has to decide where the task descriptor should go next, each processor would contain much the same analytical facilities, with the result that much of the scheduler functions would be needlessly reproduced. The answer to this is to use a centralized, explicit scheduler. Therefore, in the generalized system, each processor has an input and an output queue. Entries are placed on the input queue by the scheduler, and processor output queues are input queues of the scheduler. The scheduler decides where a descriptor is to go next.

4.4. Queue Arrangements—Some Examples

The number of queues in both the dedicated system and the generalized system with a centralized scheduler tends to be directly proportional to the number of processors. In the dedicated system, the proportionality constant is close to 1, and in the generalized system it is roughly 2. It is the middle ground where the number of queues can be overly burdensome. The situation is shown in Figure 10.10.

The number of possible sequences in the dedicated system is small. The possibilities have been examined at design time and fixed. The output queue of one processor is the input queue of the next. Relatively few processors have branching queues. There is little to centralize in queue control. The scheme is implicit, efficient, and inflexible. The inflexibility makes this kind of queue structure inappropriate to a generalized system.

The generalized system is sufficiently complex that it is not possible to decide at design time what all the possible task sequences will be. A centralized scheduler is required. The processors are simplified because they no longer need the mechanism to decide which queue will get the output. The number of queues has been increased, and the number of explicit descriptor transfers has also been increased. The scheme takes more time and more space but is more flexible than that used in the dedicated system.

A centralized scheduler requires a common interface for all queues. All descriptors must be in the same format and, generally, all data examined by the scheduler must have a common, predefined format. This means that the processor must translate or otherwise interpret the input data for its own needs and translate the output to be suitable for the scheduler. The dedicated system does not have this problem. The formats and mode of descriptor and data transfer are decided by the two programmers who share the queue. Agreement by only a few persons is required.

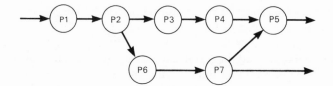

a. DEDICATED SYSTEM: 7 PROCESSORS—10 QUEUES

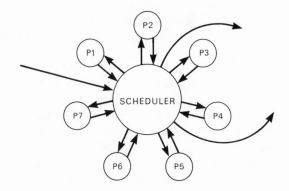

b. GENERALIZED SYSTEM: 7 PROCESSORS—17 QUEUES

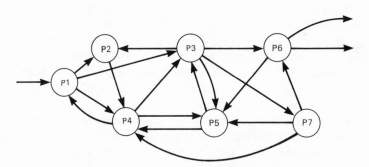

c. MIDDLE GROUND: 7 PROCESSORS—20 QUEUES

Figure 10.10. Three different queue schemes.

The kind of queue arrangement required for a centralized scheduler is not appropriate to a dedicated system where flexibility is not necessary and where most of the paths can be determined at design time. This difference is one of the primary reasons why generalized operating systems have been relatively inefficient in dedicated applications when compared to a dedicated system using the same hardware.

A third situation, shown in Figure 10.10c, is the dangerous middle ground. The various paths can be decided at design time, allowing the output queue of one processor to be the input queue of the next. However, there are too many possibilities and the result is too many queues. The system is still more inflexible, the additional queues take space, and each processor contains decision functions that could be done better by a rudimentary scheduler.

It is difficult to manage a programming effort based on a system whose queue structure is similar to that of Figure 10.10c. Agreement on queue format is needed at every interface, and is likely to be subjected to the notorious inefficiencies of design by committee. In fact, one motivation for going to a centralized scheduler is to minimize the number of queue or other interface formats.

The queue structure shown in Figure 10.10c can be avoided by drawing and comparing diagrams such as these. At the very least, the number of queues and possible interfaces arising from shared queues should be counted. One should also determine the amount of work devoted to deciding, in each processor, which queue the output is to go to and how much of that work could be incorporated in a centralized scheduler.

Unfortunately, a structure such as this can come about as a result of the successive addition of new functions over the life of the system. As the system matures, the once simple structure of Figure 10.10a approaches that of Figure 10.10c, with a resulting degradation of efficiency. Each additional function requires greater skill and knowledge of what has gone before on the part of the programmer who is to add it. If the design parameters are not well known, and if it is suspected that the system will undergo major evolutionary changes in its lifetime, it may be appropriate to start with the centralized scheduler to avoid arriving at the middle ground at a later time. Here then is a trade between efficiency now and efficiency later. The future is uncertain. Whatever the characterizing distributions of the system, the uncertainty of the future tends to broaden them. What it boils down to is that a $K\sigma$ system is more expensive than a $(K - 1)\sigma$ system. Whether the value of K is established on "day one" or whether it grows over a period of years does not much matter. In either case, the larger K will be paid for by a decrease in efficiency.

4.5. Queue Length

4.5.1. Batching Doctrines

Several doctrines can be adopted for determining how many queue entries a processor is to process at a time: it could process as many as possible until the queue is dried up and then return to the base sequencer or scheduler; it could process one at a time and return to the scheduler at the end of each entry; it could process a predetermined number of entries and then return; it could process as many as it was told to prior to returning; or it could process for a predetermined time interval. The larger the batch, the more efficient *that* processor is likely to be, but perhaps at the expense of the efficiency of the whole system. The processor must be called, work areas must be assigned and initialized, the processor itself must go through initialization steps, there are termination steps to be performed, the processor must call the scheduler or base sequencer, it must obtain the starting address of the various queues, etc. All of these are costs that can be amortized over a batch of entries. The longer any processor runs, however, the harder it is to fit into an optimum schedule. Therefore, increasing the efficiency of any one processor by allowing it to batch its work is done at the cost of decreasing the efficiency of the system as a whole. As the batch size is increased, the delay for lower-priority processors is also increased. The decision of what kind of batching to use should be made by weighing the relative importance of the processor compared to the rest of the system. If an optimization analysis has shown that the initialization or termination calculations should be placed inside the loop, there is clearly no point in going in for excessive batching. The efficiency is not there to be gained.[5]

4.5.2. Queue Length Regulation

Of the various schemes described above, the processing of a fixed number of entries is the poorest. There is no guarantee that there will be that many entries on the queue. If it is in our interest to minimize the σ of the processor by attempting to regularize the number of entries it will process, it is better done by withholding queue entries. This can be done by a centralized scheduler, but not readily by the highly implicit shared-queue scheme. What we are trying to achieve by regulating the queue length is to trade the average processing time against the deviation in processing time. By reducing the deviation, we make scheduling easier but reduce efficiency.

Queue lengths can be implicitly controlled by the original partition of processors chosen. A large processor (i.e., one that tends to take a long time) tends to increase the lengths of the output queues of the processors that feed it—that is, it tends to have a long input queue. Large partitions therefore lead to a few long queues, while fine partitions lead to many small queues.

---

[5] This can be tricky. Note that the decision to place the initialization or termination calculations inside or outside the loop depended upon the value of the looping probability. That probability is after all an expression of the number of items on the queue, which is what we are trying to decide. The analysis has to be performed parametrically, varying P and determining which should be placed where. In general, for each value of P we have a linear programming problem that will tell us the value of the optimum distribution of initialization and termination calculations. It is the parametric programming problem that we wish to solve here.

Since each queue must be administered and requires unique administration areas, fragmenting the queues tends to increase space. Since space is one of the commodities whose use must be scheduled, fragmenting may make scheduling easier from the point of view of time but more difficult from the point of view of space.

4.5.3. Dedicated Systems

The queue lengths for dedicated systems with base-sequence programs and rudimentary schedulers are relatively easy to optimize. They are deter-minded (as averages) by the time that will be allocated to each processor in the base-sequence schedule for the average system cycle. Given the system cycle length, and the number of times the particular processor will appear in that cycle, as well as the rate of generation of queue entries (usually deter-mined from the input statistics), the number of items on queue can be deter-mined. The usual practice is to clear all entries on the queue before return-ing to the base sequence. The processor partition and the way it is scheduled in the base sequence should be such that under peak loading conditions there is always at least (statistically) one item on the queue to be processed. This avoids needless examinations of empty queues under peak loading. If the probability of having one item on a queue is not sufficiently high, a less frequent schedule should be used for that processor, assuming that this is consistent with priority and delay requirements.

4.5.4. Generalized Systems

The question of queue batching doctrine for generalized systems seems to evoke as many philosophies as there are system designers. While there may be long discussions as to what is the optimum approach in any particular instance, in most cases, the designer (perhaps out of desperation) adopts the simple practice of clearing the queue in its entirety or processing one at a time—either of which is simple to mechanize—foregoing the possibility of greater potential efficiency that could be afforded through the use of a more elegant doctrine.

4.6. Priorities and Queues

Let us now restrict ourselves to examining one level at a time. At any given level, we can look upon the tasks to be performed and associate with each a priority which is generally related to the externally imposed priorities. The implementation of priorities is primarily a matter of getting the higher-priority tasks to be processed before the lower-priority tasks. There are several bad ways to do this, and several good ways, depending on the context.

4.6.1. Searching

The conceptually simpler way to handle variable priorities is to place a priority tag on each task descriptor in the queue. The processor then examines the whole queue, processing first the highest-priority item, then the next-lower-priority item, etc. This is inherently bad if the queues are long. For one thing, the processor will make many passes over the queue, only to find that the entry is not for the task priority being processed at the moment. For another, if a task for the priority being examined is not found, the system will have made a pass through the queue without accomplishing anything. The longer the queues, the worse this becomes. If the queues are so long that they cannot be stored in the main memory, this approach can lead to such a drastic overload and wasteful processing that the system may not work at all. The overall effect is to induce a term in the processing load equations that is of the order of the second or third power of the queue length.

4.6.2. Inserting and Linking

A somewhat better approach is to insert the entry into the proper place in the queue. There are two ways in which this can be done: by pushing down the lower-priority queue entries or by linking. In both cases, the task processor will not have to waste as much time re-examining the queue (except if another entry has been placed on the queue while the present entry was being processed) as it did before. Again, there is a queue length dependency, but it tends to be of the order of the second power. The queue entry to be processed is always taken from the top. The only wasted time from the point of view of the processor is the explicit examination of the priority. Pushing the queue entries around, however, is wasteful and leads to excessive queue administration. The longer the queue the more items will have to be pushed down. Again, we are imposing an extra burden at a time when the system can ill afford it. The linking approach is to string queue entries in much the same way that we allocate blocks of memory in dynamic space. To insert a new entry (say, X) in the queue, say, after A, we modify A's pointer to the address of entry X, whose pointer is set to the address of B. Typically, this scheme doubles the amount of space used for queues. This scheme is not as sensitive to queue length as the push-down scheme since only the higher-priority queue items must be examined to find the right place on the queue.

4.6.3. Separate Queues

The simplest way is to have a different queue for each priority. Queue entries need not contain priority data, as priority is implicit in the fact that the entry is on the particular queue. The queue need not be examined for either processing or for queue insertion. There is no strong queue length dependency, and the system is not penalized when the queues are long. The weakness of the scheme lies in the fact that there may be many priority levels associated with a given processor. There is a certain amount of overhead processing associated with each queue, no matter what its length, and this scheme increases the number of queues in the system. We have traded queue length for an increase in the number of queues. In most systems, in which there are only three or four external priority levels, this simple approach is fruitful.

4.7. Queue Storage and Overflow

4.7.1. Queue Storage

The queues must be stored someplace. Where they are stored and how space is allocated to the queues is a basic system design question. Queues can be stored as fixed tables, in dynamic space, as linked lists, or as linked lists within dynamic space.

The simplest example of a fixed table storage for queues are those which are normally not considered queues at all, that is, fixed schedule tables. But this is a trivial case, and we shall consider only those cases in which the queue length is not known *a priori*.

It is possible to allocate a fixed space for queues. A fixed area is set aside for each queue in the system. The size of the area is chosen on the basis of the average number of queue entries that will build up during processing intervals (e.g., a system cycle) and a judicious number of σs. Since the cycle length and the queue length are interdependent (see Chapter 13), this can be tougher analytically than it might appear to be. It is prudent to design the system such that it is possible to modify the number of entries allowed for each queue without reprogramming. The final selection of the number of queue entries for each queue may not be done till after some experience has been gained with the system—i.e., the queue length is a "tuning" factor. Fixed queues have many of the disadvantages of fixed buffers. A fixed queue table is obviously established as a circulating table. That is, we maintain separate pointers for the bottom and the top of the queue. Each new entry is placed on the current bottom and processing takes place from the current top. Circulating schemes like this are risky. More than one system has blown up because a processor placing entries on the current "bottom" of the queue inadvertently overwrote the current top.

The fixed queue scheme, despite its dangers, is not without advantages. It is much easier to store the queue for recovery (see Chapter 12, Section 6). Indexing and examination of entries is simpler. In fact, all the advantages of fixed tables accrue to us. Space, however, is wasted, since it is allocated for the worst-case situation. However, space is not wasted under heavy load, and in fact, the simpler administration required for fixed-length queue tables can result in less space under heavy load than a dynamic queue storage scheme.

As with buffers, queues can be extended to some form of dynamic space, leading to a fixed-plus-dynamic scheme similar to that used for buffers, with similar advantages and disadvantages. The queues can be placed in dynamic space proper, allocating a number of queue entries per block. Furthermore, each queue entry could be a self-contained, small block within dynamic space (e.g., a 16-character block), containing its own link to the next entry on the queue. With this, all the possibilities of shared and multiple pools can be applied.

If the total number of queue entries is insufficient to warrant a separate queue memory pool, and if there are advantages to be gained by having explicit links for queue entries, they can be stored as linked lists within dynamic space. Note that it is not normally necessary to have explicit links between queue entries. The fact that a given entry follows another implies that it is to be next in sequence. However, we saw in the case of drum and disc scheduling that it was convenient to be able to link and unlink queue entries. If the queue contains the data themselves, rather than just data descriptors, it is obvious that we are better off linking and unlinking than we are moving the queue entries about. While linked queues take additional space for the links, moving queue entries takes more space than might be supposed. There is, after all, an overlapping time interval during which the queue entry exists in two places. This simultaneous existence represents wasted space. If, for whatever reasons, it is necessary to insert queue entries into the middle of existing queues, the advantages of linked lists are again obvious. We pay for these advantages by more processing—for indexing, for linking, and for storing the queue entries on other media. If linked lists are used within dynamically allocated space, the administrative problems and the processing for indexing queue entries are compounded.

4.7.2. Queue Overflow

Queue overflow is to be avoided at all costs. It is generally preferable to curtail almost any other activity in order to free space than to allow the queues to go into overflow storage. Queue space should be given priority over data space. It may even be preferable to force data out of memory into overflow storage rather than to allow processing queues to go into overflow storage.

The logical integrity of the system is maintained by the queues. The system is lost when the queues are lost. Almost all operations in the system require the examination and manipulation of queue entries. In particular, if main memory has been so overloaded that data are out on bulk memory, recovery from the overflow will require the examination of the corresponding queue entries. If these must also be retrieved from outlying storage, the recovery time is further extended.

The queue overflow problem first manifests itself when a new entry must be placed on a queue. It is to be placed at the end of the queue, which unfortunately is on some outlying memory. This means that the memory block must be fetched, the entry made, and the block returned to that medium. Queue entries are initiated at many different priority levels. If the queue entries are contained in overflow storage, the processor that terminates its operation by placing the queue entry on the input queue of the next processor or the scheduler is blocked until the queue entry has been made and verified. This could take two revolutions of a drum, during which time, if the processor is a high-priority processor, the system is idle. Overflow occurs under high load conditions, yet the system is idle, leading to still further aggravated overflow. If enough queue entries have to be made by high-priority processors on overflow storage, the system will block itself and end up processing next to nothing. The result is a rapid, catastrophic degradation of the system throughput. The system can be choked to the point where there is not enough space available to bring in the queue blocks for modification.

If the system does not collapse totally, and if it is still possible to continue processing while placing queue entries in overflow space, the overflow problem is not solved when the main-memory-resident queues dry up and space is again available. New queue entries must still be placed onto overflow storage until all queue entries that are out there have been recovered. A stable situation can occur in which the system throughput drops following a burst which led to queue overflow, and never recovers. On the other hand, since queue entries are apt to be small, the recovery of a single entry is likely to bring back several entries. This helps somewhat but does not completely mitigate the problems associated with queue overflow.

We see from this the virtue of keeping queue entries small and avoiding data on the queue unless FIFO ordering can be ignored in overflow. If FIFO order can be ignored during and following overflow, the majority of these recovery problems do not occur.

Despite our best intentions to avoid queue overflow, it can still occur. Consequently, overflow and overflow recovery procedures must still be programmed, no matter how odious the performance of the system—for some performance is better than none. It is particularly important to give the operator warning that queue overflow may occur. He can elect to drain data, destroy data, or perhaps pick up the phone and tell those guys out there to lay off.

Just as not all data which are in space have equal priority with respect to avoiding overflow, not all queue entries are equally affected. It may be possible to relinquish FIFO for some queue entries. Some queues may be stored on outlying memories as a normal course of events—for example, the queues set up within a program by a user, or a queue that describes spooling runs, etc. In these cases, queue overflow is just another brand of memory overflow. It is the queues on which the logical integrity of the system is based that will cause the system to collapse if they are forced to overflow. Therefore, general overflow procedures can proceed from the destruction of dispensible data through usurpation of low-priority data, high-priority data, FIFO-mandatory data, low-priority queues, high-priority queues, and finally FIFO-mandatory queues. If, with all the overflow-preventive measures that should be built into the system, and the many alarms that will have sounded, the operator has not been able to prevent the overflow of FIFO-mandatory queues, the system is facing a true overload and can be expected to crash.

5. FILE MANAGEMENT

5.1. Basic Problems

A **file** is to space what a processor is to a computer. A file is a body of data rather than a collection of memory locations. A particular file may have many different existences: it may originate on paper tape, be converted to magnetic tape via a transitory existence in core, go to a drum, reside on disc, and end up as printed characters. The decision of where a particular file may momentarily reside is often not controlled directly by the job, but by the executive. Having taken on this responsibility, the executive must assure that the proper file is available in the proper form whenever a job calls for it.

A file is subdivided into **records**, which are further subdivided into characters. The record is usually the smallest unit of a file that may be retrieved or modified directly, which is to say that the retrieval of a portion of the record is tantamount to the retrieval of the whole record. Thus, a physical record such as a tape block or a drum block cannot be retrieved or written in part.

The organization and management of files centers about a four-way barter among access delay, access processing time, modification processing time, and the space taken up by the file on the various media. If we wish to obtain speedy retrieval, it will be at a cost of high processing or memory wastage. If the file is easy to retrieve, it will be difficult to modify. If the file is compact, processing time or access delay will suffer.

There are many different ways to organize a file. Some of these favor ease of processing, others compactness, and still others delay. Each particular file organization has its own advantages with respect to the characteristics discussed above.

A record is accessed by a name or a **key**. A key is any contiguous set of characters, usually in a prescribed field within a record. The key of a file could be a particular record within that file. Key retrieval is done by comparison of the key on the record to a search key. The record name could be a key within the record. To illustrate: John Doe's income tax return could be accessed by the key "John Doe." A key could be "drum block 23," which in turn could be the name of the place where an altogether different record is stored. Neither file names nor keys need be locally unique—they can be reproduced in several different jobs or within several different files of the same job. Consequently, the file management processor must have a means of assigning names to files and destroying such names when they are no longer needed lest the system run out of names.

5.2. File Structures

5.2.1. Sequential Files

A sequential file organization is the simple stringing of records at consecutive addresses of the storage media. Consecutive records on tape are the archtype of the sequential organization. In a similar way, records can be stored at successive addresses on a drum or disc. In most sequentially ordered files, the ordering of the records will not be simply the order in which the records were created. Usually the records will be sorted in the order of one or more keys: alphabetically, numerically, by street number, zip code, social security number, etc. The ordering can be nested: e.g., street order within zip code, given name within surname, bank number within social security number, etc.

The primary virtue of a sequential file organization is conceptual simplicity. A secondary virtue, for small files with simple key structures, is the ease with which keys can be searched. In most other respects the simple sequential organization is useless for large files. To see the limitations of sequential files, we must consider two things: how a record is to be retrieved and how a record is to be created, destroyed, or modified.

If the key is the address of the record, retrieval is trivial. It may be that there is a simple relation between the address of the record and its original position in the file. For example, every record takes three sectors and the file starts with sector 16, track 12, on disc 4. To obtain the 57th record we multiply 57 by 3 and add the base address of the file. In other cases we may have to find the residue of a record sequence position with respect to some number, do a few shifts, additions, etc., in order to obtain its address.

If the key is the contents of some field within the record, we can find all records satisfying that key by an exhaustive examination of the records in sequence. Finding a match between the specified key and the record field, we go to the next nested key, until we have obtained all the records that satisfy the specified keys. While this may be adequate for small files, it becomes intolerable for large files. The situation for larger files can be improved by searching for several keys simultaneously and foregoing the FIFO order of the retrieval requests. Philosophically, it is similar to the way in which we schedule a tape. We know the position of the "head" with respect to the file, e.g., it is at "Jones." Since the search is proceeding, say, in collating order, we schedule for the present pass all requests for names having a higher position than "Jones." In a single pass through the file, then, we can retrieve as many requests as came in while the pass was in progress. To do this, we must order the requests in the same manner as the file is ordered.

If the file is large, and the requests relatively sparse, an inordinate amount of time will be spent examining records which are not interesting. The number of such examinations is proportional to the file length and inversely proportional to the number of simultaneous requests being made. To reduce the number of unnecessary retrievals, we must find a better way of obtaining the proper position by means of the key. Binary halving, discussed in Chapter 6 (page 270), is one method of doing this. The file is tested near the middle and the most significant bit of the key tells us which half should be tried next. This is repeated with the next bit, each test cutting the file in half again. At the final bit of the key, the record has either been found or found not to exist.

Several assumptions are inherent in using a binary halving technique. It is assumed that the distributions of keys with requests are uniform. Key distribution uniformity implies that "Zwyan X. Zwizz" is as likely a name as "Ethan Shedley." This is patently nonsensical. Uniform distribution of requests assumes that every record in the file, even if they are uniformly distributed, is requested with equal frequency. Thus, it is assumed that a military file would be searched for the serial numbers of civil war veterans with the same frequency as for those of more recent veterans.

A knowledge of the bunching of the file and the distributions of requests allows us to be more precise about retrieval based on keys, thereby reducing the number of ineffectual fetches. The relation between the key and the position of the record in the file is considered as if it were a function. That is, the key or part of it is treated as a number. A function of that number is calculated which approximates the position of the record in the file. By retrieving *that* record we can determine if the needed file is further along the file or further back. A second function, such as the derivative of the first function, can be used for the next test. Finally, we can use interpolation and then sequential searching to find the actual record.

The frequency of the retrieval requests can be used to eliminate processing or to sharpen up the scheme used to find the initial position. For example, in a high-frequency region of the file, it might pay to use a table rather than an algebraic function.

Having ameliorated the problems of retrieval, we are still faced with the problems of updating the file. We can see just how difficult this can be by again using the tape as a model. If we wish to destroy a record, we will leave gaps in the file, or else be required to push up all entries to fill the gap. If we wish to insert records, we will have to push the file down. Similarly, the extension of a record requires that we push other records down, and the contraction requires that we push the records up. This is done on tape by recopying the tape. Again, batching can aid us. We can save the changes, creating an ordered file of new records, destroying or marking as invalid the old records. If the record is not found on the main file, the change file is examined. When enough changes have been made to warrant restructuring the file, the change file is sorted in the proper order and merged with the old file. Discarded entries are eliminated and the entire file is recopied onto the storage media in proper order.

The problems of sequential files begin to become intolerable when we have large files that must be accessed on the basis of more than one key. It is unlikely that the relation between the different keys will help us. As an example, there is little or no correlation between zip code and social security number, or between street number and name. In some special cases a nice relation may exist, so that the sequential file organization can be extended to two, three, or more keys. For example, if the file contains the elevation of geographic points, a sequential file organization based on geographic coordinates can be effective. In such cases, the search function is a function of two or more variables. Since nice functional relations between keys do not usually exist, multiple keys present a problem. One way, is to resort the file according to the desired key. If there are enough requests for two different keys, we can keep multiple copies of the file. This, however, increases the updating problem.

Files in which twenty or more keys can be used independently or in concert are not unusual. A national data bank might allow thousands of different keys to be used. If one considers files in which each record consists of several thousand characters, and in which there are tens of millions of records, the inadequacies of sequential files become apparent.

5.2.2. Indirect Methods

In **randomly organized files**, the records themselves are stored in the arbitrary locations assigned by the memory management processor. It is clear that there is no need to push things around if records are modified. The creation of new records is equivalent to assigning a new block of space. The destruction of a record is done by returning the memory block to the pool.

While these problems have been solved, there now appears to be a retrieval problem. The retrieval problem is solved through the use of dictionaries or functional calculations.

We can establish a table consisting of ordered keys called a **dictionary**. Associated with each key is the address at which the record is to be found. Since many keys can be stored in one block, this sequential file is relatively small. The same file search procedures can be used for the dictionary as were used for sequential files. This approach is sometimes called an **indexed sequential** file structure. Since keys take up less room than records, we can afford to have several sets of sequentially keyed dictionary files or cross-indexes.

If a file is created or destroyed, the dictionary is modified. If there are several dictionaries, each must be modified to reflect the changes in the file.

One error made in the design of files is to forget about the number of accesses that may be needed for the dictionary. The fact that a block will contain several entries reduces the number of fetches. In particular, it makes a calculated address more attractive. The key is again used as the variable in a function. The value calculated, however, is the sequential location of the block in which the dictionary entry is to be found. Since the block contains many entries, the probability of obtaining it on the first try is higher than if we had sequentially stored records.

It is possible to use a table as the first step in finding the approximate location of a record. The most significant bit of the key is used as an index of the table, which in turn points to the approximate location of the record. If the dictionary is large, the cost of searching for the key in the dictionary itself may be odious. One can then treat the dictionary as a set of records, store those blocks randomly, thereby alleviating the dictionary updating problem. The table then becomes the first level of the dictionary, which again can be treated as a sequential file. In this way, a tree structured file can be organized in which keys or parts of them point to yet more detailed keys, which finally point to the actual records. As more levels are added, the *minimum* number of fetches is *increased*, but the *average and maximum* numbers of fetches are *decreased*. Furthermore, as levels are added, the updating problem becomes tougher.

5.2.3. Nonmonotonic Methods

The functional relation between the key and the location or approximate location of the file discussed above was implicitly assumed to be monotonic. The function was used to improve the search by taking advantage of local bunching of keys. However, there is no need to use a monotonic function. What is sought is a mapping of the numerical value of part of the key onto addresses. Those addresses could either be of dictionary entries or of the actual records. If the function is not monotonic (e.g., a random but unique mapping), we shall have to forego the possibility of searching from an approximately derived location. The function must lead us directly to the record or dictionary block sought. If the distribution of keys were truly uniform, this would be simple. An arbitrary function would be calculated that uniquely mapped the, say, 64 bits of the key onto a 16-bit block address. This might mean that some blocks would never be used since no key value would yield those particular block addresses. The cost then is a certain memory wastage. It is possible to perform this kind of mapping even if the keys are not uniformly distributed. Again, a certain amount of memory may be wasted.

While each key produces a unique address, it is not necessarily true that a given address is accessible by only one key. There could be several keys that produce the same address. Let us assume that we are performing this kind of key-to-address conversion in order to obtain a dictionary entry, at whatever level that dictionary might be. Two keys point to the same entry. In this case, the entry in the dictionary does not point to the record, but to a list of dictionary entries which satisfy the same key. If the function is properly chosen, the memory wasted and the number of multiple entries will be minimized. Again, we obtain rapid access at the cost of a difficult problem when we wish to change keys or records.

5.2.4. Linked Lists and Inverted Lists

As the number of possible keys is increased, the space for the dictionaries begins to approach or exceeds the space taken up by the data. A totally different approach can be taken in which the data are stored randomly but are still organized sequentially with respect to specified keys. In much the same way that blocks in dynamic space pointed to the next block in the chain, records can be linked according to the order of a key. Associated with each key there will be a pointer to the record that contains the next key in the sequence. This would at first seem to be a giant step backward, for in order to find a record we would have to painfully crawl down the list, fetching each block in succession until the one with the desired key was found. There is no need to limit ourselves to a single thread of this sort. We could establish chains of links for every key or key value of interest. A given record, then, could contain N pointers, corresponding to N different keys. The advantage of this method is that records that do not contain a particular key are bypassed in that list. If there are many keys (e.g., 10,000), but any one record will have only a few of these, or the number of records corresponding to a particular key is small, the sequential search through the key is not so painful after all. The cost then is in the extra space required for the links.

Retrieval is done by using the key type to find the address of the first record having that key. We can number the keys such as ADDRESS = 1, ZIP CØDE = 2, NAME = 3, STATE = 4, etc., and request the retrieval on the basis of the number corresponding to that key. Alternatively, we can use the key description (e.g., "Address," "Zip Code," etc.) as a key to a table which is searched to determine the beginning address of the chain corresponding to that kind of key. The number of fetches can be reduced by establishing a dictionary for the elements in the chain. Thus, if there are 90,000 different zip codes for a file of 200,000,000 names, we could establish 90,000 separate lists, one for each zip code. If all records that had zip codes as keys were linked into one list, it would be 200,000,000 records long. We see, therefore, that as we increase the number of separate lists, we decrease their length. If we continue in this fashion, we have a large dictionary, and all lists are exactly one record long. We are then back to the random file structure with as many dictionaries as there are keys.

This file structure is called an **inverted list**. Since every key is indexed, and associated with every value of every key is a list of all records that satisfy that key, it is no longer necessary to look at the record. The first key's dictionary is searched to produce a list of records that satisfy that key value. The second key's dictionary is then searched to produce another list of records that satisfy it. The intersection of these two lists is smaller yet. Continuing in this manner, we finally obtain only those record addresses that satisfy all the key values. At that point, those records only are fetched. If, as is usually the case, the dictionaries themselves must be stored on the same media as the records, the number of fetches for a totally inverted list could substantially exceed the number required by a less elegant scheme.

Linked lists are difficult to administer. Every record change requires that multiple links in both directions be modified. This means that both forward and backward pointers are needed. Furthermore, if an inverted or partially inverted structure is used, a means for getting back to the dictionary block is needed as well. Therefore, not only must the dictionaries point to the record, but the record must point to every dictionary that refers to it. If these multiple pointers are not provided, updating a record, removing a record, or creating a record could require long sequential searches.

5.3. File Control

5.3.1. File Names and Directories

A file record is accessed by name. The name is usually local to the job or the processor making the file request. The name may not be unique. Ultimately, there is a level of indirect naming at which the "name" is the location of the file in a physical memory. But since this may change from moment to moment, any given file may have several names, one for each device in which it may reside during the course of a job. The maintenance of these names at each level of storage is a task of the file control processor. The collection of such lists of names is called the **directory**.

Files are in a constant state of modification and consequently their space requirements may change from moment to moment. The request for additional space as well as the release of space is ordered by the file processor and executed by the storage allocation processor. At some point in the history of a job, file names must be purged by the file processor. If they were not, the system would quickly be glutted with stale names. One way of obtaining implicit file name purging is to let the file name be the concatenation of the storage medium addresses it uses. Once that block of storage is released, its name, or rather, address, is also released.

5.3.2. File States

The file control processor keeps track of the location of the most recent copy of the file in each medium in which the file appears. Depending on the method used for storage control, duplicate copies of a particular file may have simultaneous existence on the same medium. For example, assume that a file is extended by the addition of several words within the file. A new copy of the file will be created in core, that copy transmitted to the outlying media, as required, and only after the copy has been successfully transmitted and verified will the old copy be deleted. The file then has a transitory dual existence. The file processor must maintain the state of the file, and every copy thereof, on every medium, so that if a failure were to occur at any time, the most recent, reliable copy of the file would still be available upon recovery. The states of a file that is being updated are:

1. File is being modified (copy in core being changed).
2. Modification completed.
3. Space for new copy on medium X requested.
4. Space granted.
5. Address of file placed in temporary directory.
6. Placement verified.
7. New copy transmitted to medium X.
8. Transmission verified.
9. Release of old file space on medium X requested.
10. Release verified.
11. Old file name marked stale on directory.
12. New file name installed in directory.
13. Old file name purged.
14. File transaction completed.

The reason for step 6 is that the directory itself may be located on a different medium—and verification of the directory change may be required as well. Some of the above steps may be implicit. For example, most of the verifications can be implemented by re-entering the program through a special entrance appropriate to what it is that must be verified. The particular states of the file may vary from system to system. The mechanization can be explicit by having an actual state counter, or may be implicit by the existence of a file name on a file processing queue.

5.3.3. File Security

A file security hierarchy may be superimposed on the file management processor. In large complex systems, not all files may be equally accessible. A file may have several restrictions, such as:

Directory restrictions: Only users with appropriate authority will see the file listed in the directory. All other users will not be aware of the file's existence.

Execution restriction: The file may be executed only by those with appropriate authority. Nothing else may be done with the file. This applies to program files.

Listing restriction: The file may be listed only by those users with appropriate authority.

Copy restrictions: The file may be copied or transferred to other media only by authorized users.

Modify restriction: Only users with appropriate authority are allowed to modify the file.

There may be a record for each file that specifies the passwords or authority level of other users and the kinds of things they can do with the file. Typically, that record will also have security restrictions. One would expect that the file that contained the passwords of the users that are allowed to modify the passwords would require the highest authority.

6. COMMUNICATIONS

6.1. General Objectives and Elements

Communication has increasingly become part of every computer complex. The economies of scale, reduced operational costs, increased viability, and reduced hardware and software redundancy contribute to the desirability of centralized computer complexes. If the conveniences of a local processing facility are to be retained while obtaining the benefits of the centralized complex, some means of communication must be supplied between the outlying terminals and the complex. In some complexes, communication is the main or one of the major functions. This is obvious for a communications system, but less obvious for a reservation or stock quotation system. Communication functions tend to have higher urgencies and higher priorities than other processing functions. In most cases this is due to the cost of lines and the impatience of man. In popular terms, communication functions operate in "real time."

Since most communication functions appearing in a noncommunications system can be recognized as parts of what appears within a communications system, it is expedient to examine communications systems *per se*. The communication functions of a noncommunications system are often referred to as **front-end** functions of the system. The associated processors may be grouped into explicit communications computers, or may merely be higher-level programs within a main computer or complex.

A model of a typical communications system is shown in Figure 10.11. Messages enter the system through line termination units. They convert the incoming bit stream into discrete characters and deposit them into the input buffers for that line. The messages are analyzed and perhaps converted to a uniform internal code and format by the input processor. They then go to the message input processor, where further analysis is done to determine the subsequent disposition of the message. The message input processor may store a copy of the message in one or more places. It may go to an **in-transit**

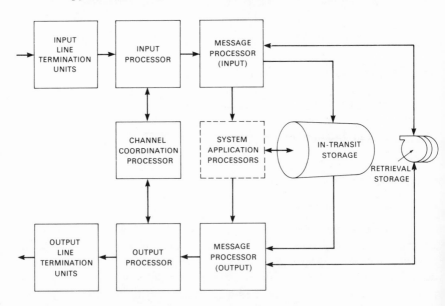

Figure 10.11. Communication functions.

storage area, typically on a disc or drum, where it will be queued until the appropriate outgoing line is free. It may be written onto a retrieval storage unit if the system is such that a message originator must be able to request a copy of a previously transmitted message. Alternatively, it may go directly to the message output processor if the message priority is high enough.

We can interpose the noncommunication functions between the message input and the message output processors, as shown in Figure 10.11.

In a reservation system, the input message may be a request for an available seat, car, or room, which is then manipulated by the reservation processors to produce the output message. In the general sense, the difference between a communications system and a noncommunications system is a matter of degree rather than kind.

The message output processor schedules messages for output on the appropriate lines as determined from information explicitly in the message or implicit in the source of the message. A copy of that message may again go to retrieval storage. The message processor gives the message to the output processor, which converts it to the proper code and format. Finally, the line termination unit converts the parallel characters into a bit stream.

We note that there is a processor interposed between the input and output processors. Communication is a bidirectional process. Many systems require some form of coordination between the input and the output. In addition to these functions, we have operator procedures, the system executive functions, and the complete gamut of syntactic processors common to most systems.

6.2. Lines and Signaling

6.2.1. Synchronous Transmissions

Two basic modes of transmission are used in communications systems; synchronous and asynchronous. In synchronous transmission, the incoming character is a stream of bits of equal length. Typically 5-, 6-, 7-, and 8-bit codes are used. Given the first bit of a message, and a code length of n bits, every nth bit is assumed to delimit a new character. Once it is known where the first character in the message starts, it is easy to distinguish successive characters. However, some means of synchronizing the line must be provided. A special character, the **synch character**, precedes the transmission. A number of such characters will be sent before the actual message starts.

The line termination unit detects the synch characters and establishes sychronization, so that when the actual characters come, they will be properly detected. Another function commonly embodied in the input line termination unit is the elimination of synch characters, so that the input buffer will not constantly be filled with synch characters that have only to be discarded.

The outgoing line termination unit may insert synch characters on command of the output processor.

If characters should be garbled, or if transmission should be interrupted, synchronization may be lost. This means that new synch characters must be transmitted. Synchronous lines are efficient from the point of view of line utilization, but are not applicable to noisy lines, since each error may require the retransmission of all or a part of the message.

6.2.2. Asynchronous Transmission

In asynchronous transmission, the synchronization information is contained in each character. The typical structure is shown in Figure 10.12. The idle line is interrupted by a start signal which is as long as a data bit. The length of the start polarity is fixed for the line. The conclusion of the start polarity is followed by a predetermined number of bits that make up the character. They are in turn followed by a stop polarity, which is 1.42 times as long as a data pulse. The stop polarity could be continued into another idle-line polarity or followed immediately by a new start polarity. The predetermined pattern allows the input line termination unit to synchronize on that character. The unit samples the line at a frequency which is some odd multiple of the bit frequency, and thereby determines if a start polarity has been received. It strips off all but the data and parity bits, which are assembled into characters and then relayed to the input buffers. Similarly, the output unit converts the character into a sequential stream of bits with the appropriate start and stop polarities for that line. It is instructive to note that the actual pulses received by the line termination unit are typically distorted.

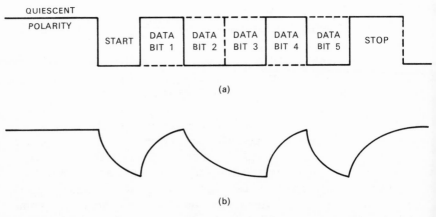

(a)

(b)

Figure 10.12. Asynchronous transmission: (a) ideal asynchronous transmission; (b) real asynchronous signal.

They appear more like those shown in Figure 10.12b than those shown in Figure 10.12a. Asynchronous transmission, while using more bits per character, does allow the repetition of a single character at a time. It has the further and more important advantage of not losing synchronization if a single character or any part thereof is lost. It originated with manual tele-printer transmission, where the sender could not be assumed to maintain synchronism.

6.2.3. Other Modes, Codes, and Mixed Modes

Many other forms of transmission can be used. Among the more common (other than the standard asynchronous and synchronous transmissions) are various multiple-line schemes. For example, two lines can be used, one providing the synchronization information and the other providing the data. Similarly, multiple lines may be used that transmit the character in parallel. The parity (odd or even) can be chosen such that there is at least one bit that differs from the idle polarity.

While it is possible to intermix synchronous and asynchronous trans-mission modes or 5-bit and 8-bit codes on the same lines, it is almost never done. The reason is the increased cost in the line termination units and input processing. Sychronization is no longer a matter of detecting character delimiters. It may require extensive bit-by-bit processing to determine what the proper code and format is. While it is not too difficult to detect the difference between asynchronous and synchronous transmissions when there is no distortion, the inevitability of noise makes this a haphazard procedure.

Similarly, different speeds of transmission are not intermixed on the same line. Consider the confusion that could occur if a formerly 1200-baud synchronous line were suddenly to start transmitting at 600 baud. Where there is an advantage to using a line for different modes, codes, and speeds, it is usually done by prearrangement. The transmitter informs the receiver that a mode shift will occur following a certain distinguishing character, or follow-ing the acknowledgment of the mode shift request by the receiver. It is then up to the receiver to make what changes he must, either manually or auto-matically, to accommodate the shift. Without this, the cost of input processing will be inordinate.

6.2.4. Controlled and Uncontrolled Transmission

Controlled transmissions are those that are elicited by the receiver. **Uncontrolled transmissions** are those that are initiated by the transmitter. A normal telephone is uncontrolled, as we cannot dictate who is going to call us, or when. Looking into a mailbox, on the other hand, is a form of con-trolled transmission, for we can ignore its content for as long as we wish and examine it at leisure.

Polling is a form of transmission control. Each outlying station is polled by a special message which requests the transmitter to supply a message if there is one. If there is one, the message is transmitted. If not, a nonmessage indication is provided. Polling is used to advantage when several terminals share a single line in order to reduce line costs. As an example, a banking system may have several hundred teller stations attached to the same physical line. Each teller may make an inquiry or entry every three minutes. The total transmission time for each inquiry might be only a few hundred milliseconds. The communication processor transmits a polling message to each station in turn. Each station contains hardware (or software) that allows it to determine if that polling request is intended for it. If the request is so intended, and if the station has something to transmit, it will do so; otherwise the request will be acknowledged or ignored as appropriate to the doctrine implemented. The polling system is a communication bus and has all the advantages and disadvantages of bussed structures.

Controlled transmission may be used for high-speed transmission lines that would otherwise require many buffer blocks. It may be required by a quirk of the outlying equipment, with no particular processing or line efficiency advantage. The central characteristic of controlled transmission is that the receiver knows that a message is coming. It requires more complex hardware and processing. On the other hand, the fact that the transmission can be predicted allows the use of anticipatory processing and the concomitant placement of the processing at lower priority levels.

Uncontrolled transmission is just that. A message may appear at any moment. The first time that we are aware of the message's existence is the appearance of its first character. Clearly, then, uncontrolled transmission requires higher-priority processing and affords fewer opportunities for anticipatory processing. The advantage of uncontrolled transmissions is the simplicity of the terminals. In a controlled transmission, the outlying terminal must have some sort of logic (or "stunt box") that allows it to provide the proper responses to the message requests. The uncontrolled terminal needs no such equipment. The full burden of accepting the message without dropping any characters falls to the communication processor.

There is a continuum of transmission procedures between the totally controlled and the totally uncontrolled. So-called uncontrolled lines may be turned off by transmitting appropriate messages such as "WAIT BEFØRE FURTHER TRANSMISSIØNS." Similarly, a "controlled line" may have a variability of several milliseconds or seconds before the message actually starts.

Controlled and uncontrolled transmissions are rarely intermixed on the same line. To allow one terminal of several to transmit at will when all other terminals on the same line transmit only upon request would be chaotic.

6.3. Message Structure

There are almost as many message structures as there are pieces of communications gear, communication networks, and computers. However, a general structure is common to most messages. It is shown in Figure 10.13. Each entry between a pair of double lines denotes a field that may exist in a message. These entries can consist of one character, a predetermined number of characters, or a variable number of characters. The double lines denote additional delimiters which may or may not be present. Very few messages are as complex as the generic structure shown here.

6.3.1. Premessage Control

This field is sometimes called a preamble field. It occurs mostly on message output and may not appear explicitly at the receiving device. This field could contain synchronization characters, or a sequence of characters required to activate the receiving device.

6.3.2. Start of Message (SOM)

The SOM may be a single character. Some codes do not have a special SOM character. A sequence of characters is used instead. "ZCZC" is common. It is selected as being highly improbable within the text of a natural message. The SOM is the first field at which the message is said to begin. If a multicharacter SOM is used, the system should be designed to allow at least one of the characters to be garbled.

6.3.3. Start of Header (SOH)

Again, a special character may be used if available. If not, a special sequence, say, consisting of a number of carriage returns and line feeds may be used to denote the beginning of the header. The **header** is that part of the message which must be analyzed to determine the disposition of the message. It contains addressing data, status, priority, etc. The start and end of header are important as they delimit the part of the message requiring detailed analysis.

6.3.4. Message Control Data

The message control data are a grab bag of information relating to the message. They may include the time of origin, the sequence number of the message on the given line, the line number, the originator identification, priority, security, etc. Alternatively, each of these functions may be contained in separate fields within the header.

6.3.5. Start of Routing Indicators (SRI)

The SRI is a delimiter that specifies that routing data are to follow. Routing data are to be distinguished from address data. The routing

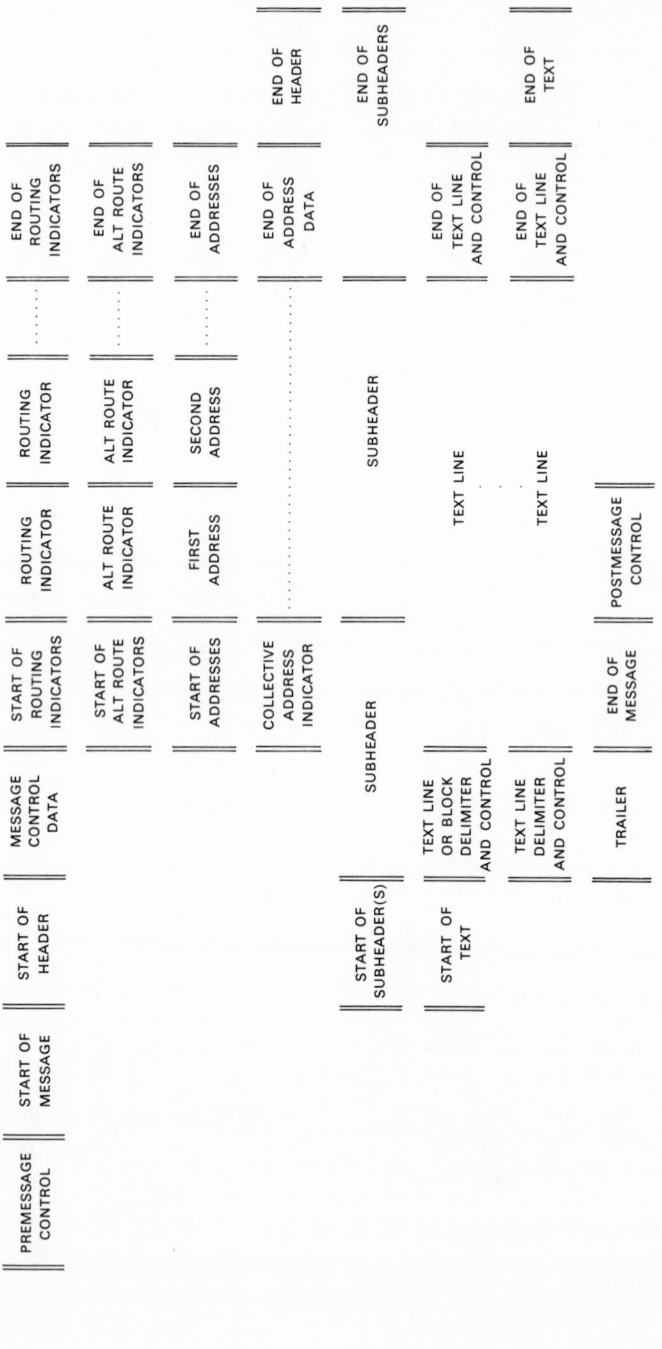

Figure 10.13. General message structure.

information specifies the path that the message will take, while address data specify the ultimate destination of the message. Thus, we might wish to transmit a message to DJAKARTA via PARIS. "PARIS" is a routing indicator while "DJAKARTA" is an address. A routing indicator can also be an address and *vice versa*.

The possibility of having several routing indicators is shown. These can be used either to dictate a detailed path for the message, or more often to indicate that the message is to be routed to all of these intermediate stations because it is to be sent to several ultimate locations.

6.3.6. Alternate Routing Indicators

The system may be designed to route messages along specified alternate routes if the primary route is not available.

6.3.7. Addresses

The general system allows multiple addressing of messages. Typically an address delimiter is used, such as a carriage-return–line-feed combination. The addresses themselves can be anything from an alphanumeric code to a full textual address in the ordinary form. Address lengths and formats can be fixed or variable. Addresses may be direct or indirect. A direct address is one of the form "377 ELM STREET." An indirect address is one of the form "JOHN SMITH (wherever he happens to be at the moment)." In the latter case, the system must maintain a table of last known locations for the addressee.

Addresses may be codes that designate distribution lists. Thus, the system accepts as an address "ALL MANAGERS," "ALL STATIONS," "LIST 23," etc. The system must distribute copies of the message to all parties named on the particular distribution list.

6.3.8. End of Header (EOH)

The header data is terminated with an EOH, which may be a special character or a special field.

6.3.9. Subheaders and Envelopes

The system may use several headers. This occurs in a network consisting of several communication centers. If the message is to be distributed to a tributary of another center, an envelope is placed around the message, header and all, and a new header created.

Consider the communication network as a hierarchy. Each time a message is passed to a higher level, another envelope may be added. Each time the message is passed down, the outermost envelope is removed, revealing the header for that level. In this way, small messages destined for the same center may be batched into longer messages for increased transmission efficiency and decreased processing. It is much the same as bagging all mail destined for the same zip code.

6.3.10. Start of Text (SOT), Text, End of Text (EOT)

The SOT and EOT delimit the message itself. The text may contain almost any character sequence except the special delimiters such as EOM, SOM, EOT, and SOT. Thus, it is not unreasonable to allow the complete repetition of the addressing and routing data within the body of the text. The existence of the SOT and EOT delimiters makes this practical.

6.3.11. Trailer, End of Message (EOM), Postmessage Control

The text may be followed by a trailer field. This field could contain special information, designate that the message should be canceled, that the message has been garbled or forcibly ended, etc. The message trailer, if any, is followed by an end of message code (EOM). Again, an unlikely sequence such as "NNNN" is used.

A postmessage control field may follow the message. This might be a sequence of characters which turns off the receiving device.

6.3.12. Format Tolerance, Delimiters, and Redundancy

It is evident from the above discussion that there is considerable redundancy with respect to delimiters. The source of redundancy is historical. The procedures and formats used in communications were established for manual systems. (A common delimiter is the carriage-return–line-feed–letter-shift sequence.) Similarly, other manual conveniences, the ease of reading the message, and such led to other character sequences which have now been adopted as part of the message format.

Another source of redundancy is more deliberate. Lines can be noisy and characters get garbled. An SOM and EOM is not really needed, for the start and end of the message can be deduced from the other delimiters. However, since one or more of these could become garbled, the use of redundant delimiters and other redundant fields allows more tolerance to errors. Where the system cannot decide what to do with a message, it prints it on an operator teleprinter for manual disposition. While it would be difficult to program a system that properly interpreted the address "N[W-XØRK," the human operator has no difficulty in distinguishing it from "N[W*RK," to come up with "NEW YØRK" and "NEWARK" respectively.

6.4. Input

6.4.1. Input

Input processing begins with the receipt of the first character of the message which has been relayed by the line termination unit to the computer.

If fixed buffers are used, there will be an immediate storage allocation problem. However, if all buffering is dynamic, there must be some place to put the first character. In systems where the line unit is capable of storing a few characters, that storage acts as the buffer. The detection of a nontrivial character is signaled by the line unit by an interrupt. This implies that the line unit is cognizant of its state (i.e., it had been in a quiescent state and is now in an active state). The urgency of supplying buffer space for the first character is alleviated if the line unit can detect the SOM or a part of it (e.g., it creates an interrupt upon receiving a "ZC" sequence). The penalty for depending upon the SOM to trigger the buffer block assignment process is that the system will not properly respond to messages in which the SOM is missing or totally garbled.

In any event, there must be a mechanism that allows the system to allocate memory for the incoming character stream. Here we see the advantage of controlled transmission. Controlled transmission allows the block to be assigned in anticipation, as the polling message is transmitted. If nothing comes back, the block is returned. Uncontrolled transmission requires either a high-priority interrupt for the first character and some method of keeping track of the fact that it was the first character, a fixed buffer area in the computer's memory or in the line unit, or anticipatory assignment of space to every input line.

While it is possible to start processing the message before it has been completely received, this is not often done. Processing may be initiated prior to the receipt of the complete message for high-speed lines or high-priority messages. In the high-speed line case, this is done to conserve memory. In the high-priority message case, it is done to reduce transmission delays. In either case, the decision of when to start processing is usually implicit in the line, or is signaled by the line unit on the basis of a detected special character. Thus, one may begin processing prior to the receipt of the EOM for all 2400-baud lines, say. As another example, the line unit might detect the fact that the priority character in the header had a certain value and create an interrupt which would be used to initiate the beginning of processing.

6.4.2. Code Conversion

One of the first steps in input processing is code conversion. A communications system may serve devices and lines that use many different codes. It is desirable to convert all codes into an internal system code. The system code is chosen as the dominant code of the network, that is, the code for which code conversion will be minimized. Thus, ASCII might be the internal code. A line using 5-bit Baudot code would have to be converted to ASCII on input, and back to Baudot for output. The choice of internal code can be readily made if we know the statistics that relate the codes of the sources to the codes of the destinations, and the probability matrix that describes how many messages of each code will go out to lines using the other codes.

Some code conversions can be done trivially by hardware, other code conversions can be expensive. For example, converting from ASCII to Baudot or *vice versa* is an expensive process because letter and figure shift characters must be inserted or deleted. It is not a one-to-one conversion. Code conversion could require the examination and moving of every character in the message.

6.4.3. Format Conversion and Editing

The system may have to respond to several different standard formats. In order to reduce the size and complexity of the various processors that will operate on the message, some sort of format conversion may be carried out in addition to the code conversion. The considerations leading to the choice of internal or standard formats are much the same as are used to decide on the internal code. It is generally not possible to convert all messages to a single master format—usually there will be several different formats in use.

Format editing is a kind of conversion in which missing or garbled fields are replaced and obviously redundant ones are removed. Thus, the format may call for six to eighteen letter shifts at a particular point. The format editing program will see to it that exactly six shifts result no matter what came in. The intention is to provide uniform formats so that subsequent processors will not have to reparse the message. Code conversion, format conversion, format editing, and header analysis (discussed below) can be combined into a single sequential pass through the message. These functions are parsing operations that can be mechanized as sequential jump tables.

6.5. Header Analysis

6.5.1. Message Control Data

The object of header analysis is to parse and interpret the header fields and determine what is to be done with the message. Priority and security data are extracted. Message control information is extracted.

6.5.2. Service Messages

Many of the messages received are not actual messages but responses to previously transmitted messages or network controls. Examples are: retrieval requests, wait before transmission, line status messages, acknowledgments, sequence numbers out of order, new sequence number series, line about to go down, line has just come up, code or format about to change, no message at this time. Each service message must be analyzed and acted upon.

Such messages typically consist only of a header, there being no explicit text. Since service messages tend to be short, it may be advantageous to rewrite them onto smaller blocks, thus freeing memory. For that matter, these messages once analyzed can be discarded and replaced by an appropriate queue entry.

6.5.3. Header Analysis Output

The result of header analysis is the placement of the message on the appropriate processing queue. If header analysis, code conversion, and format conversion singly or together take a lot of processing, the header analysis program may provide a map of the header to simplify the work of subsequent processors. Thus, one or more descriptive blocks may be produced which when examined by subsequent processors will eliminate the need for redundant header analysis.

6.6. Storage

It is not usually feasible to provide enough main memory to accommodate the traffic. A typical communications system might be required to store 8000 messages with an average length of 200 characters, 1.6 million in all. Furthermore, each message is stored at least twice to provide the required system viability.

Queues of thousands of messages can build up rapidly. Two reasons for this are that certain outgoing lines may be out of order and messages destined for those lines pile up, and that messages destined for certain outgoing lines may come in at a higher rate than they can be transmitted. Since a communications system will allow messages coming in on a high-speed line to be transmitted to a low-speed line, the possibility of temporary queue buildup for certain lines exists.

The system has a large storage area, typically on a drum or fixed-head disc (although movable-head disc and tape have been used). Most messages are transmitted to this storage to clear the main memory for the receipt of further messages. Hence, these communications systems are called **store-and-forward** message switching systems, because they first *store* the message and then *forward* it to the proper destination.

The message may also be stored in retrieval files, and on tape as a permanent record of what messages were transmitted by the system.

The in-transit memory is dynamically allocated and has extensions for overflow. Memory scheduling is accomplished by the means discussed in Section 2.4, above. While the message itself is placed in the in-transit store, a queue entry for the message remains in the main memory.

6.7. Address Analysis and Routing

This process could take place either before storage or after storage. The message analysis processor examines the messages that are queued in the system to determine where the message is to go. Using either the results of a previous parsing or a new parsing of the header, each address is extracted in sequence and used as a key in a file search to determine the line to which the message is to go. The relation between the address and the line corresponding to that address is not fixed, but may vary from center to center or from moment to moment. Thus, a switching center in New York will route messages to Washington on its line "23," but a center in Tulsa will use its line "44" for the same purpose. Since lines can fail, the operator can divert traffic destined for one location to a line other than the one normally used. Most systems will have many more addresses than lines since they act as relay centers for local distributors of messages. It is not uncommon for a message switching system with 100 lines to have a catalog of several thousand addresses. The file search techniques discussed in Section 5 above apply to this function.

To determine the identity of the line corresponding to the address is not enough. The status of that line must be examined to see if it is available. Either because of a line failure or because too many messages are queued for that line, the system may elect to send the message along an alternate line. In some systems, particularly those having many lines going to each location, the routing analysis program determines not the actual line number but the **direction number** corresponding to the address. The direction number designates a table of line numbers, any one of which can be used for that direction. In general, there will be more than one address. However, this does not necessarily correspond to more than one transmittal of the same message. Messages destined for two different addresses could go out along the same line. To illustrate, a multiple-address message originating in the U.S. and destined for several offices in Europe would all go out along the same line. The local distribution could be done by a switching center in Paris, say. The average number of addresses per message is called the **address multiplicity**, while the average number of messages transmitted per message received is called the **message multiplicity**. It is not unusual to have an average address multiplicity of 1.6, with an average message multiplicity of 1.2.

If routing analysis is done after storage, and the outgoing line is busy then, the message will either remain in the main memory until the line is free or will have to be reread when the line is about to become free. On the other hand, if the analysis is done prior to storage, and if that analysis is not to be wasted, then either redundant copies of the message will be stored or additional administrative or queue space will be used. Both may be done. High-priority messages, messages with simple formats that allow direct routing analysis, or messages known to have only one destination can be analyzed prior to storage. Other messages may be analyzed after storage.

The routing of the message may be completely implicit in the incoming line number, in the message format, or in some other aspect of the message. As an example, in an inquiry system such as a reservation system, an order-entry system, or a bank system, the routing is implicit: the response goes to the same address as the request. In those systems which are not true communications systems, there may be no routing analysis at all.

6.8. Message Exchange

A system may be required to allow a diversity of message originators to communicate with incompatible destinations. Thus, a low-speed, half-duplex line using a 5-bit Baudot code can communicate with a high-speed, full-duplex line that uses ASCII. In addition, formats may differ from one output to another. Furthermore, since a message may go to several different destinations, each of these may have a different code, format, and speed, which will require the appropriate conversion. **Message exchange** is the general term used for making such conversions. We have seen that part of message exchange can be done on input, when the message is converted to the common input format. If more than one format or code is used, some kind of message exchange will have to be performed on output as well. In order to conserve processing time, the various destinations to which the message is to go must be examined so that redundant conversions are not made. Thus, the message might have fourteen addresses, which result in eight transmissions, but only three different message exchanges. If codes and formats can be intermixed on the same line, the administration of message exchange is substantially complicated. It may then be necessary to send the same message along a given line more than once.

6.9. Output

When a copy of a message has been readied for output, its identifier is placed on the output queue of the appropriate line. Several different queues could be used for each line, corresponding to the several different priorities. The output processor assigns message sequence numbers to the message (e.g., this is the 345th message to go out on line 45). It, or a higher-priority part of it, keeps blocks linked to the chain being processed by the output multiplexer and keeps the multiplexer busy. The output processor services the alert and block-exhausted interrupts and otherwise maintains a steady stream of messages for each line. Assuming that the main memory is divided into equal-sized blocks, and that number of blocks on queue for each line is known, the output processor can determine the number of minutes that will pass before the given message will actually be transmitted. If this time is too long, the output processor, via the executive, may alert the operator. The output processor may also have the readied copy of the message written back to the in-transit store in order to conserve main memory. Alternatively, this can be done by the main memory management routine to alleviate an anticipated overflow.

6.10. Channel Coordination and Signaling

Channel coordination is the term used for those processes that require the interaction of input and output. If the system consists of nothing but full duplex lines, and there is no possibility for malfunctions, then channel coordination is minimal. However, most systems require a lot of this kind of processing. Some examples are given below.

6.10.1. Unrecoverable Errors

One or more errors are discovered in the incoming message, which cannot be corrected by the program or the operator. The message originator must be apprised of the fact and requested to retransmit. An incoming message has resulted in an outgoing message for the same line.

6.10.2. Acknowledgments

Systems using controlled transmission may require that a message be acknowledged. The sender, which is in fact another communications system, wants to purge its copy of the message. It cannot do this unless the message has been acknowledged as received by all parties to which it was transmitted. The receiver must send an acknowledgment message or a disacknowledgment message of the form

"HAVE RECEIVED MESSAGE 199 —NØ ERRØRS,"

or

"HAVE RECEIVED MESSAGE ???—SERIAL NUMBER ERRØR."

6.10.3. Half-Duplex Lines

It is not possible to transmit and receive simultaneously on a half-duplex line. Coordination is required.

Assume that the line had been in the receive position from the point of view of the communications system. The sending station wishes to accept those messages destined for it. It sends a service message to the system requesting a mode shift. The system accepts the service message. It then sends a command to a switchover unit to switch the line from receive to send. This is followed by a test message to the outlying station. The system may then switch back again to the receive mode to see if the outlying station is capable of verifying the switchover. If this is done, it switches back to the transmit mode again and proceeds to transmit. The switchover from transmit to receive is accomplished in a similar manner.

6.10.4. Dial-Up Systems

The computer may be connected to voice lines or teleprinter lines that must be dialed. A special dial unit is used that converts the various tones into appropriate characters and *vice versa*. The computer must first lift the receiver (output command), wait for a dial tone (accept an input), transmit the telephone number (output again), listen for the appropriate number of rings (input again), detect the pick-up (input), etc. The procedure may differ from network to network. Furthermore, after having reached the proper number, the computer may have to go through the same procedure with an extension number. Busy signals, misdials, etc., must be detected.

6.10.5. Device Conditioning

Initiating a connection with another device or another computer can take many steps. For example, if the outlying terminal is a magnetic tape station, the system will have to go through all the checks and steps required for writing data on magnetic tape. The main difference is that instead of simple commands, each exchange is a small message, which until it has been analyzed cannot be treated except as another, albeit short, normal message.

6.10.6. Errors and Scope

The main complications in channel coordination programs are due to the possibilities of errors. The messages used for the chitchat could be garbled, come in the wrong sequence, or be totally uncalled for. Each possible error in these sequences must be examined and an appropriate response determined. This means that channel coordination programs tend to be involved. Coordination messages must have priorities relative to normal messages. It may be desirable to interrupt an outgoing message in midstream and interpose control or coordination information. The result is that someplace, buried in the text of an otherwise normal message, there may be crucial control information. If this is allowed the input processor may have to go through every character of text to check if there is information of this kind within it.

While the channel coordination process itself may be trivial (e.g., send out a canned acknowledge message), the processing associated with it, because it is generally not known whether this is a channel coordination message or not, can be large. Special character interrupts will occur. Buffer blocks must be assigned and then released, the message must be queued, perhaps codes and formats converted, etc. In some communications systems, particularly those that are required to interface directly with computers of several different manufacturers, the channel coordination processing can account for 25% of the work required to process messages.

6.11. Retrieval

The fact that a message has been properly transmitted and acknowledged does not mean that it will never be called for again. Typically, 5% of all transmitted messages may be requested at a later time. The reasons are varied. The message may have been garbled despite the fact that it was acknowledged. After all, the garbling could be in the text, and not detected except by the ultimate recipient. Perhaps the recipient wants another copy of the message because the Xerox machine is on another floor. The request may be for legal purposes. As an example, the Federal Aviation Agency, investigating a landing accident, may request all messages pertaining to runway conditions that were transmitted to a particular station over the past 24 hours. A bank investigating a lost cash transfer may request a trace of all messages of a certain type. For whatever reasons—valid, urgent, or trivial— the system must have the ability to store and retransmit messages for some specified period past in a given amount of time. A typical requirement is the ability to retransmit any messages less than 2 hours old within 30 seconds, any messages less than 24 hours old within 3 minutes, and any messages less than 30 days old within 15 minutes.

The retrieval request enters as a service message. It contains the time of day the message was sent, the message serial number, or other identifying data. The retrieval processor is a file search processor and can be mechanized in any of the several ways discussed in Section 5 above. Retrieval is usually done on the basis of output identification and rarely required on the basis of input. That is, someone usually wants to know what was sent to him, but relatively rarely does someone want to know what it was he sent. If both types of retrieval are required, it may be necessary to have two complete files, one for messages organized according to input and one according to output. The relation between input and output sequence numbers is haphazard. Differences in line speeds, priorities, line loadings, etc., are such that only a table of correspondences can be established. Adding to this the fact that there may be some sort of message multiplicity, we find that providing two separate tables is usually the simplest approach. If the requester for messages based on input sequence is willing to accept a long wait (perhaps several hours) the dual file need not be used. The message can be retrieved by a sequential search through the file.

6.12. Operations and Controls

The system must have the ability to determine and exploit the status of all lines. A line monitor function may be used for this purpose. This can be extended to automatic tests of line noise level and distortion. The number of lines terminated at the computer may be far less than the total number of lines in the communications system. For example, there might be a whole telephone exchange in front of the message switch. The computer might be required to control this as well. The system might employ modulator–demodulator pairs, line equalizers, and the like, all of which could fail. Similarly, the lines themselves can fail. For this reason, there may be many wire patch bays that allow the operator to patch around faulty units or assign different lines to various directions. These functions can also be done by the communications system.

In much the same way that the executive optimized the resources of the complex, the operator can optimize the resources represented by the network and computer complex. He may do this by blocking certain lines, draining messages for certain destinations, overriding priorities, patching, changing the routings of messages, etc. This implies that most of the tables that establish the routing, the relation between lines and direction, or for that matter, the formats and codes associated with any given lines can be changed. Such changes must be done without interrupting the system.

6.13. Standardization

The communications system, or that part of the complex devoted to communication functions, is complicated. No small part of that complexity arises from a seeming lack of communication standards. If all lines operated at the same speed, if all users were to adopt a uniform code and format, and if all computer manufacturers agreed upon coordination chitchat, life would be much simpler. Reality, however, differs from the ideal. Communications systems typically are international, and are required to work with the standards of different countries. This alone creates standardization problems. More important, however, is the fact that there is a lot of equipment out there. One cannot ask a user to dump or modify existing equipment that has 15 more years to go before it is completely amortized. One cannot suddenly push the bandwidth of a 75-baud line up to 2400 baud. In fact, if it were not for the substantial amount of standardization that *does* exist, centralized communication complexes would be impractical. Standardization is an ongoing activity. The disparate communication formats of the past are increasingly covered by fewer and fewer standards. However, technology does not rest, and new problems always occur. A new, more effective modulation scheme is discovered, users demand cryptographic facilities, variable-length error correcting codes are introduced, present formats are found to be inadequate—thus as we lick the standardization problems of the past, the press of technology creates equally nasty new ones. Complete standardization is not possible unless there is complete stasis. Centralized communication facilities exist to solve the inevitable lack of standardization.

7. SUMMARY

Memory management exists because there is no surfeit of memory. The memory may be subdivided into blocks which by one means or another are linked together in discontiguous chains. This allows blocks of memory to be dynamically allocated to processors as they are needed. The memory management processor must keep track of what memory is available and who has it. Every finite memory is subject to overflow. This means that methods for extending the memory to another medium must be provided. The intention is to supply the system with a potentially infinite memory. In practice, nothing less will do. The best way to handle overflow is to detect its incipience and to clear out low-priority users before actual overflow takes place.

In addition to dynamic storage allocation, the system may be provided with a virtual memory capability. This is a combination of hardware and software that allows us to construct a system in which overflow is the normal mode of operation.

Rotary memories such as discs or drums may be transaction bound if not scheduled properly. A basic sacrifice is made to achieve optimum scheduling. FIFO order for memory transactions is not maintained. This allows a 20- to 50-fold increase in the number of transactions that can be consummated in each revolution.

Input-output devices require buffers. The commonly used buffer techniques are: fixed buffers, alternating buffers, dynamic buffers, or a combination of these. Two interrupts can be used to control the transfer of data to and from buffers, the alert interrupt and the fill interrupt. The position of the alert interrupt affects the priority level and the amount of space statistically used for the buffer function. The use of the alert interrupt is an example of anticipatory processing.

Jobs are coordinated by means of queues. As the job progresses, it is passed from processor to processor by placing the descriptor of the job from the output queue of one processor to the input queue of the next. The scheduler accomplishes its tasks by controlling what goes on what queue and when. Simple dedicated systems can share input and output queues. As the system becomes more generalized, this is no longer efficient and a centralized queue control is needed. Queues are normally stored in dynamic space. Therefore, it is possible that the queues will overflow and have to be extended to another memory medium. This is seen to be nothing less than catastrophic if FIFO queue management must be maintained.

A file is to memory what a processor is to a computer. Two antithetical requirements exist in the design of a file—ease of search and ease of modification. It is seen that the one is bought at the cost of the other.

While most computer complexes are not used solely for communications, communication is an important part of most computer complexes. Since a communications system has within it most communication features found within noncommunications systems, the examination of the operation of store-and-forward message switching systems is profitable. These systems exist to allow messages to be transmitted between terminals that use different codes, speeds, and formats. No small part of communications is channel coordination, taking care of the chitchat required to get disparate devices and systems to talk to each other.

8. PROBLEMS

1. In dynamic storage allocation schemes using linked lists, why is a block taken from the top of the list and returned to the bottom? Could both not be done either from the top or the bottom? What kind of linking would be needed to allow this? [*Moderate.*]

2. Flowchart a storage allocation scheme using an LAS in which links are kept separate from the block itself and in which most of the LAS is stored on drum. Show how a block is obtained and returned. Do this for the main memory dynamic storage allocation and for a similar storage allocation processor for the drum itself. [*Moderate.*]

3. Do Problem 2 under the additional assumption that the space used for the LAS is dynamically allocated. [*Moderate.*]

4. It is possible to return a connected string of blocks to the LAS at one time. If this is done, how is the new bottom of the LAS found? [*Think about it.*]

5. Assume that a bit occupancy table is used for a movable-head disc. The table is divided among three parameters: bits, words, and blocks. The blocks are dynamically allocated. Bits could be associated with tracks, sectors, or discs. Similarly, contiguous words could correspond to tracks, sectors, or discs. There are six possible assignments for this analog. Assuming that the memory allocation scheme is such that it is to assign blocks in the shortest possible time, that is, the preferred scanning order is bits, words, blocks, examine each of the six analogs to determine the advantage (if any) with respect to reducing transaction delays and maximizing the rate at which transactions can be made. Assume the average record consists of N blocks of disc. [*Long.*]

6. Flowchart a shared-pool algorithm for two different block lengths that do not nest. Flowchart the same under the assumption that the blocks do nest. Remember that somehow the blocks must be put together again. Do this problem for various probability distributions that favor either the long or the short blocks. [*Difficult.*]

7. Flowchart a code conversion which is not one-to-one, where the source data and the destination memory are both to be in dynamic space. Do this both for an expanding code and a contracting code. Assume a sequential jump table is used for conversion. [*Moderate.*]

8. Do Problem 7 under the assumption that the conversion is to be done in place. [*Moderate.*]

9. Flowchart the disc scheduling techniques described in Section 2.4.5. [*Moderate.*]

10. Why would a fixed buffer for a teleprinter that allows only 72 characters per line be made 85 characters long? [*Simple.*]

11. Given a drum with N tracks, M sectors per track, and an average of P transactions per revolution, what is the probability that a track conflict will occur (i.e., the probability that there will be two or more transactions scheduled for the same sector on different tracks)? Consider the birthday problem. [*Difficult.*]

12. Assume that the only kinds of drum conflicts that can occur are successive sector conflicts, and that there is a distribution that describes the number of sectors that will have been written consecutively. Furthermore, assume that odd sectors and even sectors will be scheduled on alternate revolutions. Devise an algorithm that provides an optimum schedule but requires only the examination of sequential sectors. If a set of linked lists (for each sector) is used, show that it is never necessary to insert dummy entries. [*Difficult.*]

13. Flowchart a disc scheduling algorithm in which transactions have two different priorities. [*Moderate.*]

14. Establish a quantitative relation between the position of the alert interrupt, the buffer fill rate, the block length, the record length distribution, and the amount of space required for the record from its initiation to its completion. Derive an expression for the space wasted as a function of alert pointer position. [*Difficult.*]

15. Examine quantitatively the effects of queue overflow on base sequence cycle length. Use an appropriately simple model system having only one queue of interest. Find the effect on space, delay, and processing time per transaction.

16. Derive a quantitative expression that relates the actual transmission rate for asynchronous and synchronous transmission modes. Assume that the probability of a character error is p and that each detected error will require the loss of N characters. Furthermore, assume that M synch characters must be transmitted after each error for the synchronous line. Establish both the effective character transmission rate and the crossover point for the two methods. [*Moderate.*]

17. Program the detection of asynchronous transmission characters. Find out how distortion is measured and the relation between the required sampling rate and distortion. Why should one use an odd number of samples per bit? Compare to an even number of samples. [*Difficult.*]

18. Flowchart a procedure for detecting characters that may be transmitted in the same code in either synchronous or asynchronous modes on the same line. Assume that at least N synch characters will appear to condition the line, or that idle line of at least M bits in length will occur. [*Moderate.*]

19. Flowchart a dial-up procedure for a computer. Both long-distance and local calls may be made. There may be extensions to dial further, and wrong numbers will occur. Suppose some unlucky human dials you and decides to retaliate by playing games with his touch tone phone. Suppose you dial the wrong computer, i.e., it speaks ASCII and you speak EBCDIC. [*Tedious.*]

20. Assume that an optimum drum transaction scheduling technique is in use. What is the expected reduction in transaction latency if the identity of the upcoming block is known, i.e., there is a drum position sensing instruction?

21. Flowchart drum scheduling techniques such as those discussed in Section 2.4.3 to take advantage of positional knowledge.

22. Consider the following four cases for a drum transaction scheduling problem:

1. Single drum, fixed number of items on queue.
2. Two drums, dual (redundant) writing of items for both drums, fixed number of arrivals on queue.
3. Single drum, arrivals at a constant average rate, i.e., n transactions per revolution.
4. Dual drums as in Case 2, with continual arrivals at the rate of n per revolution.

For all four cases, express the expected latency in fractions of a drum revolution as a function of the number items on the queue (for Cases 1 and 2) or the queue arrival rate (for Cases 3 and 4), parametric with the number of sectors on the drum. Do not attempt a formally precise solution —an approximation to 1 % will be adequate (and much easier). Cases 1 and 2 follow directly from the discussion in Reference 2 and Problems 12 and 13 of Chapter 12. [Hint for Cases 3 and 4: If the arrivals are sparse, what is the expected latency? If the arrivals are very dense, what then is the expected latency? Don't be afraid to fudge.]

23. For the four cases of Problem 22, consider the effect of positional knowledge and reduce Cases 2 and 4 to previously solved problems.

9. REFERENCES

1. Crowley, Thomas H., Harris, Gerard G., Miller, Stuart E., Peirce, John R., and Runyon, John P., *Modern Communications*, Columbia University Press, New York, 1962.

   An elementary romp through most aspects of communications—possibly an introduction for those who have no background in the subject. Primarily descriptive; no substantive techniques or "how to" information.

2. Denning, Peter J., *Effects of Scheduling on File Memory Operations*, American Federation of Information Processing Societies, Spring Joint Computer Conference Proceedings, Volume 30, April 18–20, Thompson Book Co., Washington, D.C., 1967, pp. 9–21.

   This paper is as complete a study of scheduling for drums and discs as has been published to date. The relative improvement afforded by optimum drum scheduling is developed in detail. In addition, several different disc scheduling policies are developed and analyzed.

3. "ACM Storage Allocation Symposium," *Communications of the ACM*, Association for Computing Machinery, Inc., Baltimore, Maryland, Volume 4, Number 10, pp. 416–464, October, 1961.

4. Martin, James, *Teleprocessing Network Organization*, Prentice Hall, Englewood Cliffs, New Jersey, 1970.

   This is a companion book to Martin's three other books on related subjects, *Design of Real-Time Computer Systems*, *Programming Real-Time Computer Systems*, and *Telecommunications and the Computer*. The treatment of computer-controlled communications is more detailed and more elementary than that presented in this chapter. Transmission modes, co-ordination procedures, and codes are discussed in detail. Chapter 7 is on network cost considerations and is worth reading. The glossary on communication-related terms is useful.

5. Sackman, Harold, *Computers, System Science, and Evolving Society: The Challenge of Man–Machine Digital Systems*, John Wiley, New York, 1967.

   This book would have been better titled, "Generalizations and extrapolations on human engineering problems as drawn from extensive experience with the SAGE system by an industrial psychologist." Despite this, there is a lot of valuable information on SAGE, on human engineering problems, and on system design in general in this book.

6. Stimler, Saul, *Real-Time Data Processing Systems: A Methodology for Design and Cost/ Performance Analysis*, McGraw-Hill, New York, 1969.

This is a book on how to do a timing analysis of a computer-controlled store-and-forward message switching systems reflecting a particular design philosophy. While the analysis is somewhat simplistic, it is complete and can give the reader an idea of the amount of work involved. Lots of interesting graphs, charts, and equations.

7. Uttal, William R., *Real-Time Computers: Technique and Applications in the Psychological Sciences*, Harper and Row, New York, 1968.

An elementary nontechnical exposition of computer technology for the intelligent non-computer type. Contains a good section on biological data logging, A/D equipment, teaching machines, and behavioral psychology applications.

8. Weingarten, Allen, "The Eschenbach Drum Scheme," *Communications of the ACM*, Association for Computing Machinery, Inc., Baltimore, Maryland, Volume 9, Number 7, pp. 509–512, July 1966.

This paper is primarily of historical interest, as the first known published description of the drum scheduling scheme described in this chapter.

9. Witt, B. I., "Dynamic Storage Allocation for a Real-Time System," *IBM Systems Journal*, Volume 2, pp. 230–239, September–December 1963.

An interesting approach to shared pools.

Chapter 11

VIABILITY

And on the pedestal these words appear:
"My name is Ozymandias, king of kings:
Look on my works, ye Mighty, and despair!"
Nothing beside remains. Round the decay
Of that colossal wreck, boundless and bare
The lone and level sands stretch far away.

PERCY BYSSHE SHELLEY
Ozymandias

1. SYNOPSIS

Viability is a compound probabilistic measure of the capabilities of a system. Its evaluation requires the analysis of performance, reliability, and maintainability. We shall consider what viability is, and how it is achieved, measured, and optimized. Viability design pervades the entire structure of the computer complex in much the same way that stress—and the attendant mathematics of stress analysis—dominates the design of suspension bridges. A computer complex that cannot fail is practically and theoretically unachievable. Every system can and will (eventually) fail. It remains to consider the manner and effect of those failures and the cost of minimizing them. As ever, sacrifices and trades are required.

2. BASIC CONCEPTS

2.1. The Components of Viability

Viability is a compound measure of the capability of a system quantitatively incorporating three factors: performance, reliability, and maintainability. Each factor is measured in its own way.

2.1.1. Performance

Performance is measured by the degree to which the system adequately meets the demands of its assigned tasks. Many aspects of performance are not amenable to quantitative measure. Such factors, while important, cannot now be included in a measure of viability. Only those performance factors that can be mathematically modeled or numerically expressed will be treated here.

As technology evolves, formerly subjective performance factors assume greater importance. In response to this, quantitative measures of these factors are proposed, developed, and eventually adopted. So it was with computer complex performance, reliability, and most recently maintainability and viability. The penchant for mathematical analysis that pervades the technological community is such that were aesthetics and morality contractually negotiable, universal, albeit meaningless, numerical measures for them would evolve.

2.1.2. Reliability

Reliability, as applied to computer complexes, is most often measured by the **mean time between failures** (MTBF). The MTBF is a measure of the expected time between the conjunction of events that are agreed to constitute a failure. It is usually expressed in hours. The MTBF is applicable to elements that behave as if they were new subsequent to the repair or replacement of a malfunctioning subelement. That is, the probability of subsequent failures is independent of failures in other elements, or of the history of failures of the subject element. This assumption is usually valid. It is not valid for automobile tires or other things that have pronounced irreversible wear characteristics, or for things (such as wine, women, and song) that improve with age. In such cases, the calculation and manipulation of the MTBF is more sophisticated than that presented here.

2.1.3. Maintainability

Maintainability is statistically expressed by the **mean time to repair** (MTTR). The MTTR is a measure of the expected time required to obviate those events which have been agreed to constitute a failure. The MTTR is not as simply evaluated as is the MTBF. The time to repair a malfunctioning element consists of the time to traverse a sequence of many steps of uncertain duration.

2.2. A Philosophy for Viability Design

Simply stated: *"Every system can and will fail."*

This credo must be understood and accepted by user and architect alike. Once this principle has been adopted, it remains only to negotiate the probability that the system *will* fail. Arbitrarily low failure probabilities are achievable at arbitrarily high cost. Hence the need for negotiation.

This is not a nihilistic philosophy—it is an observation of reality rather than a cause for despair.

Failures or malfunctions cannot be rationally considered unless a cost is attached to their occurrence. A momentary hesitation in processing mail orders is not critical, while an equally short hesitation is catastrophic in an air traffic control system. A system specifier who will not impose penalties on the system supplier for failures does the architect a disservice rather than a favor. It is a disservice because the architect cannot properly decide his structure, nor is he ever confident that he is designing the correct system.

We should expect performance figures to be penalized in concert with the duration and rate of occurrence of failures. The stringency of the penalty should indicate the importance that the user places on trouble-free operation. An extreme penalty implies extreme viability and commensurate system cost. The architect has the intellectual and professional duty to see to it that such penalities are realistic for the application and within the capabilities of his technology. Overemphasis on viability as on any other aspect of computer complex design is as serious an error as ignoring it totally.

2.3. Graceful Degradation

Graceful degradation[1] is a scheme whereby performance will be reduced as elements of the system fail, without a total collapse of capability, until the primal nucleus of the system no longer functions. Thus, a family sedan is not capable of graceful degradation with respect to blowouts, while a truck is. Most systems are designed with some graceful degradation capabilities. Commercial passenger aircraft are able to continue their flight with one engine failure, clear obstacles on take-off with only two engines, and land with a fair chance of success with just one engine. A piece of sandpaper exhibits almost continuous graceful degradation, while the celebrated "One-Hoss Shay" and "My Grandfather's Clock" are extreme examples of catastrophically failing systems. A system with graceful degradation is not vulnerable to the failure of one of its elements and is tolerant of multiple failures as well. The design of systems that exhibit graceful degradation is the principal approach to the achievement of high viability.

---

[1] The author has tried to trace the origin of the term "graceful degradation." The term's use predates its appearance in print by several years. The following incident is probably one of several similar ones that occurred simultaneously and independently in many places. In late 1959 the author participated in writing a proposal for a high-reliability airborne computer. He had previously used the words "degraded performance" for this concept. That term, however, lacked marketing charm. It was George Heilborn who suggested the term "graceful degradation." It has, since, always conjured up an image of the antebellum South, replete with mint juleps, faded magnolia blossoms, and the decay of a once great plantation. "Graceful degradation" is certainly a more genteel concept than the tawdry "degraded performance."

2.4. Definitions

A **subsystem** is an element of a system with the following characteristics:

The system can continue operation (possibly degraded) in the absence of any one of its subsystems.

Every subsystem is logically independent of every other subsystem, and no two subsystems have common elements.

A **unit** is an element of a subsystem with the following characteristics:

Every unit is capable of being isolated from other units in the same subsystem.

No unit is a part of more than one subsystem at any given time.

These subdivisions are specific to viability analysis and should not be confused with possibly more common usages.

The manner in which one partitions a system into subsystems and units is arbitrary, subject to the above restrictions. For example, any one battery of an artillery system might be considered a subsystem; however, the complete set of batteries could not, since the system would be inoperable in their absence. Similarly, a set of tape transports with a common power supply and control unit could be called a subsystem; however, the individual transports could not, since logical isolation is not necessarily provided.

A subsystem consisting of several units may have several levels of performance. In such cases, one can use either the statistical average performance of the subsystem, or introduce as an artifice a separate "subsystem," called a **pseudo-subsystem**, for each distinguishable level of performance. A subsystem could consist of exactly one unit. This is often the case. A computer complex consisting of memory modules, CPUs, drums, tapes, etc., each of which adheres to the definition of a subsystem is an example of a system each of whose subsystems consists of single units. A computer which consists of an ALU, a control unit, a memory, and a common power supply would have to be called a subsystem. The common power supply violates the restrictions of logical independence and performance in the absence of the subsystem; consequently, these units do not qualify as individual subsystems.

We shall for now restrict our attention to systems whose subsystems consist of single units, avoiding some of the complications which would be incurred otherwise.

The terms "element," "subelement," and "metaelement," will be used for the generic case, where we do not wish to distinguish among complex, system, subsystem, unit, or component.

3. THE MEASURE OF VIABILITY

Viability is expressed as a mathematical function of the performance, the MTBF, the MTTR, and various weighting factors that determine the importance of the performance parameters. The viability of a system cannot be described by a single number. It consists of a set of *functions*, one for each performance parameter of interest. Since the viability is a function of the MTBF, the MTTR, and the performance, a more detailed discussion of each of these is warranted.

3.1. Mean Time between Failures

The MTBF[2] is applied to the elements of the system at every level, from the basic components to the whole system itself. Two main factors are used to evaluate the MTBF:

1. The specification of the events that will be agreed upon to constitute a failure.
2. The mathematical function that describes the probability that such events will transpire.

Reliability, while having the trappings of a formal quantitative measure, is not absolute. That an event is a "failure" is decided by convention and depends upon the context of the element and the events.[3] It is not a fundamental property of an element such as its resistance, heat dissipation ability, etc. General agreement as to what constitutes the failure of a diode is not difficult to obtain—save in pathological cases where the designer insists on using it as a fuse. Diodes and fuses have complementary definitions of "failure." The "failure" of a slightly more complex component such as a transistor is not so simple. There are applications in which excessive gain can be more deleterious than an open circuit. For example, an analog system with positive feedback could be made unstable by a transistor that suddenly became overly "good." As we assemble components into circuits, circuits into subunits, and so forth to units, subsystems, systems, and complexes, the identification of those events which constitute failures, the agreement to the convention that those events are failures, and the prediction or experimental measure of the probability that those events will occur become increasingly difficult.

[2] The reliability of components that fail catastrophically and cannot be repaired is measured by the mean time *to* failure rather than the mean time *between* failures. But because most elements are repairable (e.g., computers, memories, etc.), we will deal with the MTBF.
[3] He who "comes out smelling like a rose," thereby "snatching victory from the jaws of defeat," does so by changing the context of the event, or by obtaining agreement to the redefinition of "failure."

However, the above disclaimers aside, there are in the overwhelming majority of cases effective and generally accepted measures as to what does and does not constitute a failure. Such measures, though not often explicitly specified, are an important part of the system specification.

The reliability of an element is expressed by the MTBF measured in hours, or its reciprocal, the failure rate, usually expressed in "percent per thousand hours." Thus, a metaelement with 500 subelements, requiring all of them to operate properly, with a failure rate of 0.004%/1000 hours, would have an overall MTBF of 50,000 hours.[4]

Experimental data or field failure data are the usual basis for the evaluation of the MTBF. The MTBF expresses the situation for an infinite number of elements operating for an infinite duration. However, the subelement complexity, the number of elements, the number of failures, and the duration of the test diffuse the validity of the predicted value of the MTBF. Going to extremes, a test made on no components for no time is totally meaningless, while a test made with 1,000,000 elements for 10,000 years is overly convincing (if pointless). As the duration of the test, the number of elements being tested, and *the number of observed failures* are reduced, the validity of the stated MTBF is degraded. This degrading is expressed by the **confidence level**. Thus, the same element, evaluated on the basis of the same experimental data, might have the following relation between predicted MTBF and confidence level:

Confidence level	MTBF
50%	1000 hours
80%	100 hours
90%	50 hours
95%	25 hours

A statement of reliability without a corresponding statement on confidence level[5] is meaningless. The generally accepted standard for expressing

---

[4] Life is not nearly always this simple, as any good textbook on reliability will show. Wear characteristics of components, specific failure mechanisms, component interactions, and a host of other factors can lead to models in which the simple reciprocal relation between MTBF and failure rate does not hold. The MTBF is often the single number that represents the distillation of a more complex failure model. Thus, the reliability engineer is another member of the computer complex design team and represents yet another discipline with which the architect must be conversant, perceptive, and patient.

[5] Actually, the situation is more complicated than given here. There is another term, called the **confidence interval**, which is a region about the predicted failure rate. That is, the failure rate (or rather our prediction of it) is assumed to be itself statistically distributed. The confidence interval is a region about the mean of that distribution, usually chosen to include 50% of the area. The confidence level is the probability that the predicted failure rate will fall in the given confidence interval. There is more yet of this kind of thing, but its discussion is not germane to

reliability is to state the MTBF or failure rates at a confidence level of 90 %. Reliability figures given at different confidence levels must all be translated to the same standard. The point here is to distinguish between predicted reliability and actual reliability. The actual reliability cannot be affected by the nature of the test, the sample size, or the number of observed failures, but our prediction of the reliability *is* thus affected.

3.2. Mean Time to Repair

Maintainability is statistically expressed by the mean time to repair. The MTTR is more context-dependent than is the MTBF. "Repair" can be achieved either by actual repair or by replacement. Thus, we may replace the failed element with a spare and subsequently repair it to create a new spare. Knowing the nature of the malfunction, we may choose to ignore the failure as a transient condition that will not soon recur. The MTTR is itself a compound measure consisting of the mean time to accomplish the following:

1. Detecting that the failure has occurred.
2. Isolating the malfunctioning element.
3. Removing the malfunctioning element.
4. Obtaining a replacement by either repair or from a stock of spare elements.
5. Inserting the working element.
6. Verifying that the replacement works.
7. Initializing it.
8. Initializing the system.
9. Resuming processing.

The conceptual stopwatch used to measure the MTTR is started only when the failure has been detected. A system, especially one employing self-repairing or self-correcting elements, may operate for a long time before a failure is evident. Concern over undetectable malfunctions is for the masochistically inclined. If the failure detection mechanisms cannot immediately detect a given failure, there is not much one can do about that failure. There are methods, based on a detailed knowledge of failure mechanisms, that can be used to predict incipient failures. In such cases the **mean time to detection** (MTTD) may be negative, resulting in a small, zero, or negative MTTR.

---

the central thesis of this book. Suffice it to say that without investigation, or the assurance of a knowledgeable reliability expert, a statement such as "the MTBF *is* 30,000 hours" might be meaningless, while predicted failure rates of 0.1 %, 0.01 %, or 0.001 % per thousand hours might be equivalent.

Detecting the existence of a failure does not guarantee that the cause or causes of that failure can be isolated. Until such isolation occurs there can be no repair. The failure itself is only symptomatic. Many different element failures can lead to the same symptoms, and many symptoms may occur as a result of a single failure. The time required to isolate a malfunction depends upon the diagnostic facilities of the system, the probability of simultaneous or dependent malfunctions, the structure of the system itself, and, of course, the essentially arbitrary definition of what a failure is.[6] It is theoretically possible to construct systems (albeit useless ones) in which only a complete simultaneous test of all elements will result in the isolation of the failed element. Such an example, while pathological and contrived, illustrates a situation that, to a lesser degree, can and does exist in real systems.

Removing a malfunctioning element, while seemingly a trivial thing, is not always so. We have all been shocked by the bill for repairing a $2.00 bearing in our cars. Getting there is often far more than half the job. Mechanical design is an important determinant of the time required to excise failed elements manually. Mere removal can be done with an ax. However, "removal" really means *removal without causing additional malfunctions.* Lest we lightly dismiss this point, let us observe that the single largest cause of vacuum tube failures in the Second World War was the electronic maintenance technician. Bent pins, cracked envelopes, fractured sockets, dropped chassis, improperly set test voltages, etc., all contribute to failures. If at any point in the repair procedure, further failures are induced by the repair facility, the time to correct such **derivative failures** must be included in the evaluation of the MTTR.

Removal is not always mechanical, and the time needed to remove a malfunctioning element not always dependent upon the skill of the maintenance technician. Such excisions may be done by the complex to itself under its own control. In this case the time to remove a failed element may be the time required to initiate and execute a complex sequence of events resulting in the logical but not necessarily physical removal of the failed element.

Figure 11.1 shows a complex consisting of several identical computers connected as on the surface of a sphere. Each computer can communicate with its nearest neighbors as shown. If a failure occurs in computer A, its neighbors may "remove" it by blocking A's communication with the rest of the complex. This kind of blocking may require the total capacity of the

---

[6] That the notion of what constitutes a failure is arbitrary is explicated by the following scenario. A robotic maintenance technician is given machine X to repair, being told that it is machine Y. He would methodically destroy the perfectly good machine X and after much effort succeed in having "repaired Y."

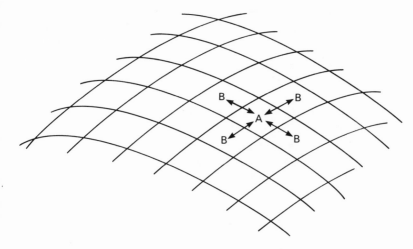

Figure 11.1. Isolation of a failed unit in an array of computers.

B computers. Prior to blocking they must (if possible) terminate their present tasks in an orderly manner. These actions could take a long time.

The time required to obtain a replacement may range from the infinitesimal to the insufferable.[7] The replacement may be permanently wired into the complex, may be in the same room, or thousands of miles away. Such choices are not made capriciously, but as a result of barters between viability and cost. The spare may itself be under repair. The key to the stock room may be lost. The repair equipment might be inoperable or uncalibrated. One should not overlook this seemingly trivial point and assume that there is an immediately available spare. Replacement is the inverse of removal and can be as difficult.

Verification of the operability of the element is done by much the same test procedure that is used to isolate the failure to that element. This is usually included in the repair time of the element. However, the element, being a subelement of the system, interacts with it. Verifying that the

[7] We are reminded of the case in which the air-data computer of a developmental aircraft had failed. The aircraft was in California, the computer manufacturer in Texas, and the aircraft factory in New York. The field engineer went to Texas to pick up the replacement, flew directly to California, and handed the spare computer to the maintenance technician. The maintenance technician took the spare up the ladder, and as he bent over to insert it into the electronics bay, dropped it ten feet to the ground. The engineer flew back to Texas, to learn that the only other spare was on its way to New York. He picked it up in New York and returned to California. He went out to the flight line, brushed the maintenance technician aside, climbed up the ladder, and dropped the computer.

interface behavior is proper may require rerunning the diagnostic program used to isolate the failed element, or at least a great portion thereof. That is to say, a test *in vacuo* may be valueless. It is sometimes possible to bypass this step. The system, if properly designed, will detect the malfunctioning replacement just as it did the original malfunctioning element. If the risk of an element working *in vacuo* but not *in vivo* is low, or if the incremental cost of yet another failure is low, the best policy may be to just accept the possible second failure.

Initialization of the element, and transition of its metaelements to full operability, as with all aspects of the MTTR, can range from simply providing power to the execution of a complex recovery program.

It is not until all these steps have been completed that the element has been "repaired." The field service organization, the quality of maintenance technicians, the physical maintenance facility, the site, the environment of the site, and all the little details required to equate the predicted MTTR to the real MTTR are proper concerns of the architect. If he ignores them, they certainly will haunt him.

3.3 Availability

A system element that does not have graceful degradation can be described as being in one of two possible states: working or not working; that is, UP or DOWN. Elements that exhibit graceful degradation can be described in one of two ways: (1) Each performance level is ascribed to a fictitious subelement or pseudosubelement, only one of which is "UP" at any given instant, the remainder being "DOWN." (2) The element has graceful degradation capabilities but is described in terms of real subelements, each of which can only be UP or DOWN.

We have used generic definitions here to emphasize that viability may be analyzed at any level. There is ultimately some level of fine detail beyond which we are willing (for the sake of analysis) to forego the apparent advantage gained by describing the performance of subelements as a continuum. If we are designing components such as diodes and transistors, we should certainly consider the degradations of gain or resistance as a continuum. If we are interested in logic design, the continuum of gain is of no interest to us, and we are satisfied to model the transistor as if it has a **binary failure** mode (UP or DOWN). Units are typically modeled as if they had a binary failure mode, while higher-level elements are accorded their continuous performance spectra. The binary failure mode assumption is pessimistic: it is used because the analysis of viability for binary failing elements is much simpler. If sufficient viability can be *proved* using the pessimistic binary model, and if the *apparent* loss of viability is not excessive, the analyst may choose the expediency of the simpler binary model. As usual, analytical simplification harbors its own dangers.[8]

The probability that an element is UP is called the **availability** of the element. Similarly, the probability that the system is UP is called the availability of the system. The availability of an element is given by

$$P_{up} = \frac{MTBF}{MTBF + MTTR}. \tag{1}$$

Strictly speaking, equation (1) is an approximation. A detailed derivation of the availability would reveal the existence of transient terms. Expression (1) is a limiting value corresponding to an infinite time. The transient term generally predicts a somewhat higher availability. The duration of the transient is usually of the order of the MTTR. As such, it is of little concern. There are cases, in which the MTTR is long relative to the MTBF and the transient may persist through a significant portion of the system's lifetime. Since the use of the limiting term is a pessimistic assumption, it can be made without penalty. It is only in those cases where the predicted viability and the system cost are so crucial that a small increase in calculated viability could reduce the system cost by a large amount (due to the quantization of computer complex elements) that the tedium of the precise calculations is warranted. However, no design should be so "close to the wire" that any one design parameter could be so critical. Certainly, no user should accept such a marginal system.

The probability that the element is DOWN is given by

$$P_{down} = 1 - P_{up} = \frac{MTTR}{MTBF + MTTR}. \tag{2}$$

The MTTR has as profound an influence as the MTBF on the viability of the system. Consequently, maintenance facilities and preventive maintenance policies have as much effect on viability as does component reliability.

There is no difference (as far as the operability of a system is concerned) if an element is disconnected because of a failure or if it is disconnected for preventive maintenance. The element is effectively DOWN in either case, and not directly available for the system. Therefore, the MTBF and the MTTR must also reflect the preventive maintenance policy used for the system. If, as in some equipment (tape transports, for example) MTBF and MTTR are strongly dependent upon the preventive maintenance, there is a barter to be evaluated.

Consider a system consisting of n subsystems. Since each subsystem can be either UP or DOWN, there are 2^n possible conditions, or **configuration states**,

---

[8] Consider the unfortunate analytical simplification of the borrower from a loan shark who equates 10% compounded monthly to 120% per annum.

for the system as a whole. Associated with each state are a number of performance parameter values which characterize the capabilities of the system in that state. Similarly, there is associated with each state the probability that the system is in that state. That probability is determined as follows.

For a given subsystem i:

$$P_{i\,up} = \text{probability that the system is UP}$$

$$= \frac{\text{MTBF}_i}{\text{MTBF}_i + \text{MTTR}_i}, \tag{3}$$

$$P_{i\,down} = \text{probability that the subsystem is DOWN}$$

$$= \frac{\text{MTTR}_i}{\text{MTBF}_i + \text{MTTR}_i}. \tag{4}$$

The probability of a given state is the product of the subsystem probabilities for that state. Thus, a system consisting of prime power, computer, and communication link in which only the computer was DOWN would have a state probability, P_s, given by

$$P_s = P_{power\,up} \times P_{computer\,down} \times P_{communication\,up}.$$

If the state were one in which all subsystems were down, P_s would be given by

$$P_s = P_{power\,down} \times P_{computer\,down} \times P_{communication\,down}.$$

Generally, we can express this as

$$P_s = \prod_{i=1}^{n} \frac{\text{MTX}_i}{\text{MTTR}_i + \text{MTBF}_i}$$

where

$$\text{MTX}_i = \text{MTBF}_i \text{ if subsystem } i \text{ is UP in state } S.$$

$$= \text{MTTR}_i \text{ if subsystem } i \text{ is DOWN in state } S.$$

It is assumed that for each configuration state of the system, there is, for each performance parameter of interest, a numerically determinable performance value peculiar to that system. A viability analysis, thus far, consists of the following steps:

1. Develop a configuration state model of the system.
2. On the basis of the MTBF and MTTR of the elements of the system, determine the availability of each configuration state, that is, the probability that that configuration state will occur.

3.4. Performance and Penalties

Let us say that there are k performance parameters of interest. Associated with each configuration state S_x there is a unique value for each performance parameter A_{kx}. Associated with each performance parameter, there is a **penalty function** which specifies the relative importance of that parameter. This penalty function is generally dependent on the configuration state, the value of the performance parameter itself, and perhaps on the values of other performance parameters as well. It may also depend on the

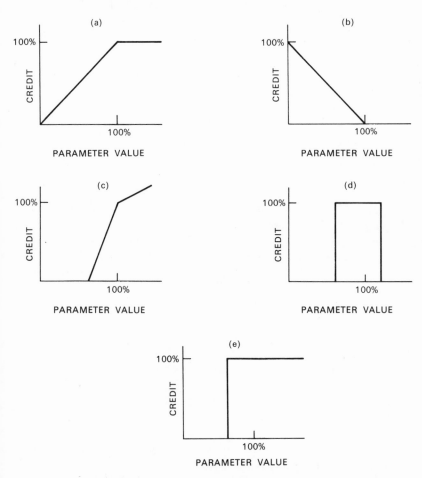

Figure 11.2. Penalty functions: (a) No bonus for overcapacity; (b) undesirable parameter; (c) no credit for minimum performance; (d) limited performance in a range; (e) binary penalty function.

length of time the system has been in a particular state. Thus, a time delay of a processing function might be of no importance until the delay had reached a threshold value. At that point, it could suddenly and discontinuously assume dominance. Similarly, overperformance could be discounted: a system with excess capacity is not given credit for it, but is still penalized when the capacity falls below the acceptable minimum. It is usually convenient to normalize performance parameters and express them as a percentage of some previously defined maximum requirement. Figure 11.2 shows some typical penalty functions. The value of the parameter is on the X axis, while the corresponding resulting value of the parameter weighted by the penalty function is given on the Y axis.

Figure 11.2a shows the penalty function for a parameter in which excess performance is not recognized but for which achieved performance up to the required maximum is given full weight. For example, the ability of a process control computer complex to handle 350 control loops is of no interest to a user whose process requires only 150 control loops. Similarly, a disc storage unit of 32 million characters has no particular advantage for a company whose active files contain 24 million characters. Since computers, storage units, and other elements of the complex are sized to meet general market requirements, and since we can hardly purchase half a disc unit, unrewarded excess performance occurs in one or more performance parameters of almost every system.

Figure 11.2b shows the penalty function for an undesirable performance parameter. Full credit is given for the absence of this factor. No further penalty is imposed after the factor reaches its maximum. An example of such a parameter is the response time in a remote-access system. Zero response time is most desirable, and a response time greater than the desperation value incurs no further penalty.

Figure 11.2c shows the penalty function for a parameter which must achieve a specified minimum value before it can be worthwhile, and for which excess performance is recognized, but not at full value. An example might be found in a servo control system or in a tracking system where a minimum number of iterations must be performed each second to keep the system stable or to form recognizable tracks.

Figure 11.2d shows a parameter with an unusual penalty function. Consider a communications system which has inadequate internal storage capacity and consequently must get rid of messages as soon as possible. To be useful it must process a minimum number of messages per second. If, however, it produces output at a higher rate, or in a momentary burst, the increased load on other elements of the network could be as deleterious as if the messages were not sent at all. The use of a high-speed line printer is another example. If the speed of the printer falls below a certain minimum, its utility as a high-speed printer is nil because a lower-cost device exists for the same task. If, on the other hand, the printer is used to produce excessively high stacks of paper, the effectiveness is again nil, because the ultimate user has no way to sift through the data.

Figure 11.2e shows a binary penalty function. If the function is performed at a certain minimum level, the system is given full credit. Further perform-ance, however, is not further rewarded. A statistics gathering system is a case in point. A minimum sample size must be used to render meaningful quality control data. Increasing the number of samples, while possible, is of no additional value since the programs and subsequent processors of the data are designed to handle the specified data acquisition rate. A synchronous data transmission system is another example. If the specified transmission rate is not maintained, the transmitted data will be garbled. The fact that the transmitting device is capable of operating at several hundred times the line speed is of no importance.

Penalty functions can take almost any form. They may be continuous, discrete, discontinuous, positive, negative, monotonic, linear, nonlinear, etc. Each such function, whether explicitly stated or implied, is part of the specification of a complex. In present practice, penalty functions are rarely given explicitly. They are usually contained in the technical evaluation guide-lines by which the proposed system will be judged. Often they are dispersed throughout the specification and alluded to, wished for, sighed about, but rarely mentioned. It is a primal responsibility of the architect to extract, formalize, and seek agreement on all explicit or implicit penalty functions. Recriminatory statements, such as the often-heard "that's not what I meant," do little good in the final design phase of the system or at the post-acceptance test post-mortem.

The penalty function need not be fixed, but can change over the system's life. The ability to handle a format that will be discontinued at a later phase in the system's life is an example. On-line gathering of operational statistics is another. The ability of the system to "grow," to "adapt," to be flexible, or to meet yet unknown challenges is an expression of shifting penalty functions.

3.5. The Performance–Probability Plot

Leaving for now the question of complicated penalty functions, let us assume that all performance values are given their full weight. Associated with each configuration state of the system, there is a probability, and for each performance parameter, a value. For any performance value, the probability of achieving it is given by the sum of the probabilities of all states in which it is achieved. In general, there are many states in which a given performance level is achieved. For example, if four computers are required to handle a particular function at full capacity and there are six computers in the system, there will be fifteen configuration states which have that performance level. Taking into account the state multiplication effect of memory failures, tape unit failures, drum failures, disc failures, etc., there may be tens of thousands of states that achieve the specified performance.

Summing the probabilities associated with each performance level of a performance parameter, we can plot the result as a probability density function such as is shown in Figure 11.3. In practice, the function is not continuous, but is a discrete distribution. However, it is convenient to deal with the performance–probability plot as if it were continuous.

There is one such performance–probability function for each performance parameter. A system that lacks graceful degradation capabilities would be represented on such a graph as a pair of points. The more general system has a distribution as shown in Figure 11.3. The viability of a system is expressed by the performance–probability curves which characterize it.

The mean value of the distribution (calculated in the normal fashion) expresses the expected performance for the parameter in question, averaged over the totality of possible states. The ratio of the mean value of the parameter to the peak value of the parameter is called the **viability efficiency** of the system. The second moment of the distribution is a measure of how

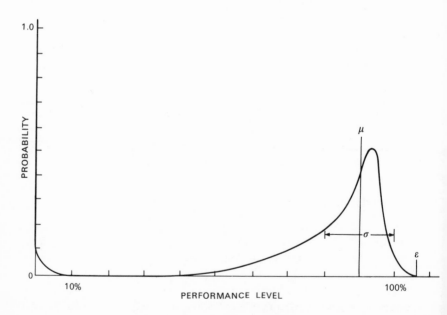

Figure 11.3. Performance–probability plot.

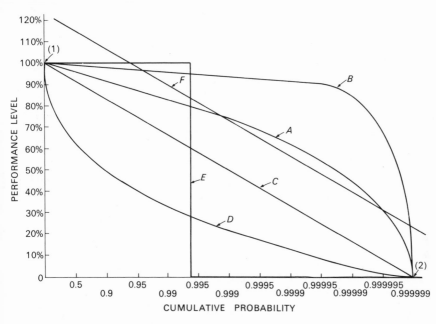

Figure 11.4. Cumulative probability.

sporadic the system behavior is. The third moment (skewness) measures just how bad things can get before the system quits altogether.

The distribution shown in Figure 11.3 is typical of a system with good viability. The higher the value of μ, the smaller the value of σ, and the smaller the peak at zero performance, the better the system. The peak near zero performance indicates that there are more states in which the system is not performing at all than states in which the system has low performance.[9]

3.6. The Cumulative Performance–Probability Plot

A more revealing method of presenting viability data is to plot the cumulative probability distributions for the performance parameters. This results in the type of curves shown in Figure 11.4.

Curve A is typical of a system with fair graceful degradation. Curve B displays better viability. Note that while the probability of achieving maximum performance (1) and zero performance (2) or better is the same for both systems, system B is more viable because its average performance is

---

[9] The distribution is similar to that which one would obtain by recording the number of cards "won" in solitaire.

better and its viability efficiency is higher. Going along in order of decreasing viability, we approach curves C and D. Curve D shows a system which attempts to maintain high performance mainly through unit reliability efforts, with relatively little emphasis placed on viability. Curve E is an example of a system with a binary failure mode (the "One-Hoss Shay"). This is an ideal system *providing the break in the curve occurs sufficiently far out*. It clearly has the highest possible efficiency. Curve F represents the achievement of viability through overdesign.

The shape of the curve required depends on the application, and should be part of the specification of a system. One should specify at least two performance levels, and the probabilities associated with each. Note that this is not enough, however, since curves A, B, C, D, and E would all meet the requirements of 100% at $P = 0$, and 0 at $P = 0.999999$. Consequently, one should also specify the mean value, the deviation, and possibly the third moment.

Viability efficiencies of 0.99 and 0.999 are achievable today with only modest requirements of MTBF (hundreds of hours) and MTTR (tens of minutes) and minimal redundancy (20–30%), for sufficiently large complexes. It is important to note that the efficiency is not strongly dependent on the unit element MTBF. *It is quite possible for a system with subsystem MTBFs of 10,000 hours to have a substantially lower efficiency than one with subsystem MTBFs of 400 hours.*

3.7. Examples of Systems

3.7.1. Store-and-Forward Message Switching System

Three basic parameters are of interest in a store-and-forward switch: message delay, line service percentage, and throughput.

The acceptable message delay is usually specified for each priority class, and may depend upon the number of messages (of that priority) in the internal message queue of the system. Extra credit is not given to short delays below a certain minimum, and heavy penalties are imposed for overly long delays.

The line service percentage is used to measure the total number of lines obtaining acceptable service. This may be further broken down into line service percentage for each of several different line types.

The **throughput** of the system is defined as the sum of the input and output rates. Throughput figures can be given for the number of bits serviced per second, the number of characters per second, message transmission blocks, and messages, separately. One might expect that these figures would be simple multiples of each other. However, there exist trades among these characteristics which the unscrupulous architect can use to advantage.

Renegotiations, recriminations, and changes of scope often center upon little known subtleties among such closely related (and, to the uninitiated, equivalent) performance parameters. The opportunities to drive a "Shylock's bargain" countered with "Portia's defense" abound—*viz.*, "80,000 characters per second, but not one message!"

3.7.2. Air Defense System

An air defense system is intended to protect an area from attack. We can consider a point ballistic missile defense, concerned with the short-range protection of a specific area. The ultimate aim of this system is to prevent an incoming re-entry vehicle from detonating its charge at a damaging altitude. Since the interceptor itself may use a nuclear charge, the altitude at which the intercept occurs is critical lest the cure be worse than the disease. Typical performance parameters are acquisition range, noise immunity, track-point-per-second, discrimination probability, kill altitude, fratricide probability, and ultimately damage probability.

The acquisition range is critical because it is this factor above all that decides the length of time over which the engagement will occur. Acquisition beyond a given range is valueless since the system may not be able to launch useful interceptors for a relatively long time. Acquisition below a certain range is equally useless since the enemy has won and the engagement is terminated.

Noise immunity is important since it is assumed that the enemy is using a variety of sophisticated noise- and confusion-inducing mechanisms. Chaff and jamming developed during the Second World War to confuse the radar operator are early examples of such techniques. Since noise immunity is translatable into processing, this becomes an important factor. Acquisition range is dependent upon the ability of the system to detect a signal buried in noise.

The system is required to keep track of all vehicles involved in the engagement. This includes the threat vehicles, decoys, debris, satellites passing overhead, the sun, the moon, scheduled airline flights, interceptors, etc. Losing a track requires the system to reinitiate the detection of the track. If tracks for certain elements of the engagement are not updated often enough, the loss of accuracy will decrease the effectiveness of the system. Since all elements of the engagement are traveling at different speeds, along different trajectories, with different maneuverabilities, the number of track points per second that the complex can calculate is another performance parameter. Discrimination probability refers to the ability of the system to distinguish among real threats, deliberate decoys, and debris. Decoys are launched and debris manufactured in an attempt to saturate the defense by forcing it to premature commitment of its interceptors, by causing a complete processing overload or an intolerable processing delay. Discrimination is merely a way of sagaciously ignoring the unimportant. Failure to discriminate between a very clever decoy and the real thing can be catastrophic. Discrimination has a nonlinear penalty function.

Kill altitude ranges from the unachievable to the intolerable. The interceptor cannot be effective beyond a certain altitude, and an intercept below a certain altitude may be useless for two reasons: the missile may be set to detonate above the lower altitude, or the interception below the lower altitude limit is as damaging as the missile itself.

The fratricide probability refers to the fact that a given interceptor may disable the interceptor of a different target. A high fratricide probability is worse than useless. However, the engagement follows a statistically determinable scenario. As the engagement becomes more crucial, more interceptors are launched. Eventually, the space in which the engagement occurs becomes crowded and fratricide increases. Here is an example of a penalty function that changes rapidly during the effective lifetime of the system.

These separate performance parameters are merely a way to approach the evaluation of the one important parameter—expected damage. One cannot do negative damage since there is no circumstance under which such an engagement would prove beneficial. Damage beyond a certain point is an instance of "overkill," for which no special bonus is granted.

3.7.3. Air Traffic Control

This is a system which consists of almost the same kinds of components as a ballistic missile defense system (except for the interceptors, despite what the air traffic controllers think about general aviation), but with the opposite objectives. Acquisition range, noise immunity, track-points-per-second, discrimination probability, collision altitude, fratricide probability, and damage probability are all valid performance parameters. The intent here, however, is to minimize intercepts.

3.7.4. Process Control

A process control system is used to control chemical and petrochemical plants such as those used to refine petroleum, fabricate plastics, or produce pharmaceuticals. Similar systems are used in food processing, steel mills, paper mills, etc. Other closely related applications include training simulators, centralized airborne computers, and navigation autopilot systems and robots. These systems are characterized by having a number of loops to control. Each loop controls a function such as temperature, move the right pinky, pressure, distance, etc. The system has sensors that must be scanned, and effectors that must be controlled on the basis of a differential equation.

These functions were initially performed by a variety of specialized instruments such as pressure regulators, temperature controllers, and level sensors. The specialized systems were later supplemented by analog computers, and latterly by digital computers. The principal performance parameters are loop service percentage, iterations per second, and control accuracy.

If critical loops are not properly serviced, the process may become unstable, losses of raw material may be incurred, or worse, the plant may be destroyed. If the number of loops and/or the quality with which the loops are serviced is degraded below a certain level, sufficient capacity must be retained to allow orderly shutdown of the process. Several levels are distinguished: full operability, productive operation with manual aid, ability to dump the process, and catastrophic failure level. The specific weight given to each level of the penalty function depends on the cost of dumping the process, the productivity under manual operation over the duration of the manual operation, and the cost (or value) of the plant—in fact, on the relative and absolute values of each of these costs.

The number of iterations performed per second is also critical. Above a certain level, no improvement is noted. Below a certain level, the control is ineffective or unstable. Iteration rate and accuracy are often interrelated and exchangeable. Thus increased iterations may be obtained at the cost of accuracy. These two parameters can be so closely linked that they cannot be dealt with separately.

3.7.5. Remote-Access Computation

A remote-access, time-sharing computer system provides computer service to several users simultaneously. Each user effectively communicates with his own computer. The number of simultaneous users may range from a few to several hundred. Since the computer complex's capabilities are being shared, the user does not have access to the full complex for more than a fraction of a second at a time. The user sees a **subjective machine** whose capabilities are far less than those of the complex were it available to him continuously. The primary performance parameters of such systems are the user service percentage, subjective response time, subjective processor rate, subjective storage, and I/O throughput capacity.

The user service percentage is directly translatable into revenue. Each line not in use represents a loss of income. If many line outages occur, or if the system is not capable of serving enough users to meet the demand, a significant number of users will receive busy signals. If this happens too often, customers will turn to competitive systems. A unit of the system not working at full capacity represents a non-income-producing unit. Given enough such units, the system will not be profitable.

The subjective response time is an example in which higher performance is not rewarded. A delay of less than 100 milliseconds between the issuance of a command by the user and its execution by the system is imperceptible to the user. Taking into account the time required to print the result, for the user to observe the result, and to respond with a new command, a perceptible time lag of 1 second is acceptable. The acceptable delay, however, is independent of the magnitude of the task. The user will accept a delay of a second for the addition of two numbers and expect a similar delay for the solution of several hundred simultaneous equations.

The I/O throughput capacity is limited in two directions. On output, the system must be capable of printing at the rate of whatever display device the user happens to be using. Any lower rate will be penalized. This can range from ten characters per second to several thousand characters per second. Input is limited by the input device and how it is used, five characters per second being effective for manual keyboards. Almost any limit on manual input speed will be severely penalized.

4. THE ACHIEVEMENT OF VIABILITY

The goals of viability design are to provide high average performance (high μ), high viability efficiency, and consistency of performance (low σ). These can be achieved by means of the following approaches individually or in concert:

High reliability,
Maintainability,
Self-repair,
Graceful degradation,
Overdesign.

4.1. Reliability

Reliability measures can be taken at several different levels, which, for convenience, we shall call the component, circuit, unit, and subsystem levels. At the system level, our concern is more with viability than reliability. There are reliability enchancement techniques applicable to each of these levels. However, the influence that the architect can exert is less at the more microscopic levels.

4.1.1. Component Level

A component, for the sake of this discussion, will include the smallest element of the system which is manufactured as a discrete element and cannot be repaired. This could be a resistor or a major part of a computer constructed of large-scale integrated circuits. Component level reliability is the controlling factor of the reliability, but not the viability, of most systems. It is the level at which the architect has the least influence. Reliability at this level is primarily a matter of what kinds of quality and production control methods the component manufacturer uses. In the overwhelming majority of cases, high-reliability components are more expensive than their lower-reliability counterparts. This is reasonable because more labor is required for quality and production control.

The failure of a properly used component is most often due to some internal or external impurity introduced during manufacture. Electron tube failures (except those induced by technicians) during the Second World War were attributed to cotton lint—hence the widespread use of synthetic fabrics in tube assembly plants. Failures of components are induced by an unbelievable array of impurities. Two of the stranger ones are the acids secreted in the fingertips of menstruating women, and the change in the composition of a well-known laxative.[10] As each failure-producing impurity or physical phenomenon is discovered by the component manufacturer, changes are made in the manufacturing process or in the selection methods to eliminate such causes of failure. As a consequence, the reliability of components has been increasing an order of magnitude every few years. No small part of this has been the influence of military programs aimed at the achievement of high reliability.

Since it is rare that the architect will have a direct influence over component reliability, the measures taken by the architect must be indirect. He can support the reliability, quality control, and purchasing departments of the company or its suppliers by encouraging realistic reliability measures, incoming inspection procedures, and the use of reliable components from reputable manufacturers. He can recognize that reliability is bought at a price and be willing to pay that price where warranted; participate in the formation and continued support of reliability committees and seminars within the organization; insist on knowing the experimental basis for manufacturer-supplied reliability data; and insist on standard methods of presenting such data. Reputable manufacturers will supply such information to qualified prospects.

The architect should be wary of components whose operating principles involve new manufacturing technologies or previously unused physical phenomena. Changes in manufacturing methods, new production facilities, and ploys like "this new component is exactly equivalent to the old one, only

---

[10] The laxative was not used in the customary manner, but was employed as an insulating coating for pulse transformers wound from steel tape.

better" (more than one project has sunk beneath the waves of disappointment caused by "equivalent" components) all warrant further investigations.

Most important, the architect can provide a climate in which the reliability engineer can do his job properly. The reliability engineer needs all the help he can get. He is similar to the apocryphal charm against tigers in an Iowa cornfield. The charm works—there are no tigers. He is taken for granted and considered superfluous when there are no failures but is severely castigated when the inevitable failure occurs. He is the statistical outcast in a binary society.

4.1.2. Circuit Level Preventive Measures

Circuit failures occur because of component failures, component drift, overstressing of components, poor solder connections, and vulnerability to failures in other circuits. Drift—and the elimination of its effects—is an important part of circuit design. There are four basic approaches to the minimization of drift-induced failures: don't care design, worst-case design, worst-worst-case design, and statistical design.

"Don't care design" or **"bogey design"** are catch-all terms that describes circuits designed merely to work, without regard to reliability. Such design practices are not acceptable for production-engineered circuits.

Worst-case circuit design is a design practice in which the end-of-life characteristics, the temperature characteristics, and other factors that affect the parameter of interest of the circuit's performance are taken into account. The circuit design is checked at the extremes of its intended temperature range. The design has sufficient tolerance that acceptable performance will occur in spite of component parameter variations. This is perhaps the most common form of reliable circuit design. Tolerance to component parameter drift is bought at a price of increasing the number and the quality of components used in the circuit. Worst-case design is an approximation to "statistical design," discussed below. The payoff, despite the increased circuit cost, has been shown to be worth it. The cost of individual circuits is increased by 30 to 40% by such design practices. The cost of a computer complex, however, is not likely to be increased by more than a few percent, while the reliability may be doubled. A large, high-speed CPU or memory would probably not work at all if worst-case or statistical circuit design were not used.

Worst-worst-case design is a misguided attempt to increase the reliability of a circuit beyond that available through the use of worst-case design. In this practice, components are assumed to simultaneously achieve both extremes of their parameter ranges. Thus, a resistor is assumed to have its maximum resistance, while a neighboring resistor of the same type assumes its minimum value. The net effect of this practice is to design a very "safe" circuit. However, this may require doubling or tripling the components.

Thus, six transistors are used for a flip-flop rather than two. The increase in the number of components can result in a *reduced* circuit reliability. The increased cost can be more profitably applied in other ways.

Statistical circuit design is a design technique wherein component parameter values are assumed to be distributed according to a calculated or experimentally derived distribution. The component's temperature characteristics are described by distributions; the end-of-life parameter values are so described, as well as internal circuit environmental factors such as load, etc. The design takes into account combinations of conditions such that the accumulated failure probabilities for these conditions are adequate. If higher reliability is required, the circuit can be designed to take further parameter extremes into account, resulting in increased tolerance to parameter drift. The statistically designed circuit may be identical to its worst-case design counterpart; however, its predicted reliability and environmental tolerance will be significantly improved. Thus, statistical design does not necessarily improve reliability but improves our knowledge of reliability. Improved knowledge about reliability can be equivalent to improved reliability (for a new system). A pessimistic reliability calculation will result in overdesign that contributes nothing to the system. A more realistic evaluation of reliability will reduce the likelihood of overdesign and therefore will result in a higher performance-to-price ratio—a better system for the money. At any given cost, this can be parlayed into higher performance.

Another source of circuit failures are construction-induced failures. Components may be subjected to higher thermal stresses during manufacture than they will encounter during operation. For instance, the careless use of a soldering iron can ruin transistors. Manufacturing techniques can reduce such stresses. Heat sinks can be used to reduce thermal stresses. Small alligator clips attached to component leads during soldering, evaporative cooling pads soaked in alcohol, carefully designed lands, and low-power soldering irons all contribute to the reduction of thermal stresses. Wave soldering, dip soldering, and other mass-production soldering techniques, when properly controlled, can reduce manufacturing thermal stresses. Mechanical stresses can be reduced and controlled through the use of automated clipping, bending, and insertion machines. The uniform shape of integrated circuit packages allows increased assembly automation and consequently decreased stresses.

Poor solder joints remain a major source of circuit failures. A properly conducted circuit reliability analysis includes the reliability of solder joints. No small part of the increased reliability of systems constructed of integrated circuits is due to the reduction in the number of solder joints. Solder joint reliability is improved by automated soldering techniques (or degraded by improperly controlled automated soldering), cleanliness, gold plating, the use of plated-through holes, proper solder, proper fluxes, proper temperature, cleanliness, careful consideration of the electrochemistry of lead–land–solder eutectics, and cleanliness.

Tolerance to failures in other circuits is achieved through circuit design and an increase in components. The prime rule, however it is achieved, is that failures in one circuit should not induce failures in another. This may lead to the use of higher-wattage resistors, additional diodes, etc. It is not necessary that an overloaded circuit continue to function during the overload, only that it should not fail as a result of the overload.

4.1.3. Circuit-Level Adaptive Measures

The preceding section was a discussion of the various methods that could be used at the circuit level to prevent failures. This section deals with the methods that can be used to increase the circuit's tolerance to failures despite their occurrence. All methods discussed in this section are redundancy methods. If applied at the circuit level or higher, the redundancy increases the system cost. This must be traded with the cost and reliability improvements achieved by higher-level measures.

Circuit-level redundancy is achieved by considering critical components and their failure modes, and replacing these with equivalent subcircuits that are failure-tolerant. An example is given by the **diode-quad** shown in Figure 11.5.

A short circuit or an open circuit in any one diode will be tolerated. The cost of a diode-quad is increased number of components, reduction of circuit speed, increased number of connections, power, heat dissipation, etc. Similar techniques can be used for resistors, capacitors, and transistors.

The effectiveness of diode-quads and similar techniques within an integrated circuit is limited. Most failures of an integrated circuit are traceable to the bonds between the external leads and the chip (internal "solder joints"). Other failures are such that the failure of one diode, resistor, or transistor on the chip will cause the whole chip to fail due to propagative effects.

4.1.4. Mechanical Units

A unit is an assemblage of circuits, designed to accomplish a specific task. It is usually the smallest element of the system for which the replace-

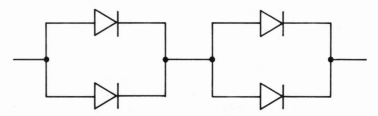

Figure 11.5. Diode-quad.

ment time is smaller than the repair time. Spare-part provisioning is often done at the unit level. A unit could be a circuit board with several integrated circuits on it, a rack of circuit boards, a core memory stack, etc.

Reliability improvement in mechanical units is accomplished by the techniques discussed in previous sections on circuit and component reliability. In addition, physical construction and connectors play an important role. Mechanical design is aimed at reducing mechanical shock to components and connectors. Many shocks occur during shipping. There are numerous stories about computers being dropped off the loading platform, being destroyed in railroad humping yards, being given standard handling by teamsters and longshoremen, etc.

One should not assume that the world is filled with malevolent beings whose only interest is to reduce a complex piece of hardware to junk while transporting it across the country. Prudence, however, is advised. Consider the apocryphal stories told about parcel post packages labeled "fragile," the improper alignment of elevators, the number of door sills between the production floor and the site, the jerky precision of fork-lift trucks, blowouts on the throughway, bumpy landings, turbulence; or, rather, consider your own composure were you shipped across the country by freight. Having considered this, the reader should gain appreciation for the specialized mechanical designs aimed at preventing such mishaps, the care and frustratingly long time required to pack and unpack computer components, the use of reliable shipping firms, and the virtue of insurance.

Mobile military systems must face the above continuum of catastrophies throughout their life. In such systems, mechanical design is proportionately more important. Good mechanical design is not achieved by building the unit as the proverbial "brick outhouse." Resonance is more important than brute strength: resilience is more effective than rigidity.

Once the system has been installed and shipping damages corrected, the real test of mechanical design begins. A pencil dropped from a height of two feet can incur shocks of 2000 Gs. A module dropped from a similar distance can be utterly destroyed. The cumulative effect of technician-induced damage makes the teamster seem like a benevolent angel suffused with the delicacy and dedication of a neurosurgeon. The technician, however, is not to be blamed if the circuit board is not provided with a handle for removal. He will, with great care, use a pair of pliers, crushing the epoxy glass board in the process and stressing nearby solder joints. Improperly balanced drawers, sticky slides, knuckle-bruising projections, exposed high-voltage lines, buried components, and the inevitable stress on maintenance personnel during a system failure all contribute to the occurrence of technician-induced failures. The equipment must be mechanically designed to withstand stress, and must be designed with the maintenance technician in mind. These requirements are sometimes contradictory. Thus, high connector insertion pressures reduce the failure of circuit board connectors but increase the difficulty of inserting and removing the board without damage. Brackets, leverage points, and specialized tools reduce the incidence of failure. "Go–no–go" design prevents the improper assemblage of elements. Keys, special slides, and built-in maintenance aids improve the situation. These methods and problems are the province of the mechanical engineer, maintenance engineer, and production engineer. These individuals, on the periphery of the glamour of system design, are often ignored, leading to low reliability and high MTTR.

Thermal design is basically a question of keeping things cool. Trivial as this may sound, many systems fail through improper thermal design. The system is designed to operate in a certain ambient temperature range. However, the highest temperatures usually occur within the unit itself. Thermal design begins with circuit designs that lead to temperature-tolerant circuits. It is then the thermal designer's job to see to it that excessive temperatures are not reached. This is done by a variety of means: card layout to induce natural convection, properly ducted forced air flow, freon-cooled mounting plates, heaters,[11] heat sinks, isolation of power-dissipating components, or air conditioning.

Temperature problems occur so frequently that they become one of the standard problems to look for in a new system. It is always safe to ask, "Have you gotten over your thermal problems yet?" Another way of judging progress on a new system is to count how many cabinet doors are open. One should beware of systems running with "open doors" during acceptance testing. Thermal design is often done by the mechanical engineer on the job. The architect who disdainfully considers the cabinet and mechanical design of a system as "mere boxes" is in for a few surprises.

Connectors and their logical extensions—backplanes, cables, and buses—are a major source of failure. Connectors fail mechanically due to improper mechanical design or handling during maintenance. They fail because a ten-pin connector is forced into a twelve-pin socket. They fail because keys have not been provided to prevent upside-down insertion. Contacts may oxidize, inducing malfunctions. Smog with a high sulfur content can contribute to this. This is a particularly serious problem in computers used in chemical and petrochemical process control, or computers used in almost any large city. Good connectors have wiping contacts that tend to rub the oxides off. If, however, the circuits are very reliable, there will

---

[11] Rather than keeping things cool, the unit is allowed to operate at a controlled temperature which is above ambient. This is often easier to accomplish than to try to keep the temperature at ambient. A temperature-controlled oven is often used in core memory stacks and other temperature-critical elements.

be no occasion to remove the card, and consequently this type of failure can increase.

Backplanes consist of many connections. Wires in the backplane may be power-wrapped and then soldered in order to reduce failures. Alternatively, large, multilayer printed circuit boards may be used, to reduce the number of wires and contacts. Printed circuit backplanes are more reliable, but have a high MTTR.

Cables present one of the knottiest problems in the design of reliable systems. Electronic considerations require that they be short and rigid. Mechanical considerations dictate that they be long and flexible. Electrical requirements require the use of twisted pairs of wires or concentrically wound helixes, while mechanically, untwisted parallel wires are best. A good cable is wound tight (loose), thick (thin), straight (coiled), etc. The problem extends to the subfloor of the system and is generally aggravated in systems using configuration switching.

4.1.5. Logical Units

The simplest approach toward increasing the reliability of logical units is to make them self-correcting. A common method is the use of majority vote logic with replication. This method is shown in Figure 11.6.

The units are assumed to be identical and are allowed any kind of failure mode. The majority vote circuit selects the best two out of three outputs and presents the concensus as the output of the circuit. The critical assumption is that the voter, being much simpler than the circuits, is more reliable. If the voting element is sufficiently reliable, the reliability of such replication schemes (where the circuit is repeated more than three times) can be made to approach that of the majority element. One does not have to assume that the voter cannot fail.

If it is reasonable to assume that only a single failure will occur in the unit, the above scheme can be cascaded to yield the scheme shown in Figure 11.7. Here the majority voters have themselves been triplicated, and by

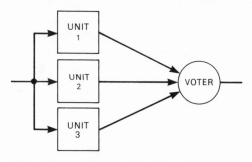

Figure 11.6. Replicated units with majority voting.

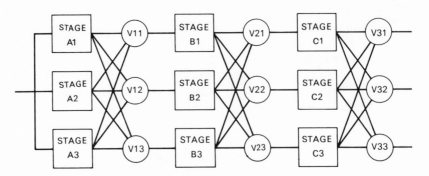

Figure 11.7. Multistage replication with replicated voting.

extension, are voted upon by succeeding majority elements. Any single failure in a stage or in a majority element will be masked. This method can also be extended by further replication. This approach, while effective, is costly. It cannot be readily applied within integrated electronic components as a single failure is likely to corrupt the complete network. Therefore its use has been limited.

Error correcting codes are another method of improving the reliability at the unit level.

In a network that implements error correction, the nature of the differences between the observed and expected values is used to correct the error. Such methods can fail because it is fallaciously assumed that no error occurs in the check or correction networks themselves. This can also be accommodated and the error rate reduced despite check-circuitry failures. Error detecting and correcting codes have been applied mostly in long-haul data transmission, or in vulnerable elements of a complex, such as memories. Applications of error correcting codes within the computer itself are rare and of marginal utility. The internal structure of a computer is sufficiently complex that the circuitry required to implement elaborate error correcting schemes is better used in providing redundancy at higher levels. Another limitation of the applicability of error correcting networks within a computer is the difficulty of designing them. The logic designer must take into account the failure modes of every logic element used. Even restricting his attention to a single failure at a time drastically increases the cost of logic design.

One weakness of adaptive measures that mask the failures which occur (such as quads or majority voting) is that a portion of the system does not work. A highly redundant system with universal triplication would probably arrive in the field with 30 % of its circuitry inoperable. The MTBF would be high. However, when an element failure occurred that could not be masked, the repair time would be enormous. The net effect would probably be to reduce the viability. The approach is valid in a satellite. If a MTBF of ten years is predicted and a life of two years expected, the trade is a good one. The MTTR is effectively infinite for most satellites, so that its increase is of no consequence.

4.1.6. Subsystem Level

The reliability enhancement techniques discussed above apply at the subsystem level as well. Additional factors, however, come into play.

The subsystem level is usually the lowest level at which power supply reliability must be considered. With it, the complete power distribution, protection, and regulation networks must be evaluated. The power supply of a computer subsystem should not be thought of as the simple rectifier, choke, and filter capacitors of a home radio. It is in reality a high-power, broad-band, precision DC amplifier.[12] Failure of one of the several power supplies in a subsystem is tantamount to the failure of the entire subsystem. Redundant power supplies are provided for critical subsystems. The power distribution and protection networks in such applications are designed to prevent the propagation of a malfunction in one power supply to its standby.

The primary consideration in subsystem reliability is the isolation of failed units from properly functioning ones. This requires careful design of all interface circuits. A common failing in subsystem design is the inability to remove malfunctioning units without damaging good ones. Thus, the removal of a bad unit, or the insertion of a good replacement, can induce transients that will cause the good units to either temporarily malfunction or to fail. In some systems, it is necessary to cut power to carry out such replacements. This is not desirable.

The problem is avoided by proper logic design of the units and the subsystem. All interfaces to units are designed so that the interface leads when left floating assume the logical values and loads of the reset state (or initial state) of the unit. Resetting the unit allows it to be removed without inducing possibly damaging transients. Unit interfaces with these safe characteristics are achievable at little or no extra production cost. The ability to remove or insert units into a running subsystem clearly contributes to a reduced MTTR. Consider the problem of testing and replacing 30 circuit boards if the power must be cycled up and down and allow the subsystem to thermally stabilize each time.[13]

---

[12] One manufacturer offers his computer power supplies for either application.

[13] The architect can use a simple, effective, but unpopular test for this capability. The architect, being a "system" or "software" type, is often considered ingenuous by the more knowledgeable engineers and technicians. We normally advise him to keep his hands in his pockets during an inspection tour. If, however, this type of problem is suspected, let him make motions as if to remove a module or circuit board in a working subsystem. The horrified expression of the maintenance technician or site engineer is a fair gauge of the degree to which the problem exists.

4.2. Maintainability

Good maintainability is the achievement of a low MTTR. The MTTR consists of the time required to accomplish the following:

1. Detect the failure.
2. Isolate the malfunctioning element.
3. Remove the malfunctioning element.
4. Obtain a replacement for it.
5. Replace it.
6. Verify its operability.
7. Initialize the replacement.
8. Transfer to the operable state.

Many factors contribute to a reduction of time in each of these steps. The probability that a particular subsystem will be down is affected as much by the MTTR as by the MTBF. Most military programs aimed at the improvement of viability have stressed the MTBF over the MTTR. This is perhaps appropriate in a guided missile or satellite in which repairs cannot be made. Recently, the emphasis has shifted to the consideration of the MTTR. The accomplishment of the above actions is influenced by the physical construction, the level at which replacements can be made, the training of the maintenance technicians, the ability to detect and isolate malfunctions, the extent and quality of diagnostic tools provided, the built-in test and diagnostic facilities of the system, and the repair facilities of the complex.

4.2.1. Mechanical Construction

The detrimental effects that poor physical construction can have on reliability through increased technician-induced failures was discussed in Section 4.1. However, it is not enough to merely prevent technician-induced failures. That only reduces secondary failures but does not help directly in the repair of a malfunction.

Let us not forget that the maintenance technician is human. He is adept, practical, and patient. He has had technical high school training and perhaps the equivalent of two years of college education and three years of experience. His theoretical knowledge of systems is limited, and he is not inclined toward the consideration of deep intellectual problems. Years of living with poor maintainability design has made him somewhat cynical. Still, his intuitive knowledge of the system or the subsystems in his charge is often superior to that of the designer of that subsystem. The designer is typically concerned with the system as it works—the maintenance technician is concerned with all the malfunctioning variations thereof. The designer builds one system with n components—the maintenance man tries to understand 2^n or more systems.

As a human being, the technician should not be asked to expose himself to lethal voltages, remain stooped in a cramped position, exert forces beyond his ability, use mirrors or cystoscopes to check connections, read backwards and upsidedown, distinguish among several subtly different colors, use impossible tools in ridiculous places and positions, wear gloves, search for dropped tools, or work in poor light. The aspects of mechanical design that lead to low repair times can be in direct contradiction to electrical requirements. A trade is implied here. The compromise is achieved by the mutual action of the designers, engineers, maintenance engineers, and human factors engineers.

4.2.2. Replacement–Repair Levels, Facilities, and Policies

An element that fails can either be repaired in place or be replaced with a functioning spare. The removed element may subsequently be repaired or discarded. From the point of view of system viability, the act of replacement is tantamount to repair if there are enough spares. The idea of what constitutes replacement and what constitutes repair depends on the level at which the maintenance is carried out. Thus, a computer complex is "repaired" when the spare computer is switched into the functioning position occupied by the failed computer. The computer is "repaired" when the faulty power supply is replaced. The power supply is repaired when the malfunctioning circuit module is replaced, which is itself repaired when the malfunctioning rectifier has been replaced.

Replacement–repair policies define a hierarchy, ranging from the largest element to the smallest (which is usually discarded upon failure). At the highest level, the elements are complex, costly, and specialized. At the lowest level, the elements are simple, inexpensive, and generalized. These characteristics of cost, complexity, and specificity are distributed continually from the simplest to the most complex elements of the system.

The mean time to repair generally increases as the lower element levels are reached. An increasingly longer chain of diagnostic tests is required to isolate the malfunctioning element. Similarly, the cost of keeping an adequate supply of spares is decreased. If all repairs are to be made at the component level, the MTTR will be maximized but the spares cost will be minimized. A realistic system design will include a set of policies for replacement and repair at every level, the mix and amount at any level being selected on the basis of maximizing the viability for a given cost. The cost of the spares, the repair facilities, and tools is no small part of the total hardware cost. Five to ten percent is not unusual.

When we evaluate the MTTR at a given level, there is an implicit assumption of an infinite source of spares at the next lower level. The next lower level is itself a complex, with its own MTBF and MTTR. That level's function, however, is not the performance of the system's tasks, but rather the production of working spares. That system has a performance measured in terms of the repair time for the elements it is repairing. If test equipment fails, or if sublevel spares are lacking, the repair time will increase. These so-called "off-line" repair facilities are structured to give immediate replacement. This is assured by making the statistical repair rate of a failed element higher than the failure rate of such elements. A complete viability calculation for the repair facilities is not usually required. Often a verification of the repair rate is sufficient.

Another important assumption, and often an insidious one, is that a qualified maintenance man will be available to make the repairs. In military systems or those operating in a military-like urgency situation (high penalty for failure), maintenance personnel is provided on a 24-hour basis, with a sufficient number of "spares" to assure the quality of the repair facility. Such heavy staffing can dominate the operational cost of the system. The increasingly common practice is to consider the total cost of the system over its expected lifetime. The cost of maintenance personnel can exceed the cost of the system with a service life of ten years. The following example shows this. A minimum crew of one man, on a 24-hour, seven-day basis, allowing for vacations and illness, requires five men. At a cost (including overhead) of $15,000 per man per year, this is $750,000 over a ten-year period. It is not unusual for a large complex to require a maintenance crew of four men. This raises the cost to $3,000,000 over a ten-year period. It is possible to reduce the maintenance crew by either increasing the MTBF of the elements, decreasing the MTTR of the elements, or increasing the number of spares kept at each level. A cost can be associated with each of these factors. The cost of a spare consists of its initial cost plus the cost of the capital it represents over the ten-year period, as well as the cost of keeping it on the shelf. A $1.00 part, on this basis, could represent a cost of $2.25 for the ten-year period. The evaluation is based on representative storage cost and compound interest at 1.5% per quarter.

From this, we see that for a given viability, the larger complex is achieved at a lower cost than several independent smaller complexes. Similarly, the manufacturer who is adding a capability to an existing complex offers a significant long-term advantage to the user over the new supplier, even if the new supplier's price is substantially lower than that of the original supplier's.

There is a trade, then, between the number and cost of maintenance technicians, the number of spares, the expected lifetime of the system, and the MTTR, and, thereby, the viability. The high-viability system may be selected not because viability itself is a requirement, but because high viability may be a way to reduce the total operational cost over the life of the system.

4.2.3. Documentation and Training

The maintenance technician, who is the prime determinant of the MTTR, is called upon to detect and correct a virtual infinity of malfunctions. It is unlikely, even for a modest computer complex, that he will be able to retain all the required information in his head. He relies on two things: general training applicable to all failures and specific classes of common failures, and documentation of the system and associated maintenance procedures.

We have tacitly assumed that the MTTR and the MTBF are independent. In reality, they are not. As the MTBF is increased, the MTTR is also increased. As any particular failure becomes less probable, the technician's ability to deal with it is degraded through lack of familiarity. A similar situation occurs in medicine. Most physicians have never seen a case of smallpox or rabies. Similarly, polio, diphtheria, beriberi, erythroleukoblastosis, and a host of other diseases are rapidly becoming "textbook cases." As these diseases are conquered, the probability of a proper and timely diagnosis when the unexpected occurs is decreased. This possibility is recognized and compensated through mandatory training in the diagnosis and treatment of such diseases, and in the existence of reference books which detail symptoms, treatment, and prognosis.

We have seen that the critical factor in viability is the ratio of MTTR to MTBF. If the degradation of the MTTR increases faster than the gain in MTBF, the system viability may be statistically decreased rather than increased. Thus, the periods of proper operation may be longer, but when failures occur, "all hell breaks loose."

Just as most of the system's program is concerned with events that may never occur, the bulk of the technician's training is concerned with unlikely but serious failures. The key to this dilemma lies in the kinds and quality of maintenance manuals that are provided. The manuals should be written from the point of view that the technician has had little or no training; that is, they should be as self-contained and complete as possible, leaving little assumed outside the scope of the manual. The detail should be written under the assumption that the failure described has never occurred before, and will probably never occur again. The procedures used to correct these failures must be sufficiently well worked out that a technician with only general training will be able to make the repair successfully. Maintenance manuals are considerably more detailed than operating principles manuals, or design documentation. If top caliber technicians are not used to staff the maintenance facility, then even greater care must be taken in writing the manuals. The technical publication group is the vital link between the designer and the maintenance man. The technical editors and writers are thus invited into the design team as well.

A common approach to the reduction of the MTTR for unlikely failures is through the simulation of such failures. Training exercises may be run during periods of low activity, major failure situations simulated, malfunctions induced, etc. The maintenance technician should be encouraged to use the time during which he is not maintaining the equipment in training and study.

5. MALFUNCTION DETECTION

The start of any repair procedure is that point at which it has been recognized that repair is required, that is, the detection of a present or impending malfunction. Detection is in itself a probabilistic thing. There are two reasons for this. For one thing it is not possible to ascertain all failure modes. For another, the malfunction detection hardware and software are themselves subject to failure. They too must be provided with malfunction detection.

5.1. Malfunction Indicators

A malfunction indicator is any method which is used to detect a malfunction, without making an attempt to correct the source of the malfunction. Malfunction detection is not concerned with the problem of isolating the component, unit, or subsystem in which the failure occurred. It may often take a combination of detected malfunctions to isolate a failed element. A malfunction is a symptom of a failure and bears the same relation to failures that physiological symptoms bear to diseases. The prevalent approaches to malfunction detection are discussed below.

5.1.1. Parity Schemes and Error Detecting Codes

Parity checks are employed in memories, tapes, and drums, but are not restricted to them. A common form of parity check used in a tape transport is called an "echo check." In this procedure, the word which has just been written onto the tape is read and its parity checked. A parity error indicates that the word was not properly written (or read). Similar schemes can be used with other memories.

Parity is normally destroyed in most arithmetic or logical manipulations of data. That is, there is no simple relation between the parity of the operands and the parity of the results, such as "the parity of the sum equals the sum of the parities," or "the parity of the union equals the union of the parities," etc. Some relations do exist. For example, the parity of a sum is determined by modifying the sum of the parities according to whether the number of carries in the addition was odd or even. This is probably one of the simplest such relations. Because of the complexity of parity correction, parity checks are generally restricted to data transfers and only occasionally used within arithmetic units.

Parity checks are a simple example of the more general error detecting codes or multiple parity methods. These techniques can be used to generate codes that detect and/or correct any number of errors in a word. Such codes are generally useful or worthwhile where the transmission channel is noisy, for example, in long-haul data transmission or in magnetic tapes. The most common example of a multiparity scheme is the use of longitudinal as well as horizontal parity in a block of words. This provides an effective multiple-error-detection, partial-error-correction scheme for large groups of data at a minimal cost.

Parity checking is an essential feature of intersubsystem communications, and is an important way of enhancing the viability of the system as a whole.

5.1.2. Check Sums

A **check sum** is another type of longitudinal parity check used for block transfers of data. Parity is a modulo-2 sum. Check sums are made modulo the range of the data unit, e.g., modulo 256 for 8-bit characters, or modulo 2^n for an n-bit data element. The arithmetic sum of all characters or words in the block is calculated, either by hardware or software. A comparison is then made with the check sums in the block (usually the last character).

5.1.3. Check Programs

The system executes a check program and generates one or more numbers. That number is compared with a previously stored result and if different indicates that the subsystem has malfunctioned. The resulting number may or may not serve diagnostic purposes. An example of a check program is to run through a given program twice; a disagreement in the results indicates that an error has been made. Periodic check programs are effective in detecting malfunctions. However, one should be cautious about using the processor under test to do the comparison, because while the lack of an error will yield a positive indication (no malfunction), the existence of an error may yield no indication.

5.1.4. Replicated Hardware

Another method of detecting malfunctions in the main frame of a computer is to provide replication of hardware. A comparison of the outputs of replicated units is made to determine whether or not a malfunction has occurred. This method was used in UNIVAC I. Replication of equipment, while detecting the overwhelming majority of errors, is expensive. Once it has been decided to incorporate redundancy, there are more effective ways of applying it toward the enhancement of viability.

5.1.5. Through-System Checks

A through-system check is an extension of a check program in which input signals simulated by the system are applied to the front end of the system along with normal inputs, and traced through from beginning to end. While this provides the most complete check of system health, there are difficulties associated with the approach. In some systems it may not be possible to simulate meaningful input signals, or a simulated signal may be interpreted as a real signal (due to a malfunction) and cause an inappropriate action to take place. Care must be taken to assure that no adverse actions can occur as a result of through-system checks.

5.1.6. Confidence Messages

A confidence message scheme is one in which the various subsystems are required to report their status at predetermined periodic intervals. Failure of a subsystem to report on time is construed as a malfunction of that subsystem. A combined hardware and software approach is usually used. This method is particularly effective as an overall failure indicator. The probability that a computer will be able to report when it has incurred a failure (in software as well as hardware) is small.

5.1.7. Level Checks

A level check is one in which critical system voltages or currents are monitored and compared against predetermined limits. They are not only indicative of actual failures, but can warn of impending failures. The effectiveness of level checks depends upon the meaning that these variations have with respect to system malfunction. Applicability of such checks in digital systems is limited. They have some utility in monitoring power supply voltages, low-level amplifiers, and other nondigital circuits.

5.1.8. Marginal Testing

Marginal testing is a technique for the detection of impending malfunctions which is a holdover from the days of vacuum tube computers, and has little or no validity when applied to solid state computers using worst-case or statistical circuit design. In practice it consists of the lowering and raising (as appropriate) of power supply voltages, and of monitoring the resulting malfunctions (if any) by other means. Since worst-case design is generally used in present-day computers, and due to the particular failure modes of semiconductors, this type of testing in computers has fallen out of use. Marginal tests can cause unnecessary stresses to components, and can thereby induce premature malfunctions. Marginal voltage checks have limited applications within computers in the case of sense amplifiers for core and film memories, particularly when coupled with level checks.

5.1.9. Cumulative Checks

A cumulative check is one in which the rate of transient malfunctions within a subsystem is continually monitored. That is, a memory location is incremented for each detected malfunction of a given type. This can serve as an indicator of impending malfunctions. The details and applicability are closely tied to the particular application.

5.1.10. Reasonableness Checks

The results of a given calculation may be checked against previously stored values or by a simpler routine, to determine if the number is within reasonable bounds. If such methods are incorporated in the software, they take the form of data validation checks, benchmark checks, and the like. The most elaborate reasonableness check is to do the whole computation independently in several different computers. A reasonableness check should be significantly less complicated than the actual calculation if it is to be effective. The use of reasonableness checks is dangerous. It presumes that proper bounds for calculated results have been established and that inputs that would drive the system outside these bounds cannot exist.

5.2. Malfunction Detection Hardware

The total cost of malfunction detection hardware is of the order of 3 to 5% of the uninstalled hardware cost. This includes the parity check and generation networks at each interface and such other special check networks as may be included. The additional hardware is dispersed throughout the system and is probably paid for in reduced production debugging time. Therefore, built-in automatic malfunction detection equipment may reduce the system cost.

5.2.1. Functional Indicators

The following is a nonexhaustive catalog of the functional alarms that could be used:

○ *Central Processing Unit*

Illegal Instruction Detection—Attempt to execute an op code not corresponding to an instruction. The illegal operation is usually interpreted as a no-op.

Invalid Instruction—Attempt to execute an instruction or instruction option not applicable to the options provided in this computer.

Overflow—Arithmetic unit overflow. Not ordinarily considered a malfunction detection measure, but often used as such.

Underflow—Loss of significance in one of two floating point operands during normalization.

Parity Errors

Arithmetic Errors

Nonexistent Address—An attempt to modify or read the content of a memory address that does not exist. This can be extended to indirect and/or index-modified addresses.

Illegal Address—The same as above, except for predetermined addresses or address segments. Some words may be read or written, some only read, some only written. The notion of what addresses are illegal may depend on the address of the instruction used to access such words.

Cycle Alarm—An alarm that is triggered if the program counter had not changed in a predetermined number of instructions. Presumably the processor is caught in a loop. This can be tricky to implement in machines that have looping instructions.

Stall Alarm—An alarm that is triggered if an instruction is not completed in a predetermined time.

Watchdog Alarm—An alarm that is triggered if the processor fails to reset the watchdog timer on time.

○ **Memory Switch**

Skip Alarm—Indicates that the memory channel was sufficiently overloaded that a request was not honored. The alarm should signify which request.

○ **Interrupt System**

Multiple Interrupt—Indicates that more than one unserviced interrupt occurred in a given interrupt channel.

Missed Interrupt—Indicates that a required interrupt, for example a watchdog alarm, has not occurred.

○ **Input/Output**

Illegal Device—No such device.

Illegal Command—Command given to a device that is not interpretable by that device. Could be broken down into many substatuses.

Improper Sequence—A second command occurs that cannot directly follow the previous command. For example, fast-forward on a tape directly after a rewind, without an intervening halt.

○ *Drum:* Parity error, bearing temperature, vibration, invalid command (e.g., REWIND, EJECT PAPER), illegal command, command sequence error.

○ *Disc:* Same as for drum, plus improper seek commands.

○ *Tape:* Broken tape, reel full, reel empty, vacuum loss, tape on leader, excessive skew, parity.

○ *Card Device:* Stuck card, double feed, skew, hopper full, hopper empty, punch solenoid current excessive.

While some of these indicators are not incorporated for the sole purpose of malfunction detection, the existence of some of these status signals in a given context may be indicative of a malfunction.

5.2.2. Built-in Test Facilities

Test points, indicator lights, push buttons, test switches, test signal generators, test logic, built-in go–no-go tests, error-forcing logic, meters, and displays are part of the built-in test facilities appropriate to good maintainability design. These facilities are not solely for detection, but play an equally important role in isolation.

A test point is any logical signal that has been brought to a convenient place. The technician uses it to observe signal levels, the existence of signals, wave forms, etc. Test points should be supplied liberally for almost any logic signal that makes sense. The existence of test points, however, tends to slow circuits and increase noise and cost. The lowest level of test points is provided by an extender card (shown in Figure 11.8), which allows the technician to monitor all inputs and outputs of the module.

The built-in test points provide access to internal signals not normally available. The selection of the test points is usually made by the logic designer. They should be chosen to give the maximum amount of information, both functional and electrical. Test points do increase cost, but reduce the MTTR of the system and the MTTR of the failed element itself. Other test points may be brought to local test-point panels, if the impedance of the dangling wires can be tolerated (a nonterminated dangling wire at high frequencies is as much a load as another circuit). Indicator lights were an early form of testpoints.

The MTBF and MTTR of early computers were so poor by present standards that many indicator lights and control switches were provided.

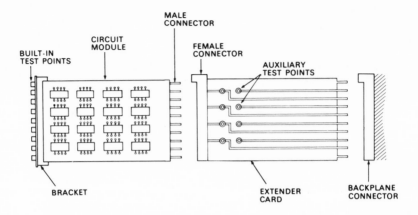

Figure 11.8. Circuit card and extender card with test points.

The more prevalent approach today is to provide three levels of indicators: on individual cards or units, directly related to the unit's function but not necessarily meaningful on an overall functional basis; on a maintenance panel or console, to be used in repairs; on the system console, relating to purely functional indicators. Thus, every circuit card of the program counter may have indicators and every flip-flop of a two-rank register may be brought out to the maintenance panel, while only the prime rank is shown on the system console (probably as an alphanumeric, hexadecimal, or octal character display).

Test switches and push buttons are used to generate signals that are normally generated by the circuitry. They appear in much the same hierarchy as do the testpoints and indicators. Switches can be used to bypass or cutoff certain signals for diagnostic purposes. Test signal generators are extensions of pushbuttons. They generate sequences of test signals rather than single signals. Test logic is included to detect conditions of several signals simultaneously, or to detect critical signal sequences.

Go–no-go tests and associated logic is designed to give positive indications of failure. This may be a small built-in test network whose output is "one" only if the network it is testing is working properly. Error-forcing logic is used to test the proper functioning of built-in test circuits, such as parity check networks. The built-in test facility may range from nonexistent to complex signal generators and logic that allows a unit or subsystem to simulate the response of every subsystem it interfaces with. Each element introduced as a built-in test facility will decrease the MTBF, increase the cost, and, it is hoped, decrease the MTTR.

5.2.3. Malfunction Indication Concentration

The outputs of malfunction indicators must be centralized and brought to the system's attention. Concentration of indicator lights and test points is done by the eyes of the technician. Concentration can be done through the generation of interrupts or special instructions devised to determine the status of units and subsystems. Similarly, the switches, pushbuttons, signal generators, and error-forcing logic may have counterparts in special instructions for this purpose. Each indicator may be examined by means of status seeking instructions. Similarly, instructions provided to force error statuses, so as to test the validity of the malfunction indicator, may be implemented.

In order to properly reconstruct a malfunctioning system it may be necessary to collect malfunction indications at a central point for subsequent analysis by a computer. This can be done by monitor scanners. These can range in complexity from simple lines dispersed throughout a system to devices approaching the complexity of a data logging system. Fundamentally, malfunction monitoring is accomplished through the use of a scanning device of some sort. Such devices can be electromechanical or electronic or both. A combination of the two is effective. The electronic scanner can be used for monitoring malfunction indicators in groups at a high speed, while the slower and less costly electromechanical scanner is applied to the individual indicators within a group when it has been determined that an element of that group has failed.

Error monitoring, if done at an inappropriate level, adds arbitrarily much to the cost of the system. *On-line* monitoring and malfunction detection is not done at a level incompatible with automatic repair. If a trade analysis is done, it turns out for most systems that, component for component and word for word, the pay-off is far better in the detection of malfunction than in the use of error correcting codes and malfunction correction at the microscopic level.

6. FAILURE ISOLATION

We shall distinguish between two types of equipment failure isolation procedures: those intended to isolate the malfunctioning equipment to the unit or subsystem level in order to provide information required for the automatic replacement of the failed device, and those intended to find faults at a lower level to be manually repaired off-line. There is no point in performing on-line isolation at a level at which on-line automatic repair is not provided. The data are of no direct use to the system, and their interpretation and processing take time.

One of the first problems in the isolation of equipment failures is the distinction between physical and functional names of devices. Hardware malfunction indicators refer directly to the device in which the malfunction occurred, and there is no problem for these indicators. Software indicators do not relate directly to the piece of hardware in which the failure occurred. The detecting device might only know the functional or logical name of the culprit, and not the physical name. A list of physical/functional assignments must be maintained at all times. This list is one of the most important information sets to be maintained.

Detection of malfunctions in a system cannot be accepted immediately as valid. Corroborative checks are required. Consider the detection of a parity error in a transmission of data from a memory to a CPU. Furthermore, assume that the CPU is the one responsible for failure isolation. The parity error could mean one of several things: parity error in the memory, error in the parity check circuit of the memory, error in the communication channel or the memory switch, CPU parity check circuit error, malfunction monitor error, isolation program error. If a complete set of malfunction detectors has been provided, the error source can be isolated. The error could have resulted in any of five different actions, namely: another attempt at transmission if it was merely a transient parity circuit error; reloading the memory if it was a transient memory parity error; choice of an alternate communication channel if it was a channel error; removal and replacement of the memory if it was a permanent memory malfunction; or replacement of the analyzing CPU if it was a CPU malfunction.

6.1. Test Programs

On-line failure isolation can be done by test programs. The objective of the test program is to determine which of several possible units has failed, without regard to the specific cause of the failure if that cause cannot be corrected at the level of the test program. Thus, if automatic repair capabilities are provided that allows only CPUs to be automatically replaced, on-line test programs that isolate to the level of, say, an arithmetic unit, are useless. Were self-repair extended to the component level (by means of some hypothetical robot), the test program would have to be diagnostic to that level to be useful.

The simplest form of test program is one that accepts as valid, the data provided by malfunction indicators. Given that a failure has been apparently detected, the test program (trivially) initiates corrective action directly. However, if the cost of corrective action, paid for in down-time, is high, and if the probability of a malfunction indicator malfunction is significant, a more elaborate test program must be used. The variations and machinations which go into the design of a test program are legion. The test program is tailored to the system in which it resides. Its detail is dictated by the details of the logic design of the elements it tests as well as the environment of the system. We shall, however, illustrate the general philosophy used in the design of a test program by an example. Figure 11.9 shows a typical solution for magnetic tapes. We shall describe a fairly elaborate procedure, recognizing that a specific test program will often be simpler, by virtue of containing only some of these elements.

One of several central processing units in a computer complex is connected to one or more channel controllers. The channel controllers could be controlled by yet other CPUs. Each channel controller, in turn, controls one or more device controllers, among which may be several tape controllers. Each tape controller controls one or more tape transports. Switchgear is interposed between adjacent levels of this tree to allow automatic switchover and self-repair. During the course of running a program, an improper status has been detected in one of the transports, say tape unit 12. That is, it appears to the CPU program that a command issued has not been successfully completed. After the appropriate number of retries, the test program is called in to determine which of the thirty-odd devices depicted in Figure 11.9 is responsible for the apparent failure of tape unit 12.

The simplest approach is to assume that tape unit 12 has malfunctioned and, if possible, replace it with a tape unit that is known to be working.

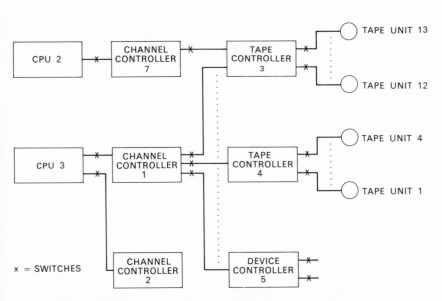

Figure 11.9. Diagnostic problem in the CPU–channel–device hierarchy.

If this does not work, the tape controller is replaced. If *that* fails to correct the apparent malfunction, the channel controller is replaced. If all else fails, the CPU aborts its functions and another CPU takes over the slot. The problem with this simplistic approach is that besides being time-consuming it does not solve the problem. Suppose that the malfunction is in the tape controller and that it results in a faulty command parameter (but proper command) being transmitted to the tape unit. Furthermore, suppose that the error is due to an improper loading of an output line driver, between tape controller 3 and tape unit 12, such that any other combination of controller and tape unit will not exhibit the malfunction. This may seem like a lot of "supposes," but is typical of the kinds of failures that a test program may be required to detect.

The first step is loading the test program. At this point in the test procedure, it is only known that there is an *apparent* tape malfunction. The failure may be in the channel, not allowing the test program to be loaded. Several alternatives are provided for loading the test program. The program used to call the test program must itself be capable of choosing among these alternatives. Furthermore, if it fails to properly load the test program, it must unambiguously indicate to either the system or the maintenance man that it has so failed. One way of doing this is to *deliberately throw the CPU into a self-loop*. If this occurs, other CPUs or equipment in the complex will surmise that there is a problem, which will lead to the manual or automatic excision of the CPU that attempted the test. That CPU, being in a loop, will display on its P register display, the address about which it is looping. The maintenance technician will then be able to look up this address in a test program dictionary, and thereby determine that the problem manifested itself in an inability to load the test program.

Assume that the test program has been loaded, and that the loader has executed a jump to the test program proper. The next question that arises is whether the test program was *properly* loaded. This can be determined by performing a check sum on the program by the program itself. This is safe because the check sum subroutine does not require the use of I/O instructions. The fact that the loader worked, and loaded something, indicates that 70 to 90% of the CPU is working properly. If the CPU is suspect, the loader and associated test bootstraps are more complicated, or occasionally impossible.

The sequence of operations that ensues is a form of crawling through, bit by bit, from the CPU to the tape. The next step might be the issuance of a known *invalid* command having the same format as the malfunctioning command. The computer should respond by ignoring the command. It may or may not indicate that a command reject has occurred. The designer of the test program must consider what registers and/or memory locations could have been modified by the CPU had it, through the agency of several possible failures, executed the invalid command. These locations are then examined.

If modified, the problem is in the CPU. One kind of invalid command used is a conditional branch instruction format. If the branch is executed, the malfunction has been identified.

Once it has been determined that the CPU seems to be working, the next step is to issue a valid command to the nearest neighbor of the suspect unit, i.e., issue the failed command to tape unit 13. If this works, one might surmise that the problem is in tape unit 12. This surmise would be wrong, since we postulated that the problem was an interactive loading problem only occurring between tape 12 and controller 3. The assumption, then, can only be tentative; it requires verification. This phase of the test could continue, testing the tape controller and the channel controller in turn. Where possible, good units could be interchanged with suspect ones, until the whole tree had been tested and it has been determined that the malfunction is indeed somewhere in the line between the CPU and tape unit 12.

The above procedure is not quite realistic, because it ignores the fact that the problem exists in a working system that cannot tolerate the borrowing and lending of so many transports, controllers, etc. Each such switch is tantamount to inducing a failure. The test program must be parsimonious with the "test spares" it uses. It may not be possible to issue valid commands to unfailed units in the tree, no matter how useful the information gained thereby would be. These units are engaged in an operational program and should not be disturbed. We are therefore back to the painful crawling through from beginning to end. Each instruction issued, whether valid or invalid, operationally meaningful or senseless, is constructed by the test program designer to detect one or more specific functional failure modes. Since we are dealing with test programs, whose intent is merely to verify the existence of a malfunction and isolate which device has failed, all failures need not be considered. There may be a hundred circuits the failure of any one of which could result in an invalid command of the type observed. Thus, the instructions used are based on functional criteria, instruction formats, and operational effects. During the course of "crawling," it may be necessary to test all error or malfunction detection circuits, by either forcing malfunctions, or executing such instructions that may be supplied for the purpose. For example, a tape parity error may be forced by writing a tape record in BCD and reading it in binary, reading and writing at different densities, using a specially constructed test tape,[14] or a host of other methods peculiar to the system being tested.

[14] A test tape is very difficult to construct. If it is to be of use, it must contain many errors that are automatically detected by properly functioning hardware. It must have parity errors, improper gap lengths, improper codes, excessive skew, drop-outs, etc. A properly functioning, normal system will simply not copy it. Writing this precious tape may require one to disable check circuits or to painfully construct the tape bit by bit on some other computer. We have heard humorous stories relating to attempts to copy a test tape.

Eventually, the program will detect that the problem is at the controller–transport interface, relates only to this specific combination of devices, and is manifested as the original malfunction as well as several others discovered along the way.

This may seem like a long and tortuous program, and it is. However, running this program may take only a few hundred milliseconds. The test program is not a diagnostic program—it does not necessarily indicate the cause of the malfunction, but only determines that the malfunction has occurred, and in which device. To that extent it can be considered as a rudimentary diagnostic program.

On-line test programs, while operationally attractive by virtue of the reduction in MTTR that they offer, are inherently dangerous. By nature, these programs require the execution of invalid commands, illegal command sequences, nonsensical commands (REWIND DRUM AND FEED CARDS, WRITE A ZERØ LENGTH RECØRD TØ NØNEXISTENT TAPE UNIT VIA WRØNG CØNTRØLLER ØN THE DISC CHANNEL, etc.), which in concert with the (unknown) malfunction could create a system situation worse than that caused by the malfunction. Test programs, typically, violate most subprogram rules and restrictions imposed by the operating system, work into and out of forbidden areas, modify interrupt priorities, in short, do anything which the ingenious mind of the test programmer deems necessary to the accomplishment of the test. If on-line test programs are required to reduce the MTTR (malfunction detection phase), they must be well specified. These specifications must be arrived at mutually by the system designers, the operating system designers, the application program designers, the user, the logic designers of the units involved, and finally and most important, the test program designer.

Off-line test programs are constructed in much the same way, but with fewer restrictions and therefore at a lower cost. The natural proclivity of the test programmer is to require all elements of the system at his sole disposal, in order to write the best possible test. This, of course, cannot be, and realistic compromises must be made.

Test programs are designed by specialists with equal training in logic design and programming. They are (with the diagnostic programmers) an elite corps, in many ways anachronistic. We have seen that contemporary programming practices frown upon the use of tricks (such as multiplying an ADD instruction by a SHIFT to obtain a DIVIDE) which lead to difficult maintenance, debugging, etc. The test programmer, however, uses such tricks along with "bad" instructions, ridiculous loop structures, redundant codes, and senseless operations as his stock in trade. Parts of the instruction sequences cannot be assembled and have to be inserted as data. He does these things not because he is perverse by nature, but because, unlike the normal programmer and logic designer, he is not working in a good machine, but in a machine that does not run. Like the maintenance man, he programs for the 2^n or more possible variations on the good machine. The test programs described above are simple in that they only consider single failures and pay minimum attention to interactions such as might be caused by computer 2 via controller 7 in Figure 11.9. A test program written to consider interactions can be orders of magnitude more complex than a single-unit test program.

The test program is a program. It must therefore be written, assembled, de-bugged, and *tested*. Testing a test program proceeds by a simulation of the malfunctions which it is intended to test.

Test program testing in a system under construction or in a new (previously unbuilt) configuration is often a comedy of errors. The test program will discover logic design bugs, engineering bugs, operating system bugs, and, occasionally, bugs in the assembler. Nor is it to be assumed that a tried and true system is free of bugs. The test program may turn up a few of these as well. When a logic bug is detected, the test program may be suspected. Disentangling the test program bugs and the system bugs and the messes created by their interactions becomes part of the test programmer's way of life.

6.2. Diagnostic Programs

> **Diagnosis:** A physician's forecast of disease by the patient's pulse and purse.
>
> AMBROSE BIERCE
> *The Devil's Dictionary*

A diagnostic program is like a test program, only more so. Its intent is to further isolate the malfunction, through interactions with the maintenance technician or maintenance facility, down to the lowest replacement level. The diagnostician differs from the test programmer in one important respect. While the test programmer is content to find one sure way of detecting and isolating a malfunction, the diagnostician tries to find *every* way. Given seven alternatives for simulating a parity error, the test programmer will generally use the single best one, or occasionally two or three. The diagnostician, given seven ways, will discover twelve more and implement them all. His concern does not stop at the functional level, but goes down to the logic level of the machine. Every logic element is examined and considered in each sensible failure mode. The failure is traced to determine what symptoms will result. Code is then structured to verify the existence of those symptoms.

The diagnostic programmer typically has five years of experience in logic design and five or more in programming. He is hardly ever to be found outside of his natural habitats—software houses and computer manufacturers. Being a former logic designer, he is knowledgeable of their foibles and tricks. Devices are rarely designed with the diagnostician in mind, and the logician only pays minimum attention to the kinds of things his device will do when it fails. The diagnostician requires the mentality of a paranoid; he follows unseeming and strange paths with the logical tenacity and intensity of a man attempting to prove that the universe has plotted to destroy the machine. His appearance is, to say the least, traumatic to the logic designer. He asks innumerable embarrassing questions, unanswerable questions, and pointless questions, that may leave the logician with a deep sense of inferiority if not awe. His mentality and the difficulty of his task are best appreciated when one considers that he is asked to run his programs in a machine that does not work.

A diagnostic program is similar in philosophy to a test program, except that when a malfunction has been detected, the program does not stop, but continues down another branch of the tree to find another way of detecting the malfunction. Having gone down the various paths relating to the detected failure, the program indicates the malfunction (usually by a simple code number). The program has the same kinds of bootstrapping problems that the test program has, but often they are worse.

Communication with the outside world (the maintenance man) is a problem. The diagnostician cannot take for granted that he has a typewriter, a printer, a CRT, or anything, for that matter, except the maintenance panel.[15] He will use several alternative methods to communicate with the technician, depending on a copious and well-written manual to allow the interpretation of the cryptic messages he produces. The documentation of a diagnostic program is part of the diagnostic program. Without documentation to translate every halt or message, the diagnostic program is useless. Furthermore, the diagnostic program cannot detect every malfunction and will occasionally be misleading. For this reason, the technician must be thoroughly trained in the logic of the program, and know its limitations and how to interpret occasionally oracular messages.

Test and diagnostic programs are fitted with controls which allow the printing or suppression of error printouts, bypassing tests or portions of tests, entrance at almost any point, halting or continuing on errors, looping on errors (to allow synchronization and use of an oscilloscope), etc.

Testing a diagnostic program is generally more difficult than testing a test program. Many more failures must be simulated. This is done by placing a small piece of paper on the logic module's connector pin to suppress the signal. One does not methodically destroy the machine to test the diagnostic program.

Bootstrapping is another problem in the design of a diagnostic program.

---

[15] Among diagnosticians, this is called the "Help, help, I am being held prisoner in a Chinese fortune cookie factory" problem.

The diagnostician cannot use an instruction (and, by extension, an element) that has not been tested. Thus, he starts his program design in the smallest portion of the logic that he can (called the **core**). The core may be up to 90 % of the CPU hardware. Having successfully executed and tested an instruction, he adds it to his repertoire, giving him a slightly more powerful machine to work in. Only when he is almost done does he have the full facilities of the system at his disposal.

These factors and difficulties in the design of test and diagnostic programs make them just about the most expensive programs that can be bought. Instruction for instruction, they require more analysis than any other program. The cost of a diagnostic program may be more than three times the cost of the logic design of the machine.

6.3. Hardware Aids to Test and Diagnostic Programs

The complexity and efficacy of a test or diagnostic program is affected by the logic design of the element being tested. The requirements of diagnosis are contradictory to tight logic design resulting in low hardware production costs. We have seen in Chapter 3 that the logic designer strives for efficient usage of his components. This will mean that any given circuit may be used in the execution of many different instructions. This results in a large diagnostic core. Disentangling the failure modes of such tight designs is difficult. Similarly, diagnosis of malfunctions during operation or production check-out is difficult. The tight design may therefore be self-defeating, lowering component cost at the expense of production and operational costs. The design of CPU and peripheral equipment with the diagnostician in mind has been increasing. Overly tight logic is no more welcome than overly tight software. This is manifested in the inclusion of special test instructions, the separation of functional subunits that could be constructed as a single logical entity, increased clarity in the functional/logical structure of the computer, the avoidance of tricks, etc. All of this is to be considered indirect forms of redundancy—either in hardware or in engineering, or both.

The kinds of things which can be done to aid the diagnostic programmer are tied to the specifics of the machine. The following are a few examples: special instruction modes that allow an instruction to be partially executed, or to be entered in the middle; accessibility under program control of internal registers; special test modes.

The test mode of a computer could lead to substantially different behavior than the normal mode. One common example is the step-by-step *vs.* the run mode, available on most CPUs. This is a rudimentary aid to the maintenance technician. If the step mode is further broken down into internal substeps, a useful tool has been created. A test mode might disable illegal instruction traps, unlink normally dependent functions, suppress error and malfunction indicators, allow the execution of special test instructions, etc. If the test mode itself can be initiated or terminated under program control, a simpler diagnostic program may ensue.

A working computer would appear to be a powerful aid to the diagnostic programmer. A properly functioning computer can, when communicating with a malfunctioning computer, be used to perform diagnostic functions. This is hardly ever done, as attractive as it might seem. The first "if" is the question of proper communications. By shifting to an external CPU, we have merely shifted the core from the CPU control logic to the complex of I/O control/memory switch/interrupt structure, which we have seen is more complex than the CPU. The second big "if" concerns the availability of another CPU. Removing the capability of a running CPU by using it to diagnose a malfunctioning CPU reduces the available time and space of the complex. This is effectively an additional malfunction and must be entered in the accounts as such. We have effectively halved the MTBF and doubled the MTTR. The break-even point will be reached only if the MTTR can be reduced to one quarter of what it would be if the external CPU were not used.

Most of the expected benefits arising from the use of an outside CPU can be obtained through the use of a specialized test unit. The unit, under program control, stimulates various portions of the logic which could not otherwise be affected. In a sense, the test box is the external provision of the hardware required for a test mode. If the application of the CPU is typically a multicomputer complex, the test unit cost will be amortized over the several CPUs; it will be possible to reduce internal test logic, contributing to a lower CPU cost for a given MTTR and increased MTBF.

7. REPAIR AND TEST FACILITIES

The repair and test facilities of a computer complex could range from a telephone to a factory. The extent is decided upon the importance of the MTTR. A typical facility for a large complex will have the ability to test and repair elements to the lowest replacement level, i.e., that level at which the component is discarded rather than replaced. Thus, the facilities for replacing a transistor or an integrated circuit will exist, but will rarely be used. Typically, the maintenance technician will have enough spares of each type to provide an effective infinite supply. If the supply of spares is exhausted, he will be able to repair the element at a lower level. Thus, spare circuit boards are kept, as well as the components on those boards. If a circuit board fails, it is shipped back to the manufacturer for repair. It is repaired at the site only if there are not enough spares.

The repair facility must be supplied with the normal test equipment, including circuit testers, card testers, component testers, oscilloscopes, meters, decade boxes, and all the normal appurtenances of electronics laboratories. The card tester is itself a diagnostic device that can stimulate and evaluate the response of the various kinds of circuit cards used in the system. It is in essence an overgrown tube tester.

8. SPARES PROVISIONING

A sufficient number of spares must be provided to constitute an effectively infinite supply. If this is not done, the MTTR will be increased accordingly. A typical policy is to supply three spares or 3% of the total of such elements, whichever is higher. Fewer spares are supplied for higher-reliability items, or for costly items such as disc or drum motors. The required number of spares can be evaluated on the basis of the number of elements of a given type in the system, the MTBF of these elements, and the effective MTTR of the element. The effective MTTR of the elements might be the time required for the factory to ship a new spare.

9. SELF-REPAIR

Viability can be achieved by increasing performance, thereby raising the average performance; increasing the MTBF, thereby increasing the probability of the system being in a useful state; or by decreasing the MTTR, resulting in a decreased probability for degraded states. The increase of MTBF is limited by technological factors and production control methods. The experience of the past several years has shown that we are rapidly approaching a point of diminishing returns with respect to viability, if we insist on doing it by increasing reliability alone. At present, it seems that the effort (money) is better spent on a decrease in MTTR than on an increase in MTBF. As the complexity of the system increases (an apparently inevitable condition), the payoff for high reliability will decrease further.

Self-repair is nothing more than a method of using the system to decrease the MTTR of its units. Perfect self-repair, as perfect self-diagnosis, is a practical and theoretical impossibility. One has only to consider the "repair" of a system wrecked by a bomb to see this point. Self-repair, to a degree sufficient to allow effective failure-free operation over the economic lifespan of the system, is not only possible, but desirable. Self-repair, however, is the culmination of a set of simpler abilities, described below. Systems having one or more of these capabilities are said to be **proprioceptive systems**, i.e., systems with (nonanthropomorphic) self-awareness.

9.1. Reflexive Systems

A **reflexive system** is one capable of storing for self-examination a complete description of its own structure. Thus, a system equipped with a large disc file or magnetic tape file, which carries the complete system configuration, the detailed logic design of each card, and the wiring lists of each unit, is reflexive.

The system must either explicitly or implicitly store its own description, or it cannot determine when its behavior is correct or false. That description must be accessible in order to be useful. The system itself is its own representation and, therefore, an adequate description of itself. That particular description is useless, however, as it is not accessible to the system. The more implicit the self-description is made, the simpler it becomes and the less accessible it is. Conversely, the more explicit it is made, the more complex it becomes and the more readily it is examined. Almost every system in operation today carries within it a partial description of its structure or desired behavior, or both. Benchmarks of various kinds, the system library tape, and the copies of the operating system are more mundane forms of self-descriptions. If the system is to have the ability to initiate and complete its own recovery from a particular failure, then someplace within the system there must be memory allocated to the description of the present and desired structure. If such space cannot be found, there is good reason to doubt the ability of the system to recover from the particular failure.

It is not presently possible to construct a reflexive system smaller than a complete general-purpose computer with associated memory. This is by no means a theoretical limitation; the theoretical limits are still an open problem. One should not be hasty about the impossibility of self-description—every biological system contains within each cell a description of its own structure.

9.2. Self-Failure Detecting Systems

The previous sections have dealt at length with providing the system with the ability to detect its own malfunctions. Self-failure detection is a step upward in the hierarchy of proprioceptive systems. The self-failure detecting methods described above are all of the form of specific answers to specific failure conditions and problems. They are not implemented within the framework of an encompassing theory. They work, but they appear independent of each other. What we are saying is that there is not now a universal methodology for implementing self-failure detection. We have of course been considering the realistic situation in which any and all self-failure detecting circuits or hardware are as prone to failure as the networks they test. Masking methods, typified by diode quads, do not count because, while they increase the reliability, they only mask the error, without detecting it. The system, after a while, has a rapidly degrading reliability. It cannot be made as good as new. When a system using error masking schemes finally does fail, it is almost impossible to repair it, since so little of it is working. Furthermore, error masking techniques make self-error or self-malfunction detection almost impossible. Pain is the biological system's answer to self-failure detection.

9.3. Self-Diagnostic Systems

The next step in the hierarchy of proprioceptive systems is the self-diagnostic system. The problems of bootstrapping the diagnostic (i.e., getting past the core) and of communications with the remainder of the system appear to be very difficult. There is no doubt that a computer complex could be constructed which has considerably more self-diagnostic ability than normally provided. Modifications could be made in the hardware design that would allow automatic self-diagnosis of the majority of malfunctions. Since the systems have not been provided with the ability to respond to such diagnosis (i.e., to make the repair), vast extensions of self-diagnostic ability seem to be pointless. Yet, as complexes evolve and become logically larger, the programs for malfunction isolation to the replacement level may approach or exceed the complexity of present diagnostic programs. This is particularly true if isolation of interacting dependent malfunctions is required. Diagnostic facilities, like failure detecting facilities, are individually designed to the specifics of the system. As in other areas related to proprioceptive abilities, there is no theoretical framework that can be used in developing practical solutions to this problem. Since crabs do not grow new claws at random, or on the wrong leg, they clearly have effective self-diagnostic abilities.

9.4. Self-Repairing Systems

With the self-diagnostic system as a start, attach an arbitrarily large store of spare parts (or an equivalent, robotic, repair shop), and the switching network (or automated repair robot) required to make use of these parts. The spares, the connection/disconnection network, and the controls are prone to failure as well. A trivial solution, in which we keep a large number of copies of the system, is not allowed. The self-repairing system, figuratively, reaches out with its hairy arm, removes its malfunctioning module, and replaces it with a working spare.

Limited self-repair is achievable and has been implemented in many systems. Every software recovery procedure, and every system with an automatically actuated standby, has self-repair capabilities.

9.5. Beyond Self-Repair

As we proceed upward in our description of the proprioceptive hierarchy, we of necessity become more vague and less substantive in our discussion. The notion of proprioception can be carried on to two more levels.

The self-repairing system had as objectives the maintenance of its structure according to some previously specified ideal. We are, however, interested not in homeostasis of structure, but in homeostasis of function. Such a system would use what spares it had and reorganize itself, possibly changing its structure (hardware or software) to maintain its ability to achieve its present goals. We can call such systems "self-organizing."

The final foreseeable level for proprioceptive systems is the "self-actualizing" system. This system strives neither for homeostasis of structure nor homeostasis of goals, but changes its goals in response to its internal activity and the pressures of its environment. Self-actualization is a laudable capability in human beings, all too rarely present.

9.6. How Far and Whereto?

As the level of proprioceptive ability is increased, the vessel for its execution becomes more complex. Almost nothing can be done at the component level, while even a modest degree of self-repair or self-organization cannot now be done by less than a multicomputer complex. The cardinal rule is "provide the least proprioceptive ability consistent with the system's self-repair ability." Thus, do not diagnose what you cannot repair, do not detect the undiagnosable, and do not describe the undetectable.

10. GRACEFUL DEGRADATION

The rationale of graceful degradation as a viability enhancement technique is clearly displayed in the following equation:

$$W = \sum_{i=1}^{2^n} p_i w_i,$$

where W is the mean value of a performance parameter, w_i the level of performance of the parameter in the state i, p_i the probability of state i, and n the number of subsystems in the complex.

A system without graceful degradation is one in which there is a single state with full performance. Let that state be called state 1. Most systems will achieve maximum performance in the state in which all subsystems are up, that is, state 1. Reliability and maintainability methods are generally aimed at making state 1 the most probable state. The mean value of the performance then, for a system without graceful degradation, is $p_1 w_1$. Since probabilities are positive, and since the performance parameter can be normalized to a positive number, it is clear that any performance whatsoever, no matter how slight, in states other than 1 *must increase the average performance*. If we operate under the philosophy that some performance is better than none, a system that can take advantage of partial performance in partially failed states is better than one that cannot.

Graceful degradation is not so graceful as we would wish it to be. Unfortunately, we are dealing with discrete elements that rarely exhibit continuous failure modes or continuous levels of performance. The applicability of graceful degradation to a computer complex is derived from the large number of units that such a complex has. It is generally not feasible to implement graceful degradation in a single-computer system. However, the long-term technological trend is toward the increased use of smaller computers in the design of a system. This will lead to complexes consisting of many CPUs, memories, and associated devices. As the number of elements is increased, the number of states in which the system could be structured so as to have partial performance is exponentially increased. The tendency is to achieve a continual range of performance which approaches continuous graceful degradation. However, as the number of elements in the complex is increased, the cost of implementation of graceful degradation increases as well. At any given time in the development of technology, there will exist a level of complexity, at which further attempts at graceful degradation will lead to reduced system performance. Thus, not every possible state will have the ability to perform, even though there might be sufficient working hardware to make this possible. Furthermore, many potentially available configuration states will be disallowed, while other configuration states, of lower performance, may be deliberately induced. This is the familiar barter situation in which we sacrifice little in one area in order to gain greatly in others.

10.1. Partition and the Domain of Sacrifice

Partition was discussed with the intent of maximizing system performance *in the ideal state*. It is not obvious that the partition scheme that is ideal for the ideal state is ideal for a system with graceful degradation.

Consider the system shown in Figure 11.10. We have here a typical example of an extensive and functional partition. The system has graceful degradation capability with respect to the front-end functions. There are sixteen configuration states, with the capabilities shown in Table 11.1. We have arbitrarily said that the large number cruncher provides a capability of 2 units, while each front-end computer has a capacity of 1. We have further assumed that the complex is functionally down if either the number crunching

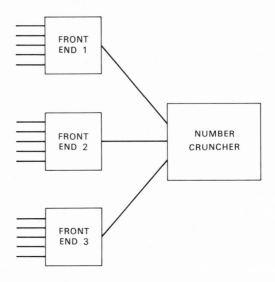

Figure 11.10. Typical system with extensive and
functional partitions.

Table 11.1. Capabilities of System Shown in Figure 11.10

Configuration state				Front-end function	Number crunching functions
FE1	FE2	FE3	NC		
1	1	1	1	3	2
0	1	1	1	2	2
1	0	1	1	2	2
1	1	0	1	2	2
0	0	1	1	1	2
0	1	0	1	1	2
1	0	0	1	1	2
0	0	0	1	0	0
1	1	1	0	0	0
0	1	1	0	0	0
1	0	1	0	0	0
1	1	0	0	0	0
1	0	0	0	0	0
0	1	0	0	0	0
0	0	1	0	0	0
0	0	0	0	0	0

or the front-end functions are absent. Let us assume that each front-end computer has an availability of 0.95, while the larger central computer has an availability of 0.90. Calculating the probability of each configuration state, and obtaining the mean value of each function, we get

$$\text{Mean front-end capability} = 2.565,$$

$$\text{Mean number crunching capability} = 1.800.$$

Compare this system now with that of Figure 11.11, in which we have replaced the large number cruncher with two smaller computers, each with an availability of 0.95. The configuration states and performances are now those given in Table 11.2. The values of the performance parameters are

$$\text{Mean front-end capability} = 2.84,$$

$$\text{Mean number crunching capability} = 1.90.$$

While this is an admittedly contrived example, we see that it is possible to achieve higher viability, though at a cost of decreased performance. The second partition is *not* optimal if we consider performance in the ideal state only. There is increased overhead and intercomputer crosstell that could have gone into increased performance in the ideal state. The incorporation of graceful degradation does have a definite bias toward extensive rather than functional partitions. On the other hand, the problems associated with

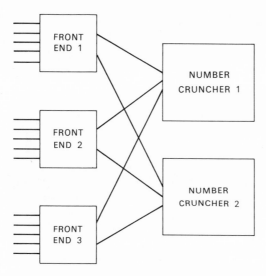

Figure 11.11. Further extensive partition of the rear end to provide higher system availability.

Table 11.2. Capabilities of System Shown in Figure 11.11

Configuration state					Front-end function	Number crunching functions
FE1	FE2	FE3	NC1	NC2		
1	1	1	1	1	3	2
0	1	1	1	1	2	2
1	0	1	1	1	2	2
1	1	0	1	1	2	2
0	0	1	1	1	1	2
0	1	0	1	1	1	2
1	0	0	1	1	1	2
0	0	0	1	1	0	0
1	1	1	1	0	3	1
0	1	1	1	0	2	1
1	0	1	1	0	2	1
1	1	0	1	0	2	1
0	0	1	1	0	1	1
0	1	0	1	0	1	1
1	0	0	1	0	1	1
0	0	0	1	0	0	0
1	1	1	0	1	3	1
0	1	1	0	1	2	1
1	0	1	0	1	2	1
1	1	0	0	1	2	1
0	0	1	0	1	1	1
0	1	0	0	1	1	1
1	0	0	0	1	1	1
0	0	0	0	1	0	0
1	1	1	0	0	0	0
0	1	1	0	0	0	0
1	0	1	0	0	0	0
1	1	0	0	0	0	0
0	0	1	0	0	0	0
0	1	0	0	0	0	0
1	0	0	0	0	0	0
0	0	0	0	0	0	0

recovery will lead us to a preference for functional partition. But, we are not to remain poised twixt Scylla and Charybdis for long, for configuration switching can give us the best of both possible worlds. However, it is still advantageous to qualitatively discuss the various forms of partition that can be employed.

If each CPU of the complex can be assigned a distinct function, and these functions are relatively independent, a sacrifice can be made of the lower-priority functions. Such functions as gathering performance statistics, updating and maintaining historical files, system status reports, and off-line program maintenance are examples of functions that may be sacrificed. Ultimately, however, this approach is merely an avoidance of the inevitable, in which a critical function will have to be degraded.

An approach which mediates between functional and extensive sacrifices is afforded by **load sharing** or **displacement sacrifice**. Assume that the system in Figure 11.11 has lost a front-end computer (number 3). It is possible to distribute the load of FE3 to FE1 and FE2. The ability to do this presumes that the front-end computers were not running at capacity in the first place. If that was the case, one might ask why FE3 was there at all. One might argue that it had been implemented to handle burst conditions or other low-probability events. If this is the case, we have sacrificed peak viability for average viability. This is often a valid sacrifice, but it must be made knowingly. If peak viability is not to be sacrificed, or if the front-end CPUs are loaded near their peak, one of three solutions must be selected:

- sacrifice of a front-end subfunction.
- extensive sacrifice within a front-end function.
- shifting of front-end load to the number cruncher.

Of these, the first two are the more commonly implemented. Thus, input and output may be serviced at a lower speed and with increased delay, operation may be throttled by slowing output and requesting the cessation of input or by ignoring certain inputs, etc.

Displacement of front-end function to the rear (or *vice versa*) is inherently difficult. The sacrificed front-end programs (probably) must be dynamically relocatable. The rear-end computer must have functions *it* can sacrifice (or else we again inquire as to why it was not fully loaded, with much the same consideration we had for the front end). It, being a piece of hardware, must have the structural ability to do both jobs. It must have a system executive capable of incorporating the many possible variations of extra load it may be called upon to handle.

The same argument holds in reverse, if we consider the system of Figure 11.11, that is, a failure of the number crunching capability to be compensated by load sharing or redistribution to functionally different (front-end) computers. Minor forms of load sharing are employed in most systems with graceful degradation. It is, however, an inherently difficult scheme to execute, and bears a substantially increased software burden. It is a scheme that has been far more often proposed, discussed, and published, than it has been successfully implemented.

Partition in extent is applicable when the system has one major task to be done repetitively for many different inputs. Tracking calculations, header analysis in communications systems, etc., are examples. The loss of a CPU or the existence of an overload may require that the extent of these computations be curtailed. Thus, if the system is capable of tracking 300 targets simultaneously, it may under failure drop to 250 targets. Generally, a system employs both modes of degradation. Ancillary functions are first dropped, with the overload distributed among the remaining computers. Further stages of degradation will begin to eat into the major processing task, dropping capabilities of extent as the overload builds up or computers fail.

Other forms of sacrifice have been attempted and suggested. Primary among these are sacrifices for delay and/or accuracy. To the extent that the system has been provided with FIFO storage schemes for incoming data, sacrifice of delay is automatic. One should tag stale data and recognize when they are of no further use. This provides an automatic sacrifice of processing delay.

Sacrifices in accuracy presume that it is possible to use a faster program with reduced accuracy. While such programs can be written, their efficacy is open to considerable question. For one thing, a sacrifice in precision may cause a fast convergent routine to converge more slowly, resulting in an overall additional degradation. For another, programs in real-time systems are written with a minimum of "fat." Finally, there is a question as to whether the less accurate data would have any meaning at all.

To reiterate the previous discussion, consider the main forms of sacrifice:

	Lose	Sacrifice
1. Extensive	part of A	part of A
2. Functional	all of A	all of A
3. Extensive displacement of functional	part of A	all of B
4. Extensive displacement of extensive	part of A	part of C
5. Functional displacement of functional	all of A	all of D
6. Functional displacement of extensive	all of A	part of E

We can continue with various levels of displacement *ad absurdum*, recognizing that each additional level requires more generality in the executive of the host computer, increased hardware symmetry of subsystems, and substantial complications in recovery procedures.

The optimum system design of the earlier chapters and the associated partition schemes are now more complex. This may lead us to partitions which, while sensible in the light of viability requirements and continued operation in the dynamically changing system configuration states, may be in direct contradiction to the apparent optima of the statically considered system.

Agreement as to the sacrifice domain is often the most difficult phase of contract negotiations. The user, justifiably, does not wish to sacrifice anything, while the architect does not relish being explicit to his client about the conditions under which his elegant house of cards will come tumbling down. The establishment of the domain of sacrifice is primarily the user's responsibility. After all, it is his system. The architect's responsibility is to make his client aware of the cost involved and to make such recommendations as he feels are in his client's best interest. It is a mutual thing, which cannot be left to the architect's convenience at the ultimate expense of the client's pocketbook.

10.2. Sacrifice Regimes

The domain of sacrifice is essentially a schedule that specifies, for each configuration state, and each load condition in each state, what the performance of the system will be. That schedule is implemented, either implicitly in the system design, explicitly as a program or table, or as a combination of both. We therefore refer to it as a **sacrifice regime** (which implies neither) rather than as a sacrifice program (which implies a program), a sacrifice schedule (which implies a table), or a sacrifice system (which implies hardware). The regime is dispersed throughout the fabric of the complex. It is difficult to modify if such modifications have not been previously considered. It is virtually impossible to implement after the fact, short of a complete system redesign.

The sacrifice regime can be as implicit as a system executive can be, consisting only of a sequence of calls and linkages. It can be as explicit as a sequential jump table, with the states corresponding to the major configuration states of the system. As usual, implicit design is fast and compact at a cost of generality and flexibility. Explicit designs are easier to design and debug. The trade here is no different than for the many other such situations that we have seen in hardware and software.

10.3. Implementation

A complete sacrifice regime is one in which every conceivable operationally distinguishable configuration state has been examined under every possible quantitative and qualitative load condition. A decision is made for each state as to what the functional capability of the system with respect to each parameter should be. From this master schedule, the desired activity of each program module, the functional assignment of each physical element, and the internal allocation of facilities such as memory can be derived. The master executive program and the executive programs of subsidiary processors each must have the ability to recognize the portions of the configuration state pertaining to its operation. The occurrence of a configuration state change (upward of downward) must be signaled via an interrupt or other means to the various processors, whereupon they will (we hope) each attain the proper condition.

The main difficulty with a complete sacrifice regime is that there is no end to it. One must consider second-order failures which could occur while configuration changes are taking place. These too must be further divided along an ever increasing tree of failures that rapidly begins to resemble a jungle. Imagine the difficulty of tracing a single path of a system with 30 subsystems and 2^{30} configuration states: "if A, B, and C have failed, and while A is recovering, but before B has recovered, D fails in such a way as to. . . ." The pragmatic impossibility of implementing this in a finite memory leads us to disregard most states and most second-order failures. The rule is: "When in trouble or in doubt—abort." This may seem drastic, until one calculates the probability of second-order failures and the probability of difficult states, sums them, and finds that adequate viability is still achieved. From this we can derive another rule: "The consideration to be given to the performance, functional configuration, and load conditions in a particular configuration state should be tempered by the probability of that state."[16] Overt consideration of statistically insignificant events is no more valid for a system than is worst-worst case design for a circuit.

Neither the physical nor the functional configuration of the system can be expected to remain static for any length of time. Operational conditions can and will change, necessitating changes in the sacrifice domain and hence the sacrifice regime. The system in question may be one of many similar but different installations, each, hopefully, running under the same software. Furthermore, the operator will have to control what functions will or will not be sacrificed. For example, on-line statistics gathering might normally be considered dispensable; yet if the situation is unusual, the operator might sacrifice some other on-line functions rather than lose valuable statistics.

While it is possible to design the system in such a way that any physical CPU can perform any functional task, the partition of functional tasks over the physical computers is generally unique. The CPU's program is structured to handle all functional tasks assigned to it. If an anisochronous executive is used, the system cycle will stretch as the overload induced by the removal of a failed CPU is applied to it. Removal of functions brings the cycle back down to the level at which it can handle its load. Thus, an individual CPU need not know the configuration state to determine which functions it should be performing. The schedule can be implemented as a bit table, which is tested by every module prior to linking to the next module (i.e., link to natural next or skip next). The linkings themselves can be changed, but this is more

---

[16] We are reminded of the story of a rather worried person who, upon hearing an astronomer lecture on the "death of the sun," exclaimed: "Ten billion years—thank heavens! I thought you said ten million."

complex since the programs may be relocatable, and since it may be desirable to purge program space as well as program time in a degraded mode. Linking can be done through a table, whose entries are supplied by the system executive to subordinate processors for each configuration state. The sacrifice regime must carry or have access to all the information that the processor must have to recover to the particular configuration state.

The use of an explicit, variable sacrifice regime practically dictates a tabular approach. This has a cost not only in space, but more indirectly *reduces the performance in every configuration state*. The problem of having the executive calculate or store all addresses which are to be modified as a result of a configuration change is readily solved by the prolific use of indirect addressing. The location of all parameters which must be changed are thereby fixed (to within relocation), the value of any given parameter need be entered only once, parameters may be arrayed in a contiguous list rather than scattered all over the memory, etc. The heavier use of indirect addressing results in greater execution time in all configuration states. This too is a form of redundancy, though not often recognized as such.

Ideally, the full set of programs is implemented in the maximum configuration state. Configuration states are grouped into sets of states that have identical performance. Such state groups are called **performance metastates**. A matrix, of performance metastates and programs is provided in the executive. Each entry specifies whether or not the program is to be used and the names of the location or descriptor of the parameter list to be used by the program in the given metastate. Modification of the matrix or its associated parameter lists is not different from any other such table. The sacrifice regime must be protected, stored in several places independently, and have built-in error detection (check sums or parities).

11. OVERDESIGN

Overdesign is a valid means of increasing viability if the penalty function allows full credit to be given to excess performance. Rather than increasing the probability of the ideal state, or providing performance in failure states, we provide excessive performance in the ideal state. High viability does not necessitate graceful degradation. Overdesign is an expression of the wish that the user will credit the system with the accumulated extra capacity it had when it was good to the nonperformance in failure states.

Whether or not overdesign is a valid method of increasing viability depends on the system application and the kinds of penalty functions used. All too often overdesign is unintentional. The computer manufacturer offers a discrete product line. He will not offer a computer that is too small, and cannot offer one that is much too large for fear of being overpriced as well as overdesigned. He offers the smallest one that will do the job. The required capacity typically falls between two of his products; hence the system has excessive capacity. However, we should not be too harsh with the supplier. He has given us the best he has. The situation is somewhat like a man going into a "Cheap John's" clothing shop to buy a size 42 suit, while the store has only a 34 and 65 in stock. Fitting the size 65 (the 34 is obviously too small), the tailor extols the fullness of the garment and hints about putting on weight. "Those extra yards of material show you that this is no cheap suit," he might say, "We can take the pants in and have enough to make a sports jacket for your son." Or, "it gives you a mature look." Try all you want, Sam, you still made the pants too long.

12. EXCHANGEABILITY

An effective way to maximize the viability of a system is to maximize the number of identical units in the system, while achieving the minimum number of different units.

Minimizing the number of physically different units reduces the spares provisioning problem. A system with ten different kinds of units requires fewer spares than one with 20 different kinds. Thus, if two different buffer units were required, for 200-baud and 2400-baud operation, the system cost might be reduced by using only 2400-baud units capable of working at lower speeds. The reduction in the cost of spares is directly translatable into a reduction of nonessential redundancy. Reducing the number of unit types has a side benefit in that it leads to reduced maintenance cost and lowered MTTR. Having fewer unit types, the maintenance technician is more effective in servicing them. A third benefit may accrue from increased production runs for the fewer unit types, resulting in a net reduction of individual unit costs and increased unit reliability. In most cases, the universal adoption of a single high-performance unit is preferable to the use of several different units of varying performance. This is not always apparent in evaluating a proposed system.

Having more units of any one given type increases the number of configuration states with identical hardware complements. This therefore increases the possibility that performance can be obtained in each of these configuration states. Exchangeability is in itself a form of redundancy. Exchangeability is obtained by upgrading units to the requirements of the maximum-performance unit of the set. There is therefore excess capacity in those units not used at their maximal capacity. Such excess capacity does not directly contribute to performance and is counted as redundancy.

We do not question the value of exchangeability in small units such as power supplies, where we will often have excess capacity. Similarly, core memories are modular, as are most logic elements. The ever decreasing cost of computer complex units has led to exchangeability at higher levels, where it is now feasible to include computers and most peripheral devices.

The preceding argument for exchangeability seems to be in direct contradiction to the argument against overdesign in Section 11. There are contradictory polarities at work here. Overdesign of the complex is to be discounted in most applications. However, overdesign of the units of the complex, to the extent that it results in lowered costs, decreased MTTR, increased reliability, increased interchangeability, and other factors that enhance the cost/viability characteristics of the complex, is welcome. Since the distinction between units, subsystems, systems, and complexes is fuzzy at best, it is sometimes difficult to properly evaluate beneficial overcapacity of an element. Element overcapacity, if accidental (e.g., the manufacturer has only the given element in his product line and cannot offer lower-capacity elements), should be distinguished from element overcapacity provided in the interest of achieving interchangeability. Certainly, the manufacturer's contention is more credible if he can also offer the lower-capacity element. The architect should therefore be ready to prove his point by a rational evaluation and presentation of the trades involved.[17]

13. REDUNDANCY

Every method thus far described for the enhancement of viability represents a form of redundancy. The three aspects of viability—MTBF, MTTR, and performance—can be improved through the use of redundancy. "Redundancy," in the broader sense in which we are using it here, means any expenditure which would be considered superfluous if the system were incapable of failing. Redundancy is not to be confused with replication, which is a limited form of redundancy. A processor cycle used for checking or protection is a redundant cycle. Tables and programs used for recovery take up memory that might otherwise be available for functional tasks. Repair

[17] A recurring problem with one manufacturer who had changed his digital module product line to take advantage of improved component price-to-performance ratios was that the new higher-capability line was actually less expensive, more reliable, and better in every respect than the older line. But in the interest of customer credibility he was required (at first) to sell the newer product at a higher price (and substantially higher profit) than the older one. The price could not be dropped until the older line had been discontinued. In some cases, the prospective client asked for a lower-speed product (hoping for a lower price thereby). It was difficult to explain that a lower-speed product would be more expensive since "slow-down" capacitors would have to be added. As it was, the product was using the cheapest possible transistors, diodes, resistors, and capacitors which would meet the required reliability and environmental standards of the market. Somehow, this real situation resulted in a difficult credibility gap.

facilities are redundant expenditures. Standby capacity is a more obvious form of redundancy.

There is not now a theoretical model that will predict how much redundancy is required to achieve a particular level of viability. While individual aspects of the complex may be rigorously analyzed, the redundancy requirements of the totality must be built-up laboriously from smaller, more elementary models. If the complex is to have a projected economic lifespan of ten years, the required redundancy expenses (measured as the excess over what would be required for nonfailing components) are of the order of 75 to 150%. Hardware redundancy alone may range from 30% to 120%. As the complex gets larger, the net redundancy required to achieve a given viability is reduced. This fact, in addition to the square law relationship of cost and performance, is a strong force for the centralization of functions and the increased complexity of digital computer complexes.

14. SUMMARY

Viability is a measure of a complex's capabilities incorporating three equally important factors: the reliability of its elements, measured by the MTBF; the maintainability of its elements, measured by the MTTR; and the performance of the complex, measured in terms peculiar to the complex's intended application. Associated with each performance parameter is a penalty function that specifies what levels of performance will be granted full weight and what will be discounted.

Reliability is achieved by many means, ranging from the component level through the system level. Maintainability is achieved by a variety of methods, including hardware, software, and operational methods. The software and the operational factors are generally under the architect's control. Performance is directly controlled by the architect.

Of the three, viability is best improved through the reduction of the MTTR and the maximization of the number of configuration states in which there is partial performance. Thus, graceful degradation emerges as the primary tool for the implementation of high viability.

The achievement of high viability requires the acceptance of the fact that every system can and will fail. The implementation of graceful degradation presumes the willingness to negotiate which *indispensable* functions will be sacrificed under what failure conditions.

15. PROBLEMS

1. Examine any well-defined computer complex, such as the CDC7600, and describe the elements of that system in terms of subsystems and units.

2. Consider a duplicated computer complex that contains a switching circuit used to switch the load from the on-line computer to the off-line computer if there should be a failure. Ignore what it is that initiates the switchover, and consider only the switchover circuit. Is that circuit a unit or a subsystem? If it is a unit, to which subsystem does it belong? What constraints on the design of the switch must be imposed if it is to be a subsystem?

3. Consider a disc pack with eight surfaces. Assume that any failure on a surface is tantamount to the failure of the whole surface. How many pseudosubsystems does the disc pack define? What are their performance levels?

4. Evaluate the mean time to repair for a flat tire, breaking it down into the basic steps involved in repair. Similarly, evaluate the MTTR for a broken pencil point under the assumption that the pencil is halfway through its life, that it is useless if it is less than 3 in. long, that 1 in. is lost every time it is sharpened, and that the pencil is originally 7 in. long.

5. Estimate the MTTR for a CPU consisting of 1500 logic modules under the assumption that the repairman knows precisely which logic module has failed.

6. Calculate the state probabilities of a computer complex consisting of 5 CPUs, 10 memory modules, 2 drums, and 2 discs, under the following assumptions:

Sub-system	MTBF	MTTR
Computer	1500 hours	0.5 hour
Memory	2000 hours	1.5 hours
Drum	500 hours	2 hours
Disc	500 hours	1.5 hours

Assume that full performance is achieved if and only if there are 3 CPUs, 7 memories, 1 drum, and 1 disc. Each CPU loss reduces performance by 1 unit, while each memory loss beyond 3 reduced performance by 0.5 units. If there is no disc, whatever performance there is is cut in half. If there is no drum, the system is down. The full system performance is 3 units. What is the mean performance and the standard deviation of the performance?

7. Define the performance parameters of interest and the associated penalty functions for any of the applications listed in Problem 1 of Chapter 9.

8. Calculate the MTBF of a diode quad assuming that the diodes fail open or closed with equal probabilities and that the failure rate is 0.0004 %/1000 hours.

9. Design a replicated AND gate with three inways, using a majority vote circuit to determine the output. Assume a perfect vote circuit and calculate the failure rate. Do the same under the assumption that the failure of the voter is finite.

10. Derive the sensitivity of the mean performance of the system of Problem 6 to changes in the MTBF and MTTR of the various subsystems.

11. Using an appropriate number representation system, design or flow chart a single error correcting binary multiplier. [*Difficult.*]

12. Do a detailed outline of the test procedure for a magnetic tape unit under the following assumptions. There is a channel controller and a tape unit controller interposed between the CPU and the tape transport. The system has several channels, the tape channel has several controllers, and these in turn have several transports. Assume that the test program has been properly loaded and verified. Start by listing the symptoms that might be observed.

13. Sketch a test program for a console switch that creates an interrupt. Sketch a test program for a console switch that must be interrogated and is reset only upon interrogation.

14. What is probably the first instruction executed in a test or diagnostic program?

15. Consider any well-defined minicomputer such as a DDP516 or PDP-8. Outline the diagnostic program for a CPU malfunction.

16. Why should the check sum character be last?

16. REFERENCES

1. Goldman, Alan S., and Slattery, T. B., *Maintainability: A Major Element of System Effectiveness*, John Wiley, New York, 1964.

This book contains much useful information on viability questions in general. The trades among failure rate, repair rate, spares, and preventive maintenance and the associated economics are discussed in sufficient detail. Guides to selecting module size, repair–discard policies, and provisioning policies are presented. Illustrative cases are worked out in detail.

2. Lechner, R. J., "Multiprocessor Design Criteria," *IEEE Transactions on Computers*, Institute of Electrical and Electronics Engineers, Inc., Volume C-17, Number 2, February 1968, pp. 187–188.

A short note on the relations among subsystem complexity, required viability, and the amount of redundancy.

3. Peterson, W. Wesley, *Error Correcting Codes*, MIT Press, Cambridge, Massachusetts, 1961.

A clear exposition of the mysteries of constructing error detecting and correcting codes. Very mathematical.

4. Pierce, William H., *Failure-Tolerant Computer Design*, Academic Press, New York, 1965.

A mathematical treatment of reliability enhancement techniques biased toward the problems of logic design. The treatment is fundamental and abstract. While the architect may not have an opportunity to employ redundancy techniques at the logic level within a computer, some elements of the complex, such as voting procedures, can be modeled on the basis of the analyses presented in this book. The book is mathematical and presumes mathematical maturity. However, it is self-contained and does not require an extensive mathematical background.

5. Seiler, Karl III, *Introduction to Systems Cost-Effectiveness*, John Wiley–Interscience, New York, 1969.

An introduction to basic concepts in systems effectiveness analysis. System effectiveness is a more general concept that embodies viability. Part IV, on system cost effectiveness models, is particularly worthwhile.

6. Wilcox, R. H., and Mann, W. C., eds., *Redundancy Techniques for Computing Systems*, Spartan Books, Washington, D.C., 1962.

A collection of early papers on redundancy as applied to computers. Quadded logic is discussed in detail, as are voting methods. The level varies with each of the over twenty papers presented. The emphasis is primarily at the logic level. The book contains many references to earlier works on reliability, self-repair, and related subjects. A number of the papers are available elsewhere or have been superseded.

Chapter 12
VIABILITY DESIGN

Redundant, *adj.,* Superfluous; needless; de trop.

The Sultan said: There's evidence abundant
To prove this unbelieving dog redundant."
To whom the Grand Vizier, with mien impressive,
Replied: "His head, at least, appears excessive."

AMBROSE BIERCE
The Devil's Dictionary

1. SYNOPSIS

High viability is achieved by the judicious use of graceful degradation. Manual implementation of graceful degradation implies a high MTTR. The most dramatic gains in viability are obtained by reducing the effective MTTR, rather than by increasing reliability or performance. Hence, viability requirements lead us to self-repair as a means of implementing graceful degradation. Self-repair implies that the complex has the ability to detect its own malfunctions, to excise malfunctioning elements, and to replace them with properly working ones. To do these things, there must be a switching network that allows the elements of the complex to be rearranged and an executive processor that controls the required actions. Both of these, being elements of the system, are themselves prone to failure. The achievement of high viability under the assumption that these elements cannot fail is trivial. The interesting questions are those that deal with the achievement of high viability despite failures in controlling elements.

2. THE DESIGN COMPONENTS OF VIABILITY

Viability is increased through increased reliability, reduced MTTR, and increased performance. The preceding chapter dealt with the factors that effect the reliability, maintainability, and performance of the system. The most dramatic improvement in viability is gained through the reduction of the effective MTTR by letting the system make its own repairs. The steps discussed in Chapter 11, starting with the detection of the failure and ending with the transition to a new operable state, can be accomplished by the system itself. A combination of hardware and software is used to detect malfunctions,

693

isolate the malfunctioning element, and verify its operability. Initializing the replacement element, and the transition to an operable state is a form of bootstrapping which in principle is not different from other bootstrap programs. What remains, then, for the system to repair itself is to provide it with the abilities to remove a malfunctioning element, obtain a replacement for it, and actually make the replacement. This is done by a physical or logical **configuration switching network**. All elements of the system can be connected through a network that allows the effective replacement of any failed element by a good one.

The maintenance facility can be automatically alerted to the failure, allowing the malfunctioning element to be repaired off-line at relative leisure. We can in this way reduce the effective MTTR from 30 or 40 minutes to a few seconds. By providing sufficient off-line repair facilities and spare elements, we obtain an effectively infinite source of spares and achieve arbitrarily high viabilities.

The above, however, is oversimplified. The configuration switching network, being an element of the system, is itself subject to failure. The configuration switching network controls, the malfunction-detecting hardware and software, in fact all the elements of the system related to automatic self-repair can fail. Despite this, the ideals of the preceding paragraph can and have been achieved. We can, so to speak, "tie the tail" of the system to itself, leaving only a small essential core, such that only *its* failure will cause the system to fail. Furthermore, we can isolate and distribute that core, so that its failure will not cause the system to fail unless there is a simultaneous failure of other elements. We cannot, however, build a nonfailing system.

Self-repair has four components which can be mechanized in hardware and/or software: malfunction detection, executive assignment, reconfiguration, and recovery. The system operates under the aegis of a **viability executive** processor (hardware and/or software, centralized or distributed, fixed or floating, implicit or explicit) which is charged with the viability of the system. That executive is to be distinguished from the system executive. Physically, these two functionally distinct processors may in fact be (and are usually) one and the same. For the sake of the present discussion, we shall consider only those aspects related to viability.

Of particular interest is the application of the various malfunction detection methods discussed in Chapter 11 to the problem of detecting malfunctions in the viability executive, configuration switching network, configuration network controls, and the processors responsible for detecting viability executive malfunctions. The means by which the viability executive is repaired or replaced, while in principle the same as the methods used for other processors, are sufficiently complex and important that a separate discussion is warranted. **Reconfiguration** is the act of performing an upward or downward transition from one configuration state to another. This occurs whenever an element fails *or is repaired.* Reconfiguration must be considered in the light of possible failures in any of its contributing elements. **Recovery** is the process by which the complex resumes functioning after it has successfully performed a configuration change. Recovery requires knowledge of the system as it was prior to reconfiguration. The information regarding the physical structure of the complex, its logical structure, the status of its subsidiary processors, tables, etc., is collectively known as the **ledger**. The ledger, also prone to failure, must also be protected.

3. EXECUTIVE MALFUNCTION DETECTION

We shall consider the problems associated with detecting malfunctions in the viability executive itself. Failures in other elements of the complex are detected and corrected under the aegis of the viability executive and have been discussed in Chapter 11. The viability executive can take on the full range of executive processor structure discussed in previous chapters. Viability executive malfunctions may be detected by the executive itself or by processors external to it.

3.1. Self-Detection

One could question the efficacy of self-malfunction detection. At first glance it does not appear reliable. That may be the case, but it is nevertheless effective. If the executive processor has not failed, there are no malfunctions for it to detect. The self-detection of a "nonexistent" malfunction is itself indicative of a malfunction, with at worst the wrong diagnosis. If the executive successfully detects a malfunction, it may or may not be able to make an orderly transfer of viability executive responsibilities to the processor that will take over in its stead. If it does perform an orderly transition, the recovery will be quicker and the effective MTTR for this failure will be short. The viability is therefore improved. If the executive cannot make an orderly transition, external means will detect the abortive attempt and recovery will be achieved anyhow.

The viability executive could detect its own malfunctions but not be capable of an orderly transition or of communicating its plight to the alternate viability executive that will succeed it. If it can communicate with the alternate, time has been saved because the alternate does not have to detect or isolate the malfunction. If it cannot communicate with its alternate, then the alternate will have to detect and isolate the malfunction. Thus, self-detection can only reduce the average MTTR and therefore can only increase the viability of the system. In fact, most executive malfunctions can be detected by the viability executive itself; an orderly transition is usually possible, and the old executive can properly communicate with its alternate.

Assume for the moment that the viability executive is also the system executive and that it is implemented in a single computer. The viability executive might detect a malfunction in one of its I/O channels which would functionally disqualify it for the executive role but not for other roles. Similarly, a malfunction could be detected in an arithmetic operation such as floating point division that is not used for the viability executive functions. There are innumerable failures in a computer that would disqualify it for certain roles in the complex but allow it to execute the steps required for an orderly transition of control.

3.2. External Detection

An **external malfunction detection** method is one in which the detection and isolation of the malfunction of the viability executive processor is accomplished by elements of the complex external to the viability executive. The processor which does the detecting is called the **monitor**. The executive can fail in three different ways: **sane**, **dead**, and **crazy**.

A **sane** processor is one which successfully communicates its plight to the monitor. This is an instance of self-detection and does not have to be considered further at this point. A **dead** processor is one which, to the external monitor, appears to be incapable of rational communication about its plight, either because it does not communicate, or because what it does transmit is garbage. An **insane** or **crazy** processor is one which communicates seemingly valid information despite its failure, but is nevertheless incapable of executing viability executive functions. If the monitor is to have the ability to detect a dead executive, it must interpret a lack of communication with the viability executive processor as failure. Thus, there must be periodic messages between the executive and the monitor. The message can be initiated by the executive, the monitor, both, or neither, but it must occur. One way or another, the executive must communicate to the monitor that it's "12 o'clock and all is well," or some such thing. The rate at which periodic check signals must be sent will depend upon the acceptable transition time from one configuration state to the next. It can range from a 100-millisecond interval to one of several minutes.

A crazy processor periodically transmits the proper message to the monitor. It can do this if it is caught in a processing loop that produces the check message. An independent check must be implemented to guard against this eventuality. The message used to detect a dead executive is called the **dead-man** signal, while the crazy processor is detected by the **crazy-man** signal.

3.3. Periodic Checks—Rationale and Implementation

Check signals must be periodically communicated between the viability executive and the monitor. If a check signal is not transmitted, or is transmitted in the wrong sequence or with the wrong value, it will indicate that the viability executive has malfunctioned. Typically, if the viability executive malfunctions in a loop, one of the check signals will be transmitted too often. A synchronous scheme for the check signal implies that there is a source of periodic signals (e.g., a clock) such that if the interval between check signals is either too small or too large, the discrepancy will be detected by the monitor and used as an indication of the failure. In synchronous schemes, the dead-man and crazy-man signals can be identical. Too long an elapsed time indicates a dead executive, while too short an elapsed time indicates a crazy executive. Presumably the probability of a loop of exactly the same duration as the check interval is small.

The problem with a synchronous check scheme is that there must be a clock, single-shot, or other processor with a time sense against which the comparison is made. Thus, in addition to possible monitor failures, we have bought possible clock failures.

If an asynchronous method is used, there must be at least two distinguishable check signals. The monitor will expect a certain number of crazy man signals for each dead-man signal, for example, "CCCCCCCCCDCCCCCCCCCD." If the dead- and crazy-man signals are generated in independent parts of the viability executive processor, it will be improbable that a failure would result in the proper sequence. A succession of crazy-man signals without intervening dead-man signals indicates a looping failure. The relation between dead-man and crazy-man signals can be made as complex as desired. Increased complexity increases the reliability of the check signals. Multiple, interlaced periodic signals can be used. These signals must be generated by independent subprocessors of the executive, should be communicated over independent channels, and use separate generation algorithms. The logical relation between the number of dead-man signals and crazy-man signals need not be fixed, nor need the value of the signals themselves be fixed. For example, we could require a prime number of crazy-man signals between dead-man signals, and the signals themselves could be successive primes. Such a sequence might be:

C1, D1, C1, C2, D2, C1, C2, C3, D3, C1, C2, C3, C5, C7, D5.

The algorithm used to generate the crazy-man and dead-man signals can be part of a test program. In fact, almost all the methods of malfunction detection described in Chapter 11 could be used. In practice, a simple, fixed relation between the crazy-man and dead-man check is adequate.

Furthermore, the check signal itself can be generated in a few well selected instructions in such a way that the probability of successful execution despite a malfunction is small.

The check signal can be initiated by the viability executive at predetermined logical points in its program; it can be initiated by the monitor, causing the viability executive to execute the programs that will generate the check signal; or it can be initiated by the clock or by another processor external to both the monitor and the viability executive, in which case both are alerted, the one to receive the signal and the other to generate it. If the signal is initiated by the clock, and the clock is not essential to the operation of the system, a failure of the clock may leave a viability executive failure or monitor failure undetected. If the clock fails dead, viability checks are suspended and the viability executive can fail catastrophically without being detected. However, this failure will not be important or affect performance unless yet another failure occurs that requires the use of the viability executive. If the viability executive places its own bounds on the expected signal from the clock, it might as well be generating the check signals itself.

A crazy clock (one which sends out too many signals) is not as harmful. The worst it can do is force the viability executive or monitor to make too many checks.

The choice between initiation of the check signal by the viability executive and the monitor is related to the problem of how failures in the monitor are discovered.

3.4. The Monitor

The monitor's functions are:

1. Detect malfunctions in the viability executive.
2. Initiate the excision of the failed viability executive.
3. Initiate the insertion of the new viability executive.

The relation between the viability executive and the monitor is as follows: the viability executive is concerned with the recovery from all failures other than its own, while the monitor is responsible for recovery from failures of the viability executive.

The monitor is not necessarily a single piece of hardware, or a single program residing in a unique memory. It can be implemented as one or several pieces of hardware or as a program residing in several memories.

The problems of executive failure, assignment, and control are different from those of other element failures. Yet, the viability executive is often the most complex processor in the system (because it is often the operational executive as well). As such, it is more likely to fail than are the simpler processors. The role of the monitor is to insure that a viable viability executive will always exist, that it has graceful degradation capabilities, and that the assignment of viability control is unambiguous and autocratic.

Autocratic control means that as long as the viability executive is in control, it is in complete control over questions relating to viability (except for its own failures). If this were not the case, a different processor could attempt to usurp control, with disastrous results to the system.

3.4.1. Human Monitor

This is the earliest and mechanically simplest, but least effective, monitor system used. Various malfunction indicators are used as appropriate to the system. The monitor periodically runs tests to validate the viability of the system. If he has detected a failure, or been alerted to an existing or incipient failure, he "throws the switch" replacing the on-line computer by its standby. He then initiates what steps he must to allow the system to recover. Both periodic and logical check signal schemes are used.

The clock, the monitor, and the viability executive are one and the same. The problem with a human monitor is that he is generally too slow to be effective, and that he cannot remember the complete algorithm required for reconfiguration of the system in a large multicomputer complex. This method was adequate for simple complexes that consisted of a pair of identical systems.

3.4.2. Check-Box Monitor

A check-box monitor is a logic network consisting of a signal receiver from the present viability executive, a single-shot to time the dead-man signal, and another single-shot to time the crazy-man signal and associated logic. If either signal fails or fails to come in the proper order, the monitor assumes that the executive has failed, causes it to be disconnected from the system and initiates a signal that will start the new viability executive. The check-box may be replicated and its operability judged by a majority vote unit or by manual checks by the system operator. This system is hierarchical or **stratified**. The system is as vulnerable as the check-box checker. Its virtue is conceptual simplicity and low initial cost. The monitor can expect temporally related check signals, in which case it is further vulnerable to clock failures, or it can be made more complex, allowing it to detect logical relations between the check signals, in which case it is even more unreliable.

The failure of the monitor does not necessarily affect the system's ability to perform its assigned tasks. The system can and does continue to operate properly despite most monitor failures. It is only when the monitor has failed *and* the viability executive processor also fails that the vulnerability of the monitor becomes a concern.

3.4.3. The Unstratified Monitor

The **unstratified** monitor is a distributed processor. It is distributed so that the failure of the monitor can occur only if the entire system has failed. The operability of the viability executive will be determined by the concensus of the remaining computers in the system. The viability executive sends its periodic check signals to all known functioning computers in the complex. These computers in turn either verify or deny the validity of the check signals. If the check signal is judged to be good, the monitoring computers each send a confidence message to the viability executive. If a monitoring computer is not satisfied with the check signal, it sends its confidence message to the computer(s) that has been designated as the successor of the viability executive. If the viability executive wins the vote, it continues to operate. If it does not win the confidence vote, it will abdicate (if it can). If the alternate executive receives a majority vote, it will assume the executive functions.

Voting can be further refined by requiring each voting processor to qualify (e.g., by means of a check message) to both the executive and the alternate executive. Failure to qualify (viewed from the viability executive and corroborated by the alternate viability executive) is an indication that that computer has failed.

If a majority of votes is required, attention must be paid to the situations in which there are an even number of computers up, and to whether or not self-voting or multiple votes are allowed for some computers. Some computers can be given more than one vote to provide for tie breaking. For example, the viability executive can be given two self-votes in cases of an even number of computers up.

If the voting procedure is detailed for every configuration state and proper attention is paid to ties, the monitor will fail only if a sufficient number of computers are down so that the system cannot process anyhow. The monitor has thus been provided with graceful degradation.

The unstratified monitor requires that all computers be capable of some intercommunication. Generally, the cost of the monitor is an increase in communication channels, additional interrupt lines, and additional space and processing time. These increases, however, are minor. A few tens of instructions are all that are required for executing the monitor functions in each computer. Tables may require of the order of 200 characters in each computer. The added channels, in most cases, will have been provided for other reasons, and since they need not be high-speed channels, they are not costly. The main cost of an unstratified software monitor is the initial programming cost. The voting procedure for each computer in each configuration state of the computers must be decided. In many cases, the action to be taken requires an operational decision and is not a clear-cut technical decision. The voting procedure, like the hardware monitor, is not infallible. Its advantage is that it can be made as infallible as practical.

As a combination of votes and configuration states are considered, the probability associated with each situation should be evaluated. If the sum of the probabilities of all such complicated situations is small, they can be treated by a simple procedure which sacrifices very little viability but reduces cost substantially. It is reasonable, in most cases, to treat all conditions in which there are two or more actual or suspected simultaneous failures by automatic reversion to a human monitor. That is, the system will not decide whether the viability executive or its alternate is in error. In practice, the treatment of second-order and multiple simultaneous failures and monitor ambiguity by reverting to manual control affects the overall viability of the system in an inconsequential manner. The designer, however, would be wise to verify this contention for his particular case.

3.5. Poisoning

Consider the shared-memory system shown in Figure 12.1. A failure or temporary malfunction in either CPU could indirectly induce the faulty operation of the other CPU. Similarly, a malfunction of any one of the memories could cause a propagation of errors that would corrupt the other memories. The very fact that units can communicate makes poisoning possible. One can conceive a highly improbable failure in one unit that results in the poisoning of every memory. It may not be possible to design a test program that could be loaded and properly executed despite the fact that one or more memories have been poisoned. To simplify the test procedures and to decrease the possibility of leaving a faulty unit on-line, a memory failure is tentatively assumed to be a CPU failure, and failure of a CPU is assumed to have corrupted all main memories to which it is connected. Since it is not generally possible to tell which of several memories has failed without executing a test program, since the memory will have to be

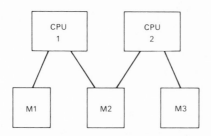

Figure 12.1. Shared-memory system.

reloaded anyhow, and since the CPU cannot be tested without a memory, taking both the CPU and its associated memories off-line does not represent a significant sacrifice.

The poisoning problem and, with it, the failure isolation problem is more acute in closely coupled systems such as shared-memory systems. Hardware malfunction isolation can only occur after the malfunction has been detected. Prior to the failure detection, we are forced to rely on software to prevent poisoning. The more checks we build into the interunit chitchat, the more isolation we provide. In the extreme case, the units are totally decoupled, the probability of poisoning is zero, but so is communication.

If the relation between each CPU and the portions of memory it has access to is fixed, then the advantages of shared memory are reduced. If, on the other hand, they are allowed unrestricted access to the other memories, the possibility of poisoning exists. Boundary violation checks can be established; they prevent poisoning but restrict CPU mobility. Similarly, assignment of CPUs to a functional role on a moment-to-moment basis gives the system high burst performance, allows parallel processing, reduces queuing delays, and reduces program and data transfers and program and data redundancy, but pays for this by significantly increasing the probability that one failure may cause the complete collapse of the system. An unstratified executive is clearly meaningless in such systems because every CPU could be the faulty one, or all could be executing the same faulty program.

4. EXECUTIVE ASSIGNMENT

The monitor determines that the viability executive has malfunctioned. It then performs the necessary actions to activate the new viability executive. The new executive assumes control and the system is again safeguarded from failures, except possibly a failure in the new executive—which is the most likely one to fail. The viability executive computer is usually the same as the system executive computer because they must both have access to and must manipulate the same information. The executive computer is often the one which is most loaded with input/output channels and peripheral devices. It has the largest tables and consequently the largest memory. The viability executive computer, considered as a subsystem, is therefore often the most unreliable one in the complex. If the system is not protected against a second viability executive malfunction, it may again break down, this time requiring manual recovery and a subsequent loss of viability.

The assignment of the next viability executive successor can be made to a functional or physical computer. It can be made before the viability executive has failed, after the failure and before the take-over by the new executive, or after the take-over by the new executive.

4.1. Physical *vs.* Functional Assignment

The alternate executive may be assigned to a physical computer (e.g., computer number 2) or to a functional computer (e.g., the statistics computer). There are advantages and disadvantages to both methods.

Since each computer is typically engaged in different functional activities, the loading on each is necessarily different. An assignment of viability roles to a physical computer then may cause extra processing for a computer which is already close to being overloaded. But the physical assignment scheme is particularly simple. If a hardware monitor is used, the assignment of the alternate can be done by a simple rotary switch. The next alternate is the next computer which is up. Thus, if there are eight computers in the complex, and computers 1, 3 and 4 are down, and the present viability executive is number 7, the alternate executive will be number 8, and the second alternate will be number 2. Physical assignment is simple, but the simplicity is bought at the expense of viability. Consider the system in Figure 12.2. If the executive (computer number 2) fails, the standby (computer number 3) will take over. The next computer to take over will be number 4, a front-end computer. However, the system is such that it should be the retrieval function that will be sacrificed and not the front-end function. The next failure will cause a break in the front-end function, while computer number 5 takes over the executive role. At that point, the system will sacrifice the retrieval function by making number 6 a front-end computer. The system will have suffered an apparent break in processing during the recovery interval. If the assignment had been made on a functional basis, it would have been the retrieval computer that would directly have taken over the viability executive function.

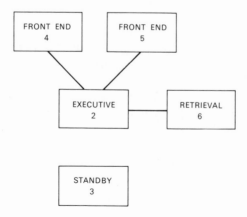

Figure 12.2. A typical two-level system.

The assignment of the alternate viability executive on a functional basis does not suffer from this problem. However, there are several disadvantages to this also. The monitor is more complex and must be updated after every configuration change. If a hardware monitor is used, the simple rotary switch is inadequate. A register holding the identification of the next physical computer that has the most dispensible functional role is needed instead. If an unstratified software monitor is used, each computer must be updated after each configuration change, and each must carry the physical identity of the new alternate executive.

A pure, fixed functional or physical assignment is not normally used. The sacrifice regime may not be fixed. It can change to adapt to changing operational conditions. Each such change will require a reassignment of the alternate executive. One way to avoid the large tables and programming costs associated with automatic viability executive reassignments is to do it manually. This is done in the Overseas AUTODIN system. After each executive failure, the system operator is requested (every few minutes) to name a successor to the viability executive. The successor's identity, once named, is transmitted to the monitor (hardware), and the system is again protected against an executive failure. Should the operator not name a successor before another viability executive failure occurs, the system may go down. The manual assignment of the alternate executive has been operationally satisfactory. If one considers that any scheme, whether manual or automatic, physical or functional, before or after the fact, must be provided with manual overrides, we can see that not much is gained by fully automatic assignment in small complexes. However, if the complex is large, consisting of hundreds of computers, and each functional processor requires several computers, manual reassignment may prove impossible. The time required for the operator to determine what the configuration is, what the momentary physical and functional relations are, and all the other data associated with the complex may be too long to be effective. If, furthermore, the physical/functional relation changes, not only due to malfunctions but due to loading, or if the executive itself floats, automatic functional assignment will be mandatory.

The ideal choice for the alternate executive is one which is physically identical to the present executive, and which is performing the most dispensible functions—that is, the executive is chosen among the functions that are next to be discarded. This is sort of like combing skid row for a new vice president who happens to wear the same size clothing as the president.

4.2. When to Assign

The question of when to assign the new alternate viability executive is as thorny as which computer should be assigned to the task. If manual reassignment is used, it should not be made during the recovery interval. It is not likely that the operator will be able to communicate with the new or old executive during recovery. Recovery can take place so quickly that it is best to lock out (except for deliberate overrides) possibly contradictory commands during this period. Furthermore, until recovery has been completed, the executive may not be able to communicate sensibly with the operator.

If automatic reassignment is to be used, the new alternate may be assigned before, during, or after recovery. The problem of assigning the new alternate before the failure is that one does not know in advance which computer will fail or be repaired next or what the final configuration will be. It could be the second alternate, the alternate, etc. Thus if the alternate viability executive were to fail, and if prior to the assignment of the new alternate, the viability executive should fail, we would again be left without a viability executive. If the assignment is made during recovery, the problem could still exist if the viability executive failure should be followed by the alternate's failure. Furthermore, it is possible that a perfectly functioning computer would not be able to take on a certain functional role, and that this could not be discovered until the attempt has been made. Thus, there is no guarantee that the alternate will be able to work, and that the configuration change will take place as planned.

For these reasons, the assignment of the new alternate is normally deferred until after the configuration changes have taken place and been verified. The system is vulnerable to a second failure while recovering from the first. However, the probability that the alternate executive will fail prior to the assignment of a new one is very small.

In general, the complications brought about by explicitly programming for the effects of failures that occur while the system is recovering from a previous failure and incorporating these into the executive reassignment programs are not worthwhile. The increased size of the programs and tables required to recover from second-order failures in every configuration state represents space of marginal utility and probably decreases rather than increases the system's viability. In keeping with this, for every step in a reconfiguration/recovery procedure, one should evaluate the reduction in failure probabilities and subsequent effects on viability. If the viability efficiency is 0.9999999990, there is no point in adding extra instructions and memory to increase it to 0.9999999992.

Executive assignment problems for computer complexes are substantially simpler than the executive assignment problems of societies. Many schemes have been tried, each with its own advantages and failings. We have described and elected deposable autocrats, reminiscent of the Roman Dictators, elected for the moment, given absolute power, but immediately deposed when found wanting. Since, however, the society of the computer

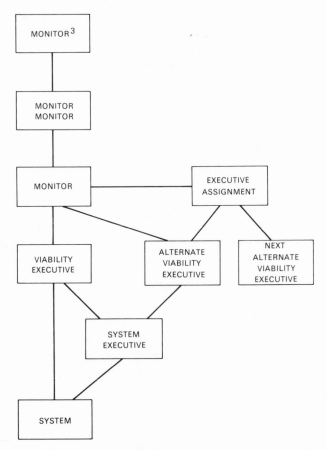

Figure 12.3. Stratified scheme for viability executive.

complex is indeed one in which every member is as capable as every other, utopian schemes can be made to work.[1]

4.3. Viability Processors in Review

The relation between the various processors participating in viability functions is depicted in Figure 12.3. The system is controlled by the system

[1] We have deliberately introduced an anthropomorphic note here to point out the dangers of thinking too much about the executive reassignment problem in human terms. We have found that in many discussions of viability executives, there is a tendency to assign human qualities to these processors. The result is an overly complex reassignment scheme, structured to take care of cases whose cumulative probability is small even compared to viabilities of the order of centuries.

executive. The system and the system executive are also controlled by the viability executive. The viability executive is responsible for all failures except its own. The monitor is responsible for failures of the viability executive. Should the viability executive fail, the monitor will direct a switchover to the alternate viability executive after the failed executive has been excised. The monitor will also direct the executive assignment processor to assign a new alternate viability executive. The monitor may in turn be overseen by a higher-level monitor, which in turn may be examined by one of a yet higher level. The system executive and the viability executive are often the same. Furthermore, executive assignment and higher-level monitoring may be done by the operator.

The unstratified scheme shown in Figure 12.4 is better. The system is its own monitor. The other units of the system, in particular, the computers, can be used to perform the various monitoring and executive assignment functions, eliminating the need for a hierarchy of monitors. The "tail is tied," so to speak.

5. THE CONFIGURATION SWITCHING NETWORK AND RECONFIGURATION

Reconfiguration is that process concerned with the ejection of malfunctioning subsystems, the introduction of spare subsystems, or the reassignment of subsystems to new functional tasks for reasons other than malfunctions. Inherent in any reconfiguration process is the assumption of a degree of interchangeability for subsystems, a switching network to allow the reconfiguration, and algorithms to control reconfiguration.

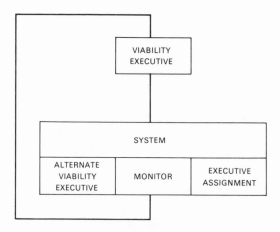

Figure 12.4. Simplified unstratified scheme for viability executive.

5.1. Partition, Similarity, and Payoff

Reconfiguration capabilities can be implemented at any hardware level —if a configuration switching network is also provided at that level. It can be shown that the size of a configuration switching network exhibits a nonlinear growth as a function of the number of elements to be connected. The nonlinear growth of the configuration switching network and the reliability and repair time of the network itself indicate that there is an optimum size for the network *beyond which further reconfiguration capabilities decrease the system viability.* The level at which the reconfiguration capabilities are supplied is called the **partition of the network**. Note that the existence of a partition at a given level, if it is to be exploited, demands automatic malfunction detection and isolation to that level.

The present technology is such that the optimum level is achieved with a partition of the system into computer main-frames (including scratch pad memories, if any), memory modules, drums or discs (with their controllers), tape transport units (with their controllers), and normal peripheral devices. That these partitions generally coincide with the usual subdivisions of a system is more than fortuitous. The usual partition of a system into units is made at points of minimum interface, "minimum" being used in a general sense here to include the number of wires, the signal levels and speeds on those wires, and functional independence from the point of view of test and debugging. To go beyond this level is to open a whole new class of switching requirements which is orders of magnitude larger. Earlier systems were partitioned at higher levels; the tendency has been toward finer partitions. The partition level, then, determines what devices will be called subsystems.

It can be shown that *for a given hardware expenditure, viability is maximized by minimizing the number of distinct subsystem types and maximizing the interchangeability of identical subsystems.* Thus, a system with two kinds of main-frames, five of one kind and three of another, is less viable than one with eight main-frames of the same kind. The payoff can be several orders of magnitude. Indirect benefits are reductions in the complexity of the configuration switching network itself, in the size of the status tables, and in the complexity of the configuration control algorithm.

5.2. Configuration Switching Network Requirements

Each element of the configuration switching network is first and foremost an element of the system. It too is capable of failure, and therefore must be replaceable. The size and complexity of the configuration switching network is such that in systems with extensive reconfiguration capabilities, this network becomes one of the predominant culprits in systems failures.

One cannot say that one shall use a configuration switch to switch malfunctioning elements of the configuration switching network; it is readily seen that this approach does not converge.

5.2.1. Modularity

Modularity of the switching elements is required in order to assure interchangeability. Furthermore, modularity is required to allow the network to be applied to systems of various sizes. In this respect, modularity of the configuration switch is not different from the modularity found in computers, memories, and other system elements.

5.2.2. Independent Failure

Every element of the configuration switching network should satisfy the criterion for subsystems. The failure of an element of the switch should not compromise the operability of other elements of the switch, or that of subsystems other than those which it is used to connect.

5.2.3. Graceful Degradation

The network structure should be sufficiently flexible to allow alternate paths and assure the connectability of critical subsystems, no matter which element of the configuration switching network has failed. This means that there will undoubtedly be some degree of redundancy in the configuration switching network itself.

5.2.4. Nonblocking

This is the most stringent requirement on the structure of the configuration switching network. A switching network is said to be **blocked** if it is not possible to connect an idle inway to an idle outway, despite the fact that some other inway–outway combination could be connected. That is, the elements of the switch path are there, but it is not possible to use them for this particular connection. A nonblocking network is one in which it is always possible to connect any idle inway to any idle outway. The simplest nonblocking network is a crossbar switch.

There are two forms of nonblocking: nonblocking without rearrangements and nonblocking with rearrangements. A switching network which is nonblocking with rearrangements is one in which it is possible to connect any idle inway to any idle outway, but the existing connections may have to be disturbed or rearranged.

5.2.5. Universal Connectability

This requirement assures that any subsystem of a given type can be connected to any other subsystem of an appropriate type, no matter what the present configuration. Interchangeability of elements imposes this requirement of universal connectability. To say that a computer can be used in any functional role is to say that it can be connected to the peripherals required for that role as well. Since universal connectability is required for every element of the system, we find that every element must have the same or analogous channel structures. The universal connectability requirement is often relaxed in practice, and is replaced by "almost universal" connectability.

5.2.6. Permutation Symmetry

Permutation symmetry is a stronger requirement than universal connectability. Universal connectability requires that the given connections can be made. Permutation symmetry requires the ability to make all such connections simultaneously. The nonblocking requirement essentially covers that of permutation symmetry. Figure 12.5 shows a simple example of a switching network that has universal connectability but not permutation symmetry.

Any memory can be connected to any computer, but only two at a time. Absolute permutation symmetry is not required in most systems. It is only necessary to provide a sufficient number of throughways to satisfy any functional configuration. The requirement for permutation symmetry is also often relaxed in real applications.

5.2.7. Speed

There are two speeds to consider in the design of a configuration switching network: the speed of switching elements and the speed of the signals being switched. These are not the same. For example, if manual connection changes are used, the switching speed is low. However, the signal speed is unaffected. The switching speed is dictated by the transition time requirements—which is to say, the effective MTTR of the complex. Since many configuration switches must be changed during a configuration change, a

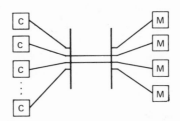

Figure 12.5. Switching network without permutation symmetry.

switching speed of 200 milliseconds per switch could result in a net configuration change time of several seconds. If configuration switching intervals of only a few hundred milliseconds are required, element switching speeds of microseconds will have to be used. Signal speed is typically that required by electronic circuits—nanosecond pulses. The configuration switching elements must pass such signals with a minimum of distortion, attenuation, and delay.

Both requirements can be met by electromechanical switches such as are used in telephone circuits; these include crossbar switches, reed relays, and electronic switching elements.

5.2.8. Path Homogeneity

This is a purely engineering consideration requiring that electrical path properties between two kinds of connected subsystems be the same no matter which particular subsystems are involved or how the connection is established through the configuration switching network. A variable (permutation-dependent) path implies variable transmission characteristics such as delay, rise time, and pulse width and amplitude. Since most subsystems will depend on fixed, known characteristics of signals and their responses, violation of this requirement would restrict the interchangeability of like subsystems.

5.2.9. Repairability

It should be possible to repair and/or replace a malfunctioning element of the configuration switching network without affecting the operability of the rest of the system. This can be done by providing alternate paths for each connection, or by reconfiguration of the complex in such a way that the switching element in question is not used in that particular configuration.

5.2.10. Simple Controls

Since the controls of the configuration switching network are themselves prone to failure, overburdening the network with complex controls might reduce the net viability. It is possible to construct configuration switching networks which, while elegant from every other point of view, fail because of the inordinate complexity of their controls.

5.2.11. Isolation

Since each element of the configuration switching network should satisfy the requirements of a subsystem, it must be possible to detect the malfunction and to isolate the failure of an element. Ideally, this ability should be provided by the system and should be automatic.

The electrical and logical isolation required for viability purposes is not necessarily absolute. The more nearly absolute it is, the simpler will be fault detection, isolation, reconfiguration, and recovery. A removable connector provides the best isolation. A relay contact or electromechanical contact is almost as good.[2] Electronic switching is less so. Weaker yet is isolation which depends upon the proper functioning of channels or central processing unit hardware. The weakest kind of isolation is that which depends upon the logical integrity of programs.

5.2.12. Cost

The use of a configuration switching network is to be weighed against other means of achieving the required viability. The configuration switching network allows the redundancy in other equipment to be reduced. If the cost of the network exceeds that of the additional redundancy required to achieve the same viability, it may not be effective.

5.3. Configuration Switching Implementation

Configuration switching as discussed above has implied automatic switching. There are, however, situations in which automatic switching is not necessarily the best. The following is a review of the factors to consider in choosing between manual and automatic switching or between electronic and electromechanical switching.

5.3.1. Manual *vs.* Automatic Configuration Switching

Manual switching requires the fewest components and is simply implemented. Manual switching is used to replace circuit cards or units. Manual switching means removing and inserting connectors. This can contribute to the failure rate. Very large connectors, with several hundred wires, cannot reliably and quickly be disconnected and reconnected. Fully manual switching by means of connectors may take several minutes for each connection. The probability that the connector will be broken or made to prematurely fail should be included in the evaluation of the viability if completely manual switching is used.

The cables used to connect the subsystems are typically routed through ducts beneath the false floor of the installation. The density of cabling in the subfloor is so great that when a cable fails (at some midpoint rather than at a connector), a new cable is passed through the floor, rather than attempting to pull and then replace the old cable. Consequently, if manual switching is to be used, all such connections should be brought to a manual patch bay. This implies additional cabling and connectors.

---

[2] Almost as good but not as good because a contact can fail closed.

A further problem with manual switchover is the density of the cabling in the patch bay. Consider a patch bay used to connect ten memories with six computers, in which every computer can be connected up to four memories. There will be twenty-four connectors for the computers and ten for the memories. Associated with each connector there will be a cable. Each cable may be one to two inches in diameter. As the cables emerge from the subfloor into the patch bay, their curvature near the connector makes the patch bay take on the appearance of a cabinet full of cobras. And the cables are about as intractable; they are inordinately stiff and their electrical properties are changed by bending and twisting. It is difficult to maintain homogeneous paths under these circumstances.

The cost of the cabling and the patch bay represents a significant portion of the cost of a configuration switching network. Furthermore, after several configuration changes have occurred, the patch bays are so tangled that status information may be lost, i.e., no one knows what is connected to what. In general, manual switching by connector changes is limited to portable units and test equipment.

Switching can be done under manual control with some sort of switch or relay replacing the patch bay and the manual connector changes. Manual rotary switches or multipoint switches are not feasible. If relays are used, and the connecting cables have been installed, the greater part of the cost of automatic configuration switching has been spent. The configuration switching network may be indirectly manually controlled via a computer. The operator dictates each configuration change to be executed. The state transition time is now reduced to the time required for the operator to recognize and isolate the malfunction, and to initiate the corrective configuration change.

5.3.2. Electronic vs. Electromechanical Configuration Switching

Electromechanical switching elements terminating a large number of parallel lines can have substantial crosstalk. This is particularly true for high-speed signals. Each path through the configuration switching network must be debugged for all pertinent configurations. If corresponding cable runs are not electrically identical, variable delays may ensue, which will cause problems. If cable runs are long, or if multiple stages are required in the network, amplifiers must be used.

Electromechanical switching presently offers the advantages of low cost, isolation between elements of the configuration switching network, feasibility for relatively high-speed circuits (750-nanosecond memories), and a long history of applications with attendant reliability data. Electromechanical switching has a further advantage in that self-latching relays are simple. Mechanical latching offers the advantage of tolerance to power failures. Configuration memory is not lost when power is lost. Electrical latching, on the other hand, is advantageous because power failures cause the system to unlatch—which is a fail–safe condition.

Electronic switching is best used where the maintenance of signal integrity is a problem. The cost, however, is high. The requirement of isolation, the ability of the system to run without the particular element, and the protection against derivative failures, all tend to further raise the cost. Protection against power loss and maintenance of configuration memory are also problems. Redundant power, independent of other power supplies, must be provided. The large number of small power supplies that must be used substantially increases the cost.

The continuing trend toward lower cost of integrated electronic circuits allows the construction of multistage networks that, for large configuration switching arrays, may turn out to be cheaper than electromechanical switching. If the elements of the complex have been designed with interfaces compatible with the requirements of configuration switching, much of the cost associated with electronic switching can be absorbed. The implementation of electronic configuration switching over an existing product line can lead to ineffectual redundancies in driver and interface circuits.

5.3.3. Implicit Configuration Switching Networks

Any communication link between units of the system can be part of an implicit configuration switching network. Channels can of course provide functions equivalent to an explicit switching network. There is then a spectrum of implementations from explicit switches to the normally existing interunit connections. The differences along this spectrum are primarily in the degree of isolation that is provided. The controls of an implicit configuration switch are programs rather than the explicit control devices discussed below.

5.4. Configuration Controls

5.4.1. Individual Switch Controls

Every switch in the configuration switching network must be controllable by the viability executive or its alternate. The following functions must be implemented:

1. Break the existing connection.
2. Make a new connection.
3. Read the position of the switch.

Disconnection is required to remove a failed element from the configuration. The break must be accomplished without disturbing or otherwise introducing transients in the existing connections; otherwise derivative malfunctions might ensue. Making a new connection is the primary function of the configuration switching network. This too must be done without disturbing existing connections.

The configuration switching network controls can also fail. Furthermore, the memory elements used to remember or latch the configuration can fail. The system must have a means by which it can read the present connections, and by which it can verify that the desired connection has been made. If this kind of feedback is not provided, the configuration stored in the ledger and the actual configuration may differ, with disastrous results. Positional feedback information is better provided on request rather than automatically. The switching time may be relatively long, and the contacts used may bounce for a few hundred milliseconds. If the feedback is provided automatically, it may occur before the switching transients have died down.

The ability to connect, disconnect, and determine the position of each switch in the network means that every switch is addressable. The individual switch elements could have their own decoding network accessed by a common bus, or the addressing logic can be centralized in an address decoding network within a configuration network controller. In either case, duplication of the bus or redundancy of the addressing network and receivers is desirable.

5.4.2. Configuration Network Controllers

A **configuration network controller** is a device used by the viability executive to control individual switches of the configuration switching network. The network controller could be part of each computer's I/O subsystem; it can be a separate device, or it can be distributed throughout the configuration switching network.

In a simple configuration switching network constructed of logical crossbar switches, control is direct. That is, it takes a single, isolated action to make, break, or read the connection between a given inway and outway. If, however, the more economical multistage networks are used, the establishment of a given inway–outway connection is the result of the action of several or almost all of the connections in the network. In such cases, the controls are best distributed among the switching elements to simplify the master control. Positional feedback must be established by a special testing network. The controller could be a small computer, or a processor within the viability executive's computer(s).

Present experience (which is based on the use of electromechanical crossbar networks) has led to the use of individual network controllers. Address decoding has been both centralized and distributed. The main function of the controller has been to provide the proper I/O chitchat with the controlling computer, the drivers for the control lines, and the receivers for the feedback information. We shall assume for the remainder of this section that there is an explicit device that can be called the configuration network controller.

The configuration network controller, being an element of the system, is itself prone to failure. Its failure, however, is a second-order failure, providing that its failure does not result in a change of the configuration. If the configuration network controller should fail, it can be repaired or replaced manually. This is effective as long as another failure requiring a configuration change does not occur in the meantime. Thus, redundancy in the configuration network controller is not absolutely essential. If redundancy is not provided, the problems attending configuration network controller failures can be partially alleviated by separating the functions of disconnection, connection, and positional feedback into three subsystems (although this is in itself a form of redundancy). The contention is that there will be many failures that require reconfiguration in which it will be possible to continue operation (probably degraded) if it is possible to excise the malfunctioning subsystem.

If the probability of a configuration network controller failure is high relative to the viability requirements, the penalty for nonprocessing is high, and/or the MTTR of the controller is high, it may be necessary to use one or more redundant network controllers. While it is possible to provide electrical and logical isolation between the controller and the computer, the interposition of isolating switches between the controller output and the switches it controls is clearly not practical. Isolation must therefore be provided by other means. The use of parity check and generate networks, error correcting codes, etc., on all control lines, and at the receivers of the individual switches, can provide excision of a faulty controller.

Higher-order replication of the configuration network controllers is not effective. The use of three controllers for one set of configuration switches and majority vote logic at each switch would be extremely reliable. However, since the configuration network controller is not needed during normal operation, the failure of two controllers and yet another subsystem leads us to probabilities that are small indeed.

Figure 12.6 shows the configuration network control scheme as described thus far. An approach to partial redundancy is shown in Figure 12.7. Each controller can control more cross-points than there are in any one configuration switching subnetwork. Controller 1 controls most of the switches in subnetwork 1 and some of the switches in subnetwork 2, and *vice versa* for controller 2. Should either controller fail, the other controller will be able to make any inway–outway connection required in either subnetwork, as long as there are no failures in those configuration switching subnetworks. The

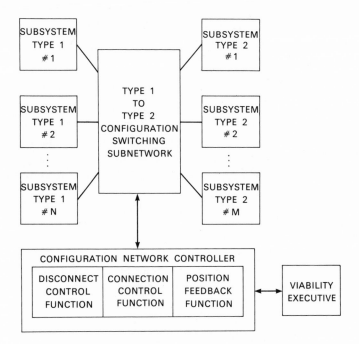

Figure 12.6. Configuration network controller.

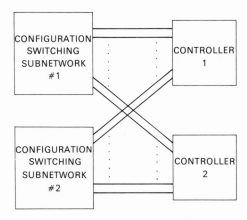

Figure 12.7. Partial redundancy in configuration network control.

alternate path capability has been sacrificed. Thus, the failure of either controller leads to a state of graceful degradation in which a subsequent failure in the switching network may disallow certain configuration changes. This does not necessarily degrade the operation of the system.

Much the same techniques used to enhance the viability of the system can be applied to the viability of the configuration switching network and its controls. The following factors, however, should be kept in mind.

1. The configuration switching network is not needed unless there is a failure (downgrade reconfiguration) or there has been a failure now corrected (upgrade reconfiguration). Failures in the configuration control are second-order failures.
2. It is not practical to provide configuration switching for the configuration switching controls.
3. Alternate routing, and the possibility of establishing alternate equivalent configurations, may allow the system to continue undegraded operation despite a configuration switch failure or a configuration switching controller failure.

5.4.3. Configuration Master Controller

The ascension of a new viability executive implies that it obtains control over the configuration, and therefore, perforce, over the configuration network controllers. The **configuration master controller** is that processor which assigns control over the configuration network controllers to the viability executive. The configuration master controller is not to be confused with the monitor, even though these can physically be the same subsystem. The configuration master controller disconnects the old viability executive from the configuration network controllers and connects them to the new viability executive. It is a miniature configuration switching network. Since its functions are relatively simple, it can be controlled directly, without yet another intervening control level (i.e., a "configuration master controller configuration controller").[3]

If the monitor is a simple (conceptual) rotary switch, we need only add a few more wafers to the switch that assigns the new viability executive to provide the configuration master control functions as well. If a more complex monitor is used, an explicit master controller will be required.

---

[3] At first blush, one might be tempted to let the master controller be one of the many configuration switches in the system, allowing it to be controlled by the configuration network controllers. This would imply that every computer would have to have continuous access to the configuration network controllers. If this were not the case, it would not be possible for the alternate viability executive to take control over the configuration network controls, and thereby the configuration. If every computer can control the network controllers, it is possible for a failed, nonviability executive to modify the configuration. To prevent this occurrence, the master controller functions are separated from those of the network controllers.

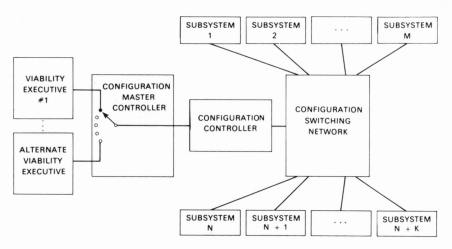

Figure 12.8. Configuration master controller.

The complete configuration control scheme as described thus far is shown in Figure 12.8. The viability executive is connected *through* the configuration master controller to the configuration network controller(s). All other potential alternate viability executives are capable of being thus connected through the configuration master controller. The configuration controller(s) in turn control the configuration switching network, which in turn determines the configuration.

The approach to configuration control described here is midway between the simple "switchover unit" used in duplex systems and substantially more complex schemes that have been implemented or proposed. Increased complexity can be used to advantage to further decrease the system's vulnerability to failure. As with "worst-worst case" circuit design, this can be carried to extremes where viability is reduced rather than enhanced.

5.4.4. Configuration Veto Controller

The configuration master controller can fail in the following ways: it fails to connect any computer to the configuration controller(s) or it connects more than one computer to the configuration controller(s). A faulty connection of one or more computers will result in a subsequently detected error, and need not be considered here. The question of what should control the configuration master controller is answered by allowing *every* computer to control the configuration master controller.

The probability of a computer failing in such a way as to properly and repeatedly move the functional position of the configuration master controller to some other computer than the viability executive is small. We are dealing here with third- or fourth-order failures. Furthermore, the failure of the master controller (as a result of which the viability executive is not connected to the configuration controllers) will become important only when a configuration change is required.

However, since the improbable will occur with embarrassingly high regularity, it behooves us to provide protection against this remote possibility. Such protection is afforded by the **configuration veto controller.**

The veto controller is a set of switches, controllable by any computer, which will disconnect all computers from the configuration controllers. This is depicted in Figure 12.9. The several computers are connected through the configuration master controller to the configuration controller(s) via the configuration veto controller. Each computer can change the position of the configuration master controller, as indicated by the conceptual OR gate shown. Each computer can also execute a veto which will disconnect all computers from configuration controllers, thus freezing the configuration. The configuration veto controller is simple—rudimentary in fact—and reliable. It should be constructed such that a total power failure will result in an automatic veto. The execution of a veto does not change the configuration. It only changes the ability of the viability executive to automatically make configuration changes. A veto can be executed for many different reasons including manual override by the operator, failure to assign a new viability executive, fight for control by two competing viability executives, configuration master controller failures, etc. Since the veto controller is a series of independent switches, and its action is to perform a disconnection, the prob-

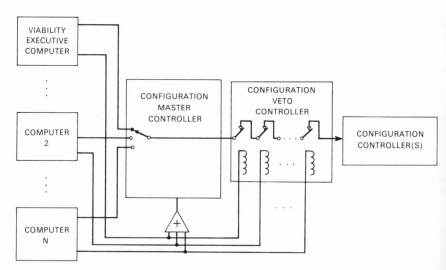

Figure 12.9. Configuration veto controller.

ability of enough simultaneous failures such that the veto will not occur is so miniscule that this occurrence is in the realm of fantasy.

The position of each switch of the veto controller should be displayed on the system supervisory console. A veto occurrence will require manual intervention. The position of the switch will also specify which computer exercised the veto. The veto action should be coupled with a loud (preferably raucous) alarm. Preventive maintenance (if applicable) or repairs, as in the case of the master controller, can be carried out while the system is operating, without changing the configuration. Should a failure occur during such an interval, the system will be under manual configuration control, which, while slow compared to automatic control, will still allow recovery and graceful degradation. The mean value of the configuration switching time is hardly affected, and the net effect on the viability is small.

The configuration master controller and veto controllers can be combined into a single switching network such that one and only one computer can be connected to configuration controllers at a time.

5.5. Reconfiguration Algorithm

The following reconfiguration algorithm is representative of the steps that could be employed in establishing a single connection directly. If the connection cannot be made, it will be attempted with an alternate controller. If the alternate controller cannot make the connection, an alternate path will be attempted. If there is no alternate path, an alternate equivalent configuration will be set up. If there is no alternate equivalent configuration and the transition was a downward transition, a further stage of degradation will be attempted. If the transition was an upward transition, the previous configuration will be maintained and the operator will be informed. If there is no available degraded state, the system will revert to manual control.

Let us assume that the switch involved in the connection has been successfully unlatched (i.e., it is open), and that it is functionally a multi-position switch. An attempt is made to set the switch to the proper position by use of the primary controller assigned to that switch. The program then waits for the interrupt that signals that that switch has responded. If the interrupt does not occur, a second attempt will be made with an alternate controller. If that does not work, something is wrong and the system must go into a test routine to establish whether the problem is in the interrupt generator, the switch itself, the commanding computer, or the configuration switch controller.

If the interrupt occurs, and it is the proper interrupt, positional feedback is requested. If the positional feedback is correct, the program can go on. If the feedback is incorrect, it can be requested by the alternate feedback network. If the new feedback is correct, then something wrong is suspected in the first feedback network, and an isolation test program will be entered to determine what may have malfunctioned. If the two feedbacks are incorrect and consistent, the failure may be in the switch itself or in the controller. A second try it made with the alternate controller to determine the possible malfunction.

The program must of course have internal switches to take care of the cases in which there is no alternate controller or alternate feedback network.

Variations on the above theme can be devised with three controllers, three feedback units, multiple tries on each controller with a consensus vote, multiple tries on feedback units, etc. Other variations include the use of error correcting codes for the commands and the feedback. The command code itself can be reflected as the feedback, to assure that the proper command has been sent to the required switch. Similarly, switch units having their own address decode networks can transmit their addresses as part of the feedback data. Comparison of transmitted code and reflected codes can be used to isolate such malfunctions. Other complications arise for multi-stage switching networks, for which the equivalent of the above procedure may have to be established for each stage.

Assume for the moment that the switch appears to have been set to the proper position. The connection must then be tested. A single wire failure (open or closed) should be detected as a parity error on one or the other side of the interface. The two communicants (this is not necessarily a computer-to-computer connection) are stimulated by the viability executive to exchange signals and transmit the results of such signals to the viability executive.

For connections not involving a computer, this may be difficult, the computer being required to determine the validity of the connection via a set of intermediaries. If the connection has been verified, the program can continue to the next correction.

If the connection is not made, or not made successfully, the viability executive must find an alternate route through the configuration switching network to establish the desired connection. If an alternate path is possible, it is set up and retried. Flags must be set to limit the number of alternate routing tries.

If an alternate path cannot be established, the viability executive will take what working subsystems it has and attempt an alternate, equivalent configuration which is as close as possible to the present configuration, that is, it will attempt to find the alternate equivalent which disturbs the present configuration least, consistent with the functional assignments of those elements that might be rearranged. The whole process is then again attempted with the new configuration. Again, flags must be established to limit the number of tries at alternate equivalent configurations.

If an alternate equivalent configuration cannot be established in the prescribed number of tries, two possible courses of action are open. If the configuration change was an upgrade change (e.g., entered because a repaired element was brought back into operation), the system can revert to the old configuration, informing the supervisor of its failure to effect reconfiguration. If the reconfiguration is a downgrade configuration change, a degraded state will be sought. The viability executive must then set up the parameters for downgrading the system and initiate the new change. In each case in which the reconfiguration algorithm strays from the normal path, additional diagnostic information is established that will be useful to the repair technician. Such information should be retained and printed or otherwise communicated to the technician.

As formidable as the above sounds, we should note that such algorithms have worked for more than 40 years.[4] We have only to examine a local telephone exchange to find most of the elements of the reconfiguration algorithm.

The action of the various configuration switches can be overlapped. Thus, a second required connection can be attempted in a different part of the network before the first connection has been completed. This is particularly important for electromechanical switches in which the switching time could be several hundred milliseconds. The required degree of overlap will be determined by the speed of the switches and the allowable transition time. If transition times of the order of several seconds are allowable, simpler algorithms that perform one connection at a time can be used. If electronic switching is used, again the more complex overlapped reconfiguration algorithms can be avoided. If the required transition time and the switching time of the individual configuration switches are comparable, extensive overlap must be used. This means that alternate paths cannot be attempted until existing connection changes have settled. Similarly, connection changes brought about by changes in the desired configuration (alternate equivalent or further degraded) cannot be initiated until previous actions have settled and been tested.

5.6. Configuration Tables

The viability executive must at all times know the exact relation between physical and functional elements of the system. This implies that there is at all times a table or set of tables that specifies all connections and assignments within the complex. If the configuration switching network is under direct

---

[4] At the turn of the last century, the old telephone engineer rebuked his younger colleague for predicting nationwide dialing, saying "But it will take billions of relays." Whereupon the youngster said "Yes!"

control of the viability executive, and if it is a multistage network, these tables can be large. Copies of the table must be safely stored before and during every configuration change. A configuration change is not considered to have occurred until the new configuration tables have been safely (redundantly) stored.

It is possible for the viability executive to reconstruct the configuration tables by a series of tests. Positional feedback information can be used to establish all physical connections. The topology of physical connections surrounding any one computer is usually sufficient to establish its functional role. If not, the viability executive should be able to obtain the functional role from the system executive (particularly simple if they are the same processor). If the functional assignments are not known to the system executive, the system is down, and due for a complete reconfiguration.

Systems employing overlapped configuration switching must maintain the intermediate status information for each switch being changed. Individual switch actions can be processed by a queue-driven processor much like any other multiprogramming executive system. If processing queues are established for configuration switching, these queue entries must also be stored.

There is one saving grace to all of this. Assume that all the required status information is lost. The worst that can happen is that the system will have to perform a complete reconfiguration, a so called "dead start." Since this can be accomplished in a few seconds, and since the likelihood is extremely small, the penalty is not statistically large. It should be recognized that, while the viability executive (combined with the functional executive) is the most likely processor to fail, the *majority of configuration changes are not viability executive reconfigurations.* This is not a contradictory statement: there are more processors and elements in the system which are not the executive. A typical example is a system which undergoes an unscheduled reconfiguration every 2 to 3 hours but a viability executive reconfiguration only every 2000 to 3000 hours.

One could establish a complex audit trail of configuration switch changes (and attempted changes), maintain accountability for all such transactions, and at all times, in every conceivable circumstance, have the ability to reconstruct the instantaneous status of the configuration switching network and its associated controllers during any configuration changes with any nth-order failure. Again, this would push matters past the point of diminishing return.

5.7. Configuration Displays

Reconfiguration as implemented is not an exciting thing to observe. But for a few light changes, clicking of relays (largely submerged beneath the constant susurrus of the air conditioners), and the notification by some tele-printer that the whole affair is over, one would not know that anything had happened.[5] However, since it is always possible that the system will have to revert to manual control, and since configuration changes can be initiated for reasons other than malfunctions, the operator must have some method of determining what the configuration is.

He must know the status of each subsystem, and its physical relation to the complex. He must also be able to determine its functional assignment. Redundant displays are required, lest the failure of one of them should lead the operator to a wrong decision. Redundancy here can take many forms: line printers, typewriters, CRT displays, indicator lamps, etc., all provide effective display redundancy. The following information must be displayed or directly obtainable in every configuration state:

○ The status of each subsystem:
  1. Up and on-line.
  2. Up and off-line.
  3. Up and available but not yet on-line.
  4. Down and off-line.
○ The functional assignment of each subsystem.
○ How it is connected to other subsystems via the configuration switching network.
○ The status and data regarding the subsystems that comprise the configuration switching network itself.

Such displays need only be meaningful when the system is not undergoing a configuration change, provided that the information can be displayed if the system has failed to effect reconfiguration.

The physical–functional relation can be displayed (or printed) as a matrix. This has the advantage that the operator can at a glance determine all conflicts as well as take note of the configuration state; that is, those functional roles which have no elements assigned have been sacrificed. If distributed processors are used, or if extensive partition is used, the operator may not be able to determine the level of degradation from such a matrix.

It is not generally possible or practical to display the specific paths through the configuration switching network by which elements of the complex are connected. The simultaneous display of all such paths would be meaningless. It is, however, advantageous to display a trace of any specific-ally named connection. That display names all interposed switches and their

---

[5] We are always surprised by the very brevity of the complicated actions we program. Something that takes so much development, thought, and time to test should be more dramatic than a few seconds' worth of blinking lights. One can do a timing analysis calculating that such and such should take 200 milliseconds, but never really appreciate how short a time that is until one does(n't) see it in action. So it is with reconfiguration.

positions. Another useful display is a list of all presently unused configuration switches. This enables the operator to specify an alternate path if the system has failed to establish one, or if one must be established to repair a malfunctioning switch.

Hardware displays on individual elements of the complex are also useful. Thus, it should be possible to determine a switch position by examining the switch itself.

Finally, all printed or graphic displays should identify themselves. Say that the system has three CRT displays, two typewriters, and a printer. The maintenance technician has been monitoring the system via a CRT, when a failure occurs. For some reason or other, the viability status information is now being typed out on a typewriter in another room. The system has been properly designed, and the failures had been such that this was the only way to communicate. The operator sitting at the typewriter may not be able to interpret a sudden printout of a matrix of ones and zeros. The display should inform the reader that this information is to be transmitted to the maintenance technician (immediately) or otherwise inform the reader of its importance.

5.8. Upgrade and Downgrade Configuration Changes

The emphasis in viability design has been on allowing the system to degrade gracefully. Graceful amelioration is also required. One is so easily entwined in the complexities of degradation that one can forget that eventually the system will get better before it gets worse. Obviously, the average number of upgrade reconfigurations should equal the average number of downgrade reconfigurations. Every sacrifice taken must be reversible; shared functions must be unshared; distributed functions must be collected.

Functional sacrifices are not difficult to undo. The recovered function is applied to new jobs, while the jobs in progress still go on as if the recovery had not occurred. Eventually the old tasks leave the system and new tasks proceed with the recovered function. In this way, the function is gradually restored with a minimum of housekeeping. Extensive partitions can be treated in a similar way.

If functions can be identified with individual computers, and if the system has a standby computer, the problem of upgrade recovery can be simplified. The standby computer is capable (by virtue of its programs) of taking over any functional role. If a single computer has failed, it is replaced in the functional standby position, and no further work is required. If two or more computers have failed, resulting in some sacrifice or another, the repaired computer is first placed in the standby position rather than directly in the functional position that has been sacrificed. The viability executive is then informed that there is a standby, whereupon the standby is placed in the functional position of the missing on-line computer. While the transition time may be increased by this, since it only occurs when there has been more than one computer failure, the simplification in upgrade recovery programs more than pays for the lost viability.

5.9. Other Uses of the Configuration Switching Network

The configuration switching network can be used to advantage for many tasks other than recovery from malfunctions. These applications include: routine switching of elements for operational reasons; bootstrapping, test, and diagnostic purposes; program check-out and modification; production testing and integration; and hardware check-out in the field.

5.9.1. Routine Switching of Elements

The tape stations of a typical computer complex are usually connected through controllers to one or more computers. Typically, a controller will control more than one tape station. This allows a tape to be rewound while another is being read from or written to. Furthermore, tape stations require routine preventive maintenance, so that several tapes are usually out of service. Some form of configuration switching has been used for tape transports for at least ten years. The tape switching network of a system employing configuration switching is a replacement for, rather than an addition to, the previously required tape switching network. The main difference is increased flexibility and generality of connections. Similarly, the programs required for tape transport assignments are included in the reconfiguration program.

A similar condition exists for disc drives, terminals, maintenance panels, and so on. In many cases, we find that a particular segment of the configuration switching network is a replacement of a previously existing switching network. Such segments do not represent an increased cost. It is not unusual to find that 30 to 50% of the configuration switching network already exists in a complex of several computers, implemented without configuration switching *per se*.

5.9.2. Bootstrapping

The configuration switching network can be used to provide an elegant bootstrap for a computer. The viability executive loads a core memory with the required program and attaches that memory to the computer requiring bootstrapping. That computer is initialized to some standard location and started. This can reduce the requirements for complex, multiple-instruction, hardware bootstraps. Similarly, loading programs can be simplified, since a self-loading loader is not absolutely essential. The various standard boot-strap and loading programs will still have to be available if the system goes down completely, that is, if it is required to perform a dead start.

5.9.3. Test and Diagnostic Purposes

The ability to change combinations and connections of elements can simplify the design of the test and diagnostic programs. If a malfunction is detected, and an ambiguity exists as to which of two elements is at fault, the test program can request substitutions of elements known to be working, and proceed to test on that basis. This can provide for relatively faster test and diagnostic routines. It does not, however, eliminate the requirements for complete self-contained test programs. The complex has presumably been designed with a minimum of fat. Consequently, the technician does not have many spare elements to work with. His only spare computer may be a bad one; similarly for his core, drum, tapes, etc. To the extent that a second spare is available, advantage can be taken of the configuration switching capabilities of the system. The ability to load a program into a good memory, with a computer known to be working, can be used to reduce the MTTR of the computer. The memory is handed over to the viability executive, which loads it with the test program. The loaded memory is returned to the suspect computer and the maintenance technician can begin his tests.

5.9.4. Program Check-out and Modification

A given complex consisting of several computers can be broken down into several smaller complexes. Each of these complexes represent a de-graded state of the system. However, they are *viable* degraded states. The system can therefore be in several states at once. Part of the complex can be removed to form an off-line complex, while the remainder continues uninter-rupted operation. This is presumably done during lightly loaded periods. Should a failure occur, the test configuration can be dissolved, and its ele-ments returned to the main configuration. Similarly, if a load burst should occur, the elements of the test configuration can be returned to the on-line configuration.

This capability is particularly important in the development of a multi-site complex such as the Overseas AUTODIN system. Eleven sites, ranging from four to six computers each, were required. A maximum test site was designed. The operational programs were written for the maximum site, the smaller sites being considered as essentially degraded versions of the maximal site. Considerable development cost was saved this way. Similarly, once the maximal site had been debugged, there was great assurance (and relatively little effort required to insure) that the individual sites would work. Staging time was reduced, with a consequent reduction in inventory cost.

Modifications required for individual operational sites were tested by using the configuration switching network to establish the configuration of the operational site at the test site.

5.9.5. Production Testing and Integration

One major part of the hardware integration effort is the testing and detection of hardware unit interaction malfunctions. The abilities of the configuration switching network can be used to reduce the effort required for this task. The system is assembled, unit tests are performed, and the nuclear configuration is debugged. At that point, all units are placed in an "available" status and the system is allowed to attempt their integration. The viability executive attempts to achieve a maximal configuration and rejects any unit that fails to work within the configuration. Since unit tests have been successfully carried out, all such failures can be construed as interaction failures. The units that are incorporated are assumed (for the moment) to work. The particular interface problems which caused a unit to be rejected are corrected and the unit (eventually) accepted by the complex.

When all units have been accepted into one maximal configuration, the test continues by changing the relation between physical and functional assignments. This continues until each unit has been accepted and served in each functional position. All malfunctions occurring along the way are corrected, the system being used to detect its own integration problems.

In this way, cabling errors, connector failures, interface incompatibilities, excessive loads, and the like are detected and corrected with relative ease. It is not, however, possible to go through every combination of physical and functional assignments. If each computer can be in one of eight functional positions, each core in one of six, each tape in one of twelve, etc., a relatively modest system would require thousands of years to test all possible assignments.[6]

If the system is part of a multiple procurement, and the configuration switching network design permits it, the site being staged can be attached to the test site (which is known to be working), and each unit brought into the test site. This will reduce unit test time. When all units of the system being staged have been accepted by the test site (with appropriate corrections made of malfunctions), the new site can then be integrated as was the single site above.

This approach is essentially an extension of the normal procedure of assembling a computer or other complex device one card at a time, by interchanging them with the cards of a computer that is known to be working.

---

[6] For this reason, one should not contract to test every possible configuration, but to test a realistic and effective sample of these possibilities. The selection is done in much the same way that we design our program test procedures.

When the interchange has been completed, the new computer is known to work, and only need go through the normal diagnostic run for verification.

6. PARTITION AND THE CONFIGURATION SWITCHING NETWORK

6.1. General

The configuration switching network is not necessarily a monolithic network capable of connecting every unit to every other unit. We cannot imagine the circumstances in which it would be desirable to connect a typewriter to another typewriter without an intervening controller. Similarly, tape–tape, tape–drum, disc–drum, line buffer–card reader, and other combinations may be unnecessary or, in the context of the particular hardware, functionally impossible. Even if all such combinations were functionally possible and desirable, they would not have to be accomplished simultaneously.

6.1.1. Growth Laws

The complexity of the configuration switching network can be measured by the number of **cross-points** it contains. A **cross-point** is a switching element which could be implemented by a simple AND gate. However, each channel through the configuration switching network is not a simple, single wire. Typically, a duplex character interface between two devices will require 24 wires. A computer–memory interface may require 120 wires. Thus, we must always keep in mind the "depth" of the cross-points as well as their number. We can afford four character cross-points for each word cross-point. The specific details will vary with the hardware set.

Even the most economical configuration switching network has a nonlinear growth. The MTBF is inversely proportional to the number of cross-points, while the MTTR is probably proportional to the square of the number of cross-points. On this basis, it would appear that the availability of the configuration switching network decreases inversely to the sixth power of N for a crossbar network (where N is the number of items to be connected). The network does increase the viability of the rest of the system. Whether or not the total viability of the system is degraded faster by the reduced availability of the configuration switching network than the increase in viability brought about by the network depends in a complex way on the particulars of the system. One can postulate parameters for which the system's viability increases indefinitely, stabilizes, or decreases as the complexity of the configuration switching network is increased.

Be that as it may, let us not forget the most important reason for introducing configuration switching: it is introduced to reduce the cost of achieving a required viability. If there are N items to be switched, and the configuration switching network grows in size (and therefore in cost) faster than N, there will be a point where it is cheaper to split the system, or otherwise reduce the cost of the configuration switching network. Thus, if K_1 is the cost of the average item switched, and K_2 is the cost of a cross-point, with amortized controls, we should re-examine the size of the network some time before the relation

$$K_1 N = K_2 N^2 \qquad (K_2 \times \text{ the cross-point count of the network used})$$

is satisfied.

Keeping in mind that not all cross-points are the same, we can observe the following characteristics of different types of networks (where N and M are the number of units of each type being connected):

Network Type	Growth Law	Comment
Crossbar	N^2 or $(N \times M)$	Suitable for electromechanical switching.
Clos	$2N \log_2 N + \dfrac{N^2}{\log_2 N}$	Nonblocking, complex controls.
Symmetric	$2N(2 \log_2 N - 1)$	Nonblocking with rearrangements, complex controls, economical for large N.

It is interesting to observe that for N less than 36 the crossbar is more economical than the Clos. Similarly, the crossbar is more economical than the symmetric network for values of N less than 10. Since the maximum number of units to be switched in existing systems with configuration switching has been small ($N = 16$), the potentially more economical Clos and symmetric networks have not been used.

The requirements of alternate routing, configuration switching network viability, repairability, and other similar practical factors, have conspired to deliberately avoid the construction of minimal configuration switching networks. The reasoning here is almost identical to that used by the telephone company. The minimal network, while meeting some hypothetical figure of merit, is liable to provide maximal headaches.

6.2. Configuration Switching Networks

Several different methods can be used to reduce the size of the configuration switching network without reducing the viability of the system. These include dedicated subnets and channel restrictions.

6.2.1. Functional Groupings and Dedicated Subnets

One approach to reducing the size of the configuration switching network is to group things by what can be sensibly connected to what. We employ a separate, independent, configuration switching network for each such grouping. The Philco Overseas AUTODIN System shown in Figures 1.5 and 1.6 of Chapter 1 has the following sets of configuration switching sub-networks: computer–computer, core–computer, drum–computer, tape controller–computer, tape–tape controller, computer–I/O, as well as several other smaller subnets.

Each such subnet has a modest number of elements to be connected, allowing the economical use of crossbar switches. The virtue of such functional groupings is that they sacrifice nothing of viability and only disallow the connectability of units whose connection would have been senseless anyhow.[7] An ancillary benefit of functional grouping is that it eliminates failure modes in which inappropriate connections could be made.

6.2.2. Channel Restrictions

Consider the problem of connecting a drum to a computer. The computer might have four channels of the correct kind available. A complete configuration switching network would require that the particular drum be connectable to all four channels of that computer. This effectively increases the network fourfold. There may be no need to allow the drum to connect to all four channels of the computer since it can only be connected to one of them at a time. The existence of two channels provides an alternate path, whose reliability is not significantly increased by a third path from the drum to that computer. If a channel has failed, it is not likely that the computer will be retained. Therefore, two channels are adequate. Many devices in the complex can be connected to each other by more than one channel. Multiple channels may not be needed in every functional position. Consequently, we can limit the combination of channels that can be used for their connection. A typical restriction would be to allow even-numbered devices to be connected to all even-numbered channels, and odd-numbered devices to all odd-numbered channels. Every device can be connected to every other device, but not by all combinations of channels. Since the MTBF of the devices is calculated on the basis of any failure in the device (e.g., a computer is considered to have failed if a channel goes out, even though it is capable of working in a particular functional role despite the failure), the calculated viability is not affected. The availability of the configuration switching network (through a reduction in alternate route capabilities) is affected. In practice, this kind of restriction has an insignificant effect on system viability.

---

[7] It is sometimes necessary to disallow the connectability of two units which could be logically connected and whose connection might prove an occasional convenience, because the cost of allowing the connection outweighs the advantages gained.

6.2.3. Permutation Restrictions

We can allow all units of a type to be connectable to all units of a compatible type, but not in any permutation. Assume that N units are to be connected to N other units. There are $N!$ possible permutations with which this can be done. Considering now all possible configuration states, in which there are N, $N - 1$, $N - 2$, ... units up, we find that there are orders of magnitude more permutations that could come up. The number of cross-points used can be reduced by reducing the number of such permutations implemented. Thus, we can implement only even permutations (those requiring an even number of interchanges from the rest state, where 1 is connected to 1, 2 is connected to 2, etc.).

In general, only K out of the N devices need be connected simultaneously. Thus, only those permutations need be established. The possibility of reducing the complexity of the configuration switching network by reducing the number of possible permutations is not applicable to crossbar networks. It can be applied to networks such as the Clos, or the symmetric net. The saving, however, is not large for large networks. This approach is most applicable to small networks, where the increased complexities of design, analysis, control, and viability evaluation do not destroy the gain obtained through the use of the smaller network.

Typically, permutation restrictions are more stringent. That is, the network will simply not allow the connection of certain compatible units to others. For example, a simple rule might be: even cores to even computers and odd cores to odd computers. This essentially cuts the network in half, and the cross-point count is divided by 4.

6.2.4. Tessellation Schemes

As the complex gets larger, it pays to subdivide it into quasi-independent subcomplexes, with limited interchangeability. Figure 12.10 shows alternate interchange schemes for a complex of eight units.

The vertices of the graph represent the units that are to be interchangeable. The links represent the ability to interchange them. Thus, in Figure 12.10a all units are completely interchangeable. In Figure 12.10b each unit can be interchanged with five other units. In Figure 12.10c the interchangeability has been reduced to four other units, while in Figure 12.10d the interchangeability has been reduced to three. The extreme cases, represented by Figures 12.10e, f, and g, show a simple linear exchange, four duplex systems, and, finally, the null case, in which no interchange is provided.

For any number N of elements to be interchanged, one can devise tessellation schemes which allow interchangeability with $N - 1, N - 2, \ldots,$ 2, 1, 0 other units of the same type. As the degree of interconnectability is reduced, the number of cross-points and the viability are reduced.

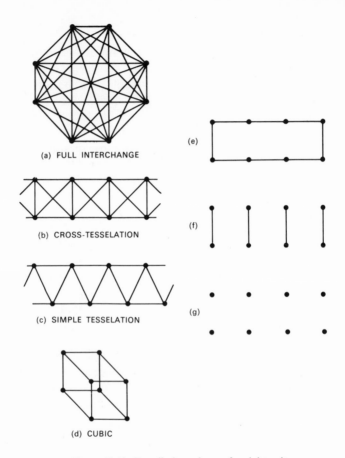

Figure 12.10. Tessellation schemes for eight units.

The idea of tessellating can be applied to the interconnection of compatible unlike units. Consider a case in which three units of one type are to be connected to six units of another type. Possible schemes are shown in Figure 12.11. The six-, four-, and two-way schemes are symmetric. However, the three-way scheme is not symmetric, since each A' unit can only be connected to one B unit.

In general, tessellation schemes should be symmetric. The extent of asymmetries (such as the A–A' situation in Figure 12.11c) should be kept to a minimum and be consistent. Asymmetry will require more complex controls (to eliminate impossible configurations), viability is lower than for symmetric schemes, and the calculation of viability far more complex.

Asymmetric tessellations are nevertheless useful on occasion. They typically arise in a multiple procurement. The system is designed for the

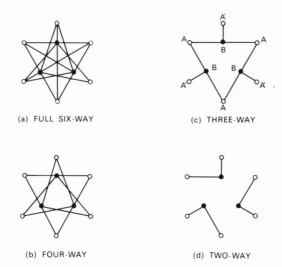

(a) FULL SIX-WAY   (c) THREE-WAY

(b) FOUR-WAY   (d) TWO-WAY

Figure 12.11. Tessellations of dissimilar compatible
units.

maximum installation, and the smaller installations are cut-down versions
of the largest. This may result in asymmetries of the configuration switching
network as the lowest-cost way of building the various sites. In such cases, the
control can be implemented by setting some nonexistent units to a permanently "down" state, and "failing" some of the links of the network. A
pessimistic viability calculation can be made by ignoring the interchange
capability of the asymmetric links such as in Figure 12.11c. Present technology
seems to place a practical limit on interchangeability at about eight. Figure
12.12 shows several approaches to the interchangeability of elements for
different numbers of elements. The reader will note that Figures 12.12f and
12.12g, while appearing different, are in reality the same scheme. This could
be readily seen by considering the connection matrix of both figures. The
theoretical treatment of configuration switching network designs leads one
rapidly into some very elegant but somewhat obtuse higher mathematics.

7. THE LEDGER

7.1. The Ledger—Why and How

Four sets of things must be correct if a system is to function: hardware,
software, data, and control. The recovery of hardware is accomplished by the
viability executive through the action of the configuration switching network
or by such other hardware recovery procedures as may be used. Programs are

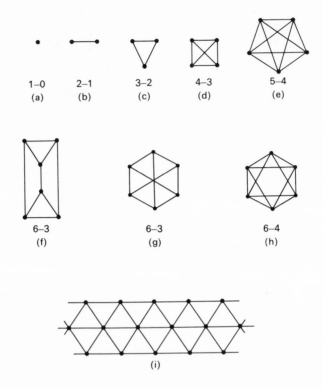

Figure 12.12. Interchangeability schemes.

recovered by reloading them from a program library. There remain only data and control to recover. The set of information required for recovery is called the **ledger**.

If it were possible to maintain a complete record of the content of all memory locations in the complex (including core, drums, discs, internal computer registers, transient registers, control flip-flops, etc.), and if the external environment did not change between the time of failure and the time of recovery, then recovery of control and data would be simple. Duplexing schemes with a primal system "ghosted" by a secondary one are an approach to the total maintenance of the data (operational and control) required for recovery. However, several factors make the problem more difficult.

1. A complete record cannot be maintained.
2. The external environment changes.
3. The internal environment changes.
4. Recovery need not be to an equivalent configuration state.

7.1.1. Pinch Points

It is possible (with certain limitations) to turn the clock back and restart the system at a point just prior to the failure. Every time we restart a program, we are doing just that. The original copy of the program, given the same input data, will produce exactly the same output each time it is started. In principle, then, one might assume that it would be sufficient to maintain a complete record of every intermediate result—an instantaneous snapshot of the system —load the program counters to the values specified by the snapshot, and thence continue as if a failure had not occurred. While this is sufficient, it is neither necessary nor possible.

There exist one or more points in the system cycle at which a minimal amount of data can be used for data and control recovery. Such points can be called **pinch points** of the cycle. We can examine the program flow chart and conceptually determine the width of every point on that chart, where the width is measured by the number of bits that would be required to restart the program at that point. The points of minimal width provide natural places for recording data required for recovery. Pinch points quantize time. If the ledger consists only of data gathered at pinch points, then the system will be able to recover only to within the nearest pinch point.

A pinch point is not necessarily a functionally recognizable or meaningful program point. However, the interfaces between programs and the pinch points can coincide because the factors that lead to program partitions and to the selection of ledger data are similar. Program partitioning can be looked upon as a process that discovers and intensifies the pinch points of the program. In previous chapters, the partition was chosen on the basis of what could be conveniently managed by one man, programmed by one group, stored in one memory segment, executed in less than a predefined time interval, independent of other programs, etc. Such partitions, however, and their naturally occurring pinch points may not be suitable for recovery. There may be too many of them; there may not be enough; the time quanta they represent may be too coarse or too fine; they may be overly redundant; they may not be reproduceable (i.e., redundant storage may be impossible). Many pinch points do not imply a fine time quantization of the possible recovery points. Similarly, a sparseness of pinch points does not imply a coarse time quantization. For example, the program might consist of many iterative routines whose individual execution times are very long. On the other hand, the program might consist of a few often used, short-duration routines.

The existing pinch points will typically provide an overly fine time quantization. The problem lies not in finding a sufficient number of such points, but in choosing which ones should be used. It is relatively rare that the program partition will have to be made finer than it would be were it not for the problems of recovery. There are some examples of this, however. Large-scale scientific and commercial programs, such as linear programming problems, charge account processing, and banking applications, whose completion may take many hours, are designed to periodically dump **benchmark** data to save running and elapsed time if a failure occurs. The benchmarks points are typically taken at pinch points: before the start of a new iteration, at a discrete record, at the beginning of a set of records, after a certain group of operations have been completed, etc.

In systems consisting of a single computer, working on a single program, independent of external effects (other than inputs), the ledger and benchmarks are the same.

7.1.2. Impossibility of a Complete Ledger

A complete ledger would be a continual snapshot of every memory location in the system, together with all synchronization data required to properly re-establish the timing relation between electromechanical elements. A complete ledger can be maintained only by simulating the system's operation and continually dumping the results to a memory. That is to say, the programs must be run interpretively bit by bit. An interpretive trace that dumps the system's every step would take ten or more instructions for each executed instruction. The system would then spend 90% of its time writing the ledger. This means that in the overwhelming majority of cases, a failure would occur while an entry to the ledger was being made.

The simplest complete simulator of a system is another copy of the system. Thus, we duplicate the system, having a redundant (**ghost**) reproducing each action of the on-line system. Were it not for electromechanical components, such a system might work. However, electromechanical components such as tapes, drums, discs, printers, readers, typewriters, etc., have variable response times. The only way to assure that two drums (say) will remain in synchronism is to place them on the same physical shaft. If this is done, they are no longer independent subsystems, and are not effectively redundant. The existence of electromechanical components means that there will be interrupts in the one computer that will occur at a different time in the ghost. The two are therefore out of synchronization. Each new interrupt will further disperse the two systems, till the desired coincidence no longer occurs, and the ideal, unquantized recovery is not achieved. The two systems can be kept synchronized if every action involving unsynchronizable devices is artificially synchronized by making the two processors wait for each other. That is, if A must write a record, it will wait (in a do-nothing loop) for B to complete the same action before going on to the next item. Waiting for the other processor can more than double the processing time. The artificial synchronization of many devices will so degrade the system that its processing efficiency may be less than 10%. Note that (so far) this may be an improvement over the interpretive ledgering scheme, because benchmark data of the do-nothing loops need not be maintained. If the two systems are to be synchronized, they must communicate, or they must receive and process each other's interrupts. If they receive and process each other's interrupts, logical isolation may be compromised. If they communicate, the veracity of those communications must be established. Thus, even the "simple" lock-step synchronism is not so simple. Practically speaking, the reconciliation of the problems of synchronizing two systems to achieve "lock-step" ghosting are such that they can recover only to within an I/O operation of each other. The continuous recovery interval is not achieved.

Ghosting systems (simple duplication) are designed to recover to predefined benchmarks, structured at natural pinch points. Though there have been several attempts at lock-step ghosting for systems using synchronous peripheral devices, there are no known successfully operating systems whose recovery is based on such schemes.

7.1.3. The Changing External Environment

It is rarely possible or desirable to reconstruct the system to the precise conditions that existed prior to the failure. System inputs can be categorized from the following points of view:

1. Can the input be reproduced?
2. What is the cost of reproducing the input?
3. If reproduced, is it meaningful?
4. What is the value of reproducing the input?
5. Is there a penalty for lost input?
6. Is there a penalty for duplicate inputs?
7. Can the input be replaced?

Not all inputs can be reproduced. For example, the particular track point resulting from a specific radar return cannot be reproduced. The same traffic pattern will not recur, the automobiles having moved on despite the system's failure.

For those data which can be reproduced, one must determine the cost of such reproduction. Rarely is the instantaneous cost of a single retransmission significant. However, the equipment or labor cost of one retransmission, multiplied by one or two thousand, may be excessive.

Reproduced data need not be meaningful. A late message can be of historical importance only.[8] Late data may be more confusing than the correct data,[9] if not totally misleading.

---

[8] The telegram warning of the attack on Pearl Harbour was delivered several hours after the start of the attack by a boy on a bicycle.

[9] Consider, for example, the telegram: "IGNORE PREVIOUS TELEGRAM."

The meaningfulness and value of late data saved through ledgering will depend on the particular application. One does not ledger data that could be recovered at a lower cost by other means, or whose recovery would be meaningless or valueless.

Recovery of the input by ledgering is not always desirable. In some systems, a duplicate input is of no concern. Thus, two identical track points in a radar system will not generally be significant, since the system is already dealing with a multiplicity of track points, some of which could be identical. On the other hand, a duplicate entry in an airline reservation system is considered less desirable than a lost entry. A duplicated bank draft, while recoverable, is generally more dangerous than a missing one.[10]

It is possible that even though the input cannot be duplicated, it can be replaced. Thus, the loss of a single track point in an air defense or air traffic control system is automatically corrected by the next return. Similarly, feedback data in a process control system can be delayed or skipped, with no long-term deleterious effects. A momentary lapse in processing of a time-shared computer system will be recovered when the user re-enters the previous line. The data being supplied are not the same as those which were lost, but they are effectively the same. A factory control system in which the inputs are part counts and other numbers affecting the inventory cannot tolerate such losses unless corroborative checks are employed which counts at other stations.

Missing or duplicated outputs are to be considered much the same way as were inputs. Thus, there may or may not be a penalty for missing outputs. It may or may not be meaningful to reproduce an output. A duplicated output may or may not be undesirable.

We see that the environment in which the complex operates is a continuously changing one. While it is possible to turn the clock back on the system, it is not possible to stop the world. The system may recover anachronisms, creating more problems than if it were totally out of commission.

7.1.4. The Changing Internal Environment

The most drastic internal environment changes occur when the system recovers to a configuration state not equivalent to the one it was in at the time of failure, that is, in an upgrade or downgrade recovery. However, recovery to an equivalent configuration state is not without internal changes.

---

[10] There is the apocryphal story about a man who deposited a large amount of money in a small bank. He informed the manager that he would hold the money there only a few days, as he was just passing through town. The manager directed all tellers to accept the gentleman's identification and to give him the money when requested. On the appointed day, five "gentlemen" entered the crowded bank, displayed proper identification to five different tellers, and simultaneously received the deposited cash.

The temporal relations between electromechanical devices have changed. Thus, one drum may be slightly ahead of another before but slightly behind it after the failure.

The new configuration has different delays for the various paths. Not all memories operate at the same speed, etc. The conjunction of these effects is such that it is not possible to base a recovery scheme on the assumption that the system will be identical to what it was before the failure. The changes in inputs will inevitably cause some changes in the running time of various programs. The system is inevitably anisochronous. The several programs running in each computer at different priority levels assume different orders. Each independently operating computer assumes a different temporal relation with the other computers of the complex.

7.1.5. Reconfiguration to a Nonequivalent State

It is not possible to know what the next configuration state will be. All failed equipment may simultaneously be repaired, or many units may simultaneously fail. It is clear, then, that since the next state might be any state, the ledger must at all times contain the information required in every state, even though those data may not be needed in the present state.

A configuration change may imply functional or extensive sacrifices, or resumption of functions or extents that had previously been sacrificed. The ledger must contain the status information regarding those functions, even though that information cannot be used or even generated in the present state. For example, suppose that the ledger included the status of communication lines. Furthermore, assume that service of those lines had been suspended. The program that generated the status data is not active, and consequently the status data can be neither used nor generated. Yet, the status data must be maintained, if only by blind recopying of that portion of the ledger. Eventually, the functions will be resumed, and the system will have to recover from the failure that caused the sacrifice of the lines in the first place. Thus, the ledger must provide the information required to recover from a failure that may have been followed by many other failures and/or repairs. If the ledger at all times contains all the information required to recover from all dead states to the maximal state(s), then it will have sufficient data to recover from any state to any other state.

7.1.6. Multiple Ledgers

We have discussed the ledger as if it were a single table, produced by a single program in one computer; the ledger is not so restricted. Each computer in the complex could maintain a ledger of the functions peculiar to it. Just as we have tended to a single viability executive residing in a momentarily fixed computer, the ledger, for the same reasons, will usually be implemented in a single undistributed program, acting within one computer. If ledgers are distributed, there will have to be some master index of the various ledgers, a central place where the recovery program can determine what data are valid and what invalid. That central ledger, then, takes on the function of "*the* ledger*.*" There is a hierarchy of data which must be preserved if the system is to recover from malfunctions. Each level in that hierarchy provides control of qualifying information relevant to the data at the next lower level of the hierarchy.

7.1.7. Ledger Cycle Cost

The ledger quantizes the system cycle, allowing recovery only to within certain predetermined points in the cycle. Typically, the point is a complete cycle. The ledger is a snapshot of the system as it existed at the time the ledger was taken. The act of recording the ledger is called **roll-off**. The roll-off is not instantaneous. If the ledger is recorded on a disc, many milliseconds may elapse between the initiation of the roll-off and its completion. The roll-off interval may require several seek times, and the time required to write many tracks of data. The ledger may range from 2500 characters for a small system to 50,000 characters for a large system. The elapsed time for the transmission of these data may be a significant portion of the system cycle. It is clear that any processing that could affect the content of the ledger must be suspended at the time that the content is being written. Since the ledger writing is most often done by a contentious transfer, it will occur independently of the various processors that could modify it. The simplest, though not necessarily best or even necessary, approach to the avoidance of possible conflicts is to suspend all processing that could affect the ledger throughout the roll-off period. Typically, this means that between 5 and 15% of the available memory cycles are discarded. The main program goes into a waiting loop, doing nothing until the ledger write is complete. The ledger is often duplicated, increasing the loss to 10 to 30%. The ledger is therefore another form of redundancy, with a hidden but nevertheless high cost.

7.2. Roll-Off Implementation

The conceptually simplest approach to implementing the ledger roll-off is to suspend all processing, initiate the ledger write, and resume processing only after the complete ledger has been safely stored. The cost of the roll-off can be reduced by various means without compromising the validity of the ledger.

7.2.1. Snapshot Ledgers and Frequency of Ledgering

Consider a simple, instantaneous, scheme in which all processing is suspended during roll-off. This is called **snapshot ledgering** (processing is suspended in order not to blur the "snapshot"). The simplest programs will ensue if the roll-off is done at a fixed point in the system cycle. A good choice is in the neighborhood of the dead-man or crazy-man generation routine, that is, generate the check signal as a result of receiving a valid interrupt for the I/O operation that performed the actual roll-off. If we wish to reduce the overhead associated with ledgering, we can simply not roll-off every cycle. Thus, the ledger could be written every tenth cycle, every hour, etc. The longer the interval between ledgers, the more noticeable the processing interruption will be. The choice is based on the probability of failures (i.e., the probability that a nontrivial reconfiguration will be required), the penalty associated with stale data, and the cost of recovery with stale data. The latter enters into the problem because it is more difficult to recover properly with stale data than with fresh data.

Typically, the roll-off interval (the reciprocal of the roll-off frequency) should be comparable to the length of residency of an average transaction.

7.2.2. Phased Ledgers

A close inspection of the data to be ledgered would reveal that the timeliness is not the same for all transactions. We would in fact find that there is a distribution that specifies the number of transactions that should be ledgered at each frequency. Thus, rather than rolling off in order to meet the requirements of the worst transaction (that which requires the highest-frequency roll-off), several different ledgers could be written, corresponding to the several different populations of timeliness requirements. Some data are rolled-off every cycle, some every two cycles, and others every ten cycles. The advantage gained by this is that the individual ledgers are smaller, and consequently, the average duration of the ledger roll-off is reduced.

7.2.3. Exception Ledgers[11]

A deeper examination of items in the ledger would reveal that the rate at which the data change and the timeliness of the data are weakly related. Thus, the status of a device may not change quickly, but must be recorded as soon as the change occurs. This might mean that a device that changes relatively slowly might have to be ledgered with a high frequency. We can examine a set of tentative ledgers and consider the changes that had occurred from ledger to successive ledger. Doing this, one would find that there were relatively few changes. Therefore, much of the information that is rewritten at each roll-off need not be rewritten at all.

The roll-off time can be reduced by recording only that which has changed since the last ledger was recorded. Rather than changing the ledger

[11] Also called "incremental ledgering" or "delta ledgering."

itself, change transactions of the form

ITEM 127 SHØULD BE ABCDEGH–993
ITEM 808 SHØULD BE ***GHTX $$$
ITEM 127 SHØULD BE ABCDEGH–994

are recorded in the main memory. The roll-off then consists of such ledger changes. The viability executive can periodically update the ledger by incorporating the succession of such changes. This can be done every ten or so cycles. The changes can be kept in a change table whose size is sufficiently large to hold a worst-case number of changes. The ledger can then be updated only when the change table is filled or about to be filled. This can further reduce the average number of memory cycles required for ledger roll-off. The recovery program first accesses the freshest complete ledger and updates it according to the set of changes that have been recorded since that ledger was rolled-off. The roll-off time has been reduced at the expense of increasing the recovery time.

7.2.4. Continuous Ledgers

One can control the roll-off as a result of specific events that require ledger updates rather than as a result of having reached a predetermined point in the system cycle. Consider a table whose entries must be maintained in the ledger. The table must be considered from the point of view of the processors that modify it and the processors that use it. If the roll-off occurs prior to the initiation of such processors, there will be no problem if a failure should occur. Similarly, if the roll-off occurs after all processors that affect or are affected by the table have terminated, there will be no problem should a failure occur. It is only when the roll-off occurs while a processor might be modifying or reading that table that a failure might cause improper ledgering. The processor and the roll-off may be operating at different priority levels. The program that performs the roll-off can set flags to indicate that the ledger is being rolled-off. Thus, if the ledger were rolled-off while a processor using it was active, a test of the roll-off flag by that processor would indicate that the processing might be fallacious (if a failure should occur) and that the processing would have to be redone. Each processor can test this flag prior to completion. Alternatively, the ledger roll-off program can test the activity of every processor that has cause to use or modify the contents of that part of the ledger. Should any such processor be active (but blocked, say), the roll-off for that cycle would be delayed until all such processors had finished.

The savings is a reduced roll-off interval and consequently a reduction in wasted memory cycles. The costs are increased space, increased processing time, increased formality of interprocessor communications, a more complex recovery program, increased recovery time, and significantly increased programming difficulty. A secondary advantage is that the system cycle is no longer punctuated by the ledger interval. This will tend to reduce queue lengths and provide better burst response.

7.3. The Content of the Ledger

The specific content of the ledger will depend upon the particular application and the specific implementation of that application. There are, however, some general items and observations as to what the ledger should contain.

7.3.1. Configuration Data

The ledger should contain the complete configuration data of the system; the status of each subsystem (UP–DØWN, ØN-LINE–ØFF-LINE, AVAILABLE–UNAVAILABLE); the physical–logical assignment of every configurable unit; the physical location(s) of every processor; the complete positions and status of the configuration switching system; the status of every processor regarding all functional or extensive sacrifices that may have been made; and special modes or information not implied or derivable from the program (i.e., operator commands).

7.3.2. Memory Control

A typical system will use some form of dynamic storage allocation in its main memory and in various mass memories associated with it. Occupancy tables for core and drum or disc blocks must be maintained or else storage may be lost or inadvertently overwritten. All block links must be maintained either in the ledger, or be accessible via the ledger. Privileged areas, boundaries, partitions, relocation register values, etc., must be maintained. The data in these locations are presumably stored elsewhere, but the organization of these data, such as the correspondence between a drum address and a core address for the same information, should be maintained in the ledger.[12]

7.3.3. Processing Status

The system will typically have internal processing queues. The queue entries and linkages should be maintained in the ledger. The status of each

[12] A large freight terminal warehouse control system was implemented without a ledger scheme (or at least without one that worked). All data regarding items stored in this highly automated warehouse were kept on a disc. A simple method was used, establishing a correspondence between a disc block and a physical bin in the warehouse. Not long after the system started working, the inevitable failure occurred, and with it, correspondence between the content of the disc and that of the warehouse was lost. To make a long story short, the terminal was shut down for several months. It was not the missing corpse or the 30,000 baby chicks that was the backbreaker; it was the 15 tons of frozen liver that did not get placed in a refrigerated compartment.

job should be maintained. The present value of the program counter for that job, unfulfilled I/O commands, and auxiliary memories and devices in use or requested should be retained. In particular, operator commands that are awaiting execution should be retained, or if not the actual commands, at least indicators that point to the command or allow the system to request a repetition.

7.3.4. How Much to Store

Consider a simple implementation of a ledger, in which every memory is duplicated by a standby. Every change in the content of the primal memory is duplicated in its backup. Each computer periodically suspends processing and transmits the contents of its several registers to the "ledger memory." This is as large a ledger as possible. Recovery with such a ledger consists of a trivial change of memories. One could hardly have a more extensive (expensive) ledger. There is normally no need to maintain programs on the ledger, especially if they are available in a central library. This cuts the ledger in half or in third. If the programs are not in the hypothetical ledger, they will have to be reloaded, adding time to the recovery function. Most of the data manipulated by the system are available or can be reconstructed. Their retrieval or reconstruction will also take time.

At the other extreme, we maintain no ledger (assuming that the system had never failed). More reasonably we take a complete snapshot of the system immediately upon recovery. In addition, let us assume that we are elsewheres maintaining a complete record of every input to the system. If a failure occurs, we reload the snapshot of the system after the previous failure, rerun all inputs, until we reach the end of the data. The ledger has been trivial, irredundant, but the recovery has taken as many hours as the system operated between its last failure and the present failure. We have by this doubled the system size. Thus, we can trade ledger redundancy for system recovery time. The simpler the ledger the harder the recovery and *vice versa*. The larger the ledger, however, the more time will be wasted by suspending processing during the roll-off. Roll-off time is lost in every cycle. Recovery time is lost only after a failure. We have here a trade between performance and recovery time.

More important than recovery time may be the cost of writing the recovery program. The simpler ledger required little of the operational programs and much of the recovery program. The complex ledger adds to the programming of each program, but results in a simpler recovery program.

7.4. Ledger Implementation

The ledger is commonly stored in an auxiliary mass memory, such as a drum or disc. Fixed-head drums have predominated in the past. Since the ledger is usually confined to control data, any system with large files will have to provide a safe storage area for such data as well. Thus, duplicate safe storage of messages in a message switching system is common if not mandatory. Similarly, job status, files, etc., will be stored in one or more forms in a remote-access system. In many cases, the multiprogramming activities of the complex are so extensive that a large bulk memory would be required even if there were no failures. We shall see, in the next section, that the ledger must be duplicated if the system is to achieve acceptable viabilities. If the ledger is stored in a large disc unit, say, the cost of duplicating the complete disc for the sake of duplicating the ledger (which would use a small percentage of the available space) would be exorbitant. Therefore, a separate memory may be used for the ledger and other critical data. We shall speak of the ledger memory as if it were a separate memory, wholly dedicated to the ledger function.

7.4.1. Tapes

Tapes are not generally used for the ledger. They are too slow for most systems, and are not reliable enough. Furthermore, it is not possible to use the same area of tape for subsequent ledgers. Thus, new tapes must be mounted periodically, and several tape stations must be assigned to the task. Tape is used as a long-term backup for failure of the primary ledger. That is, if the primary ledger is taken every second, a copy of the ledger may be made on tape every few minutes or hours. Should the primary ledger fail, partial recovery can be accomplished by using the latest ledger on tape.

7.4.2. Discs

The primary limitation to the use of discs for ledgering has been the long elapsed time required to write the ledger. If processing is suspended during the ledger write interval, the apparently low cost of the disc for ledgering will have to bear the amortization of the wasted cycle time of all computers and memories in the complex. Discs can be used if a more complex ledger writing scheme is employed. The ledger writing interval must be coordinated with the processing cycle and distributed over a longer time period. In this way, the 10 to 15% (higher for disc) wasted cycle time can be reduced to more acceptable levels. Large discs are not used unless it has been decided that redundancy in the stored data is desirable. The disc can be used as a ledger backup to a drum or core ledger much in the same way as tape is used.

7.4.3. Drums

Fixed-head drums or discs are the most commonly used ledger storage media. Their high speed, relatively low cost, and high reliability have led to this dominance. Very small drums, however, are likely to be as expensive as core memories. Thus, drums are usually used in applications that require the drum and a duplicate drum for other reasons.

7.4.4. Core

One cannot use a core memory for ledgering if that memory is used operationally by one or more computers. The high probability of a computer failing in such a way as to subsequently modify memory or execute data has made core an unlikely medium for the safe storage of the ledger. It should be recognized that a copy of the ledger is normally maintained in core by the viability executive. A high-reliability core unit used only for ledger purposes can be used if it is treated as another peripheral device. This can protect it from most failures. That is, the computer is not capable of executing instructions from the ledger core.

The ledger core need not be a random-access core nor need it be particularly fast. A low-cost, low-speed (10 microseconds), sequential- or block-access core memory can be used. In practice, it must be triplicated rather than duplicated. A core ledger offers distinct advantages. It is possible to almost completely eliminate the wasted cycles associated with the disc or drum ledgering schemes. The mean time to failure and mean time to repair for such core memories are generally better than those of drums. We can expect, because the cost of core and integrated circuit memories are dropping faster than the cost of drums and discs, that core ledgers will be used more frequently in the future than they have been in the past.

7.5. Ledger Protection

There is a high probability that the viability executive will fail while it is writing the ledger. If the elapsed time for the ledger write is 10 % of the processing cycle, and the ledger is written every cycle, there is a probability of the order of 0.1 that a viability executive failure will corrupt the ledger. The ledger memory itself is just another unit of the system and can also fail. Protection against ledger memory failure is provided by having two or more independent ledger memories. The system, therefore, maintains two copies of the ledger. However, consider the case in which a ledger memory has failed, and the viability executive fails. Furthermore, it fails while writing the ledger. The system would then seem to have lost its ledger and therefore failed. This problem is met by having the system maintain *four copies* of the ledger, two in each ledger memory. The areas used are not contiguous, and other means are employed so that a failing viability executive will at worst only destroy one copy of the ledger. In practice, ledger write follows a cycle in which ledger memories and copies are alternated. Thus, the system will write: ledger A, memory 1; ledger A, memory 2; ledger B, memory 1; ledger B, memory 2. This sequence is repeated and modified only when a ledger memory failure occurs or when a viability executive failure occurs.

Assume that the viability executive has failed and that a new executive is assigned. One of its first tasks will be to recover the ledger preparatory to the resumption of processing. The old viability executive has failed, and could not communicate with the new executive. How is the new viability executive to determine that the ledger is good?

That information must be embodied in the ledger itself, since the ledger is the only means by which the old viability executive communicates with the new one. The simplest and most prevalent method used is to employ a ledger serial number. The first and last words of the ledger carry a serial number. If the viability executive should fail while writing the ledger, the probability that the first and last serial numbers will be identical is minuscule. If the serial numbers do not agree, the new viability executive will assume that the ledger is no good and will examine the previous ledger. It will continue through all four copies. If serial number checks fail for these, then recovery will be made on the basis of the last stored tape ledger (if possible).

The serial number scheme is effective and simple. It requires no great amount of processing either preparatory to roll-off or for recovery. If greater confidence is warranted, then additional protection methods such as internally generated parities or check-sums can be used. Again, the serial number need not be a simple number obtained by incrementation, but can be a number generated by an algorithm which employs most of the computer's facilities. That is, it can be generated and checked by a program similar to that used to generate dead-man and crazy-man confidence messages.

7.6. Roll-Off Order

The graph–theoretic methods discussed in previous chapters can be used to determine preferred roll-off orders for phased ledgers. The ledger can be considered as a set of tables some of which may be independent of each other.

Any one part of the ledger affects only some of the processors, and the various processors affect only some of the tables. In general, there is a dependency relation between processors and tables.

We can express such a dependency relation by a matrix. We have shown two matrices in Figure 12.13, which express the relation between the processors and the tables. The first matrix shows which processors modify what tables; call it the P matrix. The second matrix shows what tables are required by which processors; call it the T matrix. Assume that we have Processors A, B, C, and D, and Tables 1, 2, 3, 4, 5, and 6. The P matrix shows the

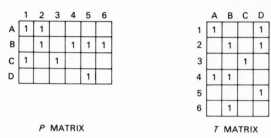

P MATRIX

T MATRIX

Figure 12.13. Incidence matrices for table–processor dependencies.

following:

Processor A can modify Tables 1 and 2.
Processor B can modify Tables 2, 4, 5, and 6.
Processor C can modify Tables 1 and 3.
Processor D can modify Table 5.

The *T* matrix shows that:

Table 1 is required by Processors A and D.
Table 2 is required by Processors B and D.
Table 3 is required by Processor C.
Table 4 is required by Processors A and B.
Table 5 is required by Processor D.
Table 6 is required by Processor B.

An ideal situation would be one in which every table is independent of every other table, and a processor modifies only its own tables. Such an example is given in Figure 12.14. This is an ideal situation because the ledger segment can be written after each processor has completed its task, without concern as to what will happen to the rest of the system. However, since this is not realistic, we must find methods for ordering the relation between the ledger and the layout of the cycle so as to achieve the greatest degree of independence.

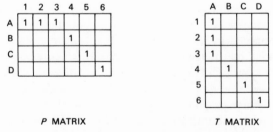

P MATRIX

T MATRIX

Figure 12.14. Incidence matrices for independent tables.

Matrices such as the *P* and *T* matrices described above are called **incidence matrices**. We can take the product of *P* and *T* in the usual way to form the matrix shown in Figure 12.15. The product matrix can be interpreted as a graph of dependencies of processors on processors. The graph

	A	B	C	D
A	1	2		1, 2
B	4	2,4,6		2, 5
C	1		3	1
D				5

P × *T* MATRIX

Figure 12.15. Dependency matrix for the incidence matrices of Figures 12.13.

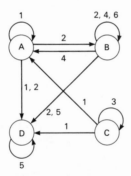

Figure 12.16. Dependency graph corresponding to the matrix of Figure 12.15.

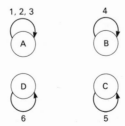

Figure 12.17. Dependency graph of Figure 12.14.

corresponding to the matrix of Figure 12.15 is shown in Figure 12.16. By contrast, we have shown (in Figure 12.17) the dependency graph for the matrices of Figure 12.14. The processors are clearly independent.

The graph of $P \times T$ can be separated into constituent subgraphs that show only the dependencies with respect to one table at a time. The result is shown in Figure 12.18. Consider the sequential ordering of the processors within the base sequences from the point of view of Table 1. It is clear that Processor B can be run at any time as far as Table 1 is concerned, since it is independent of Table 1. If C is run first, then the modifications it may make in the usage of Table 1 by Processors A and D would require us to roll-off that table only after D was over. Clearly, then, the order of processing with respect to Table 1 should be: D, A, C. Furthermore, Table 1 can be rolled-off after Processor C is through. The same analysis for Table 2 leads us to the order D, B, A, with roll-off after A is through. Table 3 can be rolled-off after Processor C is through. Table 4 can be rolled-off after B is through, and the preferred order of processing is A, B. Table 5 suggests the order of D, B, with roll-off after the completion of B; and Table 6 is independent and requires roll-off after Processor B is complete. Putting these factors in order, we obtain

Table	1	2	3	4	5	6
Execution order	D	D		D		
	A	B	A			
		A		B	B	B
			*	*	*	*
	C	C				
	*	*				

where the asterisk specifies the point at which roll-off is to occur.

We then obtain the following preferred order for the processors and ledgers:

Execute D,
Execute A,
Execute B,
Roll-off Tables 2, 4, 5, 6,
Execute C,
Roll-off Tables 1, 3.

A strict universal ordering cannot be obtained because of the interdependencies among the various processors and their associated tables. Using an analysis comparable to the foregoing, it is possible to detect the semi-independent sections of the system, and to structure the relation between the cycle and the processor sequence so as to minimize the dependencies. Minimizing these dependencies allows greater freedom in the cycle design

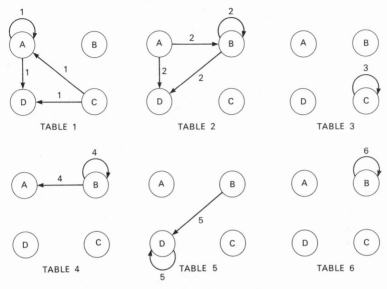

Figure 12.18. Separated graph.

and can indirectly reduce the wasted time during roll-off. The preferred ordering obtained in this way may contradict the preferred ordering obtained in the interest of a minimum time cycle design. Therefore there will be additional compromises. Wasted time due to inefficient cycle structure is traded against wasted time during ledger roll-off. The question then becomes one of which is least wasteful. The ideal isochronous cycle, and the method of designing it described in Chapter 9, must be tempered in the interest of obtaining an efficient roll-off order.

8. RECOVERY

Recovery is that process by which the system resumes operation after a failure. There is no single, universal approach to recovery, nor are there many generalized techniques. Recovery should be looked upon not so much as the action of a specialized recovery program but as the result of a philosophy which pervades the design of every program in the system. Every program must be considered from the point of view of what information would be required to resume its operation after a failure. The recovery problems associated with a program are considered at the time of design, not after the fact.

Some programs resume operation by simply restarting them with the proper information on the processing queue for that program. In general, the recovery of a program will begin at some logical starting point of that program—at a point whose parameters have been stored in the ledger. For this reason, instruction modification is not generally permitted, unless the program is designed to be the same before and after execution. Re-entrant coding may be used with parameters stored in the ledger. The necessities of recovery imposes formality in the design of the various programs. Many otherwise "clever" tricks cannot be used lest the recovery of such programs be too difficult.

Recovery itself is not a single event. The complete recovery of the system after a failure may stretch over many cycles. It may proceed at different rates for different processors and different programs within a processor. High-priority functions will be recovered first. Some functions might not be recovered until after another failure has occurred.

8.1. Recovery

The general order of recovery is: the viability executive, the system executive, high-priority functions, and then lower-priority functions. Since the viability executive failure is the most stringent case, we shall again exemplify the process in terms of viability executive failures, recognizing that other recovery functions are simplified cases thereof. Recovery begins when the new viability executive has assumed control.

8.1.1. Viability Executive Recovery

We shall illustrate the recovery of the viability executive as it is performed in a system having a complete configuration switching network. Recovery in simpler systems is correspondingly simpler. The computer(s) that assume the viability executive role must contain a system bootstrap. The first step in the recovery procedure is to obtain a configuration switching network controller. The bootstrap must be sufficiently complete to allow the use of an alternate controller or the selection of a limited number of alternate paths should the primal paths or the primal controllers fail. Having obtained and verified the operability of a configuration switching network controller, the viability executive bootstrap program can begin restructuring the viability executive.[13] The viability executive bootstrap program connects the viability executive computer to the memory that is used to store the viability executive program—typically a mass memory. Having done this successfully, the viability executive programs including the recovery and reconfiguration algorithms can be loaded. These programs must be checked (by a parity check or check-sum) before they are used. Assuming that the programs have been properly loaded, the viability executive bootstrap jumps to the initial point of a hardware recovery program. That part of the ledger that specifies the condition of the units and subsystems must then be fetched and checked.

---

[13] The computer(s) assigned to the alternate viability executive role do not normally contain the viability executive programs—it would be too wasteful.

Without this information, the new viability executive has no way of knowing what the old configuration was. The ledger specifies the last configuration known to be working. It generally cannot contain the information of what had failed that caused the viability executive change. The ledger does contain the physical identity of the old viability executive hardware. It is prudent to disassemble that hardware prior to starting reconfiguration. That is, the old viability executive hardware is dismembered by means of the configuration switching network. Connections to the mass memory, CPU-to-memory connections, tape controller connections, etc., are severed to quickly eliminate the possibility of interference from the old viability executive. The new viability executive at this point consists only of a computer, its associated main memories, a connection to one of the mass memories, connections to the configuration network controllers, and the configuration master controller.[14]

Using what spare units there are, the viability executive assembles the maximal hardware configuration that it can using as few as possible of the units that comprised the failed executive. If vital units are missing, the viability executive will have to execute test programs to determine which units of the old viability executive have failed and which can be used in the new configuration. If the new configuration is a maximal configuration, hardware recovery will stop at this point. If the new configuration is not maximal, the viability executive will then test the units of the failed executive and bring them into the configuration until a maximal configuration has been achieved, or until all units not in the configuration require human attention (standby units are part of the configuration). The old viability executive could have failed because of a momentary malfunction that led it to execute data, say, but the hardware is good and need not be repaired. Should this be the case, that hardware can be placed in a standby status (after checking it), and a further upgrade recovery may proceed from there. Viability executive recovery is complete when the maximum possible configuration has been achieved with the available working hardware.

8.1.2. System Executive Recovery

The successful completion of the viability executive recovery initiates the recovery of the system executive. The system executive programs must be fetched, loaded, and initiated. They cannot be initiated without the information contained in the ledger.

A snapshot ledger is the easiest to recover with. The queue entries, memory maps, and status data reflect the conditions that prevailed in the system prior to the failure. Since things may have been going on between the

---

[14] This last connection was made under the direction of the monitor.

time that the system executive failed and the ledger data had been reloaded, the ledger itself, while properly depicting the old conditions, does not necessarily reflect the conditions upon recovery. Not all the functions which are ledgered may be executable under the new configuration. The new system is not necessarily the same as the old. Consequently, the executive program itself may have to be modified, or at least parameters related to it brought up to date. The old executive might have been allocating space in three disc units, using a fourth for itself. In the new configuration, the fourth scratch disc might be missing. The new executive could thereby immediately find itself in overflow.

8.1.3. Cleanup

The new system executive must clean up the mess left by the failure of the old system executive. Typically, there will have been a number of I/O operations in progress between the failure and the initiation of the system executive. Those operations that concerned devices whose functions were reassigned by the viability executive because of reconfiguration will have been properly terminated or aborted. For example, a standby tape that had been moving forward would have been properly terminated and brought back to the load point prior to reassignment by the viability executive. However, those units whose functions or positions in the configuration did not change could be doing something. In particular, since recovery will take time, all other computers in the complex must be informed that the executive is undergoing recovery. In some cases, this is achieved automatically because outlying computers will have been denied data necessary to the continuation of their programs. In other cases explicit notification will be required.

The recovery in question may require functional or extensive sacrifices as a result of the configuration change. Outlying units will have to be informed of these sacrifices, lest they continue to perform tasks requiring programs that cannot be executed in the new configuration or data that are no longer available. In the most extreme case, all computers not participating in executive functions may have to be reloaded with versions of their programs appropriate to the new configuration. More practically, these computers must be given the parameters of the configuration that affect them, so that they can make the necessary sacrifices. To do this, other parts of the ledger will have to be fetched. The completion of cleanup will result in new data to be ledgered.

8.1.4. Resumption of Viability Functions

While some viability-related functions can start as soon as hardware reconfiguration has been effected, in general, it is not possible to resume viability-related processing prior to the completion of cleanup. A new ledger must be written to reflect the new hardware configuration and the new functional assignments of the units. The new alternate viability executive must be assigned. The confidence scheme used to test the viability executive can also be initiated at this point.

It is possible to delay the resumption of viability functions to a later phase of recovery. The longer the delay, the sooner will real work begin, but the more vulnerable will the system be to a subsequent failure. A new failure, occurring prior to the resumption of viability processing, will probably mean the total collapse of the system. Thus, while the probability of yet another failure is low, the penalty for that failure is likely to be very high.

8.1.5. Job Recovery

The recovery of a job implies the following sequence of events: obtain the appropriate ledger data, a new copy of the program for that job, the (possibly new) addresses of all files for that job, and the pertinent queue entries, reload the dynamic areas of memory, and return to that point of the program last known to have been successfully completed and safely stored. As a result of the configuration changes that have occurred, each of these steps may require modification of the parameters that are in the ledger. As an example, say that the program in question used blocks of dynamic memory. The old data that were in those blocks are fetched from the memory on which they were stored for safekeeping. Since the amount of dynamic space in the new configuration is not necessarily the same as the old, and since interrupts that demand space may have occurred at higher priority levels in the meantime, it is practically impossible to load the recovery data into the selfsame memory location that they had occupied prior to the failure. Typically, the program itself will have been reloaded. It is not obvious that the positions of the tasks of this job on the various task queues will be the same as they were before the failure. The total dynamics of the situation has changed. Consequently, the ledgered data for this job will have to be brought up to date.

One could avoid many recovery problems by dictating that jobs will be recovered only by starting them from the beginning. That is, the job is treated as a new one and recovery proceeds by entering the job into the job stream in the normal manner. This has several failings despite the obvious advantages. It is possible to construct a job that cannot be recovered by simply starting over again, but that can be recovered by starting at some later point in the process. The system must still contend with an incident processing load, that has been aggravated by the failure. Thus, not only is the system faced with recovery, but is facing an implicit burst at the same time—it may never catch up. Users may object to the extra delay that results from a fresh start.

It is clearly not practical to recover to within the execution of an arbitrary instruction in the program. This could only be done by running the program in what was essentially an interpretive mode. Recovery can only be quantized as finely as the ledger for that job. Roll-off is an executive function. Therefore, each point of the job that will have rolled-off to a ledger will have required some executive attention. Conversely, every instruction or action that requires executive attention provides an opportunity for ledgering and therefore recovery. Every I/O instruction, every page fetch or swap for the virtual memory, every request for or return to dynamic memory, etc., represents a point to which recovery could be made. It is possible to structure jobs for which this kind of recovery is also fallacious. In the same way that semantic processors may not be executable following a reconfiguration, actions on the part of jobs may also be senseless. Not only would the ledgers be excessively large by this approach, but the executive would have to contain considerable interpretive capabilities to allow a rational recovery for any program on this basis.

While there is a lot for the executive to do in order to recover a job, the most important thing about job recovery is that the programs be designed so that they *can* be recovered. The burden, then, is not to be placed on the executive program but on the job itself. Macro instructions are provided to allow the job to communicate to the executive what it is that has to be ledgered and where the job can be restarted. Every program then specifies its own recovery point and the data required for that recovery. This means that universal conventions must be specified and adhered to. All in all, this is the most effective approach. We can see this by considering a typical program, say, a statistical program or numerical analysis program. The inputs and outputs of this kind of program may be modest; however, a lot of intermediate data may be generated. The programmer could specify recovery to those points of his program where such intermediate data can be discarded without harm. Similarly, a payroll program can be recovered to within the processing of one paycheck; a communication program to within the reception or transmission of a complete message. The acceptability of the quantization of recovery is a semantic question. A properly designed program will contain error exits and restart points as a matter of course, independent of the configuration on which the job is to be run, and independent of system-wide viability considerations. It remains for the programmer to explicitly specify additional restart points and data that are particular and appropriate to his program. Should a restart point not be specified, the system should assume that the program is to be restarted at the beginning. If the program is a pathological one for which this cannot be done, the executive and subsequently the user will find out soon enough.

8.2. Job Recovery Schedules

A schedule must be established for recovery. Part of that schedule, as we have seen, is implicit, i.e., we cannot recover job processing until we have a viable configuration, or until the executive has been reloaded. Within job recovery there is still freedom as to what gets recovered and in which order.

A recovery schedule design is similar to the problem of establishing the operational scheduling algorithms. Generally, higher-priority processors will be recovered before low-priority processors. "Should FIFO be maintained within a priority class?" "Should old jobs be given higher priorities than new jobs?" Questions like these can lead to very complicated recovery scheduling algorithms. As in the design of scheduling algorithms, the "optimum" approach is closely tied to the specifics of the system. In dedicated systems, the typical approach is to keep things in the order in which they were prior to the failure. That is, the processing queues are used to guide the job recovery schedule.

8.3. Roll-Back

Roll-back is the conceptual complement of roll-off. Just as the ledger could be rolled-off in a snapshot, or be phased over a number of cycles, the roll-back too can be done all at once or sequenced over many cycles. The order, however, is not necessarily the same as that which is used for roll-off. The discussion of the above sections indicates a preferred ordering for the roll-back. The roll-back sequence must be compatible with the needs of the recovery sequence. Exception ledgering requires that the roll-back sequence follow the roll-off sequence. First the last complete ledger is retrieved, and then the changes to that ledger in the order in which they occurred. They are used to create the latest ledger. Recovery will be delayed until the ledger has been recreated. The penalty for saving roll-off time, is additional recovery processing and a possibly nonoptimum recovery sequence. For the more general case, in which a combination of snapshots, exception, and phased roll-off is used, the optimum roll-back order can be discovered by examining the graph that describes the precedence relation between the processors with respect to which must precede which for sensible recovery.

8.4 Upgrade Recovery

Most of the above has dealt with **downgrade** or equivalent-state recovery, that is, with the problems associated with recoveries for which the new configuration is equal to or less than the old. There is also a lesser recovery problem associated with the return of repaired equipment. This kind of recovery is called **upgrade recovery**. Fortunately, things are under control in such situations. A repaired unit is first placed in a standby position and tentatively accepted by the system. After checking, it is again available for reintegration into the working part of the complex. As with downgrade recovery, programs must be loaded, checked, and initialized. A kind of cleanup is also required here. The new device can provide an extensive or functional increase in capability, or both. All the switches that had been set to prevent the use of that unit in the degraded state must now be reset. Care must be taken to avoid critical races, particularly for controls that are manipulated at several different priority levels. Queues that had been artificially terminated can now be reopened. Previously blocked jobs are now unblocked. The major difference between upgrade recovery and downgrade or parallel recovery is that it can be done at relative leisure, over many cycles. Since the unit in question had been out of commission for a half hour or more, it will not matter if recovery takes several seconds more.

8.5. Recovery in Perspective

Other computers in the complex may continue operation throughout the reconfiguration and recovery period. In the Overseas AUTODIN system, the front-end computers continue servicing lines even though the central computer has failed. Output will continue until there are no more messages stored in the front-end computer buffer area. At that point, each outgoing line will be turned off in an orderly fashion. Similarly, input will continue until there is no more room for new messages, at which point the input lines will be advised to cease transmission. The time during which the front end can coast without an executive is greater than the worst-case reconfiguration time. Therefore, there is usually no apparent degradation in service, despite a significant malfunction.

This ability of the complex to continue much of its operations independently of the executive is very desirable. The executive is truly an executive processor, directing the processors under its control to carry out specific tasks on well specified data, and not intervening in any way, until the task has been completed.

Just as many elegant information retrieval or file searching algorithms fail because of the updating requirements, many otherwise elegant methods for improving viability fail for recovery problems. The following observations should be included in the evaluation of any viability enhancement technique:

   ○   Recovery need not occur all at once—it can and should be distributed over several cycles.

○　Processing by unfailed elements can continue during recovery of failed elements.

○　There may be yet another failure before recovery is completed.

○　Recovery may be to a higher-capability or a lower-capability state, or (in most cases) to an equivalent state.

○　It is generally neither possible nor desirable to recover the system for everything, in all possible cases.

○　The recovery "program" may have to coexist with the operational program for significantly long time intervals.

○　The recovery "program" is rarely a single identifiable program. More often than not, it is an initialization routine or a special entry to all subroutines and programs in the system. It is a prime example of a distributed processor.

○　The analytical effort required for the recovery of a particular function may equal or exceed the analytical effort required for the design of the function's processor.

○　Recovery will often occur as a result of a transient malfunction rather than as a result of a hard failure.

The problems associated with recovery can be exemplified by recounting the tribulations of a large communications system. A program modification had been made, resulting in a vulnerability of some sites to a peculiar syntax error in a message. Some of the sites in this network were not vulnerable and were able to process the message without trouble. However, the bug occurred only when the message was transmitted. The message entered the system, was analyzed, stored, and readied for relay to another site. As soon as the particular character combination that was causing the problem occurred, the bug manifested itself, and the program blew up. This system, employing a straightforward ghosting scheme, turned control over to the standby (ghost). The ghost retrieved the ledger and proceeded to continue where the prime system had left off. All was well until the bogey messages was reached, at which point the ghost blew up. In the meantime, the old prime system had gone through the test programs, had been found to be failure-free, had reloaded all programs, and has assumed the ghost position. The result was that the two systems oscillated at about 30 cycles per minute—an awesome and disturbing sight to its operators.

9. SUMMARY

Viability is increased by decreasing the effective MTTR of the units that comprise the complex. This can be done by automating part or all of the repair procedure. The viability executive processor is charged with maintaining the proper operation of the complex, except for failures in its own units.

Recovery from viability executive failures, while not different in principle, is significantly more complicated than recovery from other malfunctions. The monitor is responsible for detecting malfunctions in the viability executive should the viability executive fail to do this itself. The monitor can be implemented as hardware or software; it can be localized or distributed. The system must also be protected against monitor failures.

A configuration switching facility is employed to allow the excision of faulty elements and their replacement by standby elements of the same type. That network can be explicit or be part of the normal channel structure of the complex. The configuration network, being part of the complex, is also capable of failing. Redundancy in the form of alternate paths can be provided to overcome this potential difficulty. Additional redundancy, to protect the controls of the configuration switching, should also be provided.

Reconfiguration is a complicated process that begins with the detection of the malfunctioning element and finishes with the re-establishment of a viable configuration. The new configuration may have the same, less, or more capability than the old. Reconfiguration is followed by recovery. Recovery requires information about what it was that the system was doing prior to the failure. That information is contained in the ledger. The ledger may consist of a single table, but more likely consists of several distributed tables. Ledger roll-off can be done at discrete time intervals in the form of a snapshot, or can be done continually. There is a trade between roll-off processing, recovery processing, and time wasted ledgering. As the roll-off time is decreased, performance is increased at the expense of a longer recovery. Graph-theoretic methods can be used to obtain a guide to the optimum ledger roll-off sequence.

Reconfiguration provides viable hardware: recovery provides a viable system. Recovery is a multistep process that begins with the recovery of the viability executive, and continues in sequence through system executive recovery, cleanup, resumption of viability functions, and finally the recovery of the jobs that were in process prior to the failure.

10. PROBLEMS

1. Are periodic checks a guaranteed method of detecting viability executive failures? Would three periodic checks suffice? How many would suffice? [*Easy.*]

2. Establish the necessary and sufficient relation that must exist among periodic check signals to prevent undetected insane conditions for the following processing model. The program consists of a number of steps, with appropriate loops that generate the check signals. Consider the matrix representation of that program. A "failure" occurs when one of the *a priori* probabilities in the model has changed. The row sums of the probabilities are equal to 1 both before and after the failure. The loops are all deterministic. [*Difficult.*]

3. Why might a Fibonacci number generator be useful for a dead-man/crazy-man check scheme? [*Difficult.*]

4. Describe a general algorithm for designing voting tables for a system with n computers, of which k are required for useful work. Generate all situations for $k \leq m \leq n$, where m is the number of computers UP. [*Moderate for specific cases with small numbers; open problem for the general case.*]

5. Design an executive recovery scheme for a four-computer complex in which useful work can be done with only one computer. Assume a distributed software monitor. The backup memory is a drum. Other elements of the configuration control network are provided as required and cannot fail. Flow chart the procedure under the assumption that there will be no second-order failures. Compare the results to the same situation assuming second-order failures are possible. [*Moderate.*]

6. Prove that viability is maximized by (among other things) minimizing the number of different subsystems and maximizing the interchangeability of identical subsystems (assuming that configuration switching network failures can be ignored). Is this still true if configuration switching network failures are not trivial?

7. Consider a system consisting of N computers, each of which requires 2 memories. The performance for K computers UP is K. Compare the mean performance for each of the following cases: (a) full interchangeability; (b) odd memories to odd computers; (c) odd memories to odd channels.

8. Do Problem 7 under the assumption that half performance will be obtained if the computer has only one memory module.

9. Evaluate the probability of having N computers UP for the various tessellation schemes of Figure 12.11 (three computers, six memories, each computer must have at least one memory).

10. Prove that if the ledger contains enough information to recover from all dead states to the maximal states, then it will have sufficient data to recover from any state to any other state. [*Easy but tricky.*]

11. Construct a job to be executed by a time-sharing system that cannot be properly recovered by restarting from the beginning, but that can be recovered by restarting from some later point. Assume that you can write assembly language programs and that the system is fully protected from user program bugs. You may not have access to the operating system, nor need privileged instructions be executed. [*Easy.*]

12. The average transaction delay for a single drum is $1/2$ of a revolution. When simultaneous ledgers are written to two drums, the ledger elapsed time is the time taken by the later of the two drums. Prove that for two drums the expected latency is $2/3$ of a revolution, and that for three drums it is $3/4$ of a revolution. (*Hint:* be discrete and go to the limit.) [*Moderate.*]

13. Prove that for N drums in Problem 12 the average latency is $N/(N+1)$ revolutions. (Think geometrically.) [*Difficult.*]

11. REFERENCES

1. Rau, John G., *Optimization and Probability in Systems Engineering*, Van Nostrand Reinhold Co., New York, 1970.

An excellent book containing many things of interest to the system architect, including linear programming, Lagrange multipliers, integer programming, and queuing theory. Most of the examples and applications deal in one way or another with viability problems. Chapters 5, 6, 7, and 8 in particular discuss viability-related problems. The discussion of MTTR and MTBF trades in Chapter 7 and that of the selection of spares in Chapter 8 are particularly useful.

2. Shooman, Martin L., *Probabilistic Reliability: An Engineering Approach*, McGraw-Hill, New York, 1968.

This book covers the classic aspects of system reliability, methods for calculating MTBFs, various kinds of failure models, basic assumptions, etc. The historical introduction is good. It is followed by 100 pages of well presented mathematical preliminaries. Of particular interest to the reader should be Chapter 3, on combinatorial reliability, Chapter 5, on system reliability, and Chapter 6, on reliability improvement. Those chapters should be considered collateral reading.

3. Proceedings of the 1970 Annual Symposium on Reliability, Los Angeles, California, February 3–5, I.E.E.E. publication, 1970.

These are the proceedings of an annual symposium on system reliability and related problems. The 1970 issue contains a 15-year cumulative index that is particularly valuable. These symposia proceedings are generally a mixed bag, containing some useful theoretical work, analytical work, simulation results, philosophy, etc. On the other hand, they also contain too many papers describing "new" approaches to viability problems that not only are old, but have been discarded and surpassed by practice.

4. 1971 Internation Symposium on Fault-Tolerant Computing, March 1–3, 1971, Pasadena, California, I.E.E.E. Computer Society.

A somewhat more academic (and stratospheric) symposium than the above. The several papers on software reliability are interesting.

5. *IEEE Transactions on Reliability*, published quarterly by the Institute of Electrical and Electronics Engineers, New York.

This is the basic journal in the field. Though originally emphasizing component reliability, it has kept pace with technology and continually publishes papers of interest to the computer complex architect.

Chapter 13

SYSTEM ANALYSIS

*"I see the plan thou art pursuing:
Thou canst not compass general ruin,
And hast on smaller scale begun."*
Faust to Mephistopheles
JOHANN WOLFGANG VON GOETHE
Faust, Part 1, Act I, Scene 3

1. SYNOPSIS

The analytical techniques discussed in Chapter 7 are applied to the problem of determining the behavior of a system. Methods of establishing bounds on computer utilization, cycle length, and delays are presented. A plan of attack for the analysis of a system is discussed. Pragmatically valid simplification assumptions and their consequences are presented. The inherent nonlinearity of the behavior of a cyclically structured system with respect to processing load is derived in this chapter. The modifications required to the analysis to properly account for the ledger portion of the system cycle are also discussed.

A method for doing viability calculations that does not require the explicit examination of all the configuration states is presented. This analysis leads to an evaluation of the mean time in the various states, the mean time to recurrence for these states, and the mean time between reconfigurations. Practical problems and shortcuts in performing these analyses are also presented.

2. TIMING ANALYSIS—GENERAL

2.1. Goals, Limits, and Approach

It is neither practical nor desirable to do a complete analysis of a system by analytical means. While this may be possible for some dedicated systems, the complexity of a typical generalized system is beyond the endurance of most mathematicians. For such complicated systems, overall behavior is best obtained through simulation. Simulation cannot be done at the drop of a hat. A model must be created and programmed in the simulation language. Since the purpose of analysis is to provide answers that will guide the designer toward the achievement of an optimum complex, the simulation model and its representation as a program will not be final. To the extent that a paper and pencil analysis can result in a simpler simulation model, it is effective. For example, a particular processor after much analysis accounts for only 0.05% of the computer's capacity. It might then be possible to reduce the complexity of the simulation by ignoring this processor, using a worst-case value for it, or replacing it with an almost equivalent simpler model. It is not "analysis *vs.* simulation," but how to make the best use of each.

2.1.1. Simulation

Simulation will not be treated here in any detail. Several references to simulation have been presented. In most cases, the simulation will be done on a digital computer, will be Monte-Carlo simulation, and will require that a special simulation language such as GPSS be learned.

The common simulator, while implemented as a digital computer program, is essentially an analog of the process it represents. Characterizing distributions for input transactions are required, such as an input transaction length distribution, an arrival distribution, etc. Each process of the system is characterized by distributions as well. These could be the service time distribution (e.g., the running time of the program), memory utilization distributions, and channel utilization. The model consists of processes and events. Events are queued and passed from process to process in accordance with the characteristic behavior of these processes. The simulation language allows one to specify what kind of "statistics" is to be gathered, where, and how often. The statistics in question could be the elapsed time from transaction input to output, accumulated delay for transactions, the time spent by the computer in various programs, the time spent at various program levels, channel utilization, etc. Random number generators are used to generate events in accordance to the appropriate distributions. The events are then placed on the appropriate queues. The simulation language may allow multiple run setups so that critical factors can be examined parametrically.

If the simulation is to be reasonable, it cannot be as complex as that which it is simulating. Therefore, a certain amount of analysis and simplification will precede simulation. Some systems, particularly dedicated systems, can often be evaluated without simulation.

2.1.2. Goals and Limits

A sharp lower bound for the processing load, memory utilization, and channel utilization of the complex can be readily obtained. If the system is overloaded on the basis of a lower bound evaluation, it most certainly is overloaded on the basis of a more precise analysis. The primary difference between the lower bound presented here and the actual performance is the proper evaluation of wasted time. It is difficult to analytically evaluate the amount of time spent by processors while blocked, or the amount of time wasted by the computer in an idle loop. Under low input load, the wasted time is of little concern—there is not much to do. If the system is properly designed, there will be little wasted time under peak load conditions. The lower bounds discussed here are reasonably accurate for an *efficient* system under peak (but not crushing) load conditions. Since it is the peak conditions that concern us most, and since we will *never* design an inefficient system,[1] the lower bounds should be valid for most cases of interest.

A lower bound for time is obtained by statistically accounting for *all* processing under the assumption that no idle loops are executed. A further assumption implied by this is that any one computer of the complex does not waste time waiting for another. Therefore, the analysis is essentially of one computer at a time. Extreme nonlinear behavior such as might occur during memory or queue overflow cannot be directly obtained by this method. Again, the well designed system should not normally be in overflow.

Another shift in point of view is required. The system could be analyzed with the intent of establishing what its ultimate processing load can be (i.e., how many transactions can it handle per hour). Alternatively, it can be analyzed to obtain the number of memory cycles required to process a postulated load. The latter is much easier to do. If that postulated load is a parameter of the analysis, by numerically evaluating the time required for several different values of the load, the point at which the machine capacity has been exceeded can be found. That point represents an *upper bound* (but not necessarily a least upper bound) on the system's processing ability.

2.1.3. Plan of Attack

The immediate aim is to derive a lower bound for the length of the cycle as a function of parameters that describe the processing load. All significant processes in the computer must be accounted for. This includes contentious memory cycles, interrupt processing, and operations performed in the base sequence program. Some of these processes, for example, ledger functions and cycle initialization functions, are cycle-dependent. The more frequently the cycle is executed, the more time will be spent on cycle-dependent functions.

Other functions are load-dependent, but are initiated only once per cycle. Still other functions, typically those occurring at the higher priority levels, are executed independently of the cycle. All of this must be taken into account. Since there are cycle-length-dependent functions, the cycle length

---

[1] Shades of Gilbert and Sullivan.

will be a function of the cycle length. That is, there will be an equation to solve. The resulting equations will typically be a polynomial that can be solved numerically. It is not unusual to have a system in which most of the processing time is expressed by a quadratic equation.

A cyclically structured system obviously consists of at least one major loop. Furthermore, except for error conditions or malfunctions, the loop continues as long as the system runs: the system is not designed to work for so many seconds and then stop. A model of a cyclic system should predict an infinite processing time, and justly so for a never-ending program. Consequently, the major loop or loops must be cut to obtain a meaningful analysis. The cycle is then unfolded and is modeled as a program with a definite entrance and exit. Where this is not possible, because of shortcuts taken in the cycle, the base sequence model may have to be transformed to an equivalent one that does start and end at the same discrete point.

It is generally simpler to work from the highest priority level down, accounting first for the load-dependent processes and then for the cycle-dependent processes. A statistically valid incident load model as well as models for all major transaction flows are required for analysis or simulation. In addition to this, the processing time for each program should be known.

3. TIMING ANALYSIS

3.1 Contentious Transfers

The logically highest priority functions (from the point of view of memory access) are contentious data transfers. The incident load model specifies how many transactions of each type will occur per second. By tracing through the transaction flow model for each process the number of each kind of contentious transfer that is expected for that kind of transaction can be determined. It is advisable to establish a matrix such as is shown in Table 13.1 for the various transactions and contentious transfers that will occur. This will be useful in several other parts of the analysis. Contentious transfers can always be described in terms of a number of transfers of individual characters. Typically, input and output processes (that is, to outside of the complex) will come in variable-length blocks. Intracomplex transfers will be blocked according to dynamic memory blocks, drum blocks, disc blocks, etc. Thus, while an input message shown in Table 13.1 has an average length of 48 characters, it is transferred to and from the drum as full blocks whether or not the block is full. For this reason, transactions must be looked upon from the point of view of the number of characters they contain or generate, the number of blocks they contain or generate, and the number of transactions that occur. To assume that these have a simple relation to one another

Table 13.1. Contentious Transfer Table

Transaction type	Number per second	Characters in	Characters out	Drum block write	Drum block read	Tape block write	Disc block write	CPU block transfer in	CPU block transfer out
Message (A)	6	48	191	2	3	1	1	1.2	1
Message (B)	4	120	118	1	0	1	1	1.4	1.2
Message (C)	0.05	1800	0	14	0	2	2	0	16
ACKIN	5	8	0	0	0	1	0	0	0
ACKOUT	8	0	16	0	0	1	0	0	0
Totals		898	1746	16.7	18	23.1	10.1	13.8	12.4
μsec/transaction		0.5	0.5	64	64	32	128	64	64
Total time, μsec		449	873	1068.8	1152	739.2	129.3	883.2	793.6

Total contentious transfers: 6088.1 microseconds per second.

(such as a simple multiple) is fallacious and may lead to serious underestimation. The reader will note in the example that a lot of work has gone into what appears to be a small percentage of the processing load. If the machine can execute a million memory cycles per second, the above example represents under 1% of the total load. This is true. However, experience indicates that the typical system is not dominated by any one process, but can consist of 30 to 50 processes, the largest of which accounts for only 5% of the processing time. Intuition can be misleading.

In parametric analyses (say, where the parameters describe input load), the entries in the table are replaced by functions. That is, instead of 6 messages of type A per second, there are $6N$ messages of type A per second. Similarly, block length parameters can be introduced at this point.

Not all memory cycles taken for contentious transfers are dependent solely on the input transaction rate. Many contentious transfers are tied to the cycle itself. Ledger transfers are one example: gathered statistics, billing data, operator communications, polling sequences, computer-to-computer transfers, viability functions, etc., might all represent actions that are initiated at specific points of the cycle. As the cycle grows or contracts, the frequency of the cycle decreases and increases as does the cycle-dependent processing, and hence the number of memory cycles taken for their contentious transfers. Such contentious transfers are treated in the same way, except that instead of obtaining a number of *microseconds per second*, a number of *microseconds per cycle* is obtained. This is an important distinction which should be kept clear. The "per second" processing and the "per cycle" processing should be distinguished from each other.

3.2. Interrupts

While it is difficult to determine how often a particular program will be interrupted, it is relatively easy to estimate the number of interrupts that will lead to each program. A few simplifying assumptions are required.

1. Interrupts occur relatively uniformly throughout the cycle.
2. Interrupts are relatively rare.
3. The raw interrupt time is approximately the same for every level and from every level.
4. Every priority level will be left as often as it is entered.

The first assumption is probably the least valid. If most of the interrupts are externally derived, that is, from input transactions, this is a more credible assumption. However, a cyclic structure contributes to interrupt bunching. If assumptions 2 and 3 hold, then the effect of bunching is minimal and can be ignored.

Every interrupt consumes a number of memory cycles. The time to store and then later restore the system to the appropriate level is not trivial. If a typical instruction took two memory cycles, and a typical raw interrupt entry and exit each took ten memory cycles, and the average number of memory cycles executed between interrupts was 100, raw interrupts would consume one-sixth of the processing. This would not leave much time for doing anything. Typically, raw interrupts account for less than 1% of the total processing time. The model of interrupt acknowledge programs can be simplified if interrupts are sparse. The typical interrupt acknowledge program will acknowledge the interrupt and then check to see if another interrupt has come in at that level in the meantime. If the interrupts are truly sparse, it can be assumed that there is never another interrupt waiting to be acknowledged. This is actually a slight overestimate of the processing load since the possibly higher efficiency accorded by acknowledging several interrupts at the same level simultaneously has been ignored.

If the interrupt mechanism is primitive, i.e., only one hardware level, or if extreme bunching can occur, these assumptions may be invalid. These assumptions may also be extended to interrupt service routines. Caution must be exercised. The lower the priority level, the more likely it is that there will be several items on the queue for each entrance of the program; therefore, the less valid the assumptions becomes and the greater the overestimation.

If the interrupt hardware is sophisticated, the raw interrupt time and the return from a priority level to another level are equal for all levels. That is, the interrupt time is, say, N microseconds, and the interrupt restore is M microseconds, independent of the level at which the interrupt occurred (the destination level) or the level the machine was in at the time of the interrupt (the source level). If the interrupt hardware is primitive and the mechanization is done mostly by software, there may be differences.

The last assumption (4) is tantamount to saying that the system works. If there were not an exit for each entrance, there would be at least one favored level—that level for which the entrances were fewer than the exits. The machine would eventually settle in some state or set of states. This means that something or another would not be getting done, or that some states were transitory or superfluous. If superfluous, they should be eliminated as they only waste memory. If transitory, they do not come into the evaluation of the average cycle length.

These assumptions allow us to ignore the fact that a program is interrupted and only consider the interrupt from the point of view of the program that was entered as a result of the interrupt. The model for a typical interrupt program under these assumptions is shown in Figure 13.1. The model consists of the time to set up a new level, store registers, etc. To this is added the processing required to acknowledge the interrupt and the time to

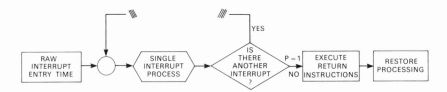

Figure 13.1. Interrupt model

ask all the questions required to terminate the routine under the assumption that there is nothing else to do. In addition, some sort of "SELECT NEXT LEVEL" or return instruction will be executed, followed by the time required to restore things to where they were prior to the interrupt.

Once we have obtained a model for each interrupt, a table is constructed for the input-dependent interrupts and the cycle-dependent interrupts. Since most contentious transfers will have resulted in at least one interrupt, the number of such transfers derived for the contentious transfers can be used to evaluate the number of interrupts that must be processed.

There may be a difference in the processing time for hardware interrupt and for internally generated interrupts as a result of blocking. Since blocking of processors occurs mostly for I/O operations, it is not unreasonable to assume that the processor is almost always blocked while waiting for an I/O operation. One should not assume blocking for simple status checks and other I/O operations that will not be terminated by an interrupt.

3.3. Non-Base-Sequence Programs

Those higher-level programs that operate on one transaction at a time can be treated as are the interrupt programs. That is, determine the number of times a second that the program will be activated and multiply by the time required for each activation. If the number of activations is cycle-dependent, then determine the number of times the program will be activated during the cycle.

If the program does batch tasks, and the start-up time for the programs is significant, the pessimistic assumption that the program will have to be restarted for each item may be overly pessimistic. A program at this level will typically have an overall structure comparable to that shown in Figure 13.2. The probability P expresses the number of items that the program will have to process. That number may depend on the incident load and on the duration of the cycle.

One tricky situation that can occur is that the program is entered twice in a cycle, the first time to do the processing for that which has accumulated during the previous cycle, and the next time to process that which has

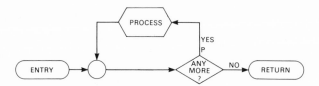

Figure 13.2. A typical higher-level program.

accumulated since the last time is was activated. The duration between the activations is again a function of the cycle length. Furthermore, since the two activations need not be evenly spaced, the queues are not the same length each time.

3.4. Input-Dependent Queues and Probabilities

Let L be the cycle length in seconds, and let $K = 1/L$ be the cycle frequency in cycles per second. If N items are queued per second, NL items will be queued per cycle. Consequently, the looping probability will be

$$P = \frac{NL}{NL + 1} = \frac{N}{N + K}.$$

Loop probabilities that describe the number of items on a queue tend to take the general form

$$\frac{aL + b}{cL + d} = \frac{a + Kb}{c + Kd}.$$

Bilinear forms of this kind show up where the queue length depends on priorities or is otherwise dependent on the number of items that are on the queue.

A possibly fallacious assumption has been made here. The assumption is that the queue buildup is linear during a cycle. The service processors (from the point of view of queuing theory) are cyclic batch processors, that is, they are activated periodically and clear all entries when they are activated. If a single program dominated the whole system, then, it could no longer be assumed that the process was effectively instantaneous, nor could the fact that new entries came onto the queue while the old ones were being cleared be ignored. The locally linear assumption is valid if the individual queue serving program is short compared to the cycle, does not in itself perturb the cycle (from the point of view of queue build-up), and despite interrupts will not be stretched out over a significant part of the cycle. If these assumptions do not properly describe the queue build-up, the analysis will have to be more complicated. The length of the queue could then be determined by a queuing theory analysis, resulting in probabilities that contain exponentials, etc. But since individual programs rarely account for more than 5% of the system capacity, the locally linear assumption is generally valid.

3.5. Cycle-Dependent and Mixed Probabilities

The cycle-dependent queue entries are those that are initiated as a result of the structure of the cycle. Here again, a lot must be known about the structure of the program in order to determine how many of these items there will be. The same kinds of local linearization assumptions are made regarding the build-up of queues for queue entries generated by the cycle. The argument, here, is weaker and more open to question. The cycle itself does not proceed uniformly. It proceeds rather as a series of fits and starts. The pace through the various functions is not uniform. The duration between the generation of queue entries is not uniform. Since input-derived queue entries are not controlled by the cycle, the length of the queue and therefore the length of the cycle does not perturb the rate at which these items build up. This is not the case for cycle-generated entries. As the system becomes more heavily loaded, the rate at which these entries build up is reduced. As the cycle is shortened, the rate increases. A cycle length dependency is expected and occurs here as well.

An interesting case is a program whose queue contains cycle-dependent entries and input-dependent entries intermixed. Storage allocation programs, and peripheral device service programs are examples. If A is the number of items generated per second as a result of the inputs, and B is the number of items generated per cycle, the total number of items on the queue in one cycle is

$$AL + B,$$

whence the looping probability is

$$\frac{AL + B}{AL + B + 1},$$

an example of the previously mentioned bilinear form.

Certain cycle-dependent queue lengths may be inversely proportional to the cycle length. A routine monitoring function may be dispensed with during peak periods. This kind of situation will occur for inescapable idle loops. This leads to a looping probability of the form $K/(A + K)$.

3.6. The Base-Sequence Program

The base-sequence program, other than the fact that it is generally more complicated than the higher-level programs, is treated in much the same way.

The difficult part of the analysis is determining what the basic cycle really is. Since the program is finite it can be unfolded, generating an ever-expanding tree. There is at least one point in this tree from which the whole tree up to that point recurs. One might object that this is not valid, since there may be user programs that are unpredictable and may never recur. This is true; however, user programs, messages, general transactions, etc., occur at lower levels. From the point of view of the executive, they are treated as objects. The process "run job number 6" may be variable and only statistically predictable. But the fact that a job is being run is a definite event at the executive level which will recur for some other job in a succeeding cycle. It should not be assumed that the point at which we *say* that the cycle begins and ends is indeed the true beginning or end of the cycle. If for example, exception ledgering is used, with a major update every tenth cycle, the recurrence period extends over ten cycles. Similarly, scheduling of alternate mass memories on alternate cycles or switches that are used to modify the basic cycle could stretch out the recurrence period over many design cycles. The point at which the entire process recurs is used as the analytical model of the cycle. The difference between two parts of a cycle defined in this way may be inconsequential. For example, if odd and even lines are alternately polled, and the statistics are the same for both types of lines, the fact that the cycles are really different is not significant. Similarly, two very different things might indeed be done in alternate cycles, but the different things might take almost the same time to perform; again the differences can be ignored. The cycle to analyze is this recurrence cycle. It is typically longer than the design cycle, i.e., an integral multiple of the design cycle. If there is a difference of this kind, then all the queue lengths should reflect the fact, as should all other significant probabilities.

A system can have two (or more) cyclic structures similar to the base-sequence program, at two different program levels. Simulation is preferable for such systems. Systems that have no well-defined cycle structure (such as asynchronous systems) are also difficult to analyze. In such cases, analysis is used as a tool to obtain a simpler simulation.

3.7. Summing Up and Solving

Having separately evaluated the time spent in each process, at each level, for those processes that occur on a cycle basis and those processes that occur as a result of the incident load, we now convert everything to a cycle basis preparatory to solving the equation for the cycle length. A process that requires A units of time per second evidently requires AL units of time per cycle. The functions thus generated are added to obtain an expression for the amount of time spent processing one average cycle. That is, of course, equal to the cycle duration. The result is an equation of the form

$$L = F(L).$$

The equation is generally nonlinear, as could be foreseen from the bilinear form of the probabilities. Additional sources of nonlinearities are: loops within loops, processes that get more efficient with increased load, anticipatory and deferred processing, nonlinear queue build-ups, priority effects, queue-length-dependent processes, etc. A typical form is

$$L^3 + aL^2 + bL + c + \frac{d}{L} + \frac{g}{L^2} + \frac{hL + k}{mL + n} + \frac{pL^2 + gL + r}{sL + t} = 0.$$

While this formidable expression can be solved by an iterative numerical procedure, it is not normally necessary to do so. Typically, the more complicated terms at the end of this expression are inconsequential for design load conditions. These nonlinear terms are significant only when the system is at or near the breaking point. A judicious examination of their values can reduce the analytical effort. The more complicated terms can also be expanded in a series by synthetic division and lumped with the more significant terms. What results after such simplifications is a quadratic or cubic equation which is then readily solved. Some pragmatic observations about the solution of such equations are worthwhile. There is usually only one real positive root. The remaining roots are either negative or complex. If there are no real positive roots, rather than having discovered something new and fundamental about system design, we have probably blundered somewhere in the analysis. We cannot at this point give physical interpretations to the negative or complex roots that may also satisfy the equations. That is not to say that such roots are meaningless or uninterpretable but that their interpretation is an open problem. Multiple real roots could come about if overflow, especially queue overflow, is properly modeled. The higher-valued roots might express steady-state conditions subsequent to an overflow.

3.8. Nonlinear Load Dependencies

There is a fundamental nonlinear relation between the cycle length and the incident load. To see this, let

L = length of the cycle in seconds (seconds/cycle)

N_c = number of items to be processed each cycle generated by the cycle itself (items/cycle).

N_t = number of new input-load-dependent transactions to be processed per second (items/second).

W_c = overhead processing time per cycle (seconds/cycle).

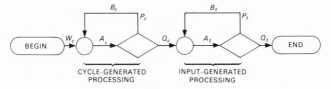

Figure 13.3. Model cycle.

Let the model of a single cycle be given as in Figure 13.3. A_c and B_c represent the work that must be done for each cycle-dependent item. A_t and B_t represent the work that must be done for each new input item. The dimensions of A_c, B_c, A_t, and B_t are seconds/item. The number of items queued in a cycle for the cycle-generated processing is N_c. The number of items queued in a cycle for the input-dependent processing is LN_t. Evidently:

$$P_c = \frac{N_c}{N_c + 1}, \qquad Q_c = \frac{1}{N_c + 1},$$

$$P_t = \frac{LN_t}{LN_t + 1}, \qquad Q_t = \frac{1}{LN_t + 1}.$$

Evaluating the model, we obtain

$$L\left[\frac{\text{seconds}}{\text{cycle}}\right] = W_c + A_c(N_c + 1) + N_c B_c + A_t(LN_t + 1) + LN_t B_t.$$

Solving for L, we obtain

$$L = \frac{W_c + N_c(A_c + B_c) + A_c + A_t}{1 - N_t(A_t + B_t)}.$$

Note that the lone A_c and A_t terms are each implicitly multiplied by 1 item/ cycle to preserve dimensionality.

N_t is a parameter that expresses the externally imposed processing load. The cycle length is a nonlinear function of the imposed load. This nonlinearity is implicit in the design of an anisochronous cyclic system. The average cycle length is not directly a measure of the utilization of the machine. As the imposed load increases, the cycle length also increases, to the point where there is not enough time to keep up with the rate at which new transactions enter the system. At that point, the cycle length is infinite. The typical relation between the cycle length and the incident load is shown in Figure 13.4.

N_t is the sole parameter in this expression that depends directly on the incident load. Furthermore, if an acceptable grade of service is to be provided under heavy load, this is one parameter that cannot be allowed to change.

The system is relatively indifferent to incremental load increases when it is lightly loaded. However, if the system is operating near the knee of the curve, a minor variation in the load could cause a catastrophic crash. The cyclic system is like the little girl in the nursery rhyme; "when she was good, she was very very good, but when she was bad she was horrid." One must get used to this inherent nonlinearity. We tend to think of systems as being described by the dashed line in Figure 13.4: if we double the load, we double the amount of processing. But that is not the case. The user, however, may be confused by this kind of seemingly irrational behavior. Three times he comes to us and asks if the system can handle another 20% increase in load; three times we magnanimously accede to his request. The fourth time, however, he requests a mere 2% increment and we blanch and splutter that the system is about to fall apart. One can readily understand the attitude of the user toward the architect under such circumstances, especially if the architect has not made the user aware of the nonlinear behavior of the system, or if the user thinks that this behavior is due to a design flaw.

If the equation for the cycle length is itself nonlinear, the nonlinearity of the relation between the cycle length and the incident load may be further emphasized. The curve will have a sharper knee and exhibit even more catastrophic degradation under extreme load. One thing is certain, however,

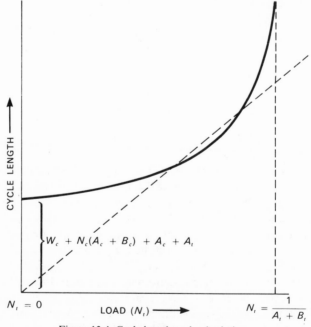

Figure 13.4. Cycle length *vs.* load relation.

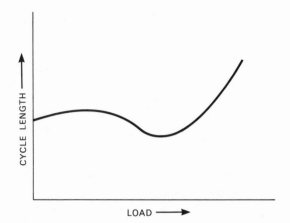

Figure 13.5. Nonmonotonic cycle length *vs.* load relation.

the curve will be monotonic increasing. That is, it will *not* be shaped like that shown in Figure 13.5. If it is, there is probably a flaw in the design. For example, an "emergency" procedure is used under heavy load which is more efficient than the normal procedure. Suspicion is warranted if the time required to process $N + 1$ tasks is less than that required to process N tasks. There are scheduling algorithms, used in systems with swapping, that exhibit non-monotonic behavior. Concomitantly, there are more efficient algorithms for which this does not occur.

3.9. Cycle Length, Delay, and Computer Loading

3.9.1. Computer Load

The cycle length is a rough measure of the delay of the system. If individual jobs have execution times that are short compared to the cycle length, and the system is so structured that the number of cycles required for a task can be determined, then the cycle length is a fair measure of the delay. The cycle length is not a measure of the degree to which the computer is being used, since the computer loading is always 100%. However, it is convenient to have a measure of how much the transaction arrival rate can be increased before the system is overloaded. A specification of maximum acceptable delay is required. As an example, refer to Figure 13.6. The incident load for which the cycle length becomes infinite is clearly an upper bound on the capacity of the system. The design load can be expressed as a percentage of the maximum load under which the specified delay is still met. Alternatively, the design load can be expressed as a percentage of the ultimate load—that load for which the delay is infinite. The measure being used should be explicitly stated. Expressing the design load conditions as a percentage of ultimate load is not realistic. There are few instances in which infinite delays are tolerable. Since the acceptable delay should be part of the specification, expressing the design load as a percentage of the maximum load for an acceptable delay is more realistic. The best method of all is to present the cycle length curve, and avoid the misunderstandings that are implicit in using simplistic measures such as "% utilization." To say without qualification that the design load represents, say, $N\%$ of the system's capacity is to imply that the load curve is a straight line through the origin.

3.9.2. Memory Limits

As the delay increases, the length of queues will increase correspondingly. Thus, as the steady-state load is increased, the available memory pool is depleted. The amount of memory in use can be determined from the delay of the transaction, how much memory is used in each phase of the transaction processing, and the length of the cycle. Alternatively, the available excess memory can be determined for each incident load condition. If the available memory is depleted prior to reaching the maximum delay, then the maximum load that the system can handle is that at which the memory is depleted. Increasing the buffer memory can insure that the memory limit point is reached only after the maximum delay point. Since memory comes in discrete modules, getting rid of a memory limitation may leave excessive memory at some point beyond the maximum load as limited by the speed of

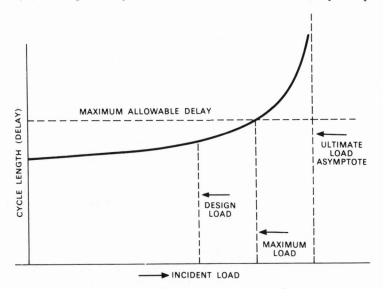

Figure 13.6. Cycle length, delay, and overload.

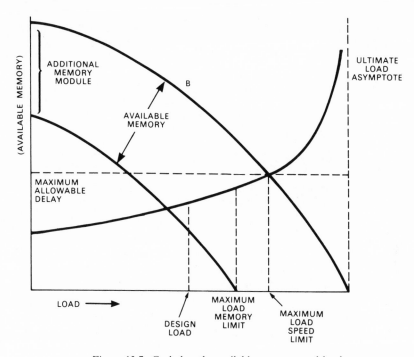

Figure 13.7. Cycle length, available memory, and load.

the CPU. This is shown by curve *B* in Figure 13.7. Space–time trades can then be used to reduce the processing time, and thereby increase the maximum load and ultimate load.

3.9.3. How Fast a Computer?

It is not unusual to have a quadratic or cubic equation in *L*. In this case, the relation between the speed of the computer and the load is not linear either. Consider a typical equation:

$$L = bL + \frac{c}{L} + d.$$

The right-hand side is the sum of the expressions evaluated to obtain the cycle length equation. If the speed of the computer were doubled, the expression on the right-hand side of this equation would be halved. Thus, a double-speed computer with the same program and load would have a cycle length expressed by

$$L = \frac{1}{2}\left(bL + \frac{c}{L} + d\right).$$

In general, if the memory cycle time of the computer is increased by a factor a (i.e., the speed increases by a factor $1/a$), the resulting equation will be

$$(1 - ab)L^2 - adL - ac = 0.$$

Solving for L, we obtain

$$L = \frac{ad + \sqrt{a^2d^2 + 4ac(1 - ab)}}{2(1 - ab)}$$

It is clear that doubling the computer's speed does not necessarily double its load-handling capacity. The minimum memory speed which will still meet the maximum acceptable delay can be found by evaluating this expression for different values of a (the memory cycle time parameter) and the load parameter(s). Alternatively, the performance advantage gained by increasing the memory speed can be determined.

Given a set of functions, which by analysis turn out to be too much for a postulated computer, we can determine how fast the computer would have to be to meet the requirement. Alternatively, we might decide to partition these tasks extensively by using more than one computer at the original speed. This is done in the same way as with increasing the computer's speed, but the increased capacity must be discounted to account for the additional intracomplex communications. This is roughly between 5 and 15% of each computer used. Thus, two computers would have an effective value of a, of, not 0.5, but 0.556.

3.10. Burst Conditions

If the incident load is steady, bursts occur relatively infrequently, and are short compared to the major cycle length, then burst effects can be calculated without simulation. Figure 13.8 is a histogram describing the load that might be incident to a system. The sample for which the system is designed should be the peak-hour period of the system, typically occurring between 11 A.M. and 4 P.M. (Time zone differences can modify this for a world-wide or nationwide system.) The load distribution over a small period of time—say, a few seconds—can be derived from such a histogram. If the bursts are short and spaced sufficiently far apart that the system can recover from each burst before another one occurs, then the load distribution can be used to determine the average system cycle length. This is done by evaluating the cycle length for each value of the incident load and obtaining the probability of that incident load from the load distribution. If the relation between incident load and the cycle length were linear, this additional calculation would not be required; the cycle length corresponding to the average incident load would be the same as that obtained by this more complicated

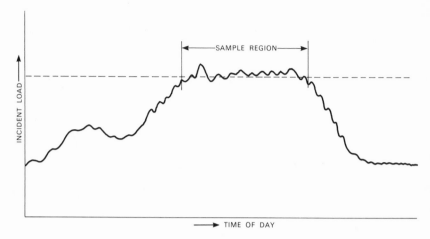

Figure 13.8. Load histogram.

calculation. The nonlinearity of the cycle length *vs.* incident load relation makes the simpler calculation invalid in general.

However, it is possible that the statistics that characterize peaks are such that the system will not have recovered from a previous burst when the next burst occurs. If this is the case, the static model that has been discussed until now is wholly invalid. A dynamic system model must be used, which takes into account the transient characteristics of queue build-up, overflow procedures, choking, etc. This type of model is best examined by simulation. The simulation must of course include a proper model of the bursts.

Here are some rules of thumb regarding the analysis of bursts. Almost anything that lasts more than 20 to 30 system cycles might as well be sustained indefinitely. The dynamics of these systems are such that if they can properly handle the load for 20 or more cycles then they can handle it indefinitely. If it is known that the bursts can last several minutes, the sample region on which the input load distribution is based should be divided at least as finely as several seconds. Clearly, the distribution for a fine division will be broader and will have sharper peaks than one obtained from a grosser sample. Bursts that last less than one or two cycles also need not be considered in the distribution if they occur sufficiently infrequently. The assumption is that the system will have sufficient time to clear the burst over the next several cycles and bring the cycle length back down to the steady-state average for that period.

It is sometimes possible to determine the effect of bursts on the system without simulation. A model of the burst is constructed. That is, a burst is considered as consisting of a succession of static input loads that last for predetermined time intervals. The resulting model should correspond

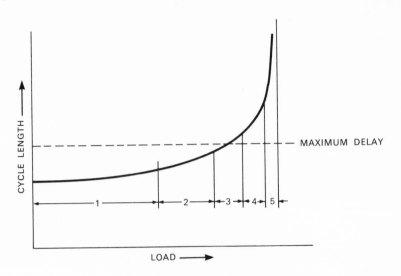

Figure 13.9. Burst model load partition.

reasonably well with the burst distribution. The static load levels can be taken far apart on the flat portion of the load *vs.* cycle length curve. Smaller increments are chosen for the steeper portions of the curve. Where it is known that the system will change its operational mode (e.g., start to choke inputs or curtail other functions), additional breaks in the load levels are created. Figure 13.9 depicts a typical partition of the load into different ranges. The relatively lengthy span given to the first range is due to the insensitivity of the system cycle to load within this range. The divisions become finer at the steeper portions of the load *vs.* cycle length curve. Figure 13.10 shows a model burst, as it might occur during the peak period. The "loads" shown here are the nonlinear regions depicted in Figure 13.9. The lowest-level load is such that the system can sustain it without building up any queues or running out of space. This level can be assumed to have gone on indefinitely. Bursts that are wholly contained within this level are

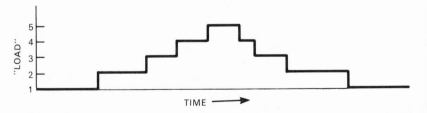

Figure 13.10. Burst model.

clearly of no concern. The second level is then assumed to occur for the prescribed time interval. The queues that build up during this time are carried forward as the initial conditions for the next interval. Note that this will in general require changes in the parameters of the model, as the queues, and hence the various probabilities do not correspond to the steady-state conditions. This procedure is carried forward to the next level of load, with the queue buildup of the previous interval used as the initial conditions for the next interval. As the burst continues, the system begins to take corrective action (such as going into overflow), and the model must again be changed to reflect the new mode of operation. The system model during the decay of the burst and the model during the buildup of the burst are not necessarily the same for the same load level. For example, level 2 of the model on the way up might not include input choking routines and overflow routines, but this might be required for the level 2 on the way down. This is not as complicated at is looks because the system model can be significantly simplified. A load *vs.* cycle length function can be derived that approximates that which was obtained from the formal analysis. This is done by the usual curve fitting procedures. Terms are added to the resulting expression to properly reflect the effects of queue build-up, overflow, etc. Furthermore, the analysis is done from the perspective of knowing what the overall behavior is. This means that the most significant parts of the processing are known. If the piecewise quasi-static model is overly fine, it will be equivalent to doing a dynamic analysis by hand. Typically, it is not practical to evaluate a burst consisting of, say, more than five levels of load and eight or ten time intervals. It is a good idea to start with a relatively crude model of the burst to see if there is anything to worry about. The results of this kind of crude analysis will give valuable guidance to a finer analysis of the burst or a full-blown dynamic simulation, should that be necessary.

3.11. Parametric Analysis

To the extent that analysis is used as a design tool, it is parametric analyses that are valuable, rather than the performance of the system at the design point. The most important thing about parametric analysis is not to overdo it. To evaluate each of four parameters at 10 points means 10,000 items of information. If done by hand, the project is over before the results are in. If done on a computer, the resulting printout is likely to be incomprehensible. The idea is to vary one or two parameters at a time, obtain a feel for the behavior of the system, and use that feel as a guide for the next parameter to evaluate.

The most important and simplest parameter to use is the incident load. That load is characterized by a distribution. Rather than start with variations on that distribution, it is best to investigate the behavior of the system in terms of simple multiples of the whole distribution. The system is evaluated at zero load, 0.5, 1, 3, 5, 7, and 10 times the nominal load. The use of a simple multiplier of the basic load allows many of the probabilities in the model to remain unchanged.

It is convenient to introduce the parameters at an early point in the model. This will result in some links that have parametric values and others that do not. The model is then reduced by eliminating all nodes that have no parametrically weighted incident or excident links. Numerical values are substituted for the parameters that will remain fixed through the analysis, and the model boiled down further. The resulting algebraic function for the cycle length (memory, channel) is a function of the cycle length and the parameter. Values are then substituted for the parameter and the equation solved for the cycle length.

Since the cycle length tends to be monotonic with respect to changes in parameters, it is reasonable to investigate the parameter first at the extreme points of its sensible range. If the difference in the system behavior across these extremes is insignificant, there may be no further need to investigate that parameter. To be on the safe side, one should investigate the derivatives of the function with respect to the parameter to see whether there are any intermediate minima or maxima. For example, a performance parameter might first increase and then decrease with increasing block size. The two extremes of block size might not tell us the true peak value of that performance parameter. The peak, as determined by investigating the derivative, will tell us. Another test for the significance of a parameter that is occasionally useful is to examine its minimal and maximal values without regard to whether they are achievable or not. Say that a performance parameter was given by the following equation:

$$P = \frac{aT^2 - bT + e^{-cT}}{1 - hT}.$$

P can be minimized by making $T = 0$ in the denominator and infinite in the exponential term of the numerator. The simpler expression resulting thereby can be examined for a minimum at $T = b/2a$.

The investigation of particular performance parameters should be weighted by the penalty function associated with that parameter. Design parameter values that lead to performance values that are totally discounted by the penalty function should not be considered in detail. For example, if the user has specified that no credit will be given if the delay exceed 30 seconds, there is not much point in investigating the detailed behavior of the system under such circumstances.

Parametric analysis is done primarily as a guide to design. Precision is rarely required, and accuracy probably not achievable since the results of the analysis may dictate changes in the system design that may render the analysis useless. It is generally better to investigate several equally important design parameters crudely than to select one to be done in glorious detail. Evaluating three or four points, estimating a few derivatives, and establishing some upper and lower bounds can often do more than an impressive printout of several pages.

4. EVALUATION OF LEDGER CONTRIBUTION

Some processing is usually suspended while the ledger is being written. In particular, those processes that could result in the modification of the portion of the ledger that is being written are curtailed during the writing interval. Other processes, however, may continue. The most prevalent mass storage devices have a significant access delay. Furthermore, these devices are designed to have transfer rates that will not take all the memory cycles of the system. Consequently, the elapsed time for writing the ledger can be significantly longer than the number of memory cycles required. A typical snapshot ledger being written to two different drums might require an elapsed time of 200 milliseconds, although the time, as measured in memory cycles, might be only 10 milliseconds. Ignoring the effect of the ledger elapsed time would lead to a serious underestimation of the cycle length and, consequently, the memory requirement. Assuming that all processing was suspended during the ledger interval could lead to an equally serious overestimate of the ledger effect. Neither of these is desirable—it is best to evaluate the contribution of the ledger elapsed time properly.

While the discussion of the succeeding sections centers about a snapshot ledger in which all executive-level processing is suspended, the same analysis applies to exception ledgering and continual ledgering.

4.1. Subsumable, Unsubsumable, and Partially Subsumable Functions

The ledger elapsed time is the time that elapses from the initiation of the ledgering function until all copies of that ledger have been stored and verified. The elapsed time can be readily determined from a knowledge of the device to which the ledger is being written and the expected condition of the device prior to the writing. Three types of processing can be considered in evaluating the ledger contributions: subsumable functions, unsubsumable functions, and partially subsumable functions.

The **subsumable functions** are those that are initiated when the ledgering process is started and terminate with the termination of the ledgering process.

Clearly, the contentious cycles taken to transfer the ledger are subsumable. Similarly, the time required to execute the I/O instructions that initiate the contentious transfer of the ledger to the mass memory and verify that the transfer has been successfully completed are subsumable. If the ledger is transferred over a noncontentious channel, and instructions must be executed for each word or character transferred, then the time required to execute those instructions is also subsumable. The memory cycles expended on subsumable functions during the ledger interval are clearly free. As long as the subsumable memory cycles take less time than the ledger interval, these cycles will not contribute to or detract from the performance of the system. The full penalty has been paid for by the ledger interval itself.

The **unsubsumable functions** are those that are suspended or cannot otherwise be executed during the ledger interval. They occur wholly outside of the ledger period. Not all unsubsumable functions result from a deliberate curtailment of processing during the ledger interval. For example, the contentious transfer of a block from memory to the drum may be usurped by the higher-priority ledger. Thus, while not explicitly curtailed, it is effectively suspended and does not occur within the ledger interval.

The **partially subsumable functions** are typically functions occurring at higher priority levels which will continue during the ledger interval. Alternatively, in a continual ledgering scheme, they are the functions that go on while part of the ledger is being written. Those memory cycles that are expended on partially subsumable functions during the ledger interval are effectively free. The total number of memory cycles spent on these functions must accordingly be reduced so that they are not overcounted. It is clear that as the processing load increases, the number of memory cycles wasted during the ledger interval will decrease because the number of partially subsumable memory cycles increases.

4.2. Ledger Analysis

Let U be the time taken in a system cycle for the unsubsumable functions, P the time taken for the partially subsumable functions, S the time taken for the subsumable functions, L the system cycle length, and M the ledger elapsed time. The portion of the cycle taken by the ledger is M/L. If the load is small, the time spent in a cycle is the sum of the unsubsumable functions, the ledger elapsed time, and the partially subsumable functions reduced to account for the "free" cycles during the ledger interval. These observations result in the following expression for the cycle length:

$$L = U + M + P\left(1 - \frac{M}{L}\right) \qquad \text{if } \frac{M}{L}P + S \le M, \qquad (1)$$

$$L = U + P + S \qquad \qquad \text{if } \frac{M}{L} P + S > M. \qquad (2)$$

The inequality in (2) expresses the fact that there are no more unwasted memory cycles—that is, all the memory cycles that were available during the ledger interval have been consumed. This condition will rarely occur over the region of interest. Consequently, the cycle length is first evaluated under the assumption that condition (1) does hold. We then substitute the value of L so obtained to see if it did indeed hold. If it does not, we re-evaluate L under the assumption that condition (2) holds. Solving equation (1) for L, we obtain

$$L = \frac{U + M + P \pm \sqrt{(U + M + P)^2 - 4PM}}{2}. \qquad (3)$$

The proper sign is determined by considering that a zero-length ledger time should not lead to a zero-length cycle length.

The effect of a change in memory speed by, say, a factor a results in

$$L = aU + aM + aP\left(1 - \frac{M}{L}\right) \qquad \text{if } a\frac{M}{L} P + aS \leq M, \qquad (4)$$

$$L = aU + aP + aS \qquad \text{if } a\frac{M}{L} P + aS > M, \qquad (5)$$

since the change in memory speed does not usually affect the ledger interval.

5. QUEUES, STRETCH, AND DELAYS

The delay of a transaction is the sum of the time expended in each queue plus the elapsed times expended in each process. While a precise determination of the delay is difficult to do analytically, the delay can be approximated by making some simplifying assumptions. These are:

1. The processes are independent; that is, what happens on one queue does not affect what happens on subsequent queues.
2. The processes are uniformly distributed throughout the cycle.
3. The characterizing distributions of the service time and the arrival rates are narrow.
4. The queue doctrine is FIFO unless otherwise stated.
5. There is only a single server for each queue.

The expected waiting time for drum or disc transactions will depend upon the scheduling routine used. These have been treated elsewhere. The concern in this section is that part of the delay that arises from internal queue waiting times.

5.1. The Stretch Factor

Consider a system operating at several different priority levels. Furthermore, assume that the transitions from level to level are random and occur uniformly throughout the cycle. Each level can be considered as if it were a separate computer operating at a somewhat slower rate than the full machine is capable of. Thus, a low-level processor might have a **subjective memory cycle** of 3 microseconds while in fact the actual memory cycle was 1 microsecond. If the priority structure is strictly ordered, the stretch is determined by the number of memory cycles taken by higher-level processors. The cycles taken by contentious transfers must be considered as being executed by a processor operating at a yet higher priority level than the highest one.

Let P_i be the probability of being in level i (where 1 is the highest level and n the lowest) and let T_i be the time (objective) expended at level i in one system cycle. Evidently,

$$P_i = \frac{T_i}{L}.$$

Let S_i be a stretch factor that described the ratio of subjective to objective time. Then, if A is the number of memory cycles taken for contentious transfers,

$$S_i = \frac{1}{1 - (A/L) - \sum_{j<i} P_j},$$

that is, the time expended at level i is stretched by the combined effect of memory cycles used at all higher levels. The service rate of a processor at level i is the rate at which that processor can service a transaction using the subjective memory cycle time.

5.2. Queues and Delays

The arrival rate of transactions is generally known from the incident load model and the cycle model. A knowledge of the arrival rate and the service rate as determined on the basis of the subjective memory cycle time allows a determination of the time spent on each queue or, better yet, the time spent in each service system (queue time plus process time). The sum of the times spent on all queues is a measure of the delay for the transaction.

These models can be refined by taking into account the variance of the service time (subjective). This model, while not precise, is adequate for a first-cut determination of delay—sufficient for the needs of initial design and for the considerations required to establish a good simulation.

6. VIABILITY CALCULATIONS

6.1. Introduction

The precise calculation of viability for a large complex, consisting of many units, each having many levels of degradation, with extensive configuration switching and complicated penalty functions, is not readily done by hand. In fact, a precise analysis of a large complex could entail 6 to 12 man-months of programming. Fortunately, the more complex calculations can be approximated to achieve a slightly pessimistic analysis that is accurate enough for most applications. However, if the viability so calculated should be inadequate or marginal, the more complex methods would have to be used. Only the simpler method will be described here.

6.2. Unit Statistics

Associated with each unit of the system there is a MTBF and a MTTR. These two numbers are the basic ones used for all further calculations. The MTBF of the unit is calculated from the failure rates and the enumeration of the number of components which make up the unit. The MTTR is based on the evaluation of the time required to repair the unit as observed over a number of failure instances. If such data are not available, the MTTR is estimated by use of generally accepted guides. The MTBF and MTTR values used in the calculation should be expressed at the same confidence level (e.g., 90%) with respect to the same interval (e.g., two-sided, 50%). Mixed confidence levels will yield meaningless results.

We shall not take into consideration the analysis of subsystems or units which exhibit many levels of degradation. Units will be assembled into subsystems, each of which will be capable of being in exactly one of two states: UP or DØWN. If a subsystem is UP, it is performing at full capacity; if DØWN, its performance is nil.

We assume that:

1. The unit failure and repair rates are independent.
2. The failure of any one unit will cause the subsystem to fail.
3. The failure rates of the units are constants.
4. The repair rates of the units are independent of the number of failures; that is, repair can proceed simultaneously on several failed units.

The mean UP and DØWN times are obtained by

$$MUT_{subsystem} = \frac{1}{\sum_{i=1}^{n} (1/MTBF_i)}, \tag{6}$$

$$MDT_{subsystem} = \frac{1}{\sum_{i=1}^{n} (1/MTTR_i)}, \tag{7}$$

where

$MTBF_i$ = mean time between failures of unit i,
$MTTR_i$ = mean time to repair of unit i,
MUT_i = mean UP time of the sybsystem,
MDT_i = mean DØWN time of the subsystem.

The summation is carried out over all the units that comprise the subsystem.

If a subsystem consisted of three units; say, a disc storage unit, a controller, and a power supply, and the parameters of each were as follows:

Unit	MTBF	MTTR
Disc	10,000 hours	1 hour
Controller	20,000 hours	0.5 hour
Power supply	20,000 hours	0.5 hour

the MUT and MDT would be

$$MUT = \frac{1}{\frac{1}{10,000} + \frac{1}{20,000} + \frac{1}{20,000}} = 5000 \text{ hours},$$

$$MDT = \frac{1}{\frac{1}{1} + \frac{1}{0.5} + \frac{1}{0.5}} = 0.2 \text{ hour}.$$

The intuitively surprising reduction in MTTR expressed by the second equation can be understood by considering the fact that there are many conditions in which simultaneous failures will occur. In such cases, all three units might be repaired within the hour. The first unit to be repaired might well take an hour. However, the next unit might be repaired within the same time or within a few seconds after the first. The apparent repair time for the second unit is therefore zero or very small. Another way to look at this is to consider the MTTR as the reciprocal of the repair rate. Thus, we have repair rates of 1/hour, 2/hour, and 2/hour respectively, leading to a net repair rate of 5/hour under the stated assumption. That yields a MDT of 0.2 hour. If the maintenance facilities are such that the repair man must repair the units in sequence, finishing the first before he can continue to the next, the formula for the MDT given here is invalid. A much more complicated expression must be used. Adequate spares provisioning and repair facilities will often result in a repair policy that will allow the use of equation (7).

If the subsystem in question has several stages of degradation, the calculation can be performed through the artifice of "pseudosubsystems." A different subsystem is created for each level of degradation. Each such "subsystem" is accorded the performance value appropriate to it. A pseudosubsystem will go "DØWN" if any of its "units" fail *or are repaired*. The calculations used to evaluate the MUT and MDT for pseudosubsystems are essentially the same as the calculations of the viability of a system. We shall not consider systems in which the analysis of pseudosubsystems are required.

6.3. States and Metastates

At any given instant of time, one can enumerate how many subsystems of each type are operational. Thus, the system might have three computers, six memories, two drums, four discs, seven tapes, etc. working. The failure or the repair of any subsystem will change this condition. The enumeration of the working and nonworking subsystems of the system is called the configuration state or, more simply, the state of the system. The state of the system is described by **state vectors**. These are defined below:

S = system vector. It enumerates the number of each type of subsystem of which the system is composed.

U_x = system UP vector. It enumerates how many subsystems of each type are UP in state x.

D_x = system DØWN vector. It enumerates how many subsystems of each type are DØWN in state x.

Consider a system consisting of 6 computers, 12 memories, 2 drums, 130 communication buffers, 18 tape stations, 1 card reader, 4 typewriters, and 1 disc file. Assume that at a given moment 5 computers, 10 memories, 2 drums, 90 buffers, 14 tapes, the card reader, and 3 typewriters are working. The system vector, the UP vector, and the DØWN vector would be:

$$S = (6, 12, 2, 130, 18, 1, 4, 1).$$

$$U_x = (5, 10, 2, \quad 90, 14, 1, 3, 0).$$

$$D_x = (1, \quad 2, 0, \quad 40, \quad 4, 0, 1, 1).$$

It is clear from the above definitions that

$$S = U_x + D_x$$

The following notation will be used to specify elements of these vectors:

n_i = the number of subsystems of type i.
u_{xi} = the number of subsystems of type i that are UP in state x.
d_{xi} = the number of subsystems of type i that are DØWN in state x.

Again,

$$n_i = u_{xi} + d_{xi}$$

for all states x and subsystems i.[2]

We normally describe a system state by an UP vector, leaving the DØWN vector and the system vector implicit. Since each subsystem can be either UP or DØWN, and since the total number of subsystems is the sum of the components of the system vector, the total number of states is given by

$$N_{\text{total}} = 2^{(s_1 + s_2 + \cdots s_m)}.$$

In the above example, then, we have a total of

$$N_{\text{total}} = 2^{(6 + 12 + 2 + 130 + 18 + 1 + 4 + 1)} = 2^{174},$$

or

$$2.36 \times 10^{52} \text{ states.}$$

If, however, subsystems of a given type are interchangeable with all other subsystems of the same type, we need not distinguish among states which differ only in that it is one rather than another subsystem of the same type that has failed. Thus, we are concerned only with how many subsystems have failed and not which specific ones. This considerably reduces the total number of effective states.

For each subsystem type, we must consider the cases in which there are $0, 1, 2, \ldots, s_i$ subsystems down. In our example, then, the number of effective states is

$$\prod_{i=1}^{m} (s_i + 1) = 7 \times 13 \times 3 \times 131 \times 19 \times 2 \times 5 \times 2 = 1.36 \times 10^7,$$

a substantial reduction, but still too large a number for an explicit evaluation of each state.

If full interchangeability has not been provided, the definition of the states and the several vectors will have to reflect this fact. This can be done by separating the groups of subsystems which cannot be interchanged. For example, if the twelve memories can only be interchanged among even- and

---

[2] This is known as the law of conservation of subsystems; i.e., subsystems are neither created nor destroyed.

odd-numbered memories, there would be two memory groups of six each rather than one group of twelve.

There is often no difference in performance among several states in a range of states. Thus, if the system can achieve full capability with 5 computers, 10 memories, 1 drum, 100 buffers, 12 tapes, 1 card reader, 3 typewriters, and 1 disc file, the states characterized by the following numbers would all be equivalent:

$$(5\text{--}6, 10\text{--}12, 1\text{--}2, 100\text{--}130, 12\text{--}18, 1\text{--}1, 3\text{--}4, 1\text{--}1).$$

On the other hand, assume that the system cannot work unless it has a drum. The following numbers would characterize equivalent states:

$$(0\text{--}6, \quad 0\text{--}12, 0\text{--}0, \quad 0\text{--}130, \quad 0\text{--}18, 0\text{--}1, 0\text{--}4, 0\text{--}1).$$

That is, as long as there is no drum, it does not matter what other subsystems are UP or DØWN, the system is DØWN.

A set of numbers such as the above is called a **metastate**. It is a shorthand for describing a set of states which are equivalent for some reason or another. The totality of states is divided into metastates such that every state included in a metastate has the same performance.

The number of states represented by a metastate is the product of ranges of the components within it. Thus, the first metastate described above represents $2 \times 3 \times 2 \times 31 \times 7 \times 1 \times 2 \times 1 = 5208$ states. Metastates will be described by a vector, each of whose elements represents a range of UP and DØWN conditions:

$$T_x = (r_1\text{--}t_1, r_2\text{--}t_2, \ldots, r_m\text{--}t_m).$$

Since the agglomeration of states into metastates requires that every state in the metastate have the same performance parameter value, the way states are combined into metastates will generally be different for each performance parameter analyzed.

6.4. Basic Approach

The method of calculating the viability of a system is trivially simple:

1. Calculate the probability of the system being in each of its states.
2. Evaluate the performance of the system in each state.
3. The average value of the performance is the sum of the products of the probability and the performance for all states.

We can then calculate the various moments (standard deviation, skewness, etc.) associated with the system. For the above example, we would have

$$W_{\text{average}} = \sum_{x=1}^{x=2.36 \times 10^{52}} w_x p_x$$

where p_x is the probability of state x, and w_x is the value of performance parameter w in state x.

But 10^{52} is a large number. At one evaluation per nanosecond, we have to grind on for about 10^{39} years. This is some 10^{29} times longer than the estimated age of the universe. If the universe were inhabited by intelligent life devoted to nothing but the calculation of this one problem, we would still be some two orders of magnitude shy of completing the task. Furthermore, we would need at least one or two redundant universes if our results were to be trusted. Dropping down to the calculation of viability using the effective number of states (1.36×10^7 for our example), and assuming one evaluation per 10 milliseconds, we still come out with 37.8 hours for these calculations—a feasible but unusable result. As it turns out, we can short-cut these calculations to the point where for a small system they can be done by hand in a few hours. More complex systems require a computer for their evaluation, the bulk of the effort being in programming the model, and not in the actual calculation.

6.5. State and Metastate Probabilities

The calculation of a state probability (i.e., the probability that the system is in a particular state) begins with evaluating the probability that the requisite number of subsystems in that state are UP or DØWN. That in turn begins with the probability that one subsystem is UP or DØWN. The probability that a subsystem is UP is

$$P_i = \frac{\text{MUT}_i}{\text{MUT}_i + \text{MDT}_i}. \tag{8}$$

The probability that a subsystem is DØWN is

$$Q_i = \frac{\text{MDT}_i}{\text{MUT}_i + \text{MDT}_i}. \tag{9}$$

Thus, a subsystem with a mean UP time of 999 hours and a mean DØWN time of one hour has

$$P_i = \frac{999}{1000} = 0.999,$$

$$Q_i = \frac{1}{1000} = 0.001.$$

Most states have several subsystems of a given type UP and DØWN at any given time. Thus, in a particular state, we might wish to evaluate the probability that exactly three out of seven subsystems are UP. In general, the probability that exactly k out of n subsystems of type i are UP is

$$P_i(k;n) = \binom{n}{k} P_i^k Q_i^{n-k}$$

$$= \frac{n!}{(n-k)!k!} P_i^k Q_i^{n-k}, \tag{10}$$

the familiar binomial expansion term. Similarly, the probability that k out of n subsystems of type i are DØWN is

$$Q_i(k;n) = 1 - P_i(k;n)$$

$$= \binom{n}{k} Q_i^k P_i^{n-k}. \tag{11}$$

In the above example, the probability that 3 out of 4 subsystems would be up is

$$P_i(3;4) = \frac{4 \cdot 3 \cdot 2 \cdot 1}{3 \cdot 2 \cdot 1 \cdot 1}(0.999)^3(0.001)$$

$$= 0.003988.$$

Metastates describe a range of numbers for UP and DØWN. The probability that k to m, inclusive, out of n subsystems of type i are UP is

$$P_i(k,m;n) = \sum_{s=k}^{m} P_i(s;n). \tag{12}$$

Similarly,

$$Q_i(k,m;n) = \sum_{s=k}^{m} Q_i(s;n). \tag{13}$$

This is the sum of the probabilities that $k, k+1, k+2, \ldots, m$ subsystems are UP (DØWN).

The probability that a system is in a given state is the product of the probabilities that the subsystems that make up that state are UP. Thus,

$$P_x = \prod_{i=1}^{m} P_i(u_{xi}; n_i), \tag{14}$$

$$Q_x = \prod_{i=1}^{m} Q_i(d_{xi}; n_i), \tag{15}$$

where m is the number of subsystems.

The probability that the system is in a particular metastate is the product of the probabilities associated with the ranges specified by that metastate. That is,

$$P_{mx} = \prod_{i=1}^{m} P_i(r_i, t_i ; n_i),$$ (16)

$$P_{mx} = \prod_{i=1}^{m} \sum_{s=r_i}^{t_i} P_i(s ; n_i)$$

$$= \prod_{i=1}^{m} \sum_{s=r_i}^{t_i} \frac{n_i !}{s!(n_i - s)!} P_i^s Q_i^{n_i - s}.$$ (17)

We can now evaluate the probabilities associated with metastates. Consider a system consisting of computers, tapes, discs, and drums. Let the system have 6, 10, 3, and 2 of these subsystems, respectively. Furthermore, assume that there are distinguishable levels of performance corresponding to 1 or fewer computers, 2 computers, 3 computers, 4 computers, 5 or more computers. With one or fewer computers, the system is assumed to be DØWN. Furthermore, if there are fewer than five tapes or fewer than one disc or drum, the system will be assumed to be DØWN. Otherwise it will be UP. These statements can be interpreted as specifying the metastates shown below:

Computers	Tapes	Discs	Drums	Performance
5–6	5–10	1–3	1–2	4
4	5–10	1–3	1–2	3
3	5–10	1–3	1–2	2
2	5–10	1–3	1–2	1
0–1	5–10	1–3	1–2	
0–6	0–4	1–3	1–2	0 (dead metastates)
0–6	0–10	0	1–2	
0–6	0–10	0–3	0	

There are four sets of states which specify dead metastates. Obtaining the dead states can be difficult, because expressions must be generated that cover each state once and only once. This will be shown in the next section.

The above table is a computation tableau. With it we can short-cut much of the labor involved in evaluating the viability. The following observations reduce the calculations considerably:

1. Evaluate the probabilities for the different subsystems separately and lay them out in a tableau (e.g., probability for 5–6 computers, 5–10 tapes, 1–3 discs, 1–2 drums, etc.).

2. The probability for large ranges is better evaluated as $1 -$ (probability of the complementary range) [e.g., $P(1-3)$ is calculated as $1 - P(0)$].
3. Probabilities associated with a full range (e.g., 0–6, 0–10) need not be calculated since they are perforce equal to 1.
4. Probabilities associated with the outer ends of large ranges, such as $P(7-10)$, $P(50-130)$, are usually so close to 1 for reasonably reliable devices that they can be replaced by 1. This has been done even when carrying out the calculations to 18 places, with no loss of accuracy.

The following table shows the MUT and MDT for the several subsystems of the previous example:

	Computer	Tapes	Discs	Drums
MUT	1500	250	3000	3000
MDT	0.5	0.5	1.3	1.5
P_{up}	0.999667	0.998004	0.999567	0.999500
P_{down}	0.000333	0.001996	0.000433	0.000500

Using equation (10) for the probabilities associated with a specific number of items UP or DØWN, and combining them as in equation (12), we obtain

Computer	Tapes	Discs	Drums
$P(5-6) = 0.999998$	$P(5-10) = 1$	$P(1-3) = 1$	$P(1-2) = 0.9999998$
$P(4) = 1.66334 \times 10^{-6}$	$P(0-4) = 0$	$P(0) = 0$	$P(0) = 2 \times 10^{-7}$
$P(3) = 7.39261 \times 10^{-10}$			
$P(2) = 1.84815 \times 10^{-13}$			
$P(0-1) = 3.36 \times 10^{-7}$			

Note that we had only eight groups of probabilities to calculate. Furthermore, we have rounded off the probabilities (by pessimistically reducing the UP probabilities), to reduce the number of significant digits required. This must be done in such a way that the sum of the probabilities is equal to one. Arranging the probabilities in a tableau, we obtain

Computers	Tapes	Discs	Drums	Probability	Performance
0.999998	1	1	0.9999998	0.9999978	4
1.66334×10^{-6}	1	1	0.9999998	1.6633397×10^{-6}	3
7.39261×10^{-10}	1	1	0.9999998	$7.3926085 \times 10^{-10}$	2
1.84815×10^{-13}	1	1	0.9999998	$1.8481456 \times 10^{-13}$	1
3.36×10^{-7}	1	1	0.9999998	3.359999×10^{-7}	0
1	0	1	0.9999998	0	0
1	1	0	0.9999998	0	0
1	1	1	0	0	0

Multiplying across the rows to obtain the probabilities of each metastate, and multiplying these by the values of the performance parameter in that metastate, we obtain an average performance of 3.9999962. Given the probabilities of the metastates and the values of the performance parameter, we can now go on in the usual way to obtain the standard deviation of the performance, as well as higher moments if desired. Similarly, the table of metastate probabilities *vs.* performance can be used to obtain the cumulative probability performance plot, which describes the viability of the system. Had we not used the idea of metastates and the methods described for short-cutting the calculations, we would have had to calculate some 924 states. As it was, we did the equivalent of calculating 8 states.

6.6. Metastate Arithmetic

The reader may have puzzled over how the dead states in the above example were obtained. While it is rather easy to specify the various performance metastates, the specification of the dead metastates can be tedious if not done in an organized way. Furthermore, it is not difficult to specify metastates in such a way that some states are left out, or some states covered more than once. This cannot be allowed—the metastates must, together, cover each state once and only once. To assure this, we shall introduce a simple kind of metastate arithmetic.

1. *Two metastates can be added if and only if they differ in only one column. The result is the sum of the ranges of the column in which they differ.* Thus,

5–6	5–10	1–3	1–2,

and

4	5–10	1–3	1–2,

can be added to yield

4–6	5–10	1–3	1–2;

but

5–6	5–10	1–3	0

and

5–6	5–10	0	1–2

cannot be added because they differ in more than one column.

2. *Any metastate can be partitioned into two or more metastates one column at a time.* Thus,

5–6	5–10	1–3	1–2

can be partitioned into

5	5–10	1–3	1–2,
6	5–10	1–3	1–2,

which could be further partitioned into

5	5–8	1–3	1–2,
5	9–10	1–3	1–2,
6	5–10	1–2	1–2,
6	5–10	3	1–2.

3. *The complement of a metastate component (but not of a metastate) is the complement of the range of that component.*

Thus, the complement of 5–10 is 0–4; the complement of 2–3 is 0–1; while (in the above example), the complement of 5–8 is 0–4 *and* 9–10.

4. *The sum of the metastates of a system is equal to the full range of each of its components.*

In the above example, we obtain the sum 0–6, 0–10, 0–3, and 0–2, which is the full range. We can see how this is done:

5–6	5–10	1–3	1–2,
4	5–10	1–3	1–2,
3	5–10	1–3	1–2,
2	5–10	1–3	1–2,
0–1	5–10	1–3	1–2,
0–6	0–4	1–3	1–2,
0–6	0–10	0	1–2,
0–6	0–10	0–3	0.

Adding the first four terms, we obtain

2–6	5–10	1–3	1–2,
0–1	5–10	1–3	1–2,
0–6	0–4	1–3	1–2
0–6	0–10	0	1–2,
0–6	0–10	0–3	0.

Adding the resulting first and second terms, we obtain

0–6	5–10	1–3	1–2,
0–6	0–4	1–3	1–2,
0–6	0–10	0	1–2,
0–6	0–10	0–3	0.

Again, adding the first two terms, we obtain

0–6	0–10	1–3	1–2,
0–6	0–10	0	1–2,
0–6	0–10	0–3	0.

Adding yet again, we find

0–6	0–10	0–3	1–2,
0–6	0–10	0–3	0,

and finally

0–6	0–10	0–3	0–2.

This last example shows how we obtained the specification of the dead metastates. We added the states in which there was some performance, and then added (one column at a time) that metastate required to make the next column equal to the full range in each component. We started with

	2–6	5–10	1–3	1–2,	the sum of the performing states.
Added	0–1	5–10	1–3	1–2,	a dead metastate,
to yield	0–6	5–10	1–3	1–2.	
Again we added	0–6	0–4	1–3	1–2,	another dead state,
to yield	0–6	0–10	1–3	1–2.	
Added	0–6	0–10	0	1–2,	a dead state,
to yield	0–6	0–10	0–3	1–2,	
and finally added	0–6	0–10	0–3	0,	the last dead state.

In this way, we developed the various dead states of the system.

The reader should note that, in general, the break-down of the system into performance metastates will differ for each performance parameter. Similarly, there may be several metastates corresponding to each performance level, and the taking of the complement to produce the dead states may be more tedious than shown here. We have found, however, that for a quick evaluation of a typical system, the manual procedure is often adequate.

6.7. Time in Metastates

Not only is the probability of being in a metastate important, but the mean time spent in that metastate is also important. The system may carry a performance penalty function which depends upon the length of stay in that state. Thus, a particular degraded metastate may cause processing delays. If the delay is less than 5 seconds, the system is not penalized. If the delay is between 5 and 15 seconds, a 25% penalty is imposed; if it is between 15 and 60 seconds, a 50% penalty is imposed; and if it is over 60 seconds, no credit is given for performance. Thus, we would have to determine the expected duration in that state as well as its probability. The duration in a degraded state is also important when the degradation leads to queue build-ups. Here the time in the metastate may be used to determine if enough storage has been provided to handle the queues. It may also be used to determine the length of time the system will take to recover once processing is resumed. If the queue build-up during a degraded state is large, and if the system does not have a chance to clean up the queues, it is entirely possible that the system will never recover; that is, it is in a continual backlog situation. In such cases, the average performance could be high, but the system is worthless despite this fact. For this reason, we shall need to determine not only the mean time in a state, but also the mean time for the recurrence of that state.

6.7.1. Border States

A **border state** of a metastate is a submetastate (that is, a portion of a metastate) such that the *failure* or the *repair* of a single subsystem will take the system out of that metastate into another metastate. For example, the metastate

4–4	5–10	1–3	1–2

has the following border states:

4–4	5–10	1–3	1–2	computer DØWN,
4–4	5–10	1–3	1–2	computer UP,
4–4	5–5	1–3	1–2	tape DØWN,
4–4	5–10	1–1	1–2	disc DØWN,
4–4	5–10	1–3	1–1	drum DØWN.

Note that a metastate can be its own border state. Furthermore, the sum of the border states does not necessarily equal the metastate. Calculating the borders of the dead states can be very difficult. It is easier to evaluate the

border of the sum of the processing states.[3] The sum of the processing states
was given as

$$2\text{–}6 \qquad 5\text{–}10 \qquad 1\text{–}3 \qquad 1\text{–}2.$$

Its borders are clearly

1, 1′)	2–2	5–10	1–3	1–2	computer DØWN,
2)	2–6	5–5	1–3	1–2	tape DØWN,
3)	2–6	5–10	1–1	1–2	disc DØWN,
4)	2–6	5–10	1–3	1–1	drum DØWN.

6.7.2. Mean Time in State

The mean time in a metastate x is obtained by evaluating the following
equation:

$$\text{MT}_x = \frac{P_x}{\sum\limits_{B(i)} P_i k_i (\text{MTX}_i)^{-1}} = \frac{P_x}{\sum\limits_{B(i)} (P_i k_i / \text{MTX}_i)}, \tag{18}$$

where

MT_x = mean time in metastate x,

P_x = probability of metastate x as determined in Section 6.5,

P_i = probability of the border metastate in which it is subsystem i
that goes UP or DØWN to make the transition,

k_i = number of subsystems of type i that are available to go UP or
DØWN in that border state to make the transition,

MTX_i = MUT_i if the subsystem goes UP to leave metastate x,

= MDT_i if the subsystem goes DØWN to leave metastate x.

$B(i)$ = indicates summation over all border states.

We can arrange the data in a tableau such as the following to simplify the
calculations as before. For example, the metastate (4–4, 5–10, 1–3, 1–2) has
the following tableau:

Border	Subsystem	UP/DØWN	k_i	P_i	MTX_i	$k_i P_i / \text{MTX}_i$
1	Computer	UP	2	–	1500	–
1′	Computer	DØWN	4	–	0.5	–
2	Tape	DØWN	5	–	0.5	–
3	Disc	DØWN	1	–	1.3	–
4	Drum	DØWN	1	–	1.5	–

[3] However, the border of the sum of the processing states is *not* the border of the dead states.
We can use the border of the processing state sum because the mean time in the dead state is
clearly the mean time to recur of the sum of the processing states, and the mean time to recur
for the dead states is the mean time in the sum of the processing states.

The border state probabilities are calculated as any other metastate probabilities would be. Note that the number of subsystems available to go UP in a metastate are the number that are DØWN, while the number available to go DØWN are the number that are UP. Note also that there are two border conditions for the computers (1 and 1'), corresponding to the case in which the computer goes UP (1) and the case in which it goes DØWN (1').

6.7.3. Mean Time to Recur

The system should be viewed as being in a particular metastate, making a transition to another, and wandering about from metastate to metastate until, at some point, the original one is reached again. We are not only interested in determining how long the system will be in a particular metastate, but how long it is likely to take for the particular metastate to recur. This concept is a generalization of the mean UP time and mean DØWN time for a single subsystem. We would expect that a good state would have a high mean time in state and low mean time to recur. Similarly, poor or dead states should have a low mean time in state and a long mean time to recur. Given any metastate, we can calculate the mean time to recur by the following equation:

$$MR_x = \frac{MT_x(1 - P_x)}{P_x}. \tag{19}$$

Thus, we can define the dead state as the complement of the processing states and evaluate the mean time to recur and mean time in state of the sum of the processing states, to obtain the dead state statistics. Let state x be the metastate corresponding to the sum of the processing metastates, and state y the dead state: then:

$$MR_x = MT_y \quad \text{and} \quad MT_x = MR_y,$$

which is to say that if the system is not processing it has failed, and if it has not failed, it is doing some processing.

6.7.4. Mean Time to Reconfiguration

The decision as to whether to use manual, semiautomatic, or automatic configuration control doctrines will depend upon the mean time to reconfiguration. Thus if a configuration change will occur every 10 days, manual methods might be usable; if a configuration change will occur every 5 minutes, semiautomatic or automatic facilities will have to be provided. For this reason, the mean time to reconfiguration (for either UPward or DØWNward transitions) is an important number. It is evaluated as follows:

$$MTE = \sum_{\substack{all \\ states}} P_s \left[\sum_i \frac{u_{xi}}{MUT_{xi}} + \frac{d_{xi}}{MDT_{xi}} \right]^{-1}, \tag{20}$$

where P_s is the probability of state x, i is the sybsystem index, u_{xi} is the number of subsystems of type i UP in state x, and d_{xi} is the number of subsystems of type i DØWN in state x.

It is fairly clear that we do not wish to calculate this number [as defined in equation (20)]. We would again be faced with the evaluation of an enormous number of states. In practice, the MTE is evaluated by taking the most probable state (everything UP) and evaluating the mean time to reconfiguration, then the next most probable state (the most likely single failure), etc. In general, it will be found that the probabilities and the mean time to reconfiguration for these states converge so quickly that only a dozen or so states actually have to be evaluated. We use the cumulative probability as a check that we have gone far enough.

7. SUMMARY

An accurate determination of the behavior of a system cannot readily be done analytically. At present, it appears that simulation is the only way to do this. However, the answers required for design need not be accurate; in fact, approximations are all that are required. It is only in the final stages of the design that we need, or in fact can formulate, a model that will give us accurate results.

The basic parameter of interest is the system cycle length. It is obtained from the processing times of all processes that are required to service the incident load. The relation between incident load and cycle length is nonlinear. This nonlinearity is basic to a cyclically structured system in which some of the transactions are externally imposed and others are generated by the cycle itself. Furthermore, the equation for the cycle length is also nonlinear, due to the effect of partially subsumable functions.

It is not meaningful to discuss percentage loading of a computer without specifying an acceptable delay level. Clearly, a computer is always 100% loaded, and can execute any reasonable task, given enough memory and elapsed time. Therefore, loading is expressed in terms of either ultimate load (that point at which the delay becomes infinite) or in terms of the maximum loading that still provides the maximum acceptable delay.

The effects of bursts can be approximated in two different ways. If the bursts are relatively sparse, and the system has time to recover before the next one occurs, the load distribution and the cycle length–load curve are used to determine the effect of bursts. If the bursts are not sparse, then a quasi-static approach can be used.

While the cycle length is a rough measure of delay, it may not be adequate for some purposes. If a finer model of the delay is required, a stretch factor can be derived from the known processing time at each priority level, and the queuing time for each process determined separately. The sum of these times plus the time spent waiting for peripheral equipment is an approximation of the transaction delay.

The viability of the system is the weighted sum of the probability of a metastate multiplied by the performance in that state and the penalty function for that performance level. The use of metastates simplifies the viability calculations to the point where realistic systems can be analyzed by hand. In addition to the viability, we can obtain the mean time in a state and the mean time for a given state to recur.

8. PROBLEMS

1. The characterizing equations of a system are

$$U = 0.210LT + 0.0355 + 0.00382LT^2 + 0.00326T^2 + \frac{0.000629L^2T}{0.000829LT + 1} \left[\frac{\text{sec}}{\text{cycle}} \right],$$

$$P = 0.001L + 0.073LT + 0.0117 \left[\frac{\text{sec}}{\text{cycle}} \right],$$

$$S = 0.0379 \left[\frac{\text{sec}}{\text{cycle}} \right],$$

$$M = 0.17151 \text{ [sec]},$$

where

U = sum of the unsubsumable functions,
P = sum of the partially subsumable functions,
S = sum of the totally subsumable functions,
M = ledger elapsed time,
T = a parameter that describes the incident load,
L = cycle length in seconds.

Calculate the value of the cycle length over the range $T = 0$ to $T = 10$.

2. For the example of Problem 1, assume that the maximum allowable delay is equivalent to three cycles and that the above equations are based on a memory cycle time of 2.2 microseconds. How slow a memory could have been used for this application?

3. Using the conditions of Problem 2, determine the maximum ledger elapsed time that would be allowable for each traffic intensity. Do the problem for several different memory speeds.

4. The characterizing equations of a system are

$$U = 0.144LT + 0.1085 + 0.00275LT^2$$

$$P = 0.470LT + 0.03475$$

$$S = 0.040 + 0.00203L$$

$$M = 0.218$$

$$M' = 0.0615$$

where M' is the length of a partial ledger taken every cycle, and M is the length of the major ledger taken every tenth cycle. The minor ledger is not taken when the major ledger is taken. Assume that the allowable delay is proportional to a 1-second cycle. Find the cycle length as a function of the incident load parameter T. Find the minimum memory speed for each load under the assumption that the given equations are based on a memory cycle time of 1 microsecond. Investigate over the range $T = 0$ to $T = 32$.

5. Assume that the system of Problem 4 requires a minimum configuration of three computers: a front-end computer, a rear-end computer, and a common standby. Assume that the load can be distributed uniformly among the on-line computers, and that 10% of each computer's capacity is taken to communicate with each other computer. Front-end computers need only communicate with the rear-end computer. Furthermore, the complex will grow by the addition of front-end computers. The following cost data are provided:

Computer with 1 microsecond memory = \$600,000.
Computer with 500 nanosecond memory = \$800,000.
Ledger memory with 218 millisecond elapsed time = \$400,000.
Ledger memory with 109 millisecond elapsed time = \$600,000.
Ledger memory with 30 millisecond elapsed time = \$950,000.

The ledger elapsed time for the interim ledger goes down proportionately. The complex must have a redundant ledger memory. For each value of the incident load, determine the lowest-cost configuration that will meet the requirements. Consider the possibility of using higher-speed memories *vs.* using more computers. Every computer in the complex must be of the same type, as must the ledger memories.

6. Do Problem 5 under the assumption that the incident load will double every two years, that the initial load is $T = 3$, and that the system is to last for 16 years. A subsystem that is replaced has no scrap value. The cost of changing any one subsystem in the field is \$75,000 per change. Find the schedule of configurations that will minimize the total cost of the system over the 16-year period.

7. Do Problem 6 under the additional assumption that there are three sites, starting with initial loads of $T = 1.5$, 3, and 4, respectively. A unit taken from one site can be used to upgrade another site, paying only the cost of changing (\$75,000) plus \$35,000 for transportation.

8. Redo Problem 6 under the assumption that the cost of a subsystem including transportation and replacement costs will be depreciated on a straight-line basis over the remaining life of the system. Furthermore, assume that any outstanding cash value will be loaded with compound interest of 2% per quarter on the remaining unamortized value of the complex.

9. Assume a penalty function of the form

$$V = 0.5 + 0.8e^{-0.5L}.$$

Ignore the realistic problems that will occur as a result of shifting the load from one computer to another. The minimum viable configuration consists of two computers and a ledger memory. Assume the following statistics for the subsystems:

	MTBF	MTTR
Computer	1400 hours	0.75 hour
Ledger memory	800 hours	1.25 hours

Find a configuration for each value of T or for ranges of values of T that maximize the expected performance as measured by the expected value of V. Find that configuration for which V/C is maximized, where C is the total cost of the complex. Use the data of Problems 4 and 5.

10. Redo Problem 6 with the additional assumptions of Problem 9.

11. Redo Problem 8 with the additional assumptions of Problem 9.

12. The mean time in metastate and the mean time to recur for a system are given below. Metastates 1 and 2 were respectively split into metastates 1A, 1B, 2A, 2B, to reflect the behavior with respect to different performance parameters. Consider metastate 1. The mean time in state is 253 years, but the mean times in its constituent submetastates are only 93.6 and 1.15 hours, respectively. No errors have been made in these calculations. Explain these phenomena.

Metastate	Mean time in state		Mean time to recur	
1	253.1	years	0.335	hour
1A	93.6	hours	0.576	hour
1B	1.15	hours	93.6	hours
2	4.5	minutes	506.5	years
2A	4.5	minutes	512.4	years
2B	4.45	minutes	39,001	years
10 (dead state)	0.339	hour	337	years

13. In Problem 13 of Chapter 12 you proved that the expected delay for the completion of redundant writing to N drums was $N/(N + 1)$ revolutions. Consider now reading those drums. The read operation is complete as soon as the first redundant copy has been fetched, whereupon the other corresponding read instructions are aborted. Prove that the expected delay is $1/(N + 1)$ revolutions, thereby proving the following law:

The sum of the read and write delays for redundant transactions to N drums is one revolution independent of the number of drums.

Which is to say, "you can't win."

14. (*Continuation.*) If more than one copy of an average block must be fetched from the storage ensemble, you can win. Do Problem 13 under the assumption that the average block will be fetched k times (ignoring the redundancies in the initial writing or the aborted read operations). The read transactions occur randomly and are sparse for any one block. That is, you cannot take advantage of the potential multiple copies that may be fetched during a given read operation. Derive a new law relating the sum of the read and write delays to k and N. For what values of $k \geq 1.0$ can delays be reduced by using redundant writes and aborted reads?

15. (*Continuation.*) Assume that each drum costs 1 unit. Let N and k be defined as in Problem 14. Let V be a value factor inversely proportional to the sum of the read and write delays (i.e., $V = a/D$, where a is proportionality constant). Derive a trade relation between V, N, k, and a, showing the range of values for which it pays to use redundant drums to improve the delay.

9. REFERENCES

1. Acton, Forman S., *Numerical Methods That* (*Usually*) *Work*, Harper and Row, New York, 1970.

   A delightful book on practical numerical methods presuming little in the way of formal mathematics. Readable, cogent, thorough, and practical. The slant is toward computers. Much practical information and nitty-gritty on numerical problems. A few typos may be misleading.

2. Anderson, Donald E., "Reliability of a Special Class of Redundant Systems," *IEEE Transactions on Reliability*, Volume R-18, Number 1, Institute of Electrical and Electronics Engineers, Inc., February, 1969, pp. 21–28.

   This paper deals with a special case in which the system is either UP or DOWN and has only one unit type. The wrinkle here is that the system is needed only for very short intervals of time compared to the time it is on standby. The question investigated is whether the system will be available when needed. Many useful charts are presented.

3. Einhorn, Sheldon J., and Plotkin, Morris, "Reliability Predictions for Degradable and Non-Degradable Systems," TR-ESD-TDR-63-642 Electronic Systems Division, Air Force Systems Command, USAF, Hanscom Field, Mass. Also, Defense Document Center, AD-426 087.

Einhorn, Sheldon J., "Reliability Prediction for Repairable Redundant Systems," *Proceedings of the IEEE*, Volume 51, Number 2, February, 1963, pp. 312–317, Institute of Electrical and Electronics Engineers, Inc.

These papers contain the derivation on which the computation technique for viability presented here is based.

Chapter 14

IMPLEMENTATION

> *"A very complete and metaphysical answer,"* said she.
> *"Seeing 'tis given on my side, I'll let it stand without*
> *question; though (to be honest) I cannot tell what the dickens*
> *it means."*
>
> E. R. EDDISON
> Lady Fiorinda, *Mistress of Mistresses*

1. SYNOPSIS

Just as the construction of a bridge is not merely a question of the shape of the finished bridge, the construction of a computer complex is not merely a question of how the hardware and software are put together. The bridge needs footings, approaches, and a complete logistics plan. Similarly, the complex is viewed as a sequence of interdependent acts, procedures, personnel, and facilities that results in the operational complex.

The typical procurement cycle for a computer complex is discussed here, as well as the kinds of purchasing policies that may be used. The physical construction of the complex and the way the old complex is phased out and the new one phased in are also topics of this chapter. The personnel required to bring all this about and the way that personnel is controlled are considered.

2. THE PROCUREMENT CYCLE

A period of four to five years may elapse from the initial recognition that a complex is needed to the time that the complex starts doing useful work. Of this time, assuming that competent persons are engaged throughout, only two to three years may be required for the actual construction of the complex. The total period from conception to operation is termed the **procurement cycle** of the complex.

2.1. The Procurement Cycle

Most complexes follow a sequence of events starting with an initial study of the job that the complex is to do, and proceeding through specification, competitive bids, evaluation of the bids, awarding of a contract, and construction of the complex, to testing and finally operating it.

2.1.1. Initial Study

The initial study, or, as it is sometimes called, the **feasibility study**, is intended to justify the complex within the buyer's organization. The questions answered by the initial study are:

1. Is the complex feasible?
2. Is it economically justified?
3. Is it operationally justified?
4. Are there intangible justifications?
5. What is it likely to cost?
6. How long will it take?
7. What will our operation be like when it is all done?
8. What is the next step beyond this complex?
9. What are the alternatives to this complex?
10. What are the contingency plans if something goes wrong before the complex is finished?

○ *Feasibility*

Technical feasibility is rarely a question. There are few jobs for which a complex cannot be constructed at some cost. It is only in the more advanced areas of computer application such as military systems, pattern recognition problems, artificial intelligence, and space exploration, that technical feasibility is questioned. More often the job is technically feasible, but the cost is not justifiable.

Feasibility may be more than a question of technology or economics. It may be a question of internal politics, departmental jurisdiction, local, state, national, or international government regulations, the attitudes of unions, and so on. A simple technical scheme may require changes in government regulatory agency policies, such as allowing a common carrier to do data processing, or a bank to do data processing for its clients. Perhaps the problem is simply that of obtaining a zoning variance so that the complex may be constructed at a particular site. Feasibility can be a question of obtaining qualified personnel to run the site—not a problem in a major city, but perhaps a problem in the Kalahari desert, at the South Pole, or on the moon.

The initial study must be addressed to the answers of all such feasibility questions, providing either an unhesitating "yes," a "yes—but" (with associated costs required to get rid of the buts), or an unqualified "no." The initial study itself may be done in two stages, the first carried out by the buyer and the second carried out by a consulting organization. If the project is expensive or crucial (e.g., a computer complex for an ABM system), the study may be done independently by several organizations, with the user obtaining a consensus.

There are several advantages to using a consulting organization for the initial study. A competent organization provides technical expertise that may not be available in the user's organization. More important, the consulting firm is objective. In most government procurements, the consulting organization is not allowed to participate in the construction of the complex except to monitor those organizations that do the implementation. In commercial procurements, the consulting organization and the implementing organization may be related or may be the same. There is a distinct disadvantage to having the feasibility study performed by the equipment supplier, though this practice is widespread. The objectivity of the supplier is open to question. There may be biases or pressures within the supplier's organization to specify the largest complex, rather than the smallest that will do the job. There is also reluctance to recommend the equipment of another vendor if it should happen to be superior.

○ *Economic Justification*

Economic justification, when available, is the strongest justification now in use. The most common errors made in such economic justifications are to ignore the following items: operating costs, maintenance costs, training costs, depreciation, residual value of the old complex that is being replaced, the cost of the procurement cycle, the return had the cost of the complex been invested elsewhere, and the risks involved in the procurement. When all of these costs are taken into account, most economical justifications are marginal. More often than not, the initial attempt to justify the complex is economical, but the final justification is operational or intangibly related to economics.

○ *Operational Justification*

The complex may be justified despite adverse economics. It may be that the complex will perform functions that cannot be done by older means because the older means will no longer be available (for example, the functions to be performed by the complex might have been done by equipment that is no longer being manufactured or serviced). It may reduce floor space or other facilities that can be better used for other purposes. It may provide information and services not feasible by other means, but to which specific values cannot be directly attributed. It may be required because the industry has adopted certain standards that can only be met through the use of a computer (e.g., sorting bulk mail in zip code order in order to qualify for lower postal rates, credit card billing, securities exchange paper work, etc.).

○ *Intangible Justifications*

The operational justifications described above are midway between the more tangible economic justification and the clearly intangible justifications described in this section. There are any number of reasons for implementing a complex. In one way or another, they are tied to the ultimate profitability of the buyer—but that tie may be indirect. The buyer may go into a complex simply because his competitors have and his customers associate computers with progress. The use of a computer complex may have publicity value far exceeding the directly tangible value of the complex: "the computer banking service," "your automated insurance company," "let our computer optimize your investment program," "computer-designed windshield wipers," "computer analysis proves that three out of four virgin tea tasters . . . ," etc. It is important not to equate "intangible" with "unreal." An intangible benefit is real, but cannot be given numerical value.

While a consulting organization or an architect can aid the user in obtaining economic justification, the justification based on the operational and intangible value of the complex is more properly done by the user because that justification will require information that the buyer may be reluctant to distribute outside of his organization.

○ *Costs and Schedules*

A properly conducted study will include cost and implementation schedule data. In both cases there are two types of numbers: the desirable and the achievable. There is the cost which the buyer would like to pay and the cost for which the vendor is willing to build the complex. Typically, the desired cost is an underestimate. Similarly, there is a desired schedule (18 months) and a feasible schedule (36 months). Cost and schedule are often underestimated because the user is more likely to overlook cost-producing and time-consuming factors than is the vendor or the consultant. The latter, having both been burned by similar underestimates, should have learned where the hidden time and dollars are.

Three sources can be used to obtain this information, and it is desirable to use all three. The buyer can make preliminary estimates. These in turn can be verified or refined by a consultant. A third source of estimates is the potential vendor. Most vendors will cooperate when told that a nonbinding estimate is required. Several potential vendors can be queried and the results compared. It is advantageous to have a consultant request an independent estimate of the same vendors that are queried directly. The consultant can do this without divulging the identity of the client. Sometimes the differences in the cost and time estimates are revealing.

○ *Impact and Alternatives*

The complex cannot be viewed outside of the organizational entity in which it will function. It will also be only the first step in a sequence of complexes that will be replaced every ten or so years. As such, it represents a continued, never-ending commitment rather than the isolated purchase of a single system. The commitment is usually large. It may create or destroy departments, change procedures, and certainly affect the budget.

There are many reasons why a computer complex can fail. Even if the work has been done competently, changes in the organization may require that the complex be abandoned prior to its completion, or in the early part of its life. Perhaps the capital is no longer available; a merger of organizations makes the complex unnecessary; the vendor is bankrupted; or some other unforeseen circumstance dictates the desirability of stopping the project. At every stage in the projected life of the complex, the consequences of being without it should be evaluated. This means determining what it would take to do the job, or to go back to doing things the way they were done prior to the implementation. If the effect is minor, the complex is probably not needed. In all cases where the total elimination of the complex is a possibility, or where a major change in the schedule or cost could have an effect on the desirability of the complex, a contingency plan should be drafted to cover that possibility. Thus, the effect of a 50%, 100%, and 200% increase in costs should be examined. The effect of inflation should be determined. The possibility of strikes or other events that could affect the delivery schedule should be explored.

Contingency plans should not be carried to extremes lest a never-ending study be initiated. They should be generic (cost, delay, elimination) rather than specific (2% increase in memory price, 37 day delay in shipping unit X, water in the basement). Furthermore, they should be tempered by the scope of the catastrophe for which they are formed.

2.1.2. Specification

The result of a study is a set of conclusions and recommendations. The conclusions specify what is to be expected for the complex, and the recommendations specify a course of action required to achieve those benefits. A specification is a document sufficiently well conceived to allow a vendor to quote firm prices and delivery dates. It should be a *pro forma* contract.

The ideal specification is functional, not biased toward any vendor or approach. One of the more common errors made in specifications is that the specifier unintentionally prejudges the solution by being overly concerned with specific technical approaches. The more constrained the mechanization, the less likely is the buyer to obtain the benefits of original thinking on the part of the vendor.

However, an unbiased specification is not loose. While a functional specification may allow freedom in implementation, there need be no doubt as to what must be done and when. Thus, one can specify file sizes, transaction delays, transaction throughput, and other performance parameters of interest, without saying that the file will be stored in such a way on a particular model number of a device. The specification is not the design of the system—it is a benchmark document by which the actual or proposed design will be judged.

Writing a specification is not trivial. It may require a few man-years of effort. If several vendors are to be involved (say, for the complex, software, terminals, communication lines, etc.), the interface and contractual responsibilities of each kind of vendor must be specified. Consulting firms can be useful in helping to write a specification because they have done more of it than the typical buyer, have evaluated more proposals, and may have written more proposals by virtue of acting as consultants to both vendors and builders.

It is often beneficial to all parties concerned to officially "leak" a preliminary copy of the specification as well as selected portions of the study. This will give the vendor more time to study the problem without being formally committed to price and schedules. The reaction of the potential vendors to the preliminary specification may help to write the final specification. It can also narrow the field to the serious potential vendors. The initial study may take three to nine months. The preliminary specification can take a similar amount of time. It will take a vendor at least two months to respond to a specification even if he has had a copy of the preliminary specifications. In all, if the time allows it, the vendor should be given four to six months to study the preliminary specification and come back with his comments. He should be made aware of (roughly) how much money has been allocated to the project and what the expected delivery schedule will be. He should be told about planned follow-on and expansions. Within the restrictions of the buyer's organizational privacy, the vendor should know as much as possible about the immediate and long-range intentions for the complex.

2.1.3. Evaluation

A clear, well written, and complete specification is lengthy. If it is sent to all possible vendors, there may be two dozen or more proposals to evaluate. This can be an overwhelming burden on the buyer.[1] Someone will

---

[1] The following story is *not* apocryphal. An agency, having created a masterful specification, distributed it to many vendors. Each vendor was required to submit much detailed information

have to evaluate those proposals. Each proposal should be given due consideration, as it may have required many man-years of effort to produce. To this end, formal evaluation criteria should be included in the specification. That is, the specification should state that so many points will be given for such and such a level of performance, for initial costs, for operating costs, for viability, etc. The vendor should, in principle, be able to grade himself as well as the competition. If the ideal is achieved, the buyer, the vendor, and a competitor would arrive at the same number of points for any given proposal.

Each vendor should be required to submit a detailed cross-reference index between his proposal and the specification. This is an important convenience, if not a necessity, for the evaluator. It also assures the vendor that the critical points of his proposal will not be overlooked because someone did not read a footnote. If evaluation criteria and cross-references are not provided, the evaluator will not be able to give each proposal the attention it deserves. The result will be that a well considered study and a careful specification will be vitiated by a cursory examination of the proposals.

2.1.4. Negotiations

It is not likely that any vendor will bid exactly what is asked for. Each proposal will offer some things that are better and others that are not as good as that which was required. Furthermore, the very fact that the buyer has examined several different proposals will make him want to change the specification. Thus, while he is interested in purchasing the system from vendor X, vendors Y and Z, though unacceptable, have desirable features in their systems that are not proposed by X. Negotiations may also be required to achieve the optimum system among the varied options offered by the bidders.

The buyer may have a staff that can be used to develop the system. Who will have responsibility for what, what documents and subsidiary specifications will be provided by whom and when, what kinds of reports will be produced, and what intermediate benchmarks are to be reached may all be part of the precontract negotiations. Precontract negotiations can last two to four months. In some cases, construction of the complex is initiated before the negotiations are over.

---

in standard form. Each vendor was also invited to submit as many alternate proposals as he wished. The procurement was large and attractive. The result was that the typical single copy of each of the ten or so vendor's proposal stretched about six feet. To make matters worse, the buyer had requested 50 copies of each proposal. On bid opening day, truck after truck loaded with the requisite number of copies arrived at the buyer's office. He was inundated with proposals to the point where concern was expressed over the permissible floor loading.

The immediate intention of these negotiations is to bring all technical, financial, and jurisdictional questions to the point where lawyers can write a contract that will be acceptable to both parties. The ultimate intention is to eliminate as many surprises as possible. Neither the bidder nor the buyer should have to say, "but you didn't tell us about that," at some later time. For all the hard-headedness that may be displayed at the negotiating table, it should be looked upon as a mutual effort in which the vendor achieves a fair profit and the buyer fair value. In most cases, the real purpose of the initial specification and the formal proposal is to decide who to negotiate with.

2.1.5. Contracts

Contracts are for lawyers, not technicians. The technician's role in the formation of the contract is to make the lawyer aware of potentially dangerous situations, of contingencies arising out of peculiarities of the procurement, and of other technical factors that may result in cost or schedule changes. The legal staffs on both sides of the table will be adept at fixing financial responsibilities, penalties for default, standard contingencies, etc. The technician should no more play at law than the lawyer at system design. The technical staffs of both sides should have the opportunity to review the final contract prior to signing.

2.1.6. Construction

By "construction" we mean all those activities required to achieve a working complex. These include hardware design and construction, software, system analysis and design, site preparation, testing, in fact the activities described in the previous chapters. Other aspects of the construction schedule are discussed in Section 3 below.

2.1.7. Acceptance Testing

At some point, the buyer must be convinced that the complex works as planned, that it is in fact the complex contracted for or a reasonable facsimile thereof. Typically, the vendor(s) will be asked to conduct a formal demonstration of that operation prior to the completion of the contract. The acceptance test is that demonstration. The system must be tested under a variety of conditions that may never occur. It may or may not be possible to test it with live data. If the designers have used a well conceived functional testing procedure, it can be a sufficient acceptance test. Thus, the vendor may write his own acceptance test. Clearly, there are some dangers associated with this.

While it is not advisable to blindly accept the vendor's proposed acceptance test, it is important to keep the acceptance test reasonable.

It is not difficult to specify a combination of conditions such that the execution of the test would take longer than the expected lifetime of the system (for example, require the system to go through every possible configuration under every possible simulated failure; demonstrate all extreme conditions simultaneously, etc.). Acceptance testing is heuristic. That is, it is over when both parties are satisfied that the system works properly, that the ability to meet the major performance criteria has been demonstrated, and that every functional requirement of the system has been met. An overly ambitious acceptance test may not prove anything, may be nothing more than a replay of the functional testing, and in any case will be paid for by the buyer.

2.1.8. Operations

Operation is what the complex is built for. Generally, the operation of the complex will initially be poorer than it will be after a few months. For one thing, everybody is playing with the system, and for another, the operators and users are still unfamiliar with it. This initial phase of operation may last three to six months. After the novelty has worn off, the system begins to do useful work.

2.1.9. Enhancements

After the system has stabilized and been thoroughly probed, deficiencies in the original specification and/or in the design may become apparent. Hopefully these are minor. Occasionally, major improvements will be possible. Sometimes after the first year of operation enhancements may be attempted, each resulting in a better system. These enhancements continue throughout the life of the complex. New functional requirements that come about, changes in the assumed load statistics, major improvements in hardware units, discovered bugs, all lead to such modifications. Each enhancement, whether done in-house or by the vendor, should go through a miniature version of the entire procurement cycle; for, just as the complex itself, it is only a minor enhancement to a much larger operation.

2.2. Procurement Policies

2.2.1. Negotiated Contracts

The most common form of commercial procurement is a negotiated contract. The first several phases of the procurement cycle may be done informally (but not necessarily carelessly), resulting in the selection of a vendor. In fact, competitive bidding may not be used at all, the vendor being selected for reasons having nothing to do with the design of the complex: for example, compatibility requirements across several divisions of an organization may dictate a particular vendor; the vendor may be a department in the buyer's organization; there may be no other capable vendor; political or overall economical considerations may disqualify certain vendors or favor others. Whatever the reasons, negotiations become increasingly important as the scope of possible suppliers is narrowed. The tightest negotiations are required if there is only one vendor.

2.2.2. Cost Plus Fixed Fee (CPFF)

The vendor agrees to supply the complex or parts thereof for an estimated cost and a guaranteed fixed profit. The submitted cost is not firm. It is only an estimate. This kind of contract carries the least risk to the supplier and the greatest to the buyer. No matter how high the overrun, the supplier is guaranteed his profit. A CPFF contract is most open to abuse on the part of the vendor; he may deliberately bid low in order to get the contract. A CPFF contract is used for large systems that cannot be clearly specified, and systems that involve unpredictable costs, research, and software. The CPFF contract is appropriate where the risks to the vendor are too high to allow him to take the contract on any other basis. The system bought under a CPFF contract tends to be late, overly expensive, and very elegant.

2.2.3. Fixed Price

The opposite extreme of the CPFF contract is the fixed price contract. The vendor agrees to supply the system at a fixed price. Should the cost be higher than anticipated, the vendor may lose his profit or his shirt. Should the costs be lower, the vendor may make a handsome profit. The vendor's risk is maximized as is his profit. The bidder's risk is minimized, as is the system's performance. The fixed price system tends to be on time, and stripped bare. A vendor's willingness to undertake a fixed price contract in what appears to be a CPFF situation is indicative of either superior knowledge of the problems or extreme ignorance thereof—and the buyer had better know which.

2.2.4. Incentive Contracts

One of the more equitable forms of contracts that tends to minimize both the bidder's and the buyer's risk is the incentive contract. It is a CPFF contract with a wrinkle. If the costs should go above the agreed figure, it will be taken out of the fee according to some predetermined schedule, possibly ending in penalties for extreme overruns. If the costs should go below the predicted values, the fee is increased to the point where the savings are distributed equally between the buyer and the vendor. The incentive contract provides a strong inducement to the vendor to produce the system at the lowest possible costs, while protecting both parties against unforeseen contingencies.

2.2.5. Two-Step Procurement

This is a form of procurement that may result in a CPFF, fixed price, or incentive contract. The bidding proceeds in three steps (despite the fact that it is called a "two-step" procedure). In the first step, potential vendors are asked to submit a technical proposal without regard to cost. These proposals are evaluated and a number of qualified vendors selected. That is, agreement is reached within the buyer's organization that any one of these vendors could do the job.

The second step is a negotiation and equalization step. This is carried out among all the vendors that qualified in the first step. Desirable features not found in some systems are made mandatory for all bidders. Options offered by some vendors are eliminated from further consideration. The result is a more detailed specification on which all vendors have agreed to submit quotations.

The third step consists of a price quotation for the revised specification. All negotiations having been completed beforehand and all bidders having been found equally acceptable, the contract is awarded to the lowest bidder.

2.2.6. Variations

Any specific procurement is a variation on the above themes. Individual contracts may carry penalties for late deliveries or bonuses for early deliveries. Various kinds of incentives may be provided. The idea behind all such variations is to achieve an equitable apportionment of the supplier's and the buyer's risks, and of the cost and profit.

2.3 Disbursement of Responsibilities

2.3.1. What Is to Be Supplied?

A physical facility to house the complex must be constructed or converted to the purpose. That facility includes the computer room, maintenance areas, offices, power plant, communication equipment room, rest rooms, vaults, filing space, storage for consumable supplies, etc. Except for the specialized power, air conditioning, and flooring peculiar to computer installations, the establishment of a physical facility is no different than setting up an office or other work area. There are the usual decisions and problems of decorating, furniture is to be purchased, delivered, and assembled, telephones are to be installed, security equipment has to be installed, etc.

The computer complex itself and its associated peripheral equipment must be installed and tested. Operating personnel must be hired and trained, as must maintenance personnel. Even if the complex itself were a routine system, requiring no special design effort—that is, if it could be purchased in its entirety as a package from the vendor—setting up the mechanical and human facility is a major logistic undertaking.

2.3.2. Turnkey Procurement

The simplest procedure from the point of view of the buyer is a **turnkey procurement**. The buyer contracts with a single vendor to install a working complex in a given location, with all personnel properly trained for the operation of the complex. All the headaches, hardware, software, training, and logistics are left to the vendor. While the vendor may subcontract portions of the job, the prime responsibility is his. This approach, while the simplest, is also the most costly. It is called a "turnkey" procurement because the operation is reminiscent of a car salesman "turning the key over to the buyer" when the car is ready, or a real estate agent "turning the key over to the new homeowner."

The advantages to the buyer are many. There is only one supplier to deal with. That supplier has presumably had much experience in solving similar installation problems. This can or should reduce the cost. The buyer does not have to mass a large specialized staff that will not be useful after the complex is in operation. Should something not work out, the buyer has a single set of penalty clauses to invoke. Whether or not the vendor will in turn sue his suppliers is not the buyer's concern. The advantages to the vendor are no less attractive. The vendor has control over the whole situation and need not rely on the vagaries of some third party. As a prime contractor, he will receive discounts from his subcontractors, which are then marked up to the advertised price. The commission received goes partly for the additional engineering and liaison required to handle a larger number of subcontractors, and partly into increased profits.

The disadvantage to the buyer other than a possible higher price is that there will be a larger single cash outlay. There will be fewer opportunities to make use of a possibly competent internal staff. The total risk, should things not work out, is also greater. The prime contractor's risk is also increased. He might have produced a serviceable building but not get paid because a minor piece of software is not working yet. His total cash outlay is greatly increased. The staff that he must commit to the project is greater, thereby reducing the ability to respond to possibly more attractive opportunities with another buyer.

While turnkey systems have been occasionally implemented in which the prime contractor has the complete responsibility of converting an empty lot into a working complex, this degree of responsibility is rare. More often than not, the buyer will separately contract for the physical facility (the building and such) and make the prime contractor responsible for getting a working complex. This division occurs because there may be an adequate building available, because the new complex is to replace one that already exists, or, more often, because the complex is to be installed as a showpiece in a much larger building that already exists. In such cases, the vendor will be asked to submit his bid on the basis of facts about the physical facilities that are presented in the specification.

Another area not normally included in a turnkey procurement is the communication lines. These are usually supplied by a common carrier. Leasing private lines from the common carrier may be part of a broader communication system that includes voice, facsimile, Telex, or other forms of communication that have nothing to do with the complex.

2.3.3. Separate Procurements

The opposite extreme of the turnkey procurement is a separate procurement for every part of the system. The buyer separately contracts for CPUs, memories, tapes, discs, flooring, lights, plumbing, software, file cabinets, etc. If he has the staff to do this, he may be able to obtain the system at a minimal cost. There is a disadvantage in that he will probably not be able to obtain the standard discount from the suppliers. The analogy to building your own home is apt. While there will be cash savings, the normal discount that the builder gets will not be available. In separate procurements, the whole headache and responsibility will be the buyer's. Few vendors will be willing to guarantee the suitability of their part of the complex to the task for which it is intended. Thus, the hardware manufacturer will guarantee that the equipment will be capable of executing so many instructions per second, but will not guarantee the ability of the system to perform its assigned tasks. After all, the software might be bad, the communications inadequate, etc. Similarly, the software manufacturer will guarantee the logical integrity of the programs as run within the specified configuration, but not necessarily that they will do the job. After all the CPU might be slower than promised, the lines inadequate, the operators unqualified, etc.

This kind of approach is not feasible unless the buyer either has or can obtain the requisite staff of specialists. If that staff must be hired, and the buyer is not likely to build several such complexes, the whole approach may be untenable. Large corporations and government agencies are the only ones with a continuing need for such a resident staff.

One error commonly made by buyers seeking to obtain the advantages of a separate procurement is to staff the project with what will eventually be operating personnel. This is like manning a ship with marine architects or a construction crew with maintenance personnel. Both jobs are spoiled.

The temperaments and knowledge of operating personnel and design personnel are different. The designer gets bored with operations and will leave when the project is over, while the operator lacks the skills to do a proper design.

2.3.4. Architectural Firms

A systems architecture firm can be used to advantage in procuring a large-scale computer complex. The architectural firm can obtain the trade discounts and thereby achieve an optimal blend of competitors' equipment. The specialized staff is there and need be used only for the duration of the contract. Once the system is working, the specialized staff is no longer a liability. Such firms can also provide complete turnkey systems. This approach has worked in other fields such as in constructing buildings, chemical processing plants, and factories.

The principal disadvantages are financial. The architectural firm may not be able to finance the large complex. If the design is bad, the company can fold, leaving nothing to collect penalties from. In other words, though the buyer's gain can be high, the risk is proportionally higher as well.

One way out of this problem is to retain the architectural firm as a consultant. In this capacity, the buyer still acts as his own prime contractor but depends upon the consultant to supply the temporarily required expertise. The consultant also monitors the subcontractors, performs liaison functions, and arbitrates disputes. In other words, the consultant acts on the behalf of the buyer as the prime contractor, but without the responsibility or additional profit.

2.4. Who Pays?

One might naively assume that the buyer pays for the system. While this is ultimately true, in practice there are several ways of purchasing, each with its advantages and disadvantages.

2.4.1. Direct Purchasing

A direct purchase is just that. Whether the complex is bought from one vendor as a turnkey system or assembled from separate purchases, the buyer pays cash on the barrel upon satisfactory delivery. The principal advantages of this kind of financing is the low total cost. Assuming that the functions of the complex are frozen, are initially correct, and that flexibility is not important, there is no less expensive way to buy the system. The principal disadvantages are the high initial cost. The complex might represent a sum of money that could be put to better uses. If the cash must be borrowed from a bank (as it often must), the interest cost tends to erode the lower cost of the direct purchase. If the requirements of the complex are only approximate and there is a likelihood that it will be rapidly obsolete, the financial risk of a direct purchase may not be attractive. Leasing is a way out of this problem.

2.4.2. Direct Leasing

The buyer leases the complex from the prime contractor. The prime contractor then finances the complex. While this is often done for a commercial installation that has predictable residual value, it is not usually done for a dedicated complex. If the complex is highly specialized, having been assembled from several different manufacturers' hardware, it may not be possible to obtain a single lease. Furthermore, since software and system design have little or no resale value, these items are not included in any but a total facility lease from a single vendor. The proclivity toward leasing on the buyer's part is a hedge against uncertainty—the uncertainty that the system will be inadequate or overly large at some point in the future. The proclivity toward leasing on the vendor's part is based on his estimation of the probable residual value of the complex at each point in its life and the probability that the lease will or will not be renewed.

2.4.3. Third-Party Leasing

This is a purely financial arrangement, with the leasing company taking over the responsibility of financing the complex. The third-party leasing company buys the complex from the vendor or vendors and then leases it to the buyer. The vendor benefits by making a cash sale and not having to worry about residual value or the termination of the lease. The buyer benefits by having flexibility, the ability to terminate the lease, and having the cash available for other activities. It is interesting to note that the leasing company may actually lease the system at a lower rate than would the prime contractor. It would seem then that the leasing company has bought all the headaches and lost the advantages.

The lease is estimated on the basis of initial costs, the cost of borrowing the money to finance the complex, and as usual the expected residual value as represented in an extension of the lease. The lease might be for a period of five years, during which time the leasing firm will recoup a major part (say, 80%) of its investment. The equipment is carried on the books of the leasing firm as an asset—it is in fact an income-producing asset. This allows the leasing company to obtain public financing (effectively a zero interest loan) to cover the purchase cost of the complex. The leasing company, given an initial bootstrap by a consortium of friendly banks, can start on a cycle of expanding business, leading to more leases, therefore to more public confidence, and therefore to a higher price for its stock on the market.

The result is that the leasing firm shows enormous growth and high initial earnings.[2] The successful leasing companies have used the large financial base obtained through computer leasing to embark upon an aggressive campaign of mergers and acquisitions into less ephemeral businesses such as real estate, oil wells, or insurance. If the second leases do not materialize, the new business areas will cover the loss. In fact, the failure of the second leases of the computers could be a useful tax loss for the more substantial aspects of the business. The lease of a computer complex from the point of view of the leasing firm is a financial arrangement, made more palatable to the buyer of the stock because of the glamour associated with computers. In the long run, the leasing of computers by a third party will be regulated by the emergence of sound amortization policies and methods for establishing residual values such as now prevail for automobiles, buildings, and aircraft.

2.4.4. Facilities Management

In this arrangement, the total responsibility is taken by the facilities management firm. The facilities management firm is the prime contractor, the financier, and the operator of the complex. In principle, facilities management is not new. It is supplied for office buildings, catering services, communications, and many other functions required in a modern business. The buyer, perhaps having made an abortive attempt to construct or run his own complex, or perhaps by observing the failure of an admired competitor at the same task, turns the whole problem over to a facilities management firm. That firm then guarantees to supply the services rendered by the complex on a certain date over a period of time. If the equipment should become obsolete, fail, or be damaged by some catastrophe, it is the facilities management firm's concern and not the buyer. The buyer has no specialized employees and can go about the business of manufacturing air conditioners, or toys, or whatever his real business is. He pays for this peace of mind, while the facilities management firm is amply rewarded for its services. After all, one man's headache is the aspirin seller's source of income.

3. THE CONSTRUCTION CYCLE

3.1. Sites and Facilities

A computer complex is rarely installed by merely placing the equipments in an unmodified existing area. The preparation of the site can be costly. The site cost is the largest part of the installation costs. However, from the time that the complex is conceived to the time that it is in operation, several different facilities, with associated costs, will be needed.

---

[2] The earnings of the leasing company can be readily adjusted by an appropriate choice of amortization policies.

3.1.1. Sites

A large complex is often installed not once, but twice or three times. A typical complex, intended for multiple installations will go through a **prototype site**, a **staging site**, and a **final site**.

○ *Prototype Site*

This is the original engineering site, in which the majority of bugs and design deficiencies will be worked out. It is designed to accommodate or to test the worst-case installation and configuration problems. It is here that the previously incompatible units will be mated, required design changes incorporated, and hardware–software interactions examined. Because of delivery problems of some items, this site may not have all the units that the various final sites will have. Consequently, some problems may be worked out with "almost equivalent" units. The final solution of such problems may have to await staging or final installation.

○ *Staging Site*

In a multiple procurement of a computer complex, each installation may be completely assembled on the factory floor and tested prior to shipping. This is called the **staging site**. After the staged complex has been debugged, with all the facilities available at the factory, it will be disassembled, crated, and shipped for final installation. Staging is intended to bring the system closer to the real problems that may be encountered. In a single complex procurement, the prototype and staging sites may be the same.

○ *Final Site*

This is the site at which the complex will reside. Since it is electrically and environmentally different from the prototype site and far removed from the mystical beneficial influence of the design engineers and "home office" maintenance technicians, a host of new problems will occur. Debugging these problems can often take several weeks, despite the very careful attention that may have been paid during staging. Occasionally the staging site is dismantled and the complex shipped before debugging has been completed. This may occur when the schedule has slipped. The contention presumably is that the user will be less annoyed with a nonworking complex on his premises than with a nonworking complex at the factory. This practice is to be avoided, as shipping creates its own malfunctions, making it more difficult to distinguish between the shipping-induced problems and those which are inherent in the configuration. The final site is also the first place where the software can be tested in its entirety, with real inputs and outputs, rather than with simulated data. Final-site debugging, therefore, is often accompanied by a largish crew of engineers and programmers. They will require more room, far more room, than will the operating personnel. Such facilities must be as close as possible to the site; otherwise we shall find programmers working in their hotel rooms and in the cafeteria, or using the console as a desk, all of which contributes to increased debugging time.

3.1.2. Site Facilities

The final site must provide power, air conditioning, heat, light, humidity control, floors, subfloors, maintenance areas, storage for tapes, discs, cards, paper, filing cabinets, toilets, lounges, reception areas, room for expansion, office space for operating and software maintenance personnel, operating records, etc. The job of preparing it is one that should be done as a cooperative effort of a site engineer, a building architect, and an interior decorator. The cost of a tasteful or even elaborately beautiful site is minuscule compared to the cost of the complex. If someone has paid 2 to 4 million dollars for the thing, he is entitled to some aesthetic gratification.

3.1.3. Other Facilities

The equipment is built in a factory. This implies many thousands of square feet of floor space. The design of that area is almost completely out of the control of the architect. A successful manufacturer, with an eye toward maximizing his productivity, will build a serviceable factory. If the factory is not up to standard, there will undoubtedly be complaints from the unions involved. It is not unusual to find that the construction of several complexes of a given type, or that of a large single complex, will impose a major temporary increase in the required factory space. The logistics of the complex's construction—the relation of the factory to the prototype and staging sites—then becomes the proper concern of the architect. One cannot take it for granted that adequate factory floor space will be available on time. This could be the critical path that determines the overall production time. The architect may decide to buy complete or subcontract an item that his own company is capable of producing in order to alleviate a critical requirement for factory facilities. Production cost is therefore increased to minimize the risk of overrunning the delivery date.

The facilities available to the engineers and programmers and associated support personnel who will design the system is to a greater extent under the control of the architect. These facilities can substantially affect the design costs. Overcrowding tends to increase the amount of time spent in unproductive bull sessions. On the other hand, completely individual soundproof offices for each member of the design team tend to cut down on communications. Generally, one-, two-, and three-man offices are desirable, with assignment of persons to offices based on the jobs they are doing, their personalities, and what they can learn from each other. A good reference library conveniently located is a necessity rather than a luxury. Copying facilities, conference rooms, and adequate telephones can contribute to the effectiveness of the design team. Desks, file cabinets, bookcases, desk lamps, and other such apparatus should be provided to meet the individual's true requirements, rather than as arbitrary status symbols. A logic designer or electrical engineer may need a larger desk than his manager because he may lay out large drawings. A mathematical analyst needs a bookcase if he is not to waste his time going through drawers for a reference book. A programmer needs a place to store cards, tapes, and disc packs. Finally, no one should be asked to sweat under a bleary light and smell last week's cigarette butts in his overflowing wastebasket.

3.2. Site Preparation, Packing, and Shipping

3.2.1. Site Preparation

Site preparation is doing all that has to be done to allow the equipment to be moved in and set to working with minimal damage. Site preparation is both a mechanical and a logistics job. The usual sequence of events is: physical building construction, followed by installation of air-conditioning equipment and ducting, elevated floor supports, power cables and grounding network, interunit cabling, the floor itself, and finally the equipment. The equipment cannot be installed in a random order. It is constrained by the room that will be available for maneuvering, the local floor loading (some equipment areas may require additional support), and the scheduled arrival of the equipment itself. Additional constraints may be imposed because it is important to get certain subsystems functioning before the complex as a whole even though this may mean a nonoptimum installation sequence.

The site must have adequate space for unpacking the equipment and getting rid of the detritus. Proper dollies must be available so that floor loadings will be distributed and the floor not marred. Facilities for hoisting the equipment and negotiating narrow corridors, adequate entrances and exits, loading platforms, etc., must also be provided. There are numerous instances on record of walls temporarily torn down, computers dropped six stories or more, floors caving in, hernias, and other miscellaneous catastrophes.

3.2.2. Crating, Shipping, and Receiving

Unless otherwise stated, prices are quoted FOB (free on board) at the factory. That is, the unit is crated and delivered to the carrier. However, it is important to know who will pay for shipping, local delivery, unpacking, and testing. The normal procedure is to ask for a complete quote for the delivery of the unit working at the site. This means that the responsibility for properly packing and shipping is left to the supplier. Similarly, the problems of getting the unit into the computer room and testing it, buying insurance, and repairing shipping damage are also given to the supplier. Nevertheless, it pays to know how much time is required for all of this.

The simplest and generally least costly method of transportation is a combination of truck and air shipment. The paperwork for air shipment is simpler than for shipping by sea. Even though the air travel time from any point on earth is less than 24 hours, the typical elapsed time for a unit leaving the factory until its acceptance on the floor is three to six weeks. The working unit is released from the factory floor and consigned to the shipping department. It then waits on queue for packing. It is not unusual to have the unit diverted to another customer whose immediate urgency is higher. In general, unless the buyer has imposed penalties for late delivery, he may have to expedite (i.e., harass the supplier) the shipment of each individual unit to assure that his unit will not be diverted. The supplier may then consign the unit to a shipper, who understandably is waiting for a full load going in the proper direction. This can entail a delay of a few more days. If shipped by air, the unit will wait on a further queue for a plane. The same procedure is repeated at the receiving terminal, with yet another delay for the local shipper. If the unit is to be shipped across international boundaries, there are additional delays, which will usually require the explicit attention of the ultimate consignee, that is, the buyer. An overzealous customs agent may decide that narcotics are being smuggled in the capacitors, that the gold plating is not covered by regulations, that there are import or export quotas or restrictions to be satisfied. All in all, it adds up to another two-week delay. Additional delays may be caused by strikes, snow, flood, rain, accidents, war, and other natural and human catastrophes.

Somehow or other, the site is always the last stop on the route, the helpers are not available, the hydraulic lift gate is inoperable, and there is no one there to sign the necessary papers. It turns out that nobody has a crowbar, the right kind of screwdriver, or the right kind of wrench. Finally, the equipment comes onto the floor but has suffered some minor shipping damage or has been knocked out of calibration. This too must be corrected.

While the above picture suggests widely distributed inspired incompetence, it need not be so prevalent in an actual case. A large complex may require several hundred individual units to be shipped from several different factories. It is not the units that arrive on time without damage that delay the implementation schedule, but those that do not arrive on time. It does not take a high shipping failure rate to seriously degrade the schedule. Planning must be based on the probable shipping delays, and controls must be instituted to see to it that the delays are not excessive.

3.3. Hardware Schedules and Development

A computer complex based *in toto* or in part on previously undeveloped hardware is the most vulnerable to schedule slippages. Since the latter phases of a new hardware development coincide with the construction of a stock unit, we shall illustrate the process with a new development.

3.3.1. Inventory Value

Manufacturers attempt to keep inventories as low as possible consistent with reasonable delivery schedules. A finished unit that has not been accepted represents cash. The higher the inventory, the higher the capital investment on the part of the supplier. Raw material in the form of components, frames, epoxy boards, and wires is converted by labor into a finished device. As labor is added, the inventory value increases. If the supplier kept standard units in stock, the additional cost of money (i.e., interest on the inventory value that is tied up) would have to be reflected in an increased price or reduced profits. Given an inventory level as measured by the accrued value of components, subassemblies, units, and subsystems, a delivery delay can be evaluated. For every delay, there is a distribution that reflects the expected loss of sales due to the delay. Ideally, the factory manager accepts some loss of sales and establishes his inventory level at the point that will maximize his profit. It is clearly in his interest to produce the equipment at the maximum rate possible consistent with his plant's capacity.

One of the *raisons d'être* of computer complexes as installed in a commercial operation is that the additional information and the reduction in data transmission delays allow a reduction in the inventory level of the manufacturer. In some cases, the interest on the value of the reduction of the inventory is sufficient to pay for the complex several times over.

3.3.2. Development

Let us say that a special device is required for the complex. The first step is an initial specification. The next step in its development will be an examination of the product line to see if an existing unit can be adapted. If this is not possible, the products of competitors will be examined. If the unit must be designed anew, a tentative specification is drawn up and submitted to cognizant departments for approval. Changes in the specification will occur, requiring resubmission. Approval is required from the production facility, and from the maintenance, documentation, human engineering, standards, purchasing and possibly other departments.

Given the initial go-ahead, the unit may be examined from the point of view of its possible application to other complexes or for possible permanent addition to the product line. Should the unit be so unfortunate as to qualify, another round of decisions may follow.

A detailed logic design is then produced. That design is partitioned into components, standard circuits, circuit boards, pans, racks, etc. The detailed logic design is also used to produce a wiring list. These last steps may be automated to some extent or may be done completely manually for smaller units (or smaller suppliers). When the card complement of the unit is known, power supplies, power sequence circuits, fuses, cabinetry, racks, and fans, are specified. The design is then reviewed to minimize the number of nonstandard parts used. Standard components are then requisitioned from the factory and nonstandard components from the purchasing department. Construction of the prototype unit begins with the arrival of the components. The prototype unit must be tested. This will lead to further changes in the design and the associated documentation. When the unit has been finally debugged, the final prototype documentation is created and released to production engineering.

The prototype unit is created by skilled technicians and engineers. The production unit will have to be constructed by semiskilled labor and machines. The production engineering department converts the prototype design documentation into a microscopically detailed set of assembly drawings and specifications. Final artwork and layout drawings must be produced for each special circuit board. Programs for automated wiring equipment must be devised. Wiring harness jigs must be built. Color photographs of subassemblies or individual assembly steps are made. Detailed mechanical specifications including heat treating, painting, drilling, finishing, countersinking, size and types of screws used, etc., must also be developed. Finally, production test procedures or specialized test equipment must be designed and constructed. The unit is then ready for production.

3.3.3. Production

A production order is received for a unit. After checking to see if the unit is in stock (it isn't), a production requisition is made. The procurement documentation is used to obtain a subassembly burst, that is, a detailed list of all standard subassemblies. The inventories of these subassemblies are checked and the existing ones routed to the assembly area for that unit. Subassemblies that are not in stock must be requisitioned. These too go through a parts burst procedure, and the required parts are ordered. Production is done on an assembly line. A given worker can assemble any number of different units. However, the worker will work in lots of several hundred identical units. Similarly, the production testing department will set up subassembly testing for one unit at a time. In fact, almost every stage of the subassembly construction will be batched to create the longest possible runs consistent with priorities. This means that each subassembly waits on a queue until the production facility (the tools, the worker, the test equipment) is ready for a run of that subassembly. Similarly, wiring machines are set up for batch runs. Thus, while the production time for a single unit might be a matter of hours, the delay can be of the order of months. To lessen that delay means either an increase in inventory value (think *space*) or a decrease in production efficiency (think *time*). The factory, then, is not much different than the computer complex, faced with similar problems and trades. The successful manufacturer, by design and by evolution, develops a close to optimum system.

Production proceeds through subassemblies, units, and finally subsystems. At each stage in the production the element in question will be tested and repaired or destroyed if found wanting. When the subsystem has successfully passed all tests, it is cleaned up, scratches are repainted, and other production-associated damages repaired. The unit is then ready for packing.

3.3.4. Why Worry?

The buyer must be aware of the steps in the prototype development and standard unit production cycle so that he can properly assess the vendor's bid. Promises of short deliveries that are not made out of stock can be indicative of efficiency, lack of work, or ignorance. Efficiency can be verified, perhaps by an inspection of the production facility. If the promise results from lack of work, then the buyer must consider the possibility that the supplier could be flooded with work and consequently choose to delay the schedule despite possible penalties. If the promise results from ignorance on the part of the supplier, the credibility of the supplier's entire bid is open to question. The buyer must know what is realistic so that he can specify properly; so that the initial studies can begin early enough; in short, so that neither the bidder nor the buyer is surprised by the other's estimate of the delivery time.

The bidder must have a realistic appraisal of the production time so that he does not promise impossible deliveries, or is forced to accelerate deliveries to the point where perturbations in the normal production cycle begin to erode the profitability of the operation.

Finally, the designer must know something about the production cycle, because it is one of his trade variables. It will affect build-or-buy decisions, the value and cost of urgent priorities, the hardware–software barters, the time–space–delay trades, and, in fact, almost every aspect of the system design. The hardware–software balance might shift toward software because of predictable demands on the factory. The space–time barter might favor space because of an excessive inventory of memories. The special purpose *vs.* general purpose trade may be influenced by available engineering manpower as a result of a recently terminated project, the absorption of another division, or an impending strike of standard unit production workers.

4. SYSTEM CUT-OVER

The system does not come into being all at once. Given the instantaneous creation of the required hardware and software properly working at the site, the system would still not go into productive work immediately after the acceptance test is passed. The cut-over from test bed operation to full working is almost always carried out in phases. There may be pre-existing conditions that force this approach. The main reason, however, is that despite the careful checking, testing, integration, acceptance testing, and still more testing, few designers and fewer buyers have the hubris required to throw the switch all at once. As with bridges, aircraft, and ships, the launching is followed by gingerly taken steps; confidence is developed gradually, and the operational risks and adverse publicity of a failure (even if only temporary) are avoided.

4.1. Pre-existing Conditions

The strongest pre-existing conditions dictating a phased cut-over come about because there is an existing complex that is replaced by the new one. The clerical procedures or other nonmechanical processes replaced by the complex are systems—viable systems at that—that cannot be suddenly terminated. Parallel operation is mandatory. If the new complex is to be housed in the same facility as the old, the old will be dismantled as the new one is assembled. Each will perform part of the work until the new complex has taken over completely. This creates additional problems regarding ducting, cabling, and the like. The problems, however, are not insurmountable.[3]

While a phased implementation is dictated by sound engineering, it may be in the buyer's and/or the builder's interest to give the appearance of an instantaneous cut-over. What this means is that the phasing will have begun earlier, so that complete confidence has been achieved at the time of cut-over. In reality, the system has been working for several months to everybody's satisfaction. Examples of this are due to seasonal variations,

---

[3] Large buildings in the center of major cities have been erected as the buildings they replaced were torn down. The construction and the destruction both proceed from the bottom floor up. If this were not complicated enough, both buildings are partially occupied throughout this process. The tenants move from the 15th floor of the old building to the 6th of the new building as the 12th floor of the old is being dismantled and the 8th of the new constructed.

the birthdays of important officials, national holidays, political events, dedication ceremonies, etc. The larger the complex, and the more public its operation, the more likely is this kind of pseudoinstantaneous cut-over. Problems will occur when the buyer is thinking in terms of a ceremonial cut-over date and the builder in terms of the acceptance test. The builder may have underestimated the schedule by a few months and the buyer may have his ceremony go sour.

4.2. Phasing Problems

The dual operation of part of two complexes is more expensive. A price must be paid for minimizing risk. During the phasing period, facilities are likely to be cramped. This means inefficiency or additional costs for temporary facilities. Two crews are doing the same job. This means that there must be administrative procedures to eliminate harmful redundancies, transactions serviced by neither, or conflicts in procedures.

Phasing can be done extensively or functionally. If the new complex is performing functions that are reasonably independent of those performed by the old complex in addition to the old functions, the new functions can be phased in first. As each function is added to the new complex, communication between the old and the new must be established. That communication can be a one-time transfer of data or may require continual communication between the two complexes required for no other purpose. There may be software modifications, or occasionally hardware modifications, to allow the systems to communicate. Some kind of parallel operation with checking is required before the old complex relinquishes a function. This too may require special software in both systems.

Extensive phasing is applied first to the new facilities being serviced and then gradually to the old. Phasing, be it functional or extensive, proceeds from the low-penalty, low-risk areas to the high-penalty or high-risk areas.

Developing a phasing plan is not unlike developing a roll-off order and a recovery schedule. Independence of processors must be detected and used to advantage. The additional complications of hardware availability, operator training, and intermediate testing and verification make the phasing problem more complicated.

5. PERSONNEL

So far we have discussed the complex in terms of its technical aspects. However, the complex does not come into being, nor can it continue successful operation, except as the result of the pooled intelligence of many different disciplines.

5.1. The Architect

We can summarize the architect's role by stating that it is synthetical, catalytic, and translative. His design is a synthesis of the substance of subordinate disciplines. He motivates and directs the efforts of those disciplines by giving their practitioners a point of view tempered by considerations outside of their domain. He is a linguist, a polyglot in a tower of Babel.

5.2. Systems Engineers

Where the architect is mainly concerned with syntheses and concepts, the systems engineer is directed toward the actual implementation. The two differ mostly in outlook and not in expertise or breadth of knowledge. As often as not, both functions are performed by the same person. The systems engineer is more realistic and willing to compromise for the achievable. The architect worries about the next ten years, the systems engineer about passing the acceptance test. The systems engineer is responsible for the execution of the architect's plan and is therefore steeped in the detail and daily decisions required for that implementation. The engineer is not subordinate to the architect. They each have a unique contribution to make. The engineer must be something of an architect and *vice versa*. When the two jobs are separated, the architect is in a staff position, while the systems engineer has the line responsibility.

5.3. System Analysts

A system analyst, as we use the term, does not mean some higher or more experienced kind of programmer. His responsibility is the analysis of the total system, hardware and software, and the traditional analysis of the trade-offs. He provides quantitative answers to questions of the form "what would happen if" posed by the architect and engineer. The architect and engineer deal with problems that are not well phrased. In fact, the posing of questions is one of their primary functions. The system analyst will provide the consequences to such questions. He determines the effect on reliability of adding another program; the amount of memory that can be saved by adding a computer; the slippage in the schedule brought about by a less costly personnel build-up. In fact, the systems analysis function is in part related to and is an essential tool of all the disciplines required to construct a complex.

5.4. Electrical and Electronic Engineers

Electrical engineers are concerned with the complex as a set of interacting pieces of hardware. While most complexes are composed of product line units, it is rare that two complexes are exactly alike. Floor layouts differ, and consequently the transmission delay between the various units will differ from installation to installation. The number of wires that a circuit will have to drive will differ. The quality of power will differ. Certain installations may have to contend with unique electromagnetic radiation and interference problems. All of these factors conspire to make the presence of such engineers mandatory.

5.5. Programmers

A programmer is a software engineer. We shall call all individuals who are directly concerned with the design and testing of programs programmers, whether they are involved in detailed, routine design, or responsible for the production of basic design flow charts. We recognize, however, that there are differences between a programmer with ten years of experience and one with three months, between graduate level education in computer and information science and a three-week COBOL course at the local business school. We cannot demean the significance of the programmer, if only for the reason that the single largest cost item in the engineering of a complex is the programming.

5.6. Logic Designers

A logic designer is a programmer whose "instructions" consist of gates, flip-flops, and connections. Few computer complexes are constructed of completely standard hardware. There are places in which the optimization of the design will require a modification of a standard item, or the wedding of units produced by different manufacturers, with not quite compatible interfaces. The logical adaptation of the units to the requirements of the complex is the responsibility of the logic designer. As most such functions can be implemented in software, there is a trade between the unique engineering cost associated with the logical design of such adaptations and the alternative implementation as a program.

5.7. Mathematical Analysts

There are many problems in the design of a computer complex that can be formulated sufficiently well to allow a mathematical solution. The overwhelming majority of these can be solved directly by the individuals who pose them. However, there are some problems that may require specialized mathematical knowledge. The idea of trading implies the use of linear and nonlinear programming. There may be differential equations to solve, matrices to invert, statistical data to be reduced, etc., of sufficient depth that a specialist is the best way to do it.

The mathematical analyst, being far removed from the actual problem, must be given the right problem to solve. The formulation of the problem in mathematical terms, usually by the system analyst, if often as difficult as the solution. The primary cause of failure of mathematical analysis is not a lack of capability on the part of the mathematician, but is giving him the wrong problem to solve. The most common error made by the system analyst in posing a problem for a mathematician is in making "simplifying assumptions," which, because of his lack of knowledge of mathematics, turn a simple problem into a doctoral dissertation. Generally it is best to pose the problem in all its glory and complexity, letting the mathematician suggest the simplifications.

5.8. Administrative Personnel

The construction of a complex is a large undertaking that can require the coordination of hundreds of individuals. Administration is to be distinguished from management. Most of the disciplines mentioned above exist at all managerial levels. Administration is not concerned with the posing of problems, the motivation of personnel, or the making of decisions. It is concerned with the provision of information and the implementation of controls that make the task of management possible. Somehow or other, one must have realistic estimates of costs, past, present, and projected. One must know if things are following a prescribed plan or schedule. People must be hired, moved, removed, housed, fed, kept healthy, and so forth. Administrative functions are often considered odious by technical people. When they are overdone, a project may be snowed under by inconsequential paperwork; when they are lacking, it may fall apart from inappropriate direction and overrun both the required time and the budget. Properly balanced administration is a flexible glue that holds the whole thing together without gumming up the works.

5.9. Production Personnel

Somehow or other, all the equipment must be built. Near-sighted little old ladies who string cores for a memory, porters who move bins of material around, test technicians, wire-harness makers, insertion tool operators, machinists, phototechnicians, and so forth, they are the ones who actually produce the tangible complex. We could ask the reader to take apart a transistor radio to the ultimate and reassemble it in working order. He might thus learn to appreciate the roles these people play. In addition, we urge him to see and spend some time on the factory floor. There was virtue in the now forgotten practice of requiring every engineer to apprentice for a while as a machinist.

5.10. Site and Installation Engineers

Consider subfloors that collapse under the weight of a disc file, mice gnawing through the insulation of a busbar, operators trying to read a printout in inadequate light in a hot and noisy room, doors and turns too small for the equipment, power requirements that exceed what the local public utility can provide, elevators that cannot take the weight, cables that are too thick to bend, roads that do not exist, low bridges, flat tires, and unknown local building regulations. *Someone* should consider these problems. They are the responsibility of site and installation engineers.

5.11. Operators

We have not yet progressed to the point that the complexes we build can run totally unattended. Since no program or design can ever be complete, some unforeseen event will always occur at some point in the life of the complex. At that point the operator is priceless. He is the insurance for all the niggling little doubts, the problems swept under the rug, and the numerous expressions of "I think it will work." If the operator's only job were to change tapes and disc packs, load paper, fill card hoppers, change printer ribbons, and stare at the console, he would soon be replaced by machines. If we are to control the machines, rather than have them controlling us, then they should always be ultimately subordinate to some human being. There will always exist a circumstance in which it is in our best interest to have the operator execute an action directly contradictory to the primal dictates of the system design. That much insurance is required. As long as the operator is there, however, we can include him in the design trades, relegating to his attention those highly improbable tasks that are more readily performed by a human.

5.12. Maintenance Technicians

Every complex can and will fail. While more and more aspects of maintenance have been automated, the increased complexity of systems have tended to keep the total amount of maintenance activity constant. The maintenance technician keeps things running—sometimes, in concert with the operator, under circumstances that tax the imagination of the designer. Without him, the whole thing would be academic, a complex being no more than a piece of particularly expensive modern art whose sole purpose is to process a while before destroying itself.

5.13. Editors, Writers, and Teachers

Shortly after the complex has been accepted, almost everyone who worked on it disappears. A problem that arises five years later must still be solved. The complex must have documents for the users, the operators, the maintenance technicians, production personnel, site engineers, and for any other foreseeable individuals who will have to use, operate, or modify the system. Documentation starts with the designers who conceive the idea. Unfortunately, technical personnel tend to communicate in a manner suitable only for others of the same ilk. The total bulk of raw documents that would allow an identical complex to be rebuilt and operated must be edited and organized into a useful form by individuals whose training differs from that of the document's originator. That organization and the production of readable manuals is the function of the editors and writers.

Operators, maintenance personnel, and users must be trained. The training ranges from a deep theoretical discourse on fine analytical points to how to change a typewriter ribbon. Large complexes, installed at many sites, may require schools with full curricula covering every aspect of the complex. In such cases, the teaching is often best done by professional technical teachers, complete with tests, grades, and homework. Sometimes, the teachers are drawn from among the design personnel. Most individuals who have a flair for teaching and who are involved in the design of computer complexes will at one time or another be required to teach a course on their aspects of the job.

5.14. Support Personnel

In addition to the above, there is an army of clerks, typists, secretaries, copy machine operators, keypunch operators, draftsmen, stock clerks, librarians, and telephone operators, without whom the design of the complex would not be possible.

6. PROJECT MANAGEMENT AND CONTROL

But Mousie, thou art no thy lane,
In proving foresight may be vain:
The best laid schemes o' mice an' men
Gang aft a-gley,
An' lea'e us nought but grief an' pain
For promis'd joy.

ROBERT BURNS
To a Mouse

Which is what project management and control is all about. Just as we accept the inevitability of component failure, we accept the inevitability of human failures and natural catastrophes that combine to extend the project duration or its cost. The mouse would have been immeasurably better off had it shifted its domicile to the base of a nearby tree; yet had it planned for lightning striking that tree, the planning or the effort to protect itself under such circumstances would also have been vain. Project management and control, then, like overdesign, redundancy, and other viability enhancement techniques, are intended to alleviate only the minor, high-probability catastrophes.

6.1. Schedules

Having seen the increased capability that can be brought about through the design of a proper processing schedule, we should expect comparable benefits from scheduling human activities, which, if anything, need it more. A schedule is a logistics program for a multiprocessor complex. Time and cost analyses are done to determine when the various elements of the complex will be available and programs devised that dictate the starting points and end points of the intermediate steps of the project. Being early will rarely cause increased cost. However, being late inevitably means increased expenditures. The schedule, then, exists not so much as a document to be slavishly followed, but as an early warning device for judging the progress of the project.

Each activity in the construction of the complex is broken down into subsidiary activities. Check points, or **milestones** (also called "millstones"), are established in advance. The failure to meet a particular milestone may not in itself be significant. However, since most elements of the complex affect subsequent elements, that failure could have repercussions totally out of proportion to its importance. A schedule should not be used to judge the effectiveness of the individuals laboring under it. It should be used primarily to detect malfunctions so that corrective actions can be initiated. If a particular element has been underestimated, it is more meaningful to adjust other efforts or to increase the manpower for that element in order to bring the project back under control. If the delay in the schedule is inevitable, and such that it will affect the overall schedule adversely, then the user is likely to be less annoyed by being told early than by being told at the last possible moment. If he is told early, then it is possible that he will voluntarily delay certain aspects of the implementation (so that his ceremony will go off as planned).

Cost control is similar to schedule control. Accounting of actual expenditures for labor, travel, supplies, and equipment is required as early as possible. The designer who is overrunning his budget may elect to bring expenditures down by eliminating fringe benefits not essential to the satisfactory completion of the contract. Cost overruns may result in re-evaluations of trades made earlier under imperfect knowledge. Again, if the cost data are not known, nothing can be done about it.

Both time and cost control are first and foremost a form of feedback. That feedback, however, should not be restricted to the implementers alone. Equally important is the feedback to the individuals who made up the schedule in the first place. If the estimators have made a mistake resulting in a longer or costlier execution, they will not be able to correct their mistakes for the next go-around without such feedback. Only when an individual does not improve in the light of continual correcting feedback is he to be judged inadequate. If he has no say in the formulation of the (time or cost) schedule, or if he has no way to judge the validity of his estimates, he is not to be blamed.

6.2. Critical Path Methods

A schedule is not a single sequential listing of events. The human organization that constructs the complex does so in parallel. Consequently, the initiation of a particular event may depend upon the successful completion of a number of previous events. This can clearly be represented by a graph.

6.2.1. Representation of Schedules

Early scheduling techniques represented the schedule as a single sequence of events; that is, the schedule was considered to be a strictly ordered graph. However, the attempt to produce complicated systems such as aircraft or large construction projects led to the gradual realization that a schedule is at best a partly ordered graph.

The **PERT** diagram is such a representation. "PERT" stands for "*P*rogram *E*valuation and *R*eview *T*echnique." The schedule is represented as a graph. Each link represents an activity or event. The link is weighted

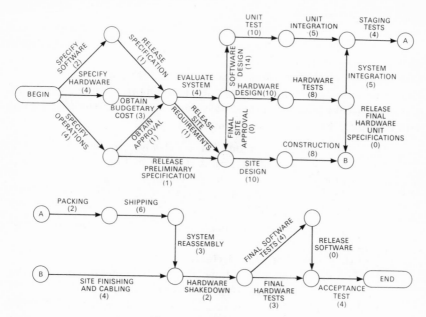

Figure 14.1. A PERT chart.

with the time expected for the completion of that activity. Nodes are used to represent conditions that must be met before the particular events can continue. Thus, each node can be considered as if it were an AND gate in a logic network.

The events in question are typically the milestones of subsidiary schedules. A typical PERT chart is shown in Figure 14.1. By convention, a PERT chart has a single inway and a single outway. Furthermore, loops are not allowed. Therefore, the time to traverse the graph is the time required to traverse the longest path on the graph. The basic PERT problem is to find that longest or **critical path**. While the critical path may be obvious in a small PERT chart of 30 to 40 events, finding it in a more realistic chart of 3000 or 4000 events is tedious and is best done by a computer. A PERT chart for a computer complex development could have several thousand events.

6.2.2. A Critical Path Algorithm

The following algorithm is readily proved to be valid for finding the length of the critical path. The star-mesh transformation is applied, using the following rules:

1. Series Rule:

$$T_{ik} = T_{ij} + T_{jk}.$$

2. *Parallel Rule*:

$$T_{ij} = \max (T'_{ij}, T''_{ij}).$$

The loop rule is not needed because loops are forbidden. The star-mesh transformation applied under these rules, retaining the beginning and end nodes, will yield the length of the critical path, but not the path itself. If the path is desired, the following algorithm can be used:

1. Using the above equations for series and parallel connections, perform the incident star-mesh transformation. This gives the longest time from the origin to every node.
2. Using the excident star-mesh transformation, obtain the longest time from each node to the terminus.
3. Add the incident and excident times for each node except the beginning and end nodes.
4. Sort the nodes in order of decreasing total time.
5. Every node having a total time equal to the longest time (also the time from the beginning to the end) is on a critical path.
6. Eliminate all nodes and associated incident and excident links that are not on a critical path. The resulting subgraph displays all critical paths (there may be more than one).

The reader should note that a link with a traverse time of zero is not the same as having no link. Zeros must be put in explicitly.

6.2.3. Variations

Charts can be constructed with different conventions. The most prevalent variation is the association of time with the nodes rather than with the links. The nodes then represent the events.

Charts can also be used to obtain the **slack time** for the various events. The slack time is the time between the latest start of the event and the earliest start of that event. The earliest start is the time to achieve the preceding node. The latest start is that for which an infinitesimal increase would place the event on a critical path. Clearly, events on the critical path have no slack. Slack can be used in conjunction with cost formulas to obtain the money lost through unexpected delays. Most increases in schedules will cause some activities to be delayed. As these activities are delayed, the wages paid to the persons engaged in those activities, as well as overhead functions associated with them may not be curtailed. It may not be possible to reassign these persons. The slack as obtained in an initial schedule can be used to modify the schedule so that there are few persons or activities with slack at any time during the project. The cost of slack can be further extended to include inventory costs and other nonpersonnel costs.

Another common variation on the theme is the inclusion of uncertainty in the schedule. Rather than state the time for the event as a single fixed number, the event is described by a distribution of times. The schedule initiator describes each activity in terms of the earliest, expected, and worst possible times for the event. The series and parallel transformation rules are changed accordingly, resulting in the earliest, latest, and expected duration of the project as well as intermediate event slacks.

6.3. Project Controls

A typical, well run, large project will institute a number of controls to provide information regarding the conduct of the project and to assure the successful completion of the contract. Design standards are established to guide hardware, software, logic, documentation, training, installation, etc. The standards are not necessarily optimum—their importance lies in the fact that they are standards. The conventional signs used in mathematics are not optimum in any sense, they are merely universally intelligible and unambiguous. So must it be with other standards implemented in the project.

Project control documents are instituted to prevent time or money overruns, or at least alert managers to them. Formal notification of changes are required once an element has been released to other parts of the project. While the designer may do as he wishes at first, once he has claimed the element to be complete, and has released the documentation, he will have to go through a formal procedure to make a change. The intent is twofold: to minimize the perturbation on dependent elements, and to limit the number of unnecessary enhancements.

Regular project review sessions are held at all levels so that parties concerned are aware of the problems and what is being done about them. If not overdone, a project review meeting can be an efficient way of informing many persons as to what is going on. If overdone, it can create unnecessary anxieties, or leave little time for honest work.

7. THE COMPLEX IN RETROSPECT

The computer complex comes into being through the mutual efforts of many different individuals and disciplines. While one person can provide the inspiration, leadership, and management that makes the successful completion of the project possible, the actual work would exhaust several lifetimes. In this respect, the construction of a computer complex is no different than that of any other large architectural project such as a dam, bridge, building, or ship. The real problems, of finding out what it is that has to be optimized, how to compare incomparables, how to sacrifice the mandatory, and how to achieve rational trades where no compromise is possible, have been with us since men first started building. Technology will change, rendering previous decisions unfortunate or making new approaches possible. Individual and collective goals will change, reflecting a difference in our notion of optima. New techniques in hardware, software, analysis, and construction will make possible a deeper examination of subtleties, allowing an even easier achievement of previous goals and the continued attempt to create yet more elegant systems.

Success in a dynamic universe is not measured against absolutes. A design is good only if the architect could not have been bettered given the same conditions and tools. The complex is never really finished and, in retrospect, could always have been done better.

8. PROBLEMS

1. Prove the validity of the critical path algorithms given in Section 6.2.2.
2. Apply these algorithms to the graph of Figure 14.1.
3. Derive an algorithm for the slack using the star-mesh transformation.
4. Use the star-mesh transformation to find the shortest path through a graph.
5. Why is finding the shortest path through a maze whose structure you do not know not the same as finding the shortest path when you do know the total structure. Look up the Fulkerson–Ford algorithm with this in mind.

9. REFERENCES

1. Archibald, Russell D., and Villoria, Richard L., *Network-Based Management Systems (PERT/CPM)*, John Wiley, New York, 1967.

   A comprehensive book on the application and implementation of PERT and related project control systems. Decision trees are also considered in this book. Contains an interesting discussion of the analytical assumptions on which PERT is based. Illustrative case histories give the book proper perspective.

2. Brandon, Dick H., *Management Standards for Data Processing*, Van Nostrand, Princeton, N.J., 1963.

   This book covers most aspects of commercial data processing. The importance of this book is not the specific standards presented, but an example of what aspects of data processing require standards. It can be used as a matrix on which a comprehensive set of standards could be built for a particular instance.

3. De Haan, Norman R., Jaeger, Dieter, Johnson, Kenneth E., Miller, Leon G., Sax, Samuel W., Torgersen, Torwald H., and Zanardelli, Henry A., *Improving Office Environment*, The Business Press, Elmhurst, Illinois, 1969.

   A set of articles on office planning that can also be applied to many aspects of physical facility planning from the point of view of its impact on personnel.

4. Enrick, Norbert Lloyd, *Management Planning: A Systems Approach*, McGraw-Hill, New York, 1967.

A general, elementary book on the application of operations research to management problems. Specific examples worked out in detail.

5. Farmer, Robert A., and Associates, *What You Should Know About Contracts*, Arco Publishing Company, New York, 1969.

A nontechnical book on contract law. It describes the more important aspects of contract law in lay terms and provides a minimum introduction to "legalese." The examples cited are clear. Not only is the law described and explained, but also the reasons behind it, that is, the justice that is attempted by the interpretation of the law. It is sufficient to allow a technical manager to hold a conversation with a lawyer with a high probability that they will both be talking the same language.

6. Grant, Eugene L., and Ireson, W. Grant, *Principles of Engineering Economy*, Ronald Press, New York, 1964 (4th edition).

This is a large book dealing with the cost and value of money, interest, depreciation, and accounting methods. It is a textbook that can be used as a reference. Definitely an "accountant's book."

7. Joslin, Edward O., *Computer Selection*, Addison–Wesley, Reading, Mass., 1968.

The orientation of this book is toward commercial data processing. Part II is an example of a selection. Despite the commercial bias, it is worth reading.

8. Levin, Richard I., and Kirkpatrick, Charles A., *Planning and Control with PERT/CPM*, McGraw-Hill, New York, 1966.

A short introduction to PERT and other project control methods. The appendix reviews other related or derivative project control methods.

9. Shedley, Ethan I., "Big System Games," *Datamation*, April 1, 1971, Volume 17, Number 7, pp. 22–25.

A list of fifteen "games" for programmers, managers and misdirected architects to be played during the implementation of a large computer complex, or to be avoided if the complex is meant to work.

10. Silverman, Melvin, *The Technical Program Manager's Guide to Survival*, John Wiley, New York, 1967.

A readable book that discusses the realities of technical program planning and implementation. The use of PERT, line of balance, and other planning aids are discussed. Much useful information on organizations, staffing, reporting, documentation, etc. If the reader could read no other book on the subject, he would do well to read this one.

11. Symonds, Curtis W., *Basic Financial Management*, American Management Association, Inc., New York, 1969.

A palatable nontechnical book on what finances are all about. Talks about what capital is, what it is used for, what it costs, and how you measure what you get for it.

INDEX

Pages 1–394 will be found in Volume 1. Bold numerals refer to the pages where terms are defined.